Infanticide

Infanticide examines medical expert evidence in infanticide cases, focusing specifically on the shifting notion of "certainty" in medical testimony. Beginning in the Early Modern period and concluding in the mid-twentieth century, it considers how courts determined whether an infant died from natural causes or other reasons, including violence.

The book explores expert evidence in cases of infanticide and examines the extent of certainty created by medical specialists who founded their testimony on anatomical exploration and science. As the book progresses, it becomes clear that medical specialists were unable to scientifically establish the cause of death and in doing so conveyed uncertainty in court proceedings. Rather than being regarded as a professional failing, Dixon argues that the uncertainty created by medical specialists redirected the outcomes of infanticide cases. The combination of uncertainty and the changing perceptions of infanticidal women by the court lead juries to find infanticidal women not guilty of a capital offence in many cases.

This book will be of great interest to students and scholars of Criminology, Law, and History.

Rachel Dixon began her career as a nurse and later a midwife before studying Law at the University of Hull, Hull, England. She is currently a lecturer in Law at the University of Hull, where she teaches Criminal Law and Criminal Justice. This book is her PhD thesis and her first publication.

Routledge SOLON Explorations in Crime and Criminal Justice Histories

This series is a collaboration between Routledge and the SOLON consortium (promoting studies in law, crime and history), to present cutting edge interdisciplinary research in crime and criminal justice history, through monographs and thematic collected editions which reflect on key issues and dilemmas in criminology and socio-legal studies by locating them within a historical dimension. The emphasis here is on inspiring use of historical and historiographical methodological approaches to the contextualising and understanding of current priorities and problems. This series aims to highlight the best, most innovative interdisciplinary work from both new and established scholars in the field, through focusing on the enduring historical resonances to current core criminological and socio-legal issues.

Edited by Kim Stevenson, University of Plymouth; Judith Rowbotham, University of Plymouth; David Nash, Oxford Brookes University and David J. Cox, University of Wolverhampton.

Parricide and Violence Against Parents
A Cross-Cultural View across Past and Present
Marianna G. Muravyeva, Phillip Shon and Raisa Maria

Policing Suspicion
Proactive Policing in London, 1780–1850
Eleanor Bland

Infanticide
Expert Evidence and Testimony in Child Murder Cases, 1688–1955
Rachel Dixon

The Limits of Criminological Positivism
The Movement for Criminal Law Reform in the West, 1870–1940
Michele Pifferi

For more information about this series, please visit: https://www.routledge.com/Routledge-SOLON-Explorations-in-Crime-and-Criminal-Justice-Histories/book-series/HCCJ

Infanticide

Expert Evidence and Testimony in Child Murder Cases, 1688–1955

Rachel Dixon

Routledge
Taylor & Francis Group
LONDON AND NEW YORK

First published 2022
by Routledge
2 Park Square, Milton Park, Abingdon, Oxon OX14 4RN

and by Routledge
605 Third Avenue, New York, NY 10158

Routledge is an imprint of the Taylor & Francis Group, an informa business

British Library Cataloguing-in-Publication Data
A catalogue record for this book is available from the British Library

Library of Congress Cataloging-in-Publication Data
Names: Dixon, Rachel (Lecturer in Law), author.
Title: Infanticide : expert evidence and testimony in child murder cases, 1688-1955 / Rachel Dixon.
Description: Abingdon, Oxon ; New York, NY : Routledge, 2022. | Includes bibliographical references and index.
Identifiers: LCCN 2021032312 (print) | LCCN 2021032313 (ebook) | ISBN 9780367438890 (hbk) | ISBN 9780367439231 (pbk) | ISBN 9781003006299 (ebk)
Subjects: LCSH: Infanticide--History. | Evidence, Expert--History.
Classification: LCC HV6537 .D58 2022 (print) | LCC HV6537 (ebook) | DDC 364.152/3083--dc23
LC record available at https://lccn.loc.gov/2021032312
LC ebook record available at https://lccn.loc.gov/2021032313

ISBN: 978-0-367-43889-0 (hbk)
ISBN: 978-0-367-43923-1 (pbk)
ISBN: 978-1-003-00629-9 (ebk)

DOI: 10.4324/9781003006299

Typeset in Times New Roman
by Deanta Global Publishing Services, Chennai, India

For Harry and Margaret

Contents

Acknowledgements viii

Introduction 1

1 A historiography of infanticide and the use of medical experts in criminal trials 23

2 Midwifery evidence in infanticide cases 58

3 The role of medical men in infanticide cases 83

4 Medical evidence and mental state of the infanticidal woman 121

5 The expert evidence of the pathologist in infanticide cases 166

6 Conclusion 189

Bibliography 197
Index 218

Acknowledgements

Firstly, I would like to acknowledge and thank the University of Hull for awarding me a PhD scholarship to fund this research. I would also like to thank (profusely) Professor Tony Ward and Professor Helen Johnston for their kind encouragement, dedicated time, advice, and continuing support on this research and subsequent manuscript. I shall always be grateful to you both.

I would also like to thank my internal PhD examiner, Professor Gerry Johnstone, and my external PhD examiner, Dr Daniel Grey, for their kind advice, and Dr Daniel Grey in particular for his support with the publication of this manuscript, and I would like to acknowledge and thank my colleagues in the Law School at the University of Hull for their valuable support and encouragement with this book. I would like to thank the series reviewers in the SOLON consortium for their comments, advice, and encouragement, and in particular Professor Kim Stevenson and Dr Dave Cox. I would also like to thank Routledge, and those who have been involved with the publication of this book, and in particular Arunima Aditya and Jayanthi Chander.

Finally, I would like to thank my family and my good friend, Rita, for their endless emotional support and encouragement, but in particular I would like to thank my husband, Simon, for believing in me.

Introduction

Mary Shirley was a young servant girl, residing and working in a house in Brixton, London, in 1873.[1] When she became pregnant, she concealed her condition from her employers and family; after delivering the child alone, she hid the corpse in a hole in the copper.[2] The case of Mary Shirley is but one infanticide case which epitomises the typical characteristics of the infanticidal woman standing trial, particularly during the nineteenth century. In many cases they were young women who, after being lured into a relationship on the empty promise of marriage, found themselves pregnant; afraid to disclose their secret, they concealed their pregnancy and delivered the child alone, concealing their secret and concealing their shame. The court had to determine whether the child had had a separate existence or, more specifically, if it had been born alive. In the absence of an independent witness to this capital offence, the court turned to medical experts to prove with certainty the extent of the woman's culpability. This was the case for Mary Shirley when the surgeon, Edmund Pope, was called to give evidence. However, he stated that:

> I can't positively say it had really a separate existence, that it was wholly born alive, it had breathed, the wound I saw would cause death, I can't say positively that it was alive when the injury was given, I cannot scarcely understand how it could be done before it was completely born, I cannot give an opinion.[3]

Mary was found "guilty of concealment of birth and she was strongly recommended to mercy by the jury on account of her age and good character – she was sentenced to two years imprisonment."[4]

Medical men were called upon to provide scientifically based proof of the cause of death from anatomical dissection: in murder trials, for example, there developed an increased involvement of medical experts as expert witnesses, basing their testimony on the body to guide and support their findings that in turn produced an expectation of certainty.[5] Whilst this notion of certainty may be true in cases of murder, this research will demonstrate that medical men were unable to meet the expectation of certainty in cases of infanticide, either through their inability or their unwillingness to say "positively" what happened, a common theme

DOI: 10.4324/9781003006299-101

of infanticide trials. This research will also demonstrate that certainty did not increase in infanticide trials with the passage of time, the introduction of scientific experiments, or through medical discourse. In most infanticide cases, medical evidence remained uncertain; medical men confirmed uncertainty through cautious answers and opinions and, in doing so, raised an element of doubt over the woman's guilt. Arguably, this uncertainty made a positive contribution to infanticide cases; the indefinite evidence allowed the jury to find these women not guilty of murder.

Arguably, this lenient, softer approach adopted by the courts not only stemmed from the personal circumstances of the infanticidal woman but also from the lack of substantive evidence establishing criminal liability. In murder cases throughout the nineteenth and twentieth centuries, the courts increasingly relied upon experts, allowing science to unearth the truth and thus in turn confirm certainty through anatomical dissection and scientific experiment. Similarly, in cases of infanticide, medical experts were also called upon to provide medical opinion and confirm certainty, establishing liability. However, this was not the case, and medical experts instead achieved the opposite, confirming uncertainty, and by doing so, allowed the jury to find the woman not guilty. It is this argument which forms the basis of this book; as the scientisation of the law became ever increasingly evident, medical men were unable to produce evidence with certainty in cases of infanticide.

Methodology

This research begins in the year 1688, 250 years before the implementation of the 1938 Infanticide Act, and a year politically noted for the "Glorious Revolution," when England experienced a coup d'état with King William III replacing King James II on the throne.[6]

This research concludes in 1955, a timescale that has allowed for the examination of a number of cases following the implementation of the Infanticide Act of 1938. As the 1960's was a decade that contained significant developments towards the empowerment of British women, concluding this research before the 1960's avoided any potential impact these developments may have had upon the results. In 1961, the contraceptive pill became available in the United Kingdom to older, married women. Controversially, in 1974 the decision was made to allow single women the contraceptive pill on prescription, a moment in time that was seen as a revolutionary victory for many women and the "greatest scientific invention of the twentieth-century,"[7] as it allowed women the liberty to legally plan childbirth.[8] Later in the decade, the Abortion Act of 1967 came into effect in England and Wales in 1968, allowing registered medical practitioners to terminate a pregnancy if the "continuation of the pregnancy would involve risk, greater than if the pregnancy were terminated, of injury to the physical or mental health of the pregnant woman,"[9] an act that not only permitted the termination of a pregnancy but also associated an unwanted pregnancy with mental state. There were clearly many changes between 1688 and 1955 within the political, legal, and social arena; those relevant to the historiography of infanticide will be discussed in Chapter 1.

This research has been carried out by examining expert testimony provided in infanticide trials held in London by accessing the online proceedings of the Old Bailey, available at www.oldbaileyonline.org,[10] as the Old Bailey is an "important part of the history of forensics, as it provided the site for extensive and specialist medical evidence."[11] In order to understand how the courts dealt with infanticide outside the London area, expert evidence in the provincial area of Kingston-Upon-Hull and the surrounding area has also been examined, and the results are included in some of the chapters. This has allowed for an additional understanding of the operation of the criminal justice process at this time and allowed the research question to be tested outside the London and Middlesex area. These cases have been accessed through newspaper articles in the British Newspaper Archive at: www.britishnewspaperarchive.co.uk.[12] The Old Bailey Online and newspaper articles were selected as opposed to archival material from depositions surviving for London and Hull because the details required for this research were adequately provided in the online sources.

Following a brief history of the cities of Hull and London, the remainder of this introductory section will explain the process a woman accused of infanticide would have experienced in the criminal justice system, beginning from the moment suspicions were raised, to the court procedure, and the role of the jury. This chapter will then continue with an explanation and analysis of the sources used within this research: the Old Bailey Proceedings Papers and newspaper articles, before concluding with an outline of each chapter.

History of Hull and London

In 1700, Hull was a fortified town, and so the majority of Hull's 6,000 residents lived within the town walls, a factor that inevitably led to overcrowded living conditions; the confines of the town walls meant limited room for expansion, and on market day people traded and physically moved around the streets with difficulty.[13] Like Hull, London was also a fortified city, houses were tightly compacted together both next to and opposite each other, and with no hygienic method of removing sewage and waste, the streets and the Thames were used for waste disposal. During the seventeenth century, the capital's population began to increase rapidly with voluminous migration attracted to the city for economic reasons, and the pull of Westminster with its growing political and legal opportunities,[14] an increasing population that has been described as causing the capital to be "bursting out of its shell."[15]

During the nineteenth century London began to flourish, as the city continued to appeal to those with aspirations to wealth and prosperity on a grand scale, and with a population of 1,000,000 recorded on the 1801 census, it was considered the largest city in Europe.[16] As the wealth of the inhabitants of London increased in size, however, so too did the size of their houses, and in 1891 there were 238,000 female domestic servants in London.[17] This rapidly increasingly wealth was not a generic factor for London; whilst some areas, for example the West End, began to flourish and prosper, other areas, such as the East End, remained poor.[18] People lived in areas described as slums, where living conditions were filthy and overcrowded; rent for such houses subsumed most of the earnings of these poor people and, in the event of any surplus money, the family may have been able to afford food.[19] For those who did not earn enough to afford the rent for houses, a two-penny hangover or a four-penny coffin could be purchased for the night.[20] These could be found in dosshouses, where either a person slept sitting upright, slumped over a rope or in a coffin; they could sleep supine, under tarpaulin, for double the price.[21] For those who could not afford the dosshouse, there were workhouses or charitable institutions, where food and accommodation were free in exchange for work; families would be separated and labour would be hard. Charles Dickens, in Oliver Twist, describes the admittance of an orphaned baby into the workhouse when he writes:

> he was enveloped in the old calico robes, which had grown old in the same service, he was badgered and ticketed, and fell into his place at once – a parish child – the orphan of the workhouse – the humble half-starved drudge – to be cuffed and buffeted through the world, despised by all, and pitied by none.[22]

For many people, it seemed that the workhouse was a place of desperation, a place to be afraid of and avoided. Workhouses were "designed to put the able bodied to work, in reality workhouses were a dosshouse for the old, the sick and single-parent families. They were often a disgrace."[23] This image was encouraged by the government stigmatising such institutions with associations of failure and idleness, characteristics that conflicted with the country's ethos of work, reward, and success.[24] Sharpe has argued that such extreme divisions between the wealthy and the poor were not only between the "rich and the poor, but also between what might be termed the respectable and the rough."[25]

The industrial revolution also had a notable effect on the town of Hull. From the late eighteenth century the whaling trade[26] began to bring prosperity to the town until the mid-nineteenth century, when the general fishing industry began to increase.[27] However, whilst Hull prospered, large numbers of Hull's citizens did not; with an increasing population of 22,000 in 1801 to 119,500 in 1870, competition for jobs, which were predominately dock-related, was hard. It led to increasing levels of poverty amongst many, and it has been stated that, in 1884, "1,000 Hull families were starving in East Hull resulting in the premature death of many children."[28] The workhouses of Hull also provided shelter for the destitute; five were built across the town.[29]

The industrial revolution had a similar effect on the people of Hull and London, bringing pollution, poverty, and ill health, particularly for the poor. With the fear of destitution, poverty, and brutal living conditions, and in the absence of reliable contraception or legal abortion, there were a predictably high number of infant cadavers discovered across England: with many mothers remaining undiscovered, the true extent of the crime is difficult to ascertain. Arnot, for example, has argued that it is impossible to determine the number of babies murdered at birth during Victorian London or indeed throughout England.[30] Similarly, in Hull, during the mid-nineteenth century, a number of infant cadavers were also discovered around the city.[31]

With people living in such close proximity, it would have been difficult to commit a crime without raising suspicions. In the seventeenth century, in cases of suspected infanticide, suspicions were raised because either an infant cadaver or evidence of childbirth had been discovered, which in turn led to an interrogation. Blood was often a crucial piece of evidence: it was difficult to conceal and difficult to remove, and so it became useful to establish that a recent delivery, or a recent death, had occurred.[32] Neighbours or members of the local community would then carry out an interrogation of the suspected woman[33] in order to establish the woman had delivered the child, a practice that continued until at least the mid-nineteenth century. For example, Elizabeth Nelson was indicted for the wilful murder of her infant, in 1867, in Hull. She had given birth in the workhouse but left suddenly when the child was five weeks old. Boarding in a lodging house, it was the landlady who raised suspicions when Elizabeth returned one day without the child, when the:

> suspicion of her neighbours were focused on Friday the 29th July and they questioned the prisoner about the child. She made excuses, and whilst pretending she was on her way out of the house to show the inquirers the dead body of the infant who she alleged died from natural causes, she ran away.[34]

Elizabeth was discovered and taken into custody; at the police station, she confessed to throwing the child into the harbour: the child's body was found on the shore near Brough; she later confessed to throwing it over North Bridge into the harbour of Hull: at the inquest, Mr Jackson, the surgeon, deposed that "the child had been severely injured … however the child was alive when it was thrown in";[35] the jury therefore returned a verdict of wilful murder against Elizabeth. At the York Assizes, "the jury, after an absence of two hours, returned a verdict of guilty with a strong recommendation to mercy, on the ground of the prisoner's youth and distress. His Lordship passed sentence of death,"[36] but Elizabeth did not seem "much to regard her position."[37]

The criminal justice process from the seventeenth century

Once questioned, a suspected woman may then have faced prosecution. Prosecutions during the seventeenth century were private, making it possible for anyone to arrest a woman on suspicion of infanticide (or any other felony).[38] However, it was advisable to firstly inform a constable or run the risk that if the Justice had no personal knowledge of the alleged crime, he had no grounds to justify an arrest;[39] the system therefore relied on willing members of the public to initiate proceedings.

Infanticide cases in London were referred to the magistrate, who assessed the evidence, committed the suspect to prison to await trial, and draw up the indictment. The trial would then have been carried out swiftly; there was a legal expectation that the woman would appear before a Justice within three days of arrest or the detention could result in false imprisonment.[40] From 1550 to 1800 the prosecution of infanticide, or any felony in the name of the king, could only proceed with an indictment.[41] As the indictment or accusation was made by "twelve or more laymen sworn to inquire in the kings behalf and recorded before a court of record,"[42] the indictment acted as a safeguard, preventing the king or his ministers from putting a woman on trial for infanticide indiscriminately. This procedure protected those accused of a felony from indiscriminate prosecutions, thus making indictments imperative as a matter of constitutional principle.

Therefore, the nature of the offence and its wording on the indictment were crucial, as they determined the punishment in the event of a "guilty" verdict.[43] The Grand Jury would discuss the indictment and the extent of the evidence; evidence would have been heard from witnesses, but not from the accused, and in the event of insufficient evidence, the case would be dropped.[44] In cases where the evidence was found to be "sufficient, to warrant a trial" and proceeded to be approved as a "true bill,"[45] the accused would be brought before the court to enter a plea during a process of arraignment. Prior to the nineteenth century the majority of suspects pleaded not guilty; this was encouraged by the courts because:

> if a defendant confessed to a crime, there was no flexibility in the punishment they could receive, whereas if a trial took place, evidence could be introduced which might determine whether the defendant merited a lesser sentence or a pardon.[46]

In cases of murder or manslaughter that had been "formulated by coroner's juries,"[47] approval by the grand jury was unnecessary; as such, cases "automatically went to trial."[48]

Pardons could be received in a number of ways, at the discretion of the judge or through the Secretary of State. By the conclusion of the Assizes, the judge had usually determined which criminals he would recommend to mercy. However, if the criminal did not receive a pardon, it was possible to petition the monarch up until the moment of execution through the Secretary of State.[49] It was therefore the monarch's prerogative to determine who should receive a pardon, and, in doing so, it was imperative that this decision was made by balancing the deterrence of crime on the one hand, and public outcry on the other. A reduction in the number of pardons would go against the grain of the principle of crime deterrence, and too many hangings would result in public outcry and disorder.[50] As many convicts did receive either a conditional pardon reducing the sentence to transportation or a free pardon, Hay has argued that, rather than terrifying criminals during the eighteenth century, the death penalty "terrified prosecutors and the jury who feared committing judicial murder on the capital statutes."[51]

There were no Assizes for London and Middlesex, because a merger existed between the two counties, allowing trials to take place for serious crimes north of the Thames in one central court with greater frequency. This central court was the Justice Hall and was attached to Newgate Prison, "where commissions to deliver that gaol were executed" and more commonly referred to as the Old Bailey.[52]

The Old Bailey consisted of eight sittings a year,[53] and, until 1737, it was an "open air edifice, almost an archaeological cutaway designed to protect the court against infectious disease that might be carried by witnesses or prisoners."[54] Onlookers at the trial stood in an open area, which resembled a courtyard called a "Sessions House Yard."[55] Oldham has noted that the trial viewed from this courtyard would "resemble nothing as much as a giant Punch and Judy show,"[56] a scene depicting an enjoyable diversion for the spectators rather than one of sorrow or dread.

During the eighteenth century criminals in Hull were dealt with by the Quarter Sessions, with more serious crimes coming before a "rather vague sheriff's court that met twice a year."[57] However, as with any suspect accused of felony until 1971,[58] the principal criminal court in England the accused woman would have appeared before was the Assizes. In most instances, women indicted through a Coroner's Inquest or Sessions Court would already be in gaol awaiting trial,[59] but as the Assizes was not a permanent court and only sat twice a year, Lent and in the summer, they may have been in gaol for some time.[60]

The Hull Assizes were held on request by the mayor but, in reality, were held only once every seven years until 1745, when the "Bench persuaded the Judges to come every three years."[61] In the nineteenth century, women accused of infanticide in Hull and the East Riding would firstly have appeared locally at the police court before being transferred to York Castle, where the Yorkshire Assizes were held. As Hull was geographically part of the county of Yorkshire, criminals awaiting trial were referred to the Yorkshire Assizes; the Yorkshire Assizes were part of a broader Assizes circuit which formed the Northern Circuit.[62]

For the purposes of Assize proceedings, the country was initially divided into six circuits,[63] when "two common law judges, a judge and a serjeant or infrequently two serjeant's rode each circuit, hearing pleas and delivering gaols in the county towns."[64] As part of the Northern Circuit, it has been highlighted by Jackson that the "majority of women tried for murder in the Northern Circuit Courts did not come from large towns such as Leeds, Sheffield or Newcastle, but from small villages and townships."[65] This raises the point that in small, close-knit communities, it was harder to escape the watchful gaze of the community. In smaller communities, women were less likely to be anonymous but more likely to experience a stain on their reputation at the prospect of delivering an illegitimate child.[66]

The day the court arrived in town brought an atmosphere of excitement and entertainment; the Assizes attracted a social spectacle on a grand scale, with the accumulation of an eclectic mix of local people from the surrounding villages and farms. The Assizes presented the people with an opportunity to meet friends or business colleagues and be entertained by the court proceedings and witnessing executions.[67] The Assizes were seen as a "formidable spectacle in country town, the most visible and elaborate manifestation of state power to be seen in the countryside"[68] because of the large presence the Assizes attracted, and its diverse blend of society with "barristers and jurors and the cream of country society attending the Assize ball and county meetings."[69] Such scenes, however, encapsulate a confused blend of emotion, with revelry and merrymaking on the one hand and the sense of foreboding on the other.

Once a prosecution went ahead, a crucial component of the trial of the woman would have been the jury. At the Old Bailey, because the court covered two jurisdictions, there were two juries, one for London and one for Middlesex; whilst one heard evidence for new cases, the other considered its verdicts.[70] In 1737, the courtroom was redesigned, which allowed the jury to present "their verdict at the end of each case without leaving the courtroom."[71]

Across the rest of the country, "trial juries were composed of men drawn from the immediate neighbourhood where the crime occurred,"[72] until the late fifteenth century, so in some cases the accused may have been known to the jury. The jury were usually male local property owners[73] and had the benefit of local knowledge of the case, giving them the advantage of accessing circumstances of the case and those responsible, in many cases from local gossip and conjecture. However, it could be argued that, in cases of infanticide, the likelihood of property owners personally knowing each infanticidal woman or girl within their community must have been rare; socially, they must have moved in very different circles within society.

Having personal knowledge of the accused or facts of the case could be seen as an advantage to the jurors. They were able to incorporate their knowledge into the verdict, arriving at their decision through common sense and common knowledge. There was an expectation that jurors would draw on this personal knowledge to reach a verdict, regardless of the circumstances of acquiring such knowledge and its unreliability; if obtained in an unofficial capacity it may have led to a false verdict.[74] In some cases, jurors were "permitted and indeed expected to consider their personal knowledge of the facts in dispute in reaching a verdict."[75] As the population grew increasingly mobile, jurors became less familiar with the facts of cases and less acquainted with the accused, leading them to rely instead on the testimony of witnesses. Attendance by witnesses in court became so important that in 1563 legislation was passed compelling the attendance of witnesses in civil cases and making perjury a crime.[76]

Throughout the seventeenth century, jurors relied on evidence presented to them in court, as opposed to information they had personally attained. Jurors had gradually become "third parties who had to employ their rational and analytical faculties to reach conclusions about facts and events they had not previously witnessed or previously known."[77] However, juries did not surrender their right to consider personal knowledge in reaching a verdict but placed a greater reliance on the testimony of witnesses and documents, which they were required to evaluate for accuracy and sincerity.

The pervasive power of the jury should not be underestimated; Loar, for example, has suggested that the conscience of the jury played a large part in the returning of many mitigated verdicts, particularly in cases where the jury faced a moral dilemma.[78] Medieval and Early Modern jurors discovered ways of mitigating the law in an attempt to prevent the accused from receiving harsh punishments to harsh laws,[79] a pervasive power that Green has argued led the courts to recognise the lesser offence of manslaughter, as opposed to the more serious offence of murder.[80] The power the jury holds "against the intervention of the judge"[81] should therefore not be underestimated or overlooked.

The landmark decision in the case of *Bushell*,[82] in 1670, further demonstrates the power of the jury; until this time, jurors could be judicially fined for reaching a conclusion with which the trial judge disagreed.[83] The *Bushell* case that was heard in the aftermath of the verdict in the case of, *The King v Penn and Mead*,[84] in which the jury went against the advice of the judge. All 12 members of the jury were not only fined, but also imprisoned without meat, drink, fire, and tobacco, until payment was duly received by the court, as it was considered that "obstinate juries as a threat to the social order and rule of law and conflict between bench and jury was not uncommon"[85] and therefore need to be punished accordingly.

When the jury foreman, Edward Bushell, appealed to the Court of Common Pleas, the case was heard before Chief Justice John Vaughan, who not only cleared them all but stated that "the jury must be independently and indisputably responsible for its verdict free from any threats from the court."[86] The case became a landmark decision for "effectively outlawing the practice of punishing conscientiously disobedient jurors."[87]

The influential power of the consciousness of the jury has also been recognised in cases of infanticide; Jackson has argued that the leniency demonstrated by juries during the eighteenth century towards infanticidal women resulted in fundamental changes in the law surrounding infanticide, with the implementation of a lesser offence of concealment of birth.[88] In infanticide cases where the jury found a woman guilty, she would be hanged, "usually within a matter of hours and nearly always within several days,"[89] an issue that undoubtedly influenced the jury's conscience, particularly in cases where the accused was known to the jury. This is reflected in a statement made by Sir Thomas Smith, Assizes Judge, to the jury:

> have an eye to your othe and to your duetie, and doe that which God shall put in your mindes to the discharge of your consciences.[90]

Towards the end of the seventeenth century the conscience of the jury was established as a right, or duty, allowing them to make:

> moral decisions based on what their own consciences told them. The objective certainty of earlier times had disappeared and been replaced by an understanding that acknowledged the individuals obligations to obey his or her own conscience regardless of what others might think.[91]

The consciousness of the jury remained at the forefront of the infanticide trial and continued to be evident throughout the nineteenth century, notably during the trial of Mary Ann Lamb from Hull, who was charged with the wilful murder of her new-born child through the administration of laudanum. At the York Assizes, Mr Dearsley, learned counsel for the defence, empathised the conscience of the jury in his address. He asked them to:

> weigh all the evidence and if they found any reasonable doubt to give the prisoner the benefit of that doubt, if the facts bring clearly home to the prisoner this fearful crime it is your duty however painful to give a verdict in accordance therein. The prisoner was accommodated with a seat at the conclusion of the opening, Mr Dearsley then addressed the jury for the prisoner, who appeared much affected during the delivery of his speech … this was a case of life or death one in which the jury must answer yea or nay and to the best of their consciousness say whether this girl should die an ignominious death on the scaffold. The jury found her not guilty.[92]

Sources

Until the nineteenth century, there was not a "single standard for the reporting of court cases."[93] The "proceedings, also known as Old Bailey Sessions Papers"[94] (OBSP) gave accounts of the trials that had taken place at the sessions or sittings at the Old Bailey, reporting the "outcome of every trial held in each session, and they contained supposedly verbatim narratives for most of the trials."[95] Based on the notes taken from shorthand reporters,[96] the OBSP were an "early species of periodical journalism, purveying a diet of true-life crime stories for the interest and amusement of a non-lawyer readership,"[97] and were available to purchase on the streets of London within days of a trial. This unique account of trials held at the Old Bailey was exclusive to cases held within London and Middlesex, and so no equivalent source for criminal trials in Hull or the surrounding area existed.

However, the OBSP were not without their deficiencies, with one crucial shortcoming being that they were edited; editing allowed each trial, held at one particular session, to be included within the pamphlet.[98] Owing to the combination of the length of the trials during the 1750s, which could amount to some three or four days' duration, and the added volume of potentially 50 cases heard over a typical session period, it is possible that most of the legal information surrounding the doctrinal and procedural detail was edited. Allowing for more entertaining content to please the non-lawyer reading public. Even from the 1780s, when the OBSP were achieving their "greatest detail, they were still omitting most of what was said at most of the trials they reported";[99] therefore, the qualitative evaluation of cases should be carried out with caution.

Beginning in 1778, and particularly after 1782, the length of the trial accounts given in the OBSP increased markedly as a result of a request of the city that a "true fair and perfect narrative of all the trials at the Old Bailey";[100] more trials were now being "reported in greater detail than ever before been the case."[101] Notwithstanding this fact, it should still be noted that even the trials that appear to have been extensively reported on might still be incomplete and not printed in their entirety.[102] In the 1802 case of Mary Lucas, for instance, who was "indicted for the wilful murder of her male bastard child," the OBSP merely reports that "the surgeon not being able to prove that the child was born alive, the prisoner was acquitted. First Middlesex Jury, before Mr Baron Hotham."[103]

Despite these shortcomings and the fact that Shoemaker argues the proceedings presented a "partial account of crime and criminal justice to their readers,"[104] it is still possible to conclude that:

> on the present state of our knowledge about the surviving sources, it has to be said that the Sessions Papers are probably the best accounts we shall ever have of what transpired in ordinary English criminal courts before the later eighteenth-century.[105]

The importance of the OBSP as a historical research source has also been emphasised by Crone, when she argues that they "tell us a great deal about the nature of crime and its punishment in eighteenth and nineteenth-century London."[106] There appear to be three reasons for the conclusion of the OBSP in 1913; the implementation of the Criminal Appeal Act in 1907, making the taking of shorthand notes a statutory requirement, giving no compelling reason to publish the papers.[107] The increasing financial implications and the added growth of the number of daily newspapers with the capacity, and ability, to publish trial reports at a faster rate than the OBSP,[108] especially the printing of cases which created sensational headlines, attracted a vast amount of public interest.

Elsewhere, until the nineteenth century, criminal law reporting failed to be common practice, when the trial became lawyer dominated. There is little literature available today on the trials and, prior to the nineteenth century, it seems there was a need for a system where both:

> statutory and case law together comprise the governing law of the land, ideally requires a thorough and authoritative set of case law reports. However, with the demise of the legal yearbooks in the early sixteenth century, law reporting was done privately where individual jurists or practitioners compiled cases for their own use and subsequently began to publish them.[109]

Following this period and throughout the nineteenth century, in particular, there are extensive newspaper articles describing the atmosphere in the courtroom, the trial, and testimony in court. This process began in the eighteenth century, when some newspaper reporters were granted special status to publish their court reports.[110] As a condition of the status permitting judges to read and amend reports prior to publication, long delays could be encountered, allowing the opportunity for unauthorised reporters to publish reports that contained varying degrees of reliability. In the years following 1790, reporters were permitted to publish "verbatim transcripts of most legal trials without interference."[111] Due to this extensive coverage of legal trials in general and medical evidence in infanticide cases in particular, newspapers have been used to source cases from Hull and the surrounding area throughout this research and for cases held at the Old Bailey between 1913 and 1955.

During the nineteenth century, as the "working class public expanded and became more diversified," an increase in literacy became evident,[112] whilst simultaneously developments in printing and an increase in the paper brought a growth in newspaper circulation. Newspaper sales began to increase dramatically and newspaper reading in popularity, despite social class, level of education, or intelligence, and so the newspaper-reading public became widespread across the population as "remarkable efforts were made to get at the news."[113] Although newspapers were "prohibitively expensive," they were freely available in coffee and public houses for customers to read.[114] Old newspapers were passed through the streets, or people clubbed together to purchase a copy, and should a newspaper appear in a shop window, a crowd soon congregated to read the headline "eager to learn what was going on."[115] To accompany this increased interest in current affairs came a corresponding increased interest in crime, which soon became a "form of entertainment for all practical purposes morally neutral and certainly popular."[116] This resulted in most newspapers feeding the hungry public's appetite for "horrible and dreadful" crimes by printing lengthy accounts to the extent that in most cases the "headlines were missing as there was not enough paper to spare for big letters."[117] As the eagerly awaiting public followed reports of criminal trials, particularly when cases were regarded as notable or notorious, newspaper editors seized the opportunity to increase circulation, with one newspaper, in particular, namely the *Times* publishing a set of formal reports, the *Times Law Reports* from 1884 to 1952.

By continuing to consider circulation and the public's enthusiasm for crime during the second half of the nineteenth century, report details were expanded to include "eyewitness accounts, investigative reports and colourful sketches,"[118] implying that some articles were written for the fundamental purpose of entertaining readers, as opposed to portraying the true facts of the case, a clear disadvantage when using newspapers for research purposes, raising concerns regarding reliability and bias. In the latter years of the nineteenth century, the proficiency of press reporting became evident with the invention of the "telegraph and the subsequent formation of collective news gathering agencies such as Reuters and the Press Association."[119]

Also evident from the mid-nineteenth century was the growth of the provincial press, and it has been identified that between "1855 and 1861, 137 newspapers were launched in 123 English towns,"[120] concentrating on particular market towns or boroughs previously without one.

The first newspaper to be published in the town of Hull was the *Courant* in 1759, renamed the *Hull Packet* in 1787; consisting of eight columns on each of its four pages, it cost 7d, a price unaffordable to many. In 1827, the *Hull Packet* was sold and once again renamed the *Hull Packet and Humber Mercury*.[121] As newspapers were an extravagance to many and unaffordable to most working-class people, the "Press Associations cheap telegraphed news and cheaper newsprint made half penny evening paper available even in small towns."[122] These evening papers were predominately aimed at the working classes and were "central to the development of gambling and professional football."[123]

As the growth of the press increased, gaining extreme audiences from a wide variety of socio-economic classes, press discourse came to be considered an educator of individuals, with the power to determine normative behaviour, in particular, a form of power operating through knowledge.

For the purposes of research, newspaper articles provide crucial background information and descriptive scene settings, which are lacking in court reports. Grey has argued that local newspapers "provide historians with key details of such cases which other sources – including national newspapers reporting on the same trial – might well omit."[124] The following accounts, for example, describe women accused of infanticide in the courtroom, and particularly the physical and emotional condition of the accused:

> this morning the unfortunate young woman (evidently in a state of great weakness) was carried into the court charged with the wilful murder of her child.[125] The Magistrate after retiring for about a quarter of an hour returned and when the mayor said, the magistrates having very carefully with the assistance of the solicitor gave into the evidence as to the charge brought against you, have come to the conclusion that there is not sufficient to justify them in sending you for trial – you are therefore discharged.[126]

A second article describes a prisoner as being:

> removed to Hull Gaol on a stretcher about ten o'clock on Tuesday night, in the care of Sergeant Cook, detective Coulson, five other constables, and the female attendant of the police station. She has, since the fearfully responsible condition in which she is placed became known to her been silent and apparently much depressed in spirits, and sobbed for hours together, but at intervals has been more lively and inclined for conversation.[127]

Newspaper articles also provide an insight into public opinion, encapsulating the public mood concerning infanticide. For example:

> the court was densely crowded, a large number of persons chiefly women remained outside unable to procure admission … the female appeared to be considerably affected.[128]

This case depicts a scene of immense female interest, which may be related to the curiosity of an infanticide case or a broader reflection of the sick civilisation, whilst at the same time reflecting the curiosity surrounding women as criminals. As female criminals after "1800 … came to be regarded as unnatural rather than criminal,"[129] their trials generated a sense of morbid curiosity amongst the public, particularly amongst other women. This is demonstrated in the case of Isabella Hewson, who was charged "on remand at the Borough Court yesterday with the wilful murder of her illegitimate child, the gallery of the court was crowded with females."[130] A further example of morbid curiously is described in the following article:

> at a very early hour on Wednesday morning the Old Bailey and all the avenues leading to it, were crowded with persons, several of whom appeared above the common grade, to witness the execution of Mary Chapman for attempting to murder her child at Hammersmith.[131]

Both newspaper articles depict a scene which encapsulates both local and national curiosity in infanticidal women from the trial to the sentence. The lower classes, according to Foucault, took an interest in crime news as they were "true stories of everyday history" and "people found in them not only memories but also precedents: the interest of 'curiosity' is also a political interest."[132]

Interestingly, the extensive coverage of crime by the nineteenth-century broadsheets coincided with the birth of detective fiction. Fictional crime literature replaced the broadsheets' role of feeding the public appetite for monstrous stories, of murder and intrigue, in the battle between two minds. The creation of the detective, and the villain or murderer, became the successful formula for bestselling novels such as the characters of Sherlock Holmes and Professor Moriarty, as portrayed by Sir Arthur Conan Doyle.[133]

Whilst crime fiction began to increase in popularity, newspapers resumed their role of "recounting the grey, unheroic details of everyday crime and punishment,"[134] and it is evident from one nineteenth-century newspaper that there were growing concerns for the increasing number of infant deaths in provincial areas. The extent of child murder in Malton, a small market town in North Yorkshire, was described as:

> becoming truly horrible. Within little more than a month there has been a case of concealment of birth at Thixendale; a verdict of wilful murder by the coroner's jury against a young woman at Aclam as to the death of her illegitimate off spring; and thirdly a new-born child found dead in a lane near the market place of Malton. The latter was wrapped up in a flannel and sewn into a pillow case, the post mortem examination showed that it had been born alive, there was a bruise on the forehead, but not sufficient to produce death, the cause of which was unknown – verdict found dead.[135]

Such articles not only reflect public opinion during the mid-nineteenth century towards infanticide but also provide a sense of the human sentiment towards infanticide. In the following article, for example, it reads:

> the public mind was most fearfully excited on Monday last, by the rumoured discovery in the hollow trunk of a tree at Kelleythrope near Driffield of the body of a child, about 6 months old. Many tongued gossip described the foundling as a beautiful creature, which, had been put away by its inhuman

> parent or parents, and speculation and wonderment ran high as to who could possibly have been the cruel perpetrators of so horrid a deed.[136]

Therefore, whilst the OBSP accurately reflect the number of cases held at the Old Bailey, it is important to highlight that newspapers may not. Newspapers provide a valuable method of encapsulating an essence of history, but for research purposes it is important to establish that a number of cases may not have been reported or printed. Articles were not written in an objective way, often "presenting a skewed view of reality, if only because a limited number of pages can never provide an accurate portrait of reality."[137] Grey has highlighted a further shortcoming of provincial newspapers, when he raises the important issue that they fail to "provide or pursue any details of the father of the child, something that was a common characteristic of reporting on infanticide cases."[138]

It is also likely that, due to the secrecy surrounding infanticide, many cases remained undiscovered. The law relied on private proceedings; therefore not all parties will have been willing to bring legal action against an infanticidal woman, whilst other women will have successfully hidden traces of their crime, escaping conviction, and contributing to the dark figure of infanticide. In other cases, as the research will demonstrate in Chapter 3, a cadaver may have been discovered and an inquest held; however, the mother remained unknown.

Chapter outline

This book will begin with a review of both themes and perceptions common to cases of infanticide. Divided into two elements, the chapter will begin with a historiography of infanticide and a review of the existing literature. In particular, it pieces together significant legal doctrine that has contributed to the historiography of infanticide, such as the 1624 "An Act to Prevent the Destroying and Murthering of Bastard Children," the Lord Ellenborough's Act 1803, and the Infanticide Acts of 1922 and 1938. It will then concentrate on medical experts and the law, with a historiography of medical experts, explaining how the role of the medical expert transpired within the English courtroom.

The following four chapters examine the testimony of a number of expert witnesses called to give evidence in infanticide cases. Chapter 2 will begin in the seventeenth century by examining the testimony of midwives, female practitioners, who were selected by the courts for their knowledge of the female anatomy and experience of childbirth. The cases throughout this chapter demonstrate the extent of the reliance the courts placed on the midwife as an expert witness throughout the seventeenth and eighteenth centuries, as she drew on her experience and training to profess her opinion. As the testimony given by midwives regarding the infant body as a source of evidence remained unsupported by scientific experiments, or testing, it could be described as raw. This chapter is therefore a useful starting point or baseline for the male medical experts throughout the remainder of this book to be measured.

The focus of this research will then turn towards the expert who relied predominantly on external examination to provide answers in court. Chapter 3 focuses on the medical, scientifically based evidence of the physician, surgeon, barber surgeon, man-midwife, and apothecary during the eighteenth and nineteenth centuries. The difference between the evidence provided by midwives and medical men lay with science in general and the lung test in particular. As the lung test proved to be inconclusive as to whether a child had had a separate existence, it became evident, over time, that there remained little difference in terms of the degree of certainty in the answers provided by the midwives and the medical men. The chapter examines the testimony provided at coroner inquests in Hull and the surrounding area, before examining the testimony within infanticide trials held at the Old Bailey.

Chapter 4 will turn away from the cadaver as the central focus of the infanticide trial, considering instead the guilty mind as a subject of evidence. The mental state of the criminal became a subject of considerable attention during the nineteenth century, when a verdict of "guilty but insane" came to be of significant use after 1883. This verdict permitted the judge to detain the criminal during Her Majesty's Pleasure, thus sparing the criminal's life. Medical evidence became crucial in insanity cases because "insanity was the easiest disease to imitate."[139] In infanticide cases, however, to plead insanity would have been detrimental to the woman, as many women either received short prison sentences or were acquitted. This chapter is supported with the testimony provided by lay witnesses and experts, analysing the mental state of infanticidal women. The chapter will draw on cases held both at the Old Bailey and in Hull and the surrounding area.

As the scientific investigation and medical discourse continued to evolve during the nineteenth century, so too did the role of the pathologist, an expert who was trained in the art of dissection and autopsy. His role was to establish cause of death and expertly present the findings in court. Chapter 5 will therefore analyse the testimony of pathologists in cases held at both the Old Bailey and Hull and the surrounding area.

This chapter began with an introduction to the notion of uncertainty in the expert evidence surrounding infanticide cases and proceeded with an explanation as to how the longevity has been divided into timeframes; it has also introduced the sources which have been drawn on to carry out the research and an explanation for their selection. The chapter has also provided an account of the procedure the prisoner would have experienced after suspicions were raised and her initial arrest, both within the areas of London and Hull. Divided into two sections, the following chapter will focus on a review of the literature with firstly the historical aspects of infanticide, and secondly experts and the law.

Notes

1 *OBP*, May 1873, Mary Shirley, t18730505-369.
2 Ibid; A copper was a deep cauldron with a lid, which supplied hot water, see: *The Copper*, available at: www.1900s.org.uk [Last accessed April 27, 2020].
3 *OBP*, May 1873, Mary Shirley, t18730505-369.
4 Ibid.

5 There was a noticeable number of murder trials held at the Old Bailey, between 1730 and 1760, in which medical testimony was given, *London Lives 1690–1800 – Crime, Poverty and Social Policy in the Metropolis,* available at: www.londonlives.org/static/CriminalTrial.jsp [Last accessed April 14, 2017]; see also J. Havard, *The Detection of Secret Homicide: A Study of the Medico-Legal System of Investigation of Sudden and Unexplained Deaths*. London: Macmillan, 1960.
6 J. Miller, *Cities Divided: Politics and Religion in English Provincial Towns 1660–1722*. Oxford: Oxford University Press. Published to Oxford Scholarship Online (eBook) (2010).
7 'How the Contraceptive Pill Changed Britain' at: www.bbc.co.uk/news/uk-15984258 [Last accessed November 18, 2015].
8 See E. M. Silies, 'Taking the Pill after the 'Sexual Revolution': Female Contraceptive Decisions in England and West Germany in the 1970s' *European Review of History*, Vol. 22, No. 1, 2015, pp. 41–59.
9 Abortion Act 1967 S1 (1) available at www.legislation.gov.uk/ukpga/1967/87 [Last accessed March 21, 2016.
10 T. Hitchcock, R. Shoemaker, C. Emsley, S. Howard and J. McLaughlin, *et al., The Old Bailey Proceedings Online, 1674-1913* (www.oldbaileyonline.org, version 7.0, 24 March 2012). All cases cited within this book, relate to the March 2012 version.
11 V. Bates, *Sexual Forensics in Victorian and Edwardian England: Age, Crime and Consent in the Courts*. Houndmills, Basingstoke, Hampshire: Palgrave Macmillan, 2016: 22.
12 British Newspaper Archive (www.britishnewspaperarchive.co.uk); The British Library Board; © 2021 Findmypast Newspaper Archive Limited.
13 Miller (2010) op. cit.: 17.
14 R. Porter, *London: A Social History*. London: Penguin, 1996: 67.
15 Ibid.: 66.
16 C. Emsley, T. Hitchcock and R. Shoemaker, "History of the Old Bailey Courthouse", *Old Bailey Proceedings Online* (www.oldbaileyonline.org, version 6.0, 17 April 2011). [Last accessed December 13, 2016].
17 Ibid.
18 See D. Gray, *London's Shadows: The Dark Side of the Victorian City*. London: Continuum, 2010: chapter 3.
19 See D. Ward, 'The Victorian Slum: An Enduring Myth?' *Annals of the Association of American Geographers*, Vol. 66, No. 2, 1976, pp. 323–336; M. McKean, 'Re-thinking Late Victorian Fiction: The Crowd and Imperialism at Home' *English Literature in Translation 1880–1920*, Vol. 54, No. 1, 2011, pp. 28; R. Porter (1996) op. cit.; G. Mooney, 'Diagnostic Spaces: Workhouse, Hospital and Home in Mid-Victorian London' *Social Science History*, Vol. 33, No. 3, 2009, pp. 357–390; S. Kearley, 'It's a Hard-Knock Life in Victorian Workhouses' *British Heritage*, Vol. 36, No. 5, 2015, pp. 50–53.
20 'A Penny for Your … Lodgings' at https://wonderfulcollection.wordpress.com/tag/penny-hang/ [Last accessed March 1, 2017].
21 Ibid.
22 C. Dickens, *Oliver Twist*. Second Edition. London: Richard Bentley, New Burlington Street, 1839: 7.
23 Porter (1996) op. cit.: 149.
24 See S. Dentith, '"Under the Shadow of the Workhouse:" The Afterlife of a Victorian Institution' *Lit: Literature Interpretation Theory*, Vol. 20, No. 1–2, 2009, pp. 79–91.
25 J. Sharpe, 'Enforcing the Law in the Seventeenth-Century English Village' in V. Gatrell, B. Lenman, and G. Parker (eds.) *Crime and the Law: The Social History of Crime in Western Europe since 1500*. London: Europa Publications, 1980: 101.
26 G. Jackson, *Hull in the Eighteenth Century: A Study in Economic and Social History*. London: Oxford University Press, 1972: 157–178.

27 Hull City Council *Hull Character Study*. Hull: Hull City Council, 2010. Available at https://cmis.hullcc.gov.uk/CMIS/Document [Last accessed April 4, 2017].
28 'Kingston upon Hull War Memorial 1914–1918' at: www.ww1hull.org.uk/index.php/hull-in-ww1/hull-before-1914 [Last accessed April 4, 2017].
29 *Hull History Centre Website* at www.hullhistorycentre.org.uk/ [Last accessed April 4, 2017]; see also F. Preston, 'The Dark Days of Hull's Lost Victorian Workhouses' *Hull Daily Mail*, 2016. Available at: www.hulldailymail.co.uk/the-dark-days-of-hull-s-lost-victorian-workhouses/story-29916122-detail/story.html [Last accessed April 4, 2017].
30 M. Arnot, 'Understanding Women Committing New-Born Child Murder in Victorian England' in S. D'Cruze (ed.) *Everyday Violence in Britain, 1850–1950*. Harlow: Pearson Education Limited, 2000: 56.
31 M. Covell, 'The Hidden Horrible Histories of Hull – From Body Snatchers to Jack the Stabber' *Hull Daily Mail*, 2016. Available at: www.hulldailymail.co.uk/the-hidden-horrible-histories-of-hull-from-bodysnatchers-to-jack-the-stabber/story-30000534-detail/story.html [Last accessed December 27, 2016].
32 S. Williams, 'The Experience of Pregnancy and Childbirth for Unmarried Mothers in London, 1760–1866' *Women's History Review*, Vol. 20, No. 1, 2011, pp. 67–86: 76.
33 M. Jackson, *New-Born Child Murder: Women, Illegitimacy and the Courts in Eighteenth-Century England*. Manchester: Manchester University Press, 1996: 17.
34 *Hull Packet and East Riding Times*, 'Yorkshire Summer Assizes' Friday August 9, 1867, p.8. British Newspaper Archive (www.britishnewspaperarchive.co.uk); The British Library Board; Image © the British Library Board. All rights reserved.
35 *The Hull Advertiser*, 'The Inquest on the Child Nicholas Nelson- Verdict of Wilful Murder' Tuesday April 23, 1867, p.5. British Newspaper Archive (www.britishnewspaperarchive.co.uk); The British Library Board; Image © the British Library Board. All rights reserved.
36 *Bradford Observer*, 'Murder at Hull' Thursday August 8, 1867. British Newspaper Archive (www.britishnewspaperarchive.co.uk); The British Library Board; Image © the British Library Board. All rights reserved.
37 'Yorkshire Summer Assizes' op. cit. Friday August 9, 1867.
38 Prosecutions remained private until 1880, when the Director of Public Prosecutions became established as part of the Home Office. Since 1986, the Crown Prosecution Service, headed by the Director of Public Prosecutions, have been responsible for prosecution. It remains possible for any person to arrest without a warrant, under section 24A of the Police and Criminal Evidence Act 1984.
39 J. Baker, *The Legal Profession and the Common Law: Historical Essays*. London: The Hambeldon Press, 1986: 281.
40 Ibid.
41 Ibid.: 263.
42 Ibid.
43 C. Emsley, T. Hitchcock and R. Shoemaker, "Trial Procedures", *Old Bailey Proceedings Online* (www.oldbaileyonline.org, version 6.0, 17 April 2011). [Last accessed January 14, 2017].
44 Ibid.
45 Ibid.
46 Ibid.
47 Ibid.
48 Ibid.
49 D. Hay, 'Property, Authority and the Criminal Law' in M. Fitzgerald, G. McLennan, and J. Pawson (eds.) *Crime and Society: Readings in History and Theory*. London: Routledge and Kegan Paul, 1981: 8; See also J. Baker, *An Introduction to English Legal History*. Fifth Edition. Oxford: Oxford University Press, 2019: 557–558.
50 See L. MacKay, 'Refusing the Royal Pardon: London Capital Convicts and the Reactions of the Court and the Press, 1789' *London Journal*, Vol. 28, No. 2, 2003, pp.

21–40; S. Devereaux, 'Imposing the Royal Pardon: Execution, Transportation, and Convict Resistance in London 1780' *Law and History Review*, Vol. 25, No. 1, Spring 2007, pp. 101–138.
51 D. Hay, 'Property, Authority and the Criminal Law' in D. Hay, et al. (eds.) *Albion's Fatal Tree: Crime and Society in Eighteenth-Century England*. London: Penguin, 1977: 23.
52 J. Baker (1986) op. cit.: 278. See also D. Gray, *Crime, Prosecution and Social Relations: The Summary Courts of the City of London in the Late Eighteenth Century*. London: Palgrave Macmillan, 2009.
53 C. Emsley, T. Hitchcock and R. Shoemaker, "History of the Old Bailey Courthouse", *Old Bailey Proceedings Online* (www.oldbaileyonline.org, version 6.0, 17 April 2011). [Last accessed November 12, 2015].
54 J. Oldham, 'On Pleading the Belly: A History of the Jury of Matrons' *Criminal Justice History*, Vol. 6, 1985, pp. 1–64: 17.
55 Ibid.
56 Ibid.
57 G. Jackson (1972) op. cit.: 319.
58 The Courts Act 1971 replaced the Assizes Courts with single permanent Crown Courts.
59 J. Baker (1986) op. cit.: 273.
60 Ibid.: 274.
61 G. Jackson (1972) op. cit.: 319.
62 M. Jackson (1996) op. cit.: 20–21.
63 J. Baker (1986) op. cit.: 274.
64 J. Cockburn, *A History of the English Assizes, 1558–1714*. Cambridge: Cambridge University Press, 2011: 23.
65 M. Jackson (1996) op. cit.: 42.
66 Ibid.
67 Hay (1977) op. cit.: 27; see also C. S. A, 'An English County Assizes' *Metropolitan*, Vol. 5, No. 17, 1832, pp. 91-98.
68 Hay (1977) op. cit.: 27.
69 Ibid.
70 C. Emsley, T. Hitchcock and R. Shoemaker, "Trial Procedures", *Old Bailey Proceedings Online* (www.oldbaileyonline.org, version 6.0, 17 April 2011). [Last accessed January 14th 2017].
71 Ibid.
72 S. Anand, 'The Origins, Early History and Evolution of the English Criminal Trial Jury' *Alberta Law Review*, Vol. 43, No. 2, 2005, pp. 407–432: 417. See also J. Cornett, 'Hoodwink'd by Custom: The Exclusion of Women from Juries in Eighteenth-Century English Law and Literature' *William and Mary Journal of Women and the Law*, Vol. 4, 1997, pp. 17–34.
73 C. Herrup, 'Law and Morality in Seventeenth-Century England' *Past and Present*, Vol. 106, February 1985, pp. 102–123. Page 108; the jury consisted of men aged between 21 and 60, with the necessary property qualifications. Until the twentieth century women were forbidden from sitting on juries until 1919; see the Sex Disqualification (Removal) Act 1919 9 & 10 Geo. 5. c. 71.
74 J. Marshall Mitnick, 'From Neighbor-Witness to Judge of Proofs: The Transformation of the English Civil Juror' *American Journal of Legal History*, Vol. 32, 1988, pp. 201–235: 203.
75 Ibid.: 201.
76 B. Shapiro, 'To a Moral Certainty: Theories of Knowledge and Anglo-American Juries 1600–1850' *The Hastings Law Journal*, Vol. 38, November 1986, pp. 153–194: 156; J. Hostettler, *The Criminal Jury Old and New: Jury Power from Early Times to the Present Day*. Winchester: Waterside Press, 2004: 41.
77 Shapiro (1986) op. cit.: 155.

78 C. Loar, 'Under Felt Hats and Worsted Stockings: The Use of Conscience in Early Modern English Coroners Inquests' *Sixteenth Century Journal*, Vol. 41, No. 2, 2010, pp. 393–414: 393.
79 Ibid.
80 T. Green, 'The Jury and the English Law of Homicide 1200–1600' *Michigan Law Review*, Vol. 74, No. 3, January 1976, pp. 413–499: 415.
81 J. Langbein, 'The Criminal Trial before the Lawyers' *The University of Chicago Law Review*, Vol. 45, No. 2, Winter 1978, pp. 263–316: 297.
82 Vaugh, 135, 124 Eng. Rep. 1006 (K. B. 1670).
83 Although it has been argued that there was little evidence of this decision until the following century, as judges continued to exercise greater control over their juries (Langbein, 1978, op. cit.: 298).
84 *The King v Penn and Mead* 6 St. Tr. 951 (1670).
85 J. Marshall Mitnick (1988) op. cit.: 207; for earlier cases of the imprisonment of jurors see R. Pugh, *Imprisonment in Medieval England*. Cambridge: Cambridge University Press, 1968: 10.
86 Vaugh 135, 124 Eng. Rep. 1006 (K. B. 1670).
87 K. Crosby, 'Bushell's Case and the Jurors Soul' *The Journal of Legal History*, Vol. 33 No. 3, 2012, pp. 251–290: 251.
88 M. Jackson (1996) op. cit.: 168–176.
89 Green (1976) op. cit.: 425.
90 Loar (2010) op. cit.: 397. Spelling and grammar are original.
91 Ibid.: 394.
92 *York Herald*, 'Yorkshire Winter Jail Delivery' Saturday December 21, 1850; see also *York Herald*, 'Child Murder at Hull' Saturday December 21, 1850. British Newspaper Archive (www.britishnewspaperarchive.co.uk); The British Library Board; Image © the British Library Board. All rights reserved.
93 M. Rubery, C. Siemann, and J. Wood, 'Court and Parliamentary Reporting' in L. Brake and M. Demoor (eds.) *Dictionary of Nineteenth-Century Journalism in Great Britain and Ireland*. Gent: Academia Press; London: British Library, 2009: 147.
94 R. Shoemaker, 'The Old Bailey Proceedings and the Representation of Crime and Criminal Justice in Eighteenth-Century London' *Journal of British Studies*, Vol. 47, No. 3, 2008, pp. 559–580: 559.
95 J. Langbein, 'Shaping the Eighteenth-Century Criminal Trial: A View from the Ryder Sources' *University of Chicago Law Review*, Vol. 50, 1983, pp. 1–136: 4.
96 Ibid.
97 Ibid.
98 See R. Shoemaker, 'Representing the Adversary Criminal Trial: Lawyers in the Old Bailey Proceedings 1770–1800' in D. Lemmings (ed.) *Crime, Courtrooms and the Public Sphere in Britain, 1700–1850*. Farnham: Ashgate, 2012.
99 J. Langbein, *The Origins of Adversary Criminal Trial*. Oxford: Oxford University Press, 2003: 185.
100 S. Devereaux, 'The City and the Sessions Papers, Public Justice in London 1770–1800' *Journal of British Studies*, Vol. 35, 1996, pp. 466–503: 467.
101 Ibid.
102 Langbein (2003) op. cit.
103 *OBP*, February 1802, Mary Lucas, t18020217-50.
104 Shoemaker (2008) op. cit.: 560.
105 Langbein (2003) op. cit.: 190.
106 R. Crone, 'Crime-and Its Fabrication: A Review of the New Digital Resources in the History of Crime' *Journal of Victorian Culture*, Vol. 16, No. 1, Spring 2009, pp. 125–134: 126.
107 C. Emsley, T. Hitchcock and R. Shoemaker, "Publishing History of the Proceedings", *Old Bailey Proceedings Online* (www.oldbaileyonline.org, version 6.0, 17 April 2011). [Last accessed October 19, 2015].

108 S. Devereaux (1996) op. cit.; See also S. Devereaux, 'The Fall of the Sessions Papers: Criminal Trial and Popular Press in Late Eighteenth-Century London' *Criminal Justice History*, Vol. 18, 2002, pp. 57–88.
109 Rubery, et al. (2009) op. cit.: 147.
110 Ibid.
111 Ibid.
112 R. K. Webb, 'The Victorian Reading Public' in B. Ford (ed.) *The New Pelican Guide to English Literature, volume 6: From Dickens to Hardy*. London: Penguin, 1982: 204.
113 Ibid.: 210.
114 R. Crone, 'Publishing Courtroom Drama for the Masses, 1820–1855' in D. Lemmings (ed.) *Crime, Courtrooms and the Public Sphere in Britain, 1700–1850*. Farnham: Ashgate, 2012.
115 Webb (1982) op. cit.: 210.
116 Ibid.: 213.
117 Ibid.
118 Rubery, et al. (2009) op. cit.: 148; for a contemporary perspective on crime and the media, see E. Einsiedel, et al. 'Crime: Effects of Media Exposure and Personal Experience on Issue Salience' *Journalism Quarterly*, Vol. 61, No. 1, 1984, pp. 131–136.
119 Rubery, et al. (2009) op. cit.: 148; for political influences on the development on the journalism see A. J. Lee, *The Origins of the Popular Press in England, 1855–1914*. London: Croom Helm, 1976.
120 A. Hobbs and M. Beetham, 'Local Press' in L. Brake, and M. Demoor (eds.) *Dictionary of Nineteenth-Century Journalism in Great Britain and Ireland*. Gent: Academia Press; London: British Library, 2009: 371; see also A. Jones, 'Provincial Newspapers' in L. Brake and M. Demoor (eds.) (2009) op. cit.
121 'From Hull Packet to Hull Daily Mail' at: www.hulldailymail.co.uk/Hull-Packet-Hull-Daily-Mail/story-18595847-detail/story.html [Last accessed October 28, 2015].
122 Hobbs, and Beetham (2009) op. cit.: 372.
123 Ibid.
124 D. Grey, 'Agonised Weeping:' Representing Femininity, Emotion and Infanticide in Edwardian Newspapers' *Media History*, Vol. 21, No. 4, 2015, pp. 468–480: 469.
125 *Hull Packet and East Riding Times*, 'Hull Police Court' Friday June 26, 1846. British Newspaper Archive (www.britishnewspaperarchive.co.uk); The British Library Board; Image © the British Library Board. All rights reserved.
126 Ibid.
127 *Hull Packet*, 'Child Murder by a Mother in Hull' Friday August 6, 1858. British Newspaper Archive (www.britishnewspaperarchive.co.uk); The British Library Board; Image © the British Library Board. All rights reserved.
128 *Hull Packet and East Riding Times*, 'Suspected Child Murder at Barrow-Upon-Humber' Friday October 16, 1857. British Newspaper Archive (www.britishnewspaperarchive.co.uk); The British Library Board; Image © the British Library Board. All rights reserved.
129 A. M. Kilday, *A History of Infanticide in Britain c.1600 to the Present*. Basingstoke: Palgrave Macmillan, 2013: 9.
130 *Hull Packet and East Riding Times*, 'The Hull Child Murder Case' Friday June 12, 1855. British Newspaper Archive (www.britishnewspaperarchive.co.uk); The British Library Board; Image © the British Library Board. All rights reserved.
131 *The Hull Packet and Humber Mercury*, 'Advertisements & Notices' Tuesday July 28, 1829. British Newspaper Archive (www.britishnewspaperarchive.co.uk); The British Library Board; Image © the British Library Board. All rights reserved.
132 M. Foucault, *Discipline and Punish: The Birth of the Prison*. London: Allen Lane, 1977: 68.

133 For example, A. Conan Doyle, *The Hound of the Baskervilles*. London: Newnes, 1902.
134 Foucault (1977) op. cit.: 69.
135 *Hull Packet and East Riding Times*, 'General Interest' Friday March 28, 1856. British Newspaper Archive (www.britishnewspaperarchive.co.uk); The British Library Board; Image © the British Library Board. All rights reserved.
136 *The Hull Packet and East Riding Times*, 'District Intelligence' Friday July 24, 1857. British Newspaper Archive (www.britishnewspaperarchive.co.uk); The British Library Board; Image © the British Library Board. All rights reserved.
137 C. Casey, 'Common Misperceptions: The Press and Victorian Views of Crime' *The Journal of Interdisciplinary History*, Vol. 41, No. 3, 2011, pp. 367–391: 385; See also J. Knelman, *Twisting in the Wind, the Murderess and the English Press*. Toronto: University of Toronto Press, 1998: chapter 3.
138 Grey (2015) op. cit.: 469.
139 K. Watson, *Forensic Medicine in Western Society: A History*. Oxford: Routledge, 2011: 78.

1 A historiography of infanticide and the use of medical experts in criminal trials

Whilst endeavouring to explore two areas of research – the history of infanticide and the use of medical experts in criminal trials, particularly during infanticide trials, this chapter locates the research question within the broader existing literature. By drawing on published research, a history of infanticide is revealed, providing crucial insight into how women came to be accused of infanticide: the process the women would have experienced, public perception towards the crime and the accused, and the punishment they received.[1] This has allowed legal historians to piece together a history that is not merely crucial to one's understanding of the historical context of infanticide but essential to one's comprehension of how medical men became involved in such cases. These published historical studies, however, tend to either concentrate on medical expert opinion, or focus more generally on the mental health element of the infanticidal woman.[2] This has led to a deficiency within the literature in terms of addressing the testimony of medical experts during infanticide trials, and the weight attached to such evidence. This research will therefore address medical testimony and specifically the element of doubt, which in turn led to uncertainty.

The first part of this chapter focuses on the history of infanticide, a timeline that will begin in 1624, and the introduction of "An Act to Prevent the Destroying and Murthering of Bastard Children," and continue in 1803, and the implementation of Lord Ellenborough's Act, an "Act for the Further Prevention of Malicious Shooting etc." It will then move onto the nineteenth century, before introducing the reforms of the twentieth century. The second section of this chapter will begin with a historiography of medical experts and continue with an examination into how the role of the medical expert transpired within the English courtroom.

Historical aspects of the crime of infanticide

Infanticide has been described as a crime as "old as human society" and a crime that has been viewed in varying degrees of severity by the English courts.[3] In medieval England, for example, infanticide, like many other crimes, was considered to be a sin rather than a crime and dealt with by the ecclesiastical court, punishable with a "form of public humiliating penance."[4] A form of humiliating punishment or atonement that was selected by societal and ecclesiastical members, which not

DOI: 10.4324/9781003006299-1

only aimed to punish the promiscuous behaviour of women within the parish but also a form of punishment that emphasised the stigma attached to illegitimate infants.[5] This act of punishment placed greater importance on the compliance of parochial or narrow-minded, normative values of society, as opposed to punishing the act or crime of infanticide per se.

It was during the seventeenth century that the criminalisation for the offence of infanticide occurred for unmarried women, with the passing of "An Act to Prevent the Destroying and Murthering of Bastard Children" in 1624. The Act was also referred to as the "Concealment of Birth of Bastards Act"[6] and the preamble of the Act reads:

> many lewd Women that have been delivered of Bastard Children, to avoid their Shame and to escape Punishment, do secretly bury and conceal the Death of their Children and after, if the Child be found dead, the said Women do alledge, that the said Child was born dead; whereas it falleth out sometimes (although hardly it is to be proved) that the said Child or Children were murthered by the said Women, their lewd Mothers, or by their Assent or Procurement.[7]

Whilst the 1624 Act specified bastard children as special victims,[8] it is also interesting to note the emphasis that the preamble places on "lewd women" and one of the fundamental reasons for its implementation. Hoffer and Hull have identified the emphasis placed on "lewd women" to be "accusatory and unrelenting."[9] An issue they believe constituted the Act's true objective: to target and punish the sexual promiscuity of unmarried women and, in particular, to deter women from entering into marriage-less relationships, which in turn could impose financial burdens on the local parish.[10] The term "lewd" from the fourteenth century was used as an expression of condemnation, such as "bad, vile, evil or wicked"; during the eighteenth century, it was used to refer to behaviour that was considered "lascivious and unchaste."[11] It also became a gender-related term, associating the aberrant sexual behaviour of women considered to be culturally unacceptable.[12]

Not only did the 1624 Act portray the infanticidal woman as lewd; it also portrayed her as promiscuous and unmarried, thus providing a strong association between illegitimacy and infanticide;[13] Arnot has suggested that this is substantiated with previous court records.[14] Married women were unable to face prosecution under the 1624 Act, and court records show a large number or over-representation of unmarried women were charged with cases of infanticide. In reality, many married women also committed infanticide, but they were more likely to escape the watchful gaze of the community. Married women were more likely to succeed in concealing a birth, hide a cadaver (corpse), and escape criminal proceedings for murder.[15] Jackson had highlighted this point, identifying that, before the implementation of the 1624 Act, women were tried for killing both legitimate and illegitimate infants equally; however, following the implementation of the Act, there were significantly more women tried for murdering illegitimate infants.[16] Jackson suggests that the reason for this anomaly in conviction rates either relates to the efforts made by the courts to ensure the successful implementation of 1624 Act, or the increased vigilance of the neighbours,[17] a significant point which supports the fact that married women may also have been committing infanticide, but were less likely to be caught and face a charge of murder. As motive made a significant contribution to the implementation of the 1624 Act, it was generally believed that married women had no motive, and if a married woman should commit infanticide, it was "so shocking and so unlikely that the only motive assigned to it was insanity."[18] As the Act only applied to unmarried women, marriage was a defence under the 1624 Act, implying unmarried women had a stronger motive for killing their infant and were therefore more likely to do so.[19] Very few men committed the offence, but for those who did, they faced charges at common law along with married mothers who were accused of killing their infants.[20]

Although the 1624 Act portrayed infanticidal women as "lewd," it seems that in reality this was not the case, but instead these women were of good character, concealing the infant corpse in an attempt to conceal their shame. Beattie showed that the unmarried women indicted for murder under the 1624 Act were far from "lewd."[21] He stated that, between 1660 and the end of the eighteenth century, there were 62 indictments in the 95-year period at the Surrey Assizes; three-quarters of these were of good character, committing infanticide to hide their shame and save their reputation.[22] Malcolmson has also suggested that the unmarried women who were "lewd" would have brazenly given birth to the illegitimate child, without a care of the repercussions of rearing an illegitimate child in a society with strict normative morals.[23]

The 1624 Act created the legal presumption that, if the mother had concealed the death of the infant, she had murdered it. In this respect, concealment was evidence of murder,[24] and the woman was expected to provide evidence to the contrary.[25] In seventeenth-century England, the presumption of innocence was not only "absent from, but antagonistic to the whole system of the penal procedure."[26] There was a need for a recognised principle of presumption of innocence, a recognition that was championed by the influential English jurist, Matthew Hale. He believed that "rather through ignorance of the truth of the fact or the unevidence of it, acquit ten guilty persons than condemn one innocent."[27] Writing in the 1670s, Hale argued that if the "scales are even … it is safer to err on the side of sympathy than severity?" and "where the evidence is obscure innocence is presumed."[28] It was not until the late eighteenth century that this principle was referred to as the presumption of innocence. It was the English lawyer, William Garrow, during the trial of George Dingler (accused of murder), who stated that it should be "recollected by all bystanders (for you do not need to be reminded of it) that every man is innocent until proved guilty."[29] Regardless of this recognition, it widely remained an unaccepted principle at the time.[30] The presumption of innocence principle was therefore not firmly established until the case of *Woolmington v DPP*, when the House of Lords clarified that, under common law in criminal proceedings, the burden of proving beyond reasonable doubt for both the actus reus and the mens rea lies with the prosecution, with the exception of statutory provisions and cases of insanity.[31] It was during this case that Viscount Sankey stated that "throughout the web of English Criminal Law one golden thread is always to be seen, that is the duty of the prosecution to prove the prisoner's guilt."[32] A statement that is arguably a "misleading figure of speech" since at least 1762, on charges of murder, once it had been established the prisoner had murdered the deceased, the onus was on the prisoner to provide a defence.[33]

The 1624 Act placed the burden of proof on the accused,[34] a fact that has led to suggestions that the defendant may have referred to or held up a few scraps of child bed linen. This demonstrated the material preparations she had made for the forthcoming delivery and also eliminated the possibility that she had intended to conceal the birth,[35] a defence which has been referred to as the "childbed linen defence."[36] Alternatively, women were permitted to produce at least one witness willing to testify that the child had been stillborn. In the event of a woman failing to meet either requirement, there was a strong possibility that she would be found guilty of murder.[37]

As the 1624 Act faced increasing criticism for its harshness towards unmarried women, it was also criticised for its lack of compassion, from both members of the judiciary and social commentators.[38] In general, eighteenth-century courts adopted a softer approach towards women charged under the 1624 Act. Rabin has identified that most women charged under the 1624 Act at the Old Bailey from the 1700s were acquitted, and there were no further convictions after 1775 under the 1624 Act.[39] Therefore the Act was gradually observed with less strictness before it became "largely disregarded."[40]

This change in sensibilities during the eighteenth century marked a period of humanitarian sentiment towards infanticidal women, as the courts began to adopt a softer, more sympathetic approach. Beattie observed that the courts were beginning to adopt a softer approach towards women on trial for infanticide, in general, and those women who were being tried under the statute of 1624 in particular.[41] He observed that women were no longer hanged in Surrey for infanticide in the second half of the eighteenth century.[42] A significant number of women were in fact young, single, and usually domestic servants, who were lured into a relationship under false pretences. Upon discovering the pregnancy, she was abandoned, left trapped between saving her respectable reputation and saving her position within the domestic sphere.[43] If her pregnancy was disclosed, Malcolmson claimed it would result in her instant dismissal and, in the absence of a character reference, her opportunities of future employment "in service" would be unlikely.[44] It could be argued that this stereotypical image was misleading. It is clear that a large number of young women who were accused of infanticide were employed as servants. Service was the most common form of employment during this period for young, single women of childbearing age, and it is also clear that living in such close proximity to others, these young servant women were at greater risk of detection.[45] They were under almost constant observation and faced the challenge of not only giving birth undetected but also smuggling a child out of the house undetected. It was much easier for women who lived in the wider community to conceal a pregnancy, deliver the child, and dispose of a body undetected, as England observes, "the old belief that infanticides were disproportionately committed by unmarried servant girls arose because other infanticides were more successfully concealed."[46]

This perception of women has also been reflected within King's research on the sentences received by women within the English criminal justice system. He states that women who were considered not to be "normal, conventional and respectable, female defendants whose lifestyles violate conventional notions of women proper roles were more likely to receive harsher treatment."[47] This reaction towards women places a significant emphasis on behaviour. The women who failed to conform to a particular form of respectable female behaviour, especially sexual behaviour, were more likely to receive a harsher punishment.[48] King's research involved the county Assizes and the Old Bailey Sessions between the late eighteenth century and early nineteenth century, and although his research is confined to property crime, it reveals a distinct pattern of gendered conviction and sentencing rates that were consistently lenient towards women on a national basis. He also found that women were more likely to receive partial verdicts from juries than men; in other words, they were more likely to be found guilty of a lesser offence.[49]

Hoffer and Hull address a number of issues surrounding infanticide during the seventeenth century, including motive; one particular combination of motives, they claim, was poverty and public disgrace.[50] They suggest that the 1624 Act encouraged the courts to pursue women who gave birth to illegitimate children and encouraged the vigilance of neighbours, which in turn led to an increasing number of women concealing their pregnancy, delivering unaided, and alone, which increased the risk of stillbirth.[51] They also identify varying degrees of punishment between men and women. For example, they claim that whilst fathers tended to escape punishment, it was women who were held to account by receiving sentences of either imprisonment or corporal punishment.[52] Hoffer and Hull included children under the age of eight or nine as infants in this study, stating that "infanticide is an effective method of population control."[53]

Hoffer and Hull have also identified that, throughout the eighteenth century, public attitudes softened towards infanticidal women, a fact they claim is evident from the verdicts and sentences in infanticide trials.[54] This softening sentiment may have stemmed from a:

> cluster of narratives that came to speak in extraordinary detailed fashion about the pains and deaths of ordinary people in such a way as to make apparent the causal chains that might connect the actions of its readers with the suffering of its subjects.[55]

Jackson states that broadsheet newspapers reported melancholy stories of the lives of women convicted of murdering their new-born children, their experiences whilst in gaol, and the confessions they were reported to have made which led to their deaths. These accounts were made with a two-fold objective: to entertain the readers and to deter women from a similar fate. In contrast to the broadsheet accounts of infanticide cases during the eighteenth century, the stories began to adopt a more sympathetic or humanitarian stance towards such women, describing how women may have been led astray and naively seduced by men, committing infanticide to save their virtue, dignity, and reputation.[56]

The character and conduct of infanticidal women were debated and discussed throughout the eighteenth century. Jackson explains how the physician Bernard Mandeville, writing in 1714, believed that "modesty and the fear of shame derived not from female nature as was commonly supposed but from female education,"[57] believing that the natural desires of young women were counterbalanced by strong notions of honour, instilled in them from their infancy. Although Mandeville believed their conduct was a result of nurture as opposed to nature, he did support the view that such women should be found guilty of murder. In contrast, the medical practitioner Erasmus Darwin, writing in 1767, believed that the excessive modesty which resulted in women committing infanticide stemmed from a woman's virtue and that such women should receive "our greatest pity rather than condemnation,"[58] a view that Jackson argued was echoed by the government in 1772. The supporters in favour of reforming the 1624 Act in the House of Commons believed that repealing the Act would serve the interests of both "justice and humanity and claimed that a woman's attempts to conceal the birth of her bastard child might proceed from the best causes, from real modesty and virtue."[59]

Darwin's opinion was reflected in the physician William Hunter's book, *On the Uncertainty of the Signs of Murder, in the Case of Bastard Children*,[60] echoing the previous arguments of both Mandeville and Darwin, and a title that explicitly links uncertainty and infanticide, thus supporting my argument. Hunter insisted that the majority of women accused of murdering their new-born child had done so out of an "unconquerable sense of shame, and pants after the preservation of character; so far she is virtuous and amiable."[61] He did not support Mandeville's view that most women accused of murder were guilty but instead believed that many women had been wrongly convicted and therefore many innocent women had been hanged.

Jackson argues that the development of the humanitarian approach rests with the evidence against the women, not only the evidence of a live birth and the evidence of signs of violence but also the weight of the evidence of concealment of birth and the responsibility of the man.[62] If women concealed the birth and death of the child because of their virtue and modesty, rather than the fact that they were monstrous and cruel, then Jackson argues that concealment could no longer be regarded as undeniable evidence of murder;[63] concealment, according to Hunter, should only be grounds for suspicion, rather than the absolute determination of a woman's guilt.[64]

It is interesting to note that it was medical writers who attempted to re-characterise infanticidal women as righteous, moral, and importantly innocent, during the eighteenth century, and yet it was also medical men who were called on by the courts to replace midwives as expert witnesses to establish the cause of death in such cases.

Throughout his work, Jackson draws on Haskell's concept that the "unprecedented wave of humanitarian reform sentiment that swept through the societies of Western Europe, England and North America in the hundred years following 1750,"[65] suggesting that the wave of sensibilities triggered many movements of reform; for example, the abolition of the slave trade. In conjunction with the wave of reform, new ideas and concepts began to emerge as to how to deal with the poor, deter criminals, and cure the insane.[66] Haskell argued that any new method of reform in such areas was considered to be an improvement, as many of the old practices were barbaric. Ward has identified that it was on this basis that Jackson established a link to infanticide, a link, he argues, which was founded on the particular notion that humanitarian reform was "understood as a by-product of the construction of (bourgeois, male) subjects under the discipline of the market."[67] A market that Ward, paraphrasing Haskell, argued "required subjects who were not only rational, calculating and self-interested, but also had a strong sense of moral obligation and an awareness of the long term consequences of their actions."[68] The latter element of this aspect, Jackson argues, created a new cognitive style in respect of the narratives of infanticide, particularly emphasising the physical and psychological suffering these women experienced that was "attributed to the faithfulness of their seducers."[69]

This period of humanitarian sentiment towards infanticide is complemented by the wider changes in attitudes within England during the eighteenth century, a period of enlightenment, scientific investigation, innovation, and, for some institutions, reform. The English criminal justice system, for example, passed through a lengthy period of major reform beginning in the eighteenth century;[70] Cairns, following Langbein,[71] has identified that, until this time, the purpose of the trial had historically been to allow the accused to speak for him or herself, and so criminal trials were conducted in the absence of counsel.[72] The trial presented the accused with the opportunity to provide answers to the charges of which they were accused; defence counsel was forbidden in such matters of fact.[73] Evidence was put forward either by the judge, who examined the witnesses and parties himself or directly by the accuser, accused, and witnesses,[74] with the expectation that the accused represented themselves.[75] The general consensus is that the accused would be more likely to tell the truth if he represented himself, by way of a form of honesty through innocence or ignorance. The absence of counsel was a common feature of the criminal trial until the "Adversarial Revolution"[76] of the eighteenth century, when prosecution counsel began to appear with greater frequency within murder trials.[77] The implementation of the Prisoner's Counsel Act of 1836 had one of the greatest impacts on the adversarial trial, as it allowed defence counsel to address the jury.[78] Towards the end of the nineteenth century, the counsel had an overwhelming effect on the overall conduct of criminal trials, as they had:

> ushered into criminal procedure the divisions between examination-in-chief and cross-examination and between evidence and argument, nourished the growth of the law of evidence, changed the nature of the judicial involvement in the trial, and supplemented the haphazard efforts of prisoners to defend themselves with professional advocacy.[79]

The end of the nineteenth century experienced a further transformation with the passing of the Criminal Evidence Act 1898, legislation that allowed prisoners to give evidence on oath, whilst also importantly enshrining their right not to give evidence. This formed part of the adversarial trial that is now considered to be at the heart of the rule of law.[80]

The nineteenth century not only saw the transformation of the criminal justice system but was a period of wider criminal law reforms. In respect of infanticide laws, the 1624 Act was repealed by Lord Ellenborough's Act, "An Act for the Further Prevention of Malicious Shooting etc." 1803, 43 Geo III c. 58, an Act that placed the burden of proof on the prosecution to establish that the infant had been born alive. The 1803 Act created the new offence of concealment of birth, which carried a maximum sentence of two years' imprisonment. Although the Act was aimed at unmarried women, it also placed the burden of proof on the prosecution: it was for the prosecution to prove murder. The implementation of Lord Lansdowne's Act, also referred to as the Offences Against the Person Act 1828, extended this provision to include married women. Smith has argued this offence was introduced in order to obtain convictions: as infanticide was punishable by death, juries were reluctant to convict women, and so by reducing the sentence, juries were more likely to convict women of concealment.[81] Arguably, the implementation of the lesser offence reflected a broader shift away from executing criminals in general, with the exception of those convicted of murder from the 1840s.[82]

The adoption of a lenient approach by the courts towards infanticidal women has been identified by Higginbotham, who argued this became increasingly evident throughout the nineteenth century. She believed that there was a surprising number of women who were treated with leniency: very few were found guilty of infanticide, and those who were tended to receive a pardon.[83] Smith has also recognised a willingness to excuse infanticidal women during this period. A willingness that he considered to be "remarkable especially as infanticide was thought to be widespread throughout the century; and further, it was a crime which drew horrified attention to itself."[84] He believed this stemmed from the fact that infanticidal women were not considered fully responsible for their actions and were the inappropriate objects of punishment: on many occasions they were the objects of mercy.

As the circumstances surrounding infant death remained difficult to ascertain, it became increasingly difficult for medical men to establish whether a child died as a result of natural causes or murder. A child may have died from complications arising from an unassisted birth and sustained similar injuries to those infants that may have been murdered; this resulted in many women being charged with concealment of birth as opposed to murder. In turn, this led to the juries adopting a compassionate approach towards the infanticidal women by considering the social pressure to which these women were subjected, sparing their lives. Ward has suggested that this compassionate view consisted of two elements: "sympathy for the physical pain of a mother giving birth unattended" and the notion of the "fallen woman," "heavily determined by social forces, the antithesis of the autonomous, rational masculine self."[85]

Towards the end of the eighteenth century, attempts were made to make wider criminal law reforms and reduce the number of capital offences, with the implementation of Acts which allowed the courts greater leniency and discretion.[86] The latter decades of the eighteenth century and the early nineteenth century were a period of significant reform in the penal system. Johnstone and Ward state that, through the application of "principles of enlightenment to thinking about crime and justice,"[87] an attempt was made to make the system more rational and humane;[88] these Acts were referred to as the "Peel Acts," named after the Home Secretary, Robert Peel. The Acts consolidated a number of previous statutes and offences and reduced the number of capital offences, for example, the Criminal Statute Repeals Act 1827, the Indemnity Act 1827, and the Offences Against the Person Act 1828.[89] This period during the late Hanoverian era marked a time prior to the Victorian era, of riches, refinement, sensibilities, and morality: a strict moral code concerning behaviour and propriety.

Particularly reminiscent of the Victorian era was the behaviour of women: they were expected to follow a strict moral code, and an ideology of a woman's appropriateness, decorum, and place within the family soon began to emerge. In contrast to this behaviour was a woman's shameful behaviour, a behaviour that involved the disobeying of strict moral values that originated from the perception of the perfect "woman," and how she was expected to adhere to strict patterns of behaviour, both in public and in private.

During the Victorian era this perception evolved into one of a "middle-class wife and mother whose asexual, morally uplifting influence"[90] emanated over both her family and society, whose antithesis was the "fallen woman." Fallen from innocence, with the loss of her chastity through corruption and degradation,[91] cast out from society, with those coming near the "fallen woman" or socialised with her, facing the risk of contamination and corruption: tainted by association.[92] This Victorian perception of the "fallen woman" stemmed from behaviour such as sexual misconduct, drunkenness, or criminality. To avoid being labelled as such, it was necessary for women to follow the strict moral code and acceptable patterns of behaviour,[93] a theme that is epitomised through Victorian art and English literature: in Dante Gabrielle Rossetti's *Found*, a painting he began in 1853, a scene is depicted whereby a farmer discovers his former sweetheart to be a prostitute. In Thomas Hardy's *Tess of the D'Urbervilles*, published in 1891, but set in the late eighteenth century, Tess is initially depicted as a weak, vulnerable character, who is raped and left pregnant.[94] In Elizabeth Gaskell's *Ruth,* published in 1853, the themes of legitimacy and Victorian values are discussed when Ruth gives birth to an illegitimate child; however, by cleverly declaring herself a widow, she avoids stigmatising her son, and she gains employment as a respectable governess.[95]

The crime rate amongst women has been identified as being considerably less than men's during the Victorian era; women were considered to be less likely to steal or cheat and be more honest than men.[96] It was also generally believed that women were morally superior to men; through their expectation and natural ability to raise children, they were expected to possess natural, maternal qualities such as "compassion and self-fulfilment which mitigate against any tendency towards crime."[97]

Women were also considered to be more religious than men,[98] a further factor which allegedly restrained criminality. This view has led to assumptions towards women's behaviour and views that female criminals were unnatural as opposed to criminals.[99] Kermode and Walker identified that men who committed crimes were labelled criminals, whilst criminal women were labelled mentally ill,[100] a fact that determined men's criminality as "normal, explicable and rational" and women's criminality as "irrational, if not pathological."[101] This combination of factors has led D'Cruze and Jackson[102] to observe that, throughout history, women have been associated with specific types of transgression, linking certain crimes to femininity.[103] These transgressions or gender-specific crimes, such as witchcraft in the Early Modern period and poisoning and infanticide during the nineteenth century,[104] have revealed that women were not necessarily labelled criminal but more likely to be referred to as abnormal or deviant.[105] An analogy that sees the criminal woman not only as committing an offence against society but also against her societal role as a woman, making her doubly deviant.[106]

The doubly deviant infanticidal woman was perceived during the nineteenth century as the antithesis of womanhood through the crime she had committed and through her failure to comply with the ideal conduct of femininity.[107] Smart has argued that infanticide was regarded to be a heathen act, "one propagated by peoples not fully civilised or human,"[108] an ideology when taken within the Imperial context, must have been shocking for people to learn that infanticide seemed as common in London as it was in Bombay.[109] In many respects public opinion towards infanticide remained divided: on the one hand there was a belief that the infanticidal woman was "motivated by the feminine quality of shame, the natural desire to save her child from a life of misery, and themselves from possible further degradation by the need to turn to prostitution to survive."[110] Employment opportunities were few and harsh; many women had little option but to enter the immoral world of prostitution, mistresses, or unmarried mothers.[111] Therefore, if a woman had respectable employment, such as that of a kitchen maid, it was important that she did not forfeit this position by giving birth to an illegitimate child; a woman with a child born out of wedlock would almost certainly be stigmatised.[112] On the other hand, there was a belief that infanticidal women demonstrated "a lack of chastity and characterised offenders as callous single mothers concerned only to get rid of an encumbrance,"[113] thus portraying the infanticidal woman as the epitome of immorality and deviance, giving birth to illegitimate infants who, born out of wedlock, were "great social evils."[114] Not only did infanticide save the young woman from an immoral lifestyle; it also relieved her of a potential financial encumbrance and the social stigma of an illegitimate child. It is therefore no coincidence that infanticide peaked during the Victorian era, a period when poverty was widespread and cultural doctrine dictated the appropriateness of women's behaviour through strict normative principles, the demeanour of unmarried women in general, and her reputation and honour within the family and community in particular.

These issues surrounding legitimacy were not exclusive to moral consideration but were also the subject of the broader legal convention. Under common law, particularly during the eighteenth and nineteenth centuries, a child born outside marriage was considered "*fillius nullius*, nobody's child," a fact that resulted in legitimacy or illegitimacy being determined within core legal battles, especially in cases involving property or inheritance rights.[115] In contrast to this under canon law, the "family" was described as an "effective and social unit underpinned by natural law principles, regarded it as a moral duty for parents to support their children regardless of legitimacy."[116] It was common practice for ecclesiastical courts during the Early Modern period to hear cases whereby suits were brought pursuing fathers for payments towards the financial upkeep of illegitimate infants.[117] A duty that was revoked by the 1834 Poor Law Amendment Act, when the obligation of financial support was removed from the father and placed entirely on the mother.[118] This Act became the inspiration behind Frances Trollope's 1843 novel, *Jessie Phillips: A Tale of the Present Day*, in which Trollope protests at the inclusion of the bastardly clause that prevented women from claiming financial support from the father of her illegitimate child. Jessie is seduced and subsequently abandoned by Frederic Dalton, the son of the squire; after giving birth in the workhouse, she is unable to seek financial support from him, because of the bastardly clause within the Poor Law 1834. Jessie is wrongly accused of infanticide when Frederic murdered the infant; this eventually leads to Frederic committing suicide and Jessie dying of natural causes.[119] The novel not only reflects the harshness of the 1834 Act but also demonstrates the seduction of a young naive woman and subsequent desertion by her seducer, common factors in many infanticide cases.

A second, albeit contentious, form of infanticide which peaked during the nineteenth century was overlaying,[120] the asphyxiation of a "child inadvertently when sleeping in a shared bed"[121] or indeed advertently, as the intention was notoriously difficult to prove. Although overlaying was included in the 1889 Prevention of Cruelty to Children Act, it was not until the Children Act 1908 that the potential neglect of parents towards their children was set out in greater detail – the risk of suffocation, for example, if the parent was drunk at the time they went to bed with the child.[122] Although historically it was considered common practice for parents to sleep in the same bed as their infant, it was also held that "those who wished to dispose of unwanted infants overlaid them,"[123] by rolling over onto the infant, suffocating them in their sleep; in many cases differentiating between intent and accident proved extremely difficult and will be discussed in Chapter 5.

Alternative methods to infanticide for the disposal of unwanted infants included abandonment, the London Foundling Hospital, and baby farming. Abandonment was a method employed to dispose of unwanted infants and could involve leaving the child in a place where it might or might not be discovered. If a mother intended the infant to be discovered and cared for, she may have left the child on the steps of a church or wealthy family. On the other hand, if the mother intended for the child to remain undiscovered, she may have abandoned the child in a woodland where, exposed to the elements, the death of the child would be expedited.[124] Abandonment is evident in George Eliot's *Adam*

Bede (1859), a novel set in 1799 within a close-knit rural community.[125] Whilst engaged to Adam Bede, Hetty Sorrel discovers she is pregnant to another man, Arthur Donnithorne, the grandson of the local squire. Hetty decides to go in search of Arthur, the child's father, to inform him of the pregnancy, but whilst away from home searching for the father of her baby, the child is born alive with the aid of a woman she encounters. Hetty abandons the child in a field but feeling guilty about her behaviour she later returns to the child, only to find the child has died from exposure. Once Adam is aware of the situation, he interestingly blames Arthur for Hetty's predicament, stating "it is his doing … if there's been any crime, it is at his door."[126] The novel Adam Bede was inspired by an anecdote, related to Mary Ann Evans (George Eliot) by her Methodist Aunt Elizabeth Evans, describing an encounter between herself and Mary Voce in prison, the day before her execution (on March 17, 1802). Mary was accused of poisoning her new-born child, a child she had conceived with another man in the absence of her husband who was away in the army; she poisoned the child to hide her infidelity and conceal her shame. The aunt had sat, praying with Mary throughout the night, heard her confession, and accompanied her to the gallows.[127]

It has been suggested by Kilday that, by the middle of the nineteenth century, more children were abandoned than were the victims of infanticide;[128] in response to this growing concern for the number of infants who were believed to be abandoned, the Offences Against the Person Act 1861 established, through clause 27, abandonment as a misdemeanour, if a person abandoned a child under the age of two. The Act also stated that it is at the "discretion of the court, to be kept in penal servitude for the term of three years, or to be imprisoned for any term not exceeding two years, with or without hard labour."[129]

It is interesting to note that, in a number of abandonment cases, women left overwhelming evidence by the child's body that could easily be traced back to her, a behaviour that Higginbotham argued showed "fear and confusion and perhaps an unconscious desire for discovery."[130] In some cases the woman may even have returned to the hidden body, a point that is reflected in the behaviour of Hetty Sorrel. In other cases, Higginbotham argued, women readily told the police or doctors about the deaths of their infants, demonstrating that these women were not the "cunning murderesses, portrayed in some Victorian accounts."[131] Ward has therefore argued that many infanticidal women were neither "mad nor bad merely sad, a social casualty driven by overwhelming stress,"[132] and in a great number of infanticide cases there was clearly a lack of mens rea.

The establishment of the London Foundling Hospital in the mid-eighteenth century allowed women to leave their illegitimate child under the age of 12 months, with "no questions asked" to be cared for and raised, with the ultimate aim of preserving the lives of those infants that may otherwise have been destroyed.[133] The many notes left with children on admittance serve as an indication of the gratitude felt by the parent towards the hospital for the care they provided.[134] Small tokens may have also been left by the parent with the child, most of which were "pieces of fabric or scraps of ribbon, some with embroidery."[135] Such tokens were considered to be symbolic of motherly love, a maternal link between the mother and her child.

Alternatively, some women turned to baby farmers, women of limited financial means who set up businesses to care for infants in exchange for a weekly monetary sum, who then neglected them or kept them in such poor conditions that they failed to thrive.[136] Baby farming could take a number of forms; in some cases, the baby farmer would offer to find adoptive parents for the child; however, in many cases this would result in the mother paying an agreed sum, the baby farmer killing the infant, and retaining the money.[137] This bad reputation that baby farmers acquired quickly turned into an established perception, associating baby farmers as villainous characters, a factor that was reflected in their title: originally named "she butchers," in the eighteenth century, and renamed "baby farmers" during the nineteenth century.[138]

The trade of baby farming was a practice that became both stigmatised and despised, as it symbolised the "contradictions between dominant images of idealised womanhood and its reality for those women whose circumstances did not fit this image."[139] An article in the *British Medical Journal* describes the "mode in which the business of baby farming is conducted,"[140] stating that the baby farmer who featured in the article had registered seven infant deaths in the last two years.[141] These deaths occurred from a variety of causes, from jaundice to lung congestion and convulsions; in many cases the child was registered as illegitimate and the children who were registered as legitimate were dubiously so.[142]

The despised practice of baby farming continued until the passing of the 1872 Protection of Infant Life Act, an Act which gave a minimum standard of care of infants and a requirement for all baby farmers to be licenced.[143] One of the most notorious baby farmers, Amelia Dyer, was described as a "wholesale child destroyer,"[144] because she refused to reveal the true number of babies she had thrown into the River Thames. She was described as a "short stout woman of middle age, who rocked herself backwards and forwards as though mentally distressed."[145] As she confessed to strangling infants in her care by tying "tape round their necks,"[146] she was found guilty of murder in March 1896 and executed within the walls of Newgate, on June 10, 1896.[147]

Whichever method of disposing of an unwanted infant a woman selected, an underlying common theme is present throughout the historiography of infanticide: desperation. An element that is reflected in the historical account of infanticide provided by Kilday,[148] when she argues that "British women committed infanticide between 1600 and 1900 when other means available to them were considered too dangerous, or too expensive."[149] Finding themselves in a desperate situation, whilst attempting to comply with strict normative principles, many women had no choice but to conceal the pregnancy and deliver the child alone, risking the lives of both mother and child. Kilday's detailed account of the history of infanticide covers four centuries in Scotland, England, and Wales, with the objective of providing "an integrated British picture of a given offence over a long period of time."[150] A history that indicates that infanticide has not always been considered as a crime in England; in early history, for example, in parts of

England and especially rural areas, Kilday suggests that infanticide was accepted as a form of population control.[151] With the passage of time and an alteration in humanitarian attitude, views towards infanticide began to change, a changing perception towards infanticide in general and towards the perpetrators of infanticide in particular.[152] Attitudes towards the perpetrators during the Victorian era took another turn when infanticide was considered to be an unnatural offence, and mothers were regarded as the antitheses of both motherhood and womanhood.[153] The unnaturalness of infanticide remained a strong theme in the late nineteenth and early twentieth centuries, when discussions began to link the crime to maternal mental state.

During the early twentieth century a number of commentators identified a strong association between infanticide and mental state,[154] a link that commentators argued to be reflected within the law: John Baker, the MD Deputy Superintendent to the State Asylum Broadmoor, was one such commentator. Baker carried out research on admitted infanticidal women, the results of which led him to conclude that common predisposing factors existed that caused women to commit infanticide. His findings indicated that most women were single and concealed their pregnancy:

> she has made no preparation for the birth, except sometimes a knife or pair of scissors is kept at hand for the purposes of severing the cord. Labour comes on, and the child is born and begins to cry. This contingency has been overlooked, and in desperation lest its wail be heard, she cuts its throat, stabs or otherwise mutilates it. In some cases this is followed by an attempt to conceal the body. It may be called transient frenzy; no doubt it is, but the mother is generally capable of afterwards detailing all the circumstances.[155]

Baker observed that there was a higher occurrence of infanticide during the period when lactational insanity was prevalent, a period he identified as being not before the first 16 days following the delivery of the child. He believed the reason for this was related to the fact that women were at greater risk of committing infanticide whilst suffering from puerperal melancholia, a condition which is prevalent in women following the first 16 days post-delivery. In particular, Baker identified a link between infanticide and post-natal psychosis, a link he believed should be implemented into legislation to allow for a defence in such circumstances.[156]

It was not until the passing of the Infanticide Act 1922 that further legislative changes came into effect, the objectives of which Grey argues were to "remedy the situation whereby those few women convicted of new-born murder in the early twentieth century were sentenced to death."[157] Nevertheless this was not what commentators during the early twentieth century were arguing for. Commentators such as Baker were arguing that it was women who were killing infants over the age of 16 days old, who were more likely to commit infanticide as a result of puerperal melancholia.

The implementation of the Infanticide Act 1922 allowed the apparently psychiatric defence for a category of women who were considered to be least likely to be insane, allowing an abnormal mental state to reduce a charge of murder to the lesser offence of manslaughter (although not considered to be insane in the *McNaughtan* sense of insanity, *McNaughtan* will be discussed further in Chapter 4).[158] This enabled a more lenient sentence to be passed; for example, section one of the Act reads:

> any wilful act or omission caused the death of her newly born child, but at the time of the act or omission had not fully recovered from the effect of giving birth to the child, the balance of her mind being disturbed, should be judged guilty of infanticide and might for such an offence be dealt with and punished as if she had been guilty of manslaughter.[159]

Cooper-Graves suggested that the research and commentary published by Baker contributed in some degree towards the passing of the Infanticide Act 1922.[160] An Act that was regarded as a milestone for infanticidal women as it allowed women accused of "killing their new-born child a partial defence for murder," if it could be proved that "she had not fully recovered from the effect of giving birth to such child, and by reason thereof the balance of her mind was then disturbed."[161] If successful, then her punishment would be reduced to manslaughter from the death penalty.

Allen describes the Infanticide Act 1922 as unique, as it is the only offence in which:

> mental abnormality is a positive precondition for conviction (as part of the mens reas of the offence) and not as a defence or partial defence against conviction, infanticide is thus an offence that can only be committed by an abnormal subject.[162]

Infanticide does not require that the killing of the child is a result of the imbalance of the woman's mind; it merely has to coincide with it, establishing a link between "female biology and legal pathology."[163] The 1922 Act implies that the normal physiological process of childbirth and lactation are disruptive of the subjectivity required by the law.[164]

Ward argues that the:

> central paradox of the 1922 Act was that it singled out the killing of newly born infants for an apparently medical defence, when this kind of infanticide was much less likely to be seen as a product of mental disease than the killing of older babies,[165]

an important point that is reflected in the results in Chapter 4. These cases demonstrate that where a mother received a "guilty but insane" verdict and was detained during His or Her Majesty's Pleasure, she had generally killed her older infant as opposed to her new-born infant. A fact that supports Baker's observations is that most infanticidal women admitted to Broadmoor acted in the later stages of the puerperal period, a period he identified as being the first two months following delivery with puerperal insanity usually diagnosed around two weeks post-delivery. Diagnosed initially with an onset of mania, puerperal insanity was followed by a period of melancholia, and it was during this time that both the child and the mother were most at risk: the child from infanticide and the mother from suicide.[166]

As the wording of the Infanticide Act 1922 was narrow, succinctly stating that "the killing of a newly born child by a mother who had not fully recovered from the effect of giving birth to such child, and by reason thereof the balance of her mind was then disturbed," difficulties were soon encountered, concerning the interpretation of the term "newly born," a question that arose in the case of Mary O'Donoghue (see Chapter 4).[167]

In 1938 a Bill was introduced, to extend the definition of infanticide to include the killing of all infants under the age of one year, where the balance of her mind was disturbed as a result of the birth or the effect of lactation following upon such birth."[168] The Bill was accepted and the Infanticide Act 1938 was implemented,[169] broadening the scope of infanticide as critics had identified a "gap between the medical view of maternal mental disorder and its legal reconstruction."[170] The 1922 Act referred to "newly born" infants, whilst the 1938 Infanticide Act identified an age range of infants up to the age of 12 months. Moreover, the 1938 Act also introduced lactational insanity, "the effects of lactation," in addition to the previous clause, which reads that the "balance of mind was disturbed by reason of her not having fully recovered from the effect of her giving birth to the child."[171]

This twentieth-century infanticide legislation allowed an "abnormal mental state that falls short of actual insanity to reduce murder to a lesser offence, on a level with manslaughter,"[172] a concept of diminished responsibility later introduced in the Homicide Act 1957. The 1957 Act makes the Infanticide Act surplus to requirement; despite this fact, the Infanticide Act 1938 remains in force today, demonstrating a "legal understanding of female mentalities and the relationship with the law."[173] Marks and Kumar have argued that English courts continue to demonstrate leniency towards infanticidal mothers, as women who commit infanticide are considered to be mentally ill, whereas fathers or any other person who commits the same crime are criminals.[174]

Ward argues that the Infanticide Act 1938 can be viewed as a result of humanitarian sensibilities, a sentiment which began to develop towards infanticidal women in the late eighteenth century. By drawing on Norrie's theory of "legal abstraction," a view that:

> common law doctrines of criminal liability contain deep contradictions which must be understood as a product of their formative period in the early nineteenth century. He discerns a fundamental conflict between the law's ideology of "abstract individualism," which envisages a world peopled by rational, calculating, responsible subjects and the concrete, social individuality of human beings operating within a conflictual society.[175]

Ward illustrates how the Infanticide Act 1938 is an example of Norrie's contradiction thesis; when infanticide is considered in isolation, it is simply a case of murder, and so the courts need to take into account the external influences which might have affected the woman's behaviour.[176] On this basis, Ward argues the "legal abstraction" which treated infanticide as murder, for example the 1803 legislation developed paradoxically as a result of humanitarian sensibilities, replaced the seventeenth-century legislation that presumed unmarried women who had given birth in secret, the infant then found dead, were guilty of murder.[177]

Medical experts

As the unease began to increase around the prosecution of infanticidal women, so too did the demand for certainty. In the absence of an independent witness it was difficult under the 1624 Act to prove that the woman had concealed the death, without first proving the child had been born alive. This book will demonstrate that in the cases where women faced criminal proceedings under the 1624 Act, there were very few occasions when witness testimony could be provided to establish a live birth; therefore, the most challenging obstacle for the courts was the lack of substantive evidence. The courts therefore relied upon circumstantial evidence to establish the child was born alive and subsequently murdered, which in many cases may have been the "neighbour's suspicions" and conjecture. In other cases, the courts relied upon the experience and opinion of the expert witness, which during this period was the female midwife, an expert on childbirth who drew on her own expertise and experience to provide evidence (see Chapter 2). As the harshness of the 1624 Act was realised, the admittance of substantive evidence became crucial to infanticide cases. It became increasingly evident that the courts required greater certainty from the expert witness, men of medicine and men of science, in the shape of medical men: surgeons, barber surgeons, man-midwives, apothecaries (which will be discussed in further detail in Chapter 3). In the latter years of the nineteenth century and into the twentieth century, the pathologist gradually began to carry out this role in infanticide cases (which will be discussed in further detail in Chapter 5).

Although expert testimony within the English courtrooms is long-established,[178] historically, it was difficult to distinguish between the jury and witnesses, as the "jurors were the witnesses."[179] The jurors were selected because of their knowledge of the case, or relevant details of the case, making the concept of expert witnesses unnecessary. Towards the end of the sixteenth century, juries became judges of the facts of the case or "judges of evidence given by others,"[180] ceasing to be selected from a group of witnesses.[181] This change in trial procedure created a void in the structure of the trial, particularly in cases where the disputed "facts were such that the jury lacked sufficient knowledge to draw an informed decision," and so the need to call expert witnesses was established.[182] A need which, Jones argued, stemmed from the "need for expert witnesses, created by the changing role of early modern juries, from repositories of local … knowledge to the trier to passive triers of fact."[183]

It has been argued by Adam that the role of the expert witness was developed in the seventeenth century, when "the men of science came to be seen as a reliable witness."[184] As the role of the expert witness grew, the court saw the role of the expert as a threat to judicial control, a concern that resulted in the expert role being purposely reduced to that of witness. In an attempt to reduce the risk to judicial control, their testimony was confined to evidence of fact, prohibiting experts from providing opinion evidence. This issue was reflected in *Wells Harbour* or *Folkes v Chadd*,[185] a case that Golan describes as the foundation of the "rules governing expert evidence as the principal precedent that shaped the most dominant option of using expert's knowledge in the modern Anglo-American courtroom."[186] The case involved a number of men of science as expert witnesses, who were called to testify on the cause of decay of a particular harbour in Norfolk. One witness in particular, Mr Smeaton, an engineer, was called to testify; however, the opposing party objected to his evidence "on the grounds of its being a matter of opinion."[187] It was as a result of this case and on a practical basis that expert evidence became an exception to the rule, "forbidding witnesses to give opinion evidence,"[188] presenting the expert witnesses as a unique witness within the trial procedure by allowing opinions of "scientific men upon proven facts may be given by men of science within their own science."[189] Golan described *Wells Harbour* as a good example of judicial trust; the experts were members of the elite Royal Society, and they were considered to be "men of honour, and their integrity guaranteed the truthfulness of their stories."[190] With the significant developments during the nineteenth century within science and industry, it is clear that the expert witness came to be regarded as a crucial figure in the courtroom.[191]

The ruling in *Folkes v Chadd*[192] remains the orthodox legal rule today as quoted in *R v Turner*,[193] when Mr Justice Lawton stated:

> an expert's opinion is admissible to furnish the court with scientific information which is likely to be outside the experience and knowledge of a judge or jury. If on the proven facts a judge or jury can form their own conclusions without help then the opinion of an expert is unnecessary.[194]

In *R v Turner* it was held that evidence provided by psychiatrists and psychologists could be excluded on the grounds of "normal defendants" that it contributes very little to the value to jury's deliberations. The case also set "strict limits to the use of psychiatric evidence in English criminal trials"[195] and remains the leading case on the admissibility of psychiatric evidence today.[196]

The use of medical experts within a legal context is referred to by Jackson and how medical evidence came to play a central role in the investigation of suspicious infant deaths in the eighteenth century.[197] He argued that medical testimony was a prominent feature of:

> coroner's investigations into new-born child murder and a regular part of trials for this offence … medical testimony as to the cause of death and the

possibility of still birth, made significant contributions to discussions of the crime both in and out of court.[198]

Through linking coroner's investigations and medical evidence, Jackson raises the important issue that, "for a number of reasons, medical witnesses were rarely able to answer such questions with any certainty."[199] Jackson continues by stating that "perhaps paradoxically it was this lack of certainty that proved most useful to the courts," as it provided the courts with the flexibility to apply a degree of leniency to their verdict reflecting public opinion and "emerging humanitarian concerns" evident in the nineteenth century.[200] A point by Jackson that is acknowledged as crucial to this research is that greater uncertainty was more advantageous to the courts.

Whereas Jones provides the "first comprehensive socio-legal analysis of experts in the legal system, studying experts as scientists, as witnesses and as an aspect of advocacy,"[201] from the seventeenth century to 1994. Adopting a "broad brush" approach to the history of the expert witness Jones particularly specifies that the history of the expert witness was not one of "unilinear progression,"[202] whilst highlighting the changing role of expert witness throughout the nineteenth and twentieth centuries. The challenge to the law this created in terms of its authority, and specifically the role of the jury, led the law to respond "by seeking to restrict the role of the expert witness by strict rules of evidence such as the ultimate issue rule."[203]

Jones argues that, beneath the current debate surrounding expert witnesses and the law, there lies an intrinsic crisis of confidence within the institutions of both science and law. In her view the historical image of each has been to portray them as privileged systems that evolve around "objective value free truth by adherence to rules methods and procedures that are inherently rational and logic."[204] She argues that there was "no rule of evidence which states experts have an overriding duty to the court,"[205] and through the use of rigid rules and procedures, she states that the "law makes it abundantly clear that experts have no independent locus."[206] In turn, this has created problems for expert witnesses, as they tend to be "victims of their own past performance,"[207] by adopting an ideology of impartially and neutrality, they created an expectation that all future expert witnesses would be viewed in this light. A fact she claims is weakened by the aspect that the "experts status is linked to the most artificial of legal distinctions, the separation between fact and opinion."[208] Jones states that, during the nineteenth and twentieth centuries, the law increasingly relied upon experts in cases where science could provide "examples of rational truth finding procedures," and within this increasing ideology, the expert witness was part of an "interpenetration of law and science. This may also be seen in the growing scientisation of law and judicialisation of science."[209] In this respect, Jones argues there is no longer a clear distinction between science and law in terms of knowledge, as one infiltrates the other, claiming that law is often the moderator of scientific practice, for example, deciding when scientific practice is ethical or not,[210] a concept that dates back at least as far as medieval times, when law regulated the profession of medicine.[211]

The so-called scientisation of law resulted in calls for the need to structure expert evidence, as there was a growing possibility that "experts would usurp the judicial role and that science would displace law as the touchstone of social order."[212] As fears were raised that the current legal procedures and rules were growing ever more scientific, a correlating fear developed that science was growing ever more powerful within the legal system. In response to this, Jones argues that the courts adopted an adversarial model, with the medical expert becoming a secondary player in the courtroom, a fact she claims is evident merely by the positioning of the expert in the witness box as opposed to the bench.[213] An issue that could be argued, is reflected in the fact that science has historically been viewed as redoubtable to the legal system however, rather than viewing the systems as rivals, expert witnesses have been used to both contribute to, and enhance, legal practices.

Jones argues that the essence to aiding one's understanding of the development of the role of the expert witness has been the "creating and sustaining the distinction between fact and value has been one of the main activities of law and science over the last two hundred years"[214] of their evidence.

A crucial concept in the sense that the law of evidence is founded on this principle as it "underwrites exclusionary rules regarding testimony based upon inferences or conclusions,"[215] with witnesses requested to give evidence based on their personal knowledge of the case or facts in issue, whereas expert witnesses were required to give evidence based on their specialised knowledge without personal knowledge of the case.[216]

It could be argued that Jones's "broad brush" claim concerning the history of the expert witness is correct in some respects; however, Ward has argued it was not necessarily true in cases involving mental state, involving contemporary psychiatrists.[217] Ward instead suggests that "her argument should be qualified to take account of the differences between different forms of expertise."[218]

As the interpretation of death became increasingly physiological "contained within the institutional and cultural apparatuses of scientific medicine,"[219] the presence of medical men as experts in murder trials became increasingly evident; however, increasing presence does not necessarily equate to increasing reliance. This increase in the presence of scientific discourse brought an anticipation of certainty for an uncertain jury in infanticide cases, an anticipation that, in reality, turned the expectation of certainty into a confirmation of doubt. As the law increasingly called experts to provide evidence on an increasing number of subjects, a correlating fear began to emerge that "science would displace law as the touchstone of social order,"[220] a fear that gradually created a rift between the experts and the law. This tension was evident when disagreements and contradictions occurred between men of science called as expert witnesses, and the court regularly dismissed expert evidence as the "weakest kind of testimony, discredited evidence, and unreliable mere opinion to be looked on with great suspicion."[221] It was therefore common practice for one party to accuse the other of partiality, whilst at the same time acknowledge their own witness as impartial. Therefore, the introduction of the expert witness into the courtroom introduced a potential partisan medical expert into the courtroom, ready to manipulate the findings in order to confirm his own belief of the accused's culpability.

The role of the expert witness has also been explored in the research carried out by Clayton, who explores the treatment of women accused of infanticide from the late seventeenth century to the beginning of the nineteenth century.[222] Through trials held at the Old Bailey, she argues that three particular developments led to the change in the treatment of these women, "the development of a range of successful defence strategies, changes in courtroom procedures and the increased participation of lawyers, and a greater use of and reliance on medical witnesses and their evidence."[223] This third key development is interesting, as she highlights the reliance on medical witnesses and their evidence. This research will argue the opposite: that there was no such increasing reliance on medical witnesses; in fact, there was a decreasing reliance on medical witnesses particularly towards the end of the eighteenth century at the Old Bailey. She identifies that coroners increasingly requested surgeons to perform autopsies on the infant's body, with a view to determining "whether the child had lived or was stillborn; whether it was full term; whether the child had any injuries and, if so, whether they could have been the caused during the birth or by the mother after the birth," highlighting the key questions medical experts were expected to answer.[224] Very little discussion is provided on whether or not the medical witnesses fulfilled this role, and instead Clayton concentrates on the lung test (this will be discussed in further detail in Chapters 3 and 5). A test that was considered to be "conclusive in 1729; its value became a matter of opinion in the 1730s and 1740s and it was discredited by the 1770s, but not before it had helped to send four women to the gallows";[225] notwithstanding this fact it continued to be carried out, until at least the early twentieth century by medical men.[226] Clayton also observed that medical experts contributed to the legal framework of questioning in infanticide cases by raising particular issues in court, such as whether the navel string was cut or torn, and the possibility that a child may have bled to death if a cord remained untied, a complication of an unassisted birth.

In her analysis on medical experts, however, Clayton argues that "considerable weight seems to have been accorded the evidence from medical practitioners, whether they were midwives (of either gender), apothecaries, or surgeons."[227] In cases of infanticide, it is clear that considerable weight was placed on uncertain medical evidence, as it allowed the jury to find the woman not guilty.

A further transformation occurred during the late eighteenth century, in the context of medical opinion, when the focus on evidence began to change course. Until this time opinion evidence largely related to the condition of the infant's body; however, Rabin has argued that the "state of the defendants mind became so privileged" that it began to carry greater weight in the determining of such cases.[228] The mental element of infanticide was recognised as early as the seventeenth century by Matthew Hale. Hale singled out infanticidal women as "a special case within the category of insanity," when he cited from a case at the Old Bailey in 1668, where a woman suffering from exhaustion and lack of sleep murdered her child whilst experiencing a temporary frenzy;[229] the following day the woman could not recall the events leading up to the attack and had no recollection of her actions.[230]

Poverty has also been a major contributing factor to infanticide.[231] Norrie, for example, has stated that an analysis of Bethlem case notes carried out by Smith indicated that juries were reluctant to convict these women and that in many cases where women were found to be insane, they were in fact sane.[232] He argues that "psychiatric discourse was a convenient aid to rescue the law from the embarrassing consequences of its harsh narrowness while at the same time avoiding any focus upon the social conditions that gave rise to the crimes in question."[233]

It was during the nineteenth century that an increasing need for evidence of the woman's state of mind was required at the time she committed the offence. Smith has argued that, for many years, medical evidence had been presented in cases of infanticide at inquests held by coroners, sessional courts, and the Assizes, and it was these courts that demanded medical evidence linking infanticide to lunacy.[234] Thus, a framework became established allowing the removal of responsibility from women in cases, regardless of whether overwhelming substantive evidence was presented; if insanity could be proved, the woman would be acquitted. It is interesting to note that Eigen argues that mental state experts were subjected to the same level of questioning as other witnesses, with the question most experts being asked, "were women diagnosed with puerperal melancholia incapable of resisting an impulse to destroy their own infant?[235] – a question that remained unanswered in many cases.

Foucault argues that in cases where medical experts are called to give evidence, they are asked to distinguish between illness and responsibility. In such cases, Foucault argues that:

> expert opinion must make it possible to distinguish between the dichotomies of illness and responsibility, between pathological causality and the freedom of the legal subject, between therapy and punishment, medicine and penalty, hospital and prison. One must choose, because madness wipes out crime.[236]

Arguing that, in France, in any crime when mental state is called into question, Foucault states that criminality disappears, because "madness cannot be crime, just as crime cannot be, in itself rooted in madness."[237] Foucault describes this thought process as a revolving door, because when "pathology comes in; criminality must go out; in the event of madness the medical institution must take over from the judicial institution."[238] In a situation such as this Foucault argues that it is the responsibility of the expert to take on the role of a doctor-judge or to facilitate the transition from being accused to being convicted.[239] Foucault was concerned with the way in which "medico-legal practice produced a psychologico-moral,"[240] a double effect of the legal offence, as it created a "dangerous individual and eventually through the functioning of power of normalization came to constitute itself as an authority responsible for the control of abnormal individuals."[241] He therefore believed that, "along with other processes, expert psychiatric opinion brought about this transformation in which the legally responsible individual is replaced by an element that is the correlate of a technique of normalization."[242] Ward has questioned how far Foucault's theory applied to England, arguing that English law and psychiatry in the nineteenth century did cross over in parts with Foucault's argument, although the "interplay between them worked out quite differently."[243]

This role of doctor-judge, Foucault argued, follows a specific process: a process which begins with an analysis of the material or substance that it is to be punished; this part of the process involves the medical expert or pathologist, who is responsible for both the analysis and the presentation of evidence of the cause of death.[244] If this evidence indicates an unnatural cause of death, this would in turn indicate a crime has been committed, which would then, Foucault argued, be the responsibility of the expert to twin the offence with criminality by providing causal explanations for the death.[245] In an attempt to establish the criminal's state of mind at the time of the offence, the expert would then be responsible for doubling the accused with a character, a role which Foucault argued was previously unknown during the eighteenth century. If it could then be determined that the accused was in what Foucault refers to as a "state of dementia," as he quotes from the Napoleonic Code (*demence*), then the accused would no longer be held responsible for the offence.[246]

It was the asylum doctors and alienists who responded to the need to fulfil the role, described by Foucault as a doctor-judge, by taking to the courtroom and using the witness box like a platform to "claim status and expertise" as they revealed their evidence.[247] Ward has argued that:

> Foucault maintained that courts and other institutions routinely accepted statements as true merely on the basis of the status of their maker, even in matters of life and death, because this was a practical necessity for the working of the machinery of power.[248]

In this respect many of the cases within this book appear to be anti-Foucauldian, unless the grounds of uncertainty were provided by the experts themselves.

The introduction of mental incapacity led to the development of psychiatric medico-legal discourse within infanticide cases, a concept that is encapsulated in the nineteenth-century research of Zedner on female criminality. She focused on the "medical professionals' remarkable achievement in persuading lawyers of the validity of this psychiatric exculpation, effectively replacing traditional legal discourse with that of psychiatry,"[249] resulting in mental incapacity "occupying a prominent place in the contemporary criminal law."[250] By medicalising deviance in this manner, Zedner's argument may be correct in many cases involving the mental state of the defendant; however, as this book will demonstrate, this was not the case in trials involving infanticide.

The role of the mental state expert is one that has developed throughout the last two centuries, with an increased understanding of diseases of the mind within anatomical research and the development of "rules of evidence and procedure (such as the reverse burden of proof)" within the courtroom,[251] which will be discussed in further detail throughout Chapter 4. The reason for the slower recognition of the mental state expert as an expert witness in court lies firmly with the fact that, although mental state experts considered themselves to be experts in the legal sense, courts did not always award them with such titles. It was judges who determined whether a witness should be considered an expert, and, in cases of lunacy, jurists argued that state of mind was a question of common sense as opposed to the expert question.[252]

Regardless of the fact that mental incapacity has been historically identified as an essential element of the crime of infanticide, and with the increased presence of asylum doctors in the courtroom, it was not until 1922 and the enforcement of the Infanticide Act that a partial defence to murder was permitted. Providing it could be proved the woman had killed her new-born child whilst the balance of her mind was disturbed as a result of giving birth.

Mental state or more specifically insanity is the core subject at the heart of the research carried out by Smith, as he focuses on two fundamental elements: the issues surrounding distinguishing different types of conduct and the nature of scientific knowledge.[253] By distinguishing between the behaviour determined by the Victorians resulting from disease and behaviour resulting from volition, Smith argues it is possible to interpret the line drawn by the Victorians between insanity and responsibility. His research begins in the mid-nineteenth century, a period when the "authority of science came to underpin medical statements on insanity" and a time when he identified that "medical men in general and alienists in particular made many rash statements about the scientific standing of their knowledge."[254] During this era it was difficult to fit infanticidal women into one specific category of either conduct emanating from volition or disease, as the line drawn between "murder and the baby not having lived independently must have been extremely fine, especially in conditions of gross poverty and undernourishment."[255] He therefore argues that infanticide was not "looked upon in the same light as other murders by the public generally … there is no crime that meets with so much sympathy."[256] An observation which links to Norrie's theory of "legal abstraction," that infanticide should not simply be regarded as murder, but external influences should also be taken into consideration by the court.[257]

Smith suggests that separating infanticide from murder led to a filtering process that could lead to four possible outcomes: the courts could "turn a blind eye" to the charge of infanticide by simply acquitting the woman, bring a "charge of concealment," give the woman the benefit of the doubt, and, in doing so, rely on the Home Secretary to ensure she was hanged. The final possible outcome was to encourage the woman to plead guilty to insanity.[258]

This distinction of infanticide from murder has been suggested for three inseparable reasons:

> to remove vagueness and inconsistency from the law; to achieve some kind of sanction against women who killed their children; finally, to appease sentiment about the special position of mothers.[259]

It has also been recognised that the legislation prevented many women from being convicted of new-born child murder when they had intended to do so. There were:

> special circumstances which should be recognized in law: a woman's mind after confinement was abnormally weak; temporary insanity was common and well known at this time; it was a less serious crime because one could not estimate the loss as it affected the child; it caused no alarm as it was committed by a restricted group; and public sympathy was heightened in illegitimacy cases because of the father's lack of accountability.[260]

Therefore, as medical discourse became ever more present in cases involving infanticide, the verdict of insanity required a sentence in need of therapy or care, as opposed to punishment. The Victorians regarded this as humanitarian and carried the express objective of preventing the woman from hanging. The psychiatric symptoms a woman presented with following childbirth gradually became enshrined into the medicalisation of infanticide, leading to the widely accepted recognition of puerperal insanity, both within medical and legal discourse. Therefore, when puerperal insanity became a recognised form of mental disorder from the early nineteenth century, it became a disorder that was rapidly acceptable as a form of defence plea.

It has been identified by Ward that "recent accounts of nineteenth century infanticide have recognised that medical explanations of the crime co-existed with socio-economic explanations, and that both influenced the decisions of the courts."[261] He argues that infanticide:

> constitutes a remarkable and perhaps unique exception to the way in which the criminal ordinarily constructs subjects. The infanticidal woman is not an abstract legal subject who acts outside any social or emotional context, but neither is she an insane non-subject.[262]

Medical concepts of puerperal or lactational insanity helped to make a legal defence acceptable but failed to reflect them all (new-born children were not the typical victims of insane mothers), so when encompassed within legal doctrine, it was deemed an acceptable solution to the antithesis of the infanticidal woman, by demonstrating a lack of maternal instincts towards her infant.

Loughnan, on the other hand, defines madness as a readable feature of the defendant's behaviour or conduct, with the conduct alone manifesting the defendant's underlying incapacity.[263] When applied to the infanticidal woman, the killing of the infant by the mother can be interpreted as a self-evident irrational act that triggers or manifests a mental disturbance, which stems either from the onset of the birthing process or as a result of lactation.

Throughout the nineteenth century, as psychiatry began to play an increasing role in the courtroom, there became increasing evidence of "clinical diagnosis based on knowledge, providing a means of accommodating the variety of exculpatory narratives that featured in the criminal trials of such women."[264] Loughnan argues that, through the development of psychiatric discourse, the diagnosis of phrenzy gradually became associated with childbirth, leading many professionals from various medical backgrounds to give evidence in court and leading expert evidence to become a distinguishing feature in infanticide trials. She claims that the reason expert evidence became acceptable stemmed from three key factors: the distinctive status of midwives, who possessed both specialist knowledge of childbirth and the death of new-born infants, combined with the fact they resided within local communities – it was broadly accepted that they should be called upon to give evidence in court. Difficulties arose when determining whether the child had been born alive and the expert evidence of surgeons and medical men was called for; their knowledge of anatomy and physiology stemmed from their ability to perform autopsies. So it should naturally follow that "medical experts had been required to give evidence in coronial inquires there was an established institutional framework into which medical evidence linking lunacy and infanticide could be placed."[265]

Therefore, in addition to the diagnosis of infanticidal women in court was the ascertainment of the level of the woman's responsibility. It was necessary to distinguish between women who were merely upset by the circumstances surrounding the birth of their illegitimate child from those who were insane. In many cases the plea of insanity was in fact extended to women who were sane but merely upset or, more specifically, "feeble minded."[266] Therefore two crucial elements needed to be established and clearly identified: distressful circumstances and distress of reason, or, more specifically, identifying women who were sad from those who were mad.[267] As the line separating the two anomalies became increasingly blurred, it became increasingly difficult to distinguish between the two elements, reflecting "ordinary or non-specialist understanding of madness, rather than a desire on the part of medical professionals to prescribe the significance of the acts of women killing their new-borns."[268] This phase establishing the rise of expert knowledge of mental incapacity and childbirth is referred to as the "medicalization of infanticide" and stems from the fact that women accused of infanticide were seen as the "subjects of medical rather than legal attention, and receive treatment rather than punishment."[269]

Ward argues that, by examining the interlinking aspects of law, medical knowledge and lay values and beliefs that contributed to the implementation of the Infanticide Act 1922, a potentially interesting relationship between Teubner's autopoiesis theory and infanticide emerges.[270] The term autopoiesis means the "self-maintenance of an organized entity through its own internal processes,"[271] and when applied to the criminal justice system, "autopoiesis proposes to identify circular relationships within the legal system … that analyze their internal dynamics and their external interactions."[272] This form of legal autonomy, Ward argues, has the potential to conceptualise the relationships between law, medical knowledge, and lay values and beliefs in general. In particular, he believes that the concepts of insanity and infanticide during the Victorian era were compatible with the autopoiesis theory, although when the concepts were applied to individual cases they were incompatible with the "view of law as an autonomous epistemic subject."[273] In respect of the mental state, by defining insanity in legal terms, the criminal justice system remained outside the bounds of scientific development, and so in turn the law relied heavily upon the common sense of judges and juries to interpret the definition and apply it to individual cases.[274]

Central to the historiography of infanticide is the issue surrounding medical experts, through the part they played in the courtroom, and in particular their ability or inability to provide testimony with certainty; their uncertainty contributed towards shaping the jury's opinion. The lack of certainty the medical experts demonstrated allowed the jury to apply leniency to their verdict, a point that is reflected in particular in the work of Higginbotham and Jones. Equally, this lack of certainty allowed the court to adopt a humanitarian approach, as identified by Jackson, allowing the jury to reach a verdict of "not guilty" that led to an "acquittal," thus sparing her life.

It is the element of certainty in cases of infanticide which underpins this book. Through an exploration of the contribution each medical expert has made to the historiography of infanticide, it will become clear that, although there was a general perception that through the development in medical discourse and scientific experiment certainty would increase, this was simply not the case. This research will therefore begin in the following chapter with the testimony of midwives by exploring their evidence within infanticide trials, arguing that the evidence they gave made a little contribution towards certainty.

Notes

1 For example: R. W. Malcolmson, 'Infanticide in the Eighteenth Century' in J. S. Cockburn (ed.) *Crime in England 1550–1800*. London: Methuen & Co LTD, 1977; A. Higginbotham, 'Sin of Age: Infanticide and Illegitimacy in Victorian London' *Victorian Studies*, Vol. 32, No. 3. Spring 1989, pp. 319–337; A. May, 'Infanticide Trials' in V. Frith (ed.) *Women and History, Voices of Early Modern England*. Toronto: Coach House Press, 1995; M. Arnot (2000) op. cit.; A. M. Kilday (2013) op. cit.; A. Cossins, *Female Criminality: Infanticide, Moral Panics and the Female Body*. London: Palgrave Macmillan, 2015.

2 T. Ward, 'The Sad Subject of Infanticide: Law, Medicine and Child Murder' *Social and Legal Studies*, Vol. 8, No. 2, 1999, pp. 163–180; D. Rabin, 'Bodies of Evidence, States of Mind: Infanticide, Emotion and Sensibility in Eighteenth-Century England' in M. Jackson (ed.) *Infanticide: Historical Perspectives on Child Murder and Concealment 1550–2000*. Aldershot: Ashgate, 2002; H. Marland, *Dangerous Motherhood: Insanity and Childbirth in Victorian Britain*. Basingstoke: Palgrave Macmillan, 2004; A. Loughnan, *Manifest Madness, Mental Incapacity in Criminal Law*. Oxford: Oxford University Press, 2012: chapter 8.

3 P. Hoffer and N. Hull, *Murdering Mothers: Infanticide in England and New England 1558–1803*. New York: New York University Press, 1984: 3; See also C. Damme, 'Infanticide: The Worth of an Infant under Law' *Medical History*, Vol. 22, 1978, pp. 1–24.

4 R. Kellett, 'Infanticide and Child Destruction – The Historical Legal and Pathological Aspects' *Forensic Science International*, Vol. 53, 1992, pp. 1–28: 2. See also J. Kermode and G. Walker, *Women, Crime and the Courts in Early Modern England*. London: UCL Press, 1994; J. Sharpe, *Crime in Early Modern England 1550–1750*. London: Longman, 1999; V. Makinen, and H. Pihlajamaki, 'The Individualization of Crime in Medieval Canon Law' *Journal of the History of Ideas*, Vol. 65, No. 4, 2004,

pp. 525–542; G. Johnstone and T. Ward, *Law and Crime*. London: Sage Publications Ltd, 2010: 36–39.

5 Kellett (1992) op. cit.: 2.

6 D. Rabin, *Identity, Crime and Legal Responsibly in Eighteenth-Century England*. Basingstoke: Palgrave Macmillan, 2004: 95.

7 M. Jackson (1996) op. cit.: 32; Grammar, spelling and capitalisation are original.

8 C. Smart, 'Disruptive Bodies and Unruly Sex, The Regulation of Reproduction and Sexuality in the Nineteenth Century' in C. Smart (ed.) *Regulating Womanhood: Historical Essays on Marriage, Motherhood and Sexuality*. London: Routledge, 1992: 16.

9 Hoffer and Hull (1981) op. cit.: 22.

10 Kilday (2013) op. cit.: 19.

11 K. Kittredge, 'Introduction: Contexts for the Consideration of the Transgressive Antitype' in Kittredge, K. (ed.) *Lewd and Notorious: Female Transgression in the Eighteenth Century*. Michigan: The University of Michigan Press, 2003: 2.

12 Ibid.: 3.

13 Higginbotham (1989) op. cit.: M. Jackson (1996) op. cit.; see also M. Francus, 'Monstrous Mothers, Monstrous Societies: Infanticide and the Rule of Law in Restoration and Eighteenth-Century England' *Eighteenth-Century Life*, Vol. 21, No. 2, 1997, pp. 133–156; Cossins (2015) op. cit.: 5: see also L. Gowing, 'Ordering the Body: Illegitimacy and Female Authority in Seventeenth-Century England' in M. Braddick, and J. Walter (eds.) *Negotiating Power in Early Modern Society: Order, Hierarchy and Subordination in Britain and Ireland*. Cambridge: Cambridge University Press, 2001.

14 Arnot (2000) op. cit.: 57.

15 See Malcolmson (1977) op. cit.: 192–193; M. Jackson (1996) op. cit.: chapter 2; Arnot (2000) op. cit.: 57.

16 M. Jackson (1996) op. cit.: 36.

17 Ibid.

18 Rabin (2002) op. cit.: 76.

19 M. Caswell, 'Mothers, Wives and Killers: Marital Status and Homicide in London 1674–1790' in R. Hillman and P. Ruberry-Blanc (eds.) *Female Transgression in Early Modern Britain: Literary and Historical Explorations*. Surrey: Ashgate, 2014: 114. [Available at https://books:google.co.uk, Last accessed February 27, 2015].

20 M. Jackson (1996) op. cit.: 35.

21 J. Beattie, *Crime and the Courts in England 1660–1800*. Oxford: Clarendon Press, 1986: 114.

22 Ibid.

23 Malcolmson (1977) op. cit.: 205.

24 A. Loughnan, 'The Strange Case of the Infanticide Doctrine' *Oxford Journal of Legal Studies*, Vol. 32, No. 4, 2012, pp. 685–711: 701.

25 Kilday (2013) op. cit.: 18.

26 C. K. Allen, *Legal Duties and Other Essays in Jurisprudence*. Oxford: Clarendon Press, 1931: 271.

27 M. Jansson, 'Matthew Hale on Judges and Judging' *The Journal of Legal History*, Vol. 9, 1988, pp. 201–213: 208.

28 Ibid; see also H. Berman, *Law and Revolution II, the Impact of the Protestant Reformations on the Western Legal Tradition*. Cambridge, MA: Belknap, 2003: 319.

29 *OBP*, September 1791, George Dinger, t17910914-1.

30 J. Hostettler, *Champions of the Rule of Law*. Hook, Hampshire: Waterside Press, 2011: 135.

31 *Woolmington v DPP* (1936) 25 Cr App R 72.

32 Ibid.: 481.

33 Lord Cooke, *Turning Points of the Common Law*. London: Sweet and Maxwell, 1997: 32.

34 J. McDonagh, *Child Murder and British Culture, 1720–1900*. Cambridge: Cambridge University Press, 2003: 4: L. Radzinowicz, *A History of English Criminal Law and Its Administration from 1750, Volume 1*. London: Stevens, 1948: 430–436.
35 A. May, 'Infanticide Trials' in V. Frith (ed.) *Women and History, Voices of Early Modern England.*. Toronto: Coach House Press, 1995: 22.
36 M. Clayton, 'Changes in Old Bailey Trials for the Murder of New-Born Babies, 1647–1803' *Continuity and Change*, Vol. 24, No. 2, 2009, pp. 337–359: 341.
37 Ibid; see also M. Jackson (1996) op. cit.: chapter 2.
38 Kilday (2013) op. cit.: 19.
39 Rabin (2004) op. cit.: 99.
40 A. Loughnan, 'The Strange Case of the Infanticide Doctrine' *Oxford Journal of Legal Studies*, Vol. 32, No. 4, 2012, pp. 685–711: 693.
41 Beattie (1986) op. cit.: 113–124.
42 Ibid.
43 See Ibid; see also L. Gowing, 'Secret Births and Infanticide in Seventeenth-Century England' *Past and Present*, Vol. 156, August 1997, pp. 87–115: 89; A. L. Masciola, 'The Unfortunate Maid Exemplified: Elizabeth Canning and Representations of Infanticide in Eighteenth-Century England' in M. Jackson (ed.) *Infanticide: Historical Perspectives on Child Murder and Concealment, 1550–2000*. Aldershot: Ashgate, 2002.
44 Malcolmson (1977) op. cit.: 192; See also L. Zedner, *Women, Crime and Custody in Victorian England*. Oxford: Oxford University Press, 1991: 68.
45 J. Beattie, 'The Criminality of Women in Eighteenth-Century England' *Journal of Social History*, Vol. 8, No. 4, Summer 1975, pp. 80–116: 84.
46 R. England, 'Investigating Homicide in Northern England 1800–1824' *Criminal Justice History*, Vol. 6, 1985, pp. 105–123: 119.
47 P. King, 'Gender, Crime and Justice in Late Eighteenth and Early Nineteenth-Century England' in M. Arnot and C. Usborne (eds.) *Gender and Crime in Modern Europe*. London: UCL Press, 1999: 63.
48 See S. Edwards, *Women on Trial*. Manchester: Manchester University Press, 1984: 185; F. Heidensohn, *Women and Crime*. London: Macmillan, 1985: 43–50; A. Morris, *Women, Crime and Criminal Justice*. Oxford: Blackwell, 1987: 82–101; King (1999) op. cit.: 62.
49 King (1999) op. cit.: 56.
50 P. Hoffer, and N. Hull, *Murdering Mothers: Infanticide in England and New England 1558–1803*. New York: New York University Press, 1984.
51 Ibid.: 13.
52 Ibid.
53 J. Einarsdottir, *Tired of Weeping: Mother Love, Child Death and Poverty in Guinea-Bissau*. Wisconsin: University of Wisconsin Press, 2005: 142.
54 Hoffer and Hull (1981).
55 T. Laqueur, 'Bodies, Details and the Human Narrative' in A. Biersack and L. Hunt (eds.) *The New Cultural History*. Berkeley: University of California Press, 1989: 176.
56 M. Jackson (1996) op. cit.: 112.
57 Ibid.: 113.
58 Erasmus Darwin, quoted in Ibid.: 115.
59 Jackson (1996) op. cit.: 115.
60 W. Hunter, *On the Uncertainty on the Signs of the Signs of Murder: In the Case of Bastard Children*. London: Callow, 1818.
61 Ibid.: 7.
62 Jackson (1996) op. cit.: 116.
63 Ibid.
64 Ibid.
65 T. Haskell, 'Capitalism and the Origins of the Humanitarian Sensibility, Part 1' *The American Historical Review*, Vol. 90, No. 2, 1985, pp. 339–361: 339.
66 Ibid.
67 Ward (1999) op. cit.: 176.

68 Ibid.
69 Ibid.
70 See D. Cairns, *Advocacy and the Making of the Adversarial Criminal Trial 1800–1865*. Oxford: Clarendon Press, 1998.
71 Langbein (1978) op. cit.: 307–316.
72 Cairns (1998) op. cit.: 3.
73 Langbein (2003) op. cit.: 2.
74 Ibid.: 13–16: see also D. Rabin (2004) op. cit.
75 T. Golan, *Laws of Men and Laws of Nature: The History of Scientific Expert Evidence in England and America*. Cambridge, MA: Harvard University Press, 2004.
76 T. Golan, 'The History of Scientific Expert Testimony in the English Courtroom' *Science in Context*, Vol. 12, No. 1, March 1999, pp. 7–32: 9. See also T. Golan, 'Revisiting the History of Scientific Expert Testimony' *Brooklyn Law Review*, Vol. 73, No. 3, 2008, pp. 879–942.
77 Langbein (2003) op. cit.: chapter 3.
78 Hostettler (2011) op. cit.: 137.
79 Cairns (1998) op. cit.: 3.
80 R. Vogler, *A World View of Criminal Justice*. Aldershot: Ashgate Publishing Limited, 2005: 142–143.
81 R. Smith, *Trial by Medicine, Insanity, Responsibility in Victorian Trials*. Edinburgh: Edinburgh University Press, 1981: 145.
82 H. Johnston, *Crime in England 1815–1880: Experiencing the Criminal Justice System*. London: Routledge, 2015: 62.
83 Higginbotham (1989) op. cit.: 323.
84 Smith (1981) op. cit.: 144.
85 T. Ward, 'Legislating for Human Nature: Legal Responses to Infanticide, 1860–1938' in M. Jackson (ed.) *Infanticide, Historical Perspective on Child Murder and Concealment 1550–2000*. Aldershot: Ashgate, 2002: 251.
86 "The Judgement of Death Act 1823 gave judge's discretion to abstain from passing the death sentence, in any crime except murder." J. Gregory and J. Stevenson, *Britain in the Eighteenth Century 1688–1820*. Oxford: Routledge, 2007: 194; see also S. James-Fitzpatrick, *A History of the Criminal Law in England Volume 3V*. London: Macmillan and Co, 1833: 190.
87 Johnstone, and Ward (2010) op. cit.: 50.
88 Ibid.
89 See M. Rustigan, 'A Reinterpretation of Criminal law Reform in Nineteenth Century England' *Journal of Criminal Justice*, Vol. 8, 1980, pp. 205–219.
90 Zedner (1994) op. cit.: 11.
91 Zedner (1991) op. cit.: 11; see also W. E. Hougthon, *Victorian Frame of Mind 1830–1870*. Boston: Yale University Press, 1957; A. Wohl (ed.), *The Victorian Family: Structure and Stresses*. London: Croom Helm, 1978; Smart (1992) op. cit.: 14.
92 See L. Bland, 'Feminist Vigilantes of Late-Victorian England' in C. Smart (ed.) *Regulating Womanhood: Historical Essays on Marriage, Motherhood and Sexuality*. London: Routledge, 1992.
93 See L. Davidoff, 'Class and Gender in Victorian England' in J. L. Newton, et al. (eds.) *Sex and Class in Women's History*. London: Routledge, 1983.
94 T. Hardy, *Tess of the D'Urbervilles*. London: Penguin, 2011; see also N. Lacey, *Women, Crime and Character: From Moll Flanders to Tess of the D'Urbervilles*. Oxford: Oxford University Press, 2008: chapter 3.
95 E. Gaskell, *Ruth*. London: Penguin, 1997; see also L. Rodensky, *The Crime in Mind: Criminal Responsibility and the Victorian Novel*. New York: Oxford University Press, 2003.
96 Zedner (1991) op. cit.: 23; see also B. Godfrey and P. Lawrence, *Crime and Justice 1750–1950*. Second Edition. Oxford: Routledge, 2011: chapter 8.
97 Zedner (1991) op. cit.: 23.

98 Ibid.
99 Kilday (2013) op. cit.: 9.
100 Kermode and Walker (eds.), (1994) op. cit.: 16.
101 Ibid.
102 S. D'Cruze and L. Jackson, *Women, Crime and Justice in England since 1660*. London: Palgrave Macmillan, 2009: 2.
103 Ibid.: 2: see also C. Smart, *Women, Crime and Criminology, A Feminist Critique*. London: Routledge & Kegan Paul, 1976: 8–13.
104 S. D'Cruze, and L. Jackson (2009) op. cit.: 2; I. Burney, *Poison, Detection and the Victorian Imagination*. Manchester: Manchester University Press, 2006: 21.
105 Kilday (2013) op. cit.: 9; see also Heidensohn (1985) op. cit.
106 Zedner (1991) op. cit.
107 The principle of double deviancy was first raised in Heidensohn (1985) op. cit.
108 Smart (1992) op. cit.: 16.
109 See J. Wilson, 'History of the Suppression of Infanticide in Western India under the Government of Bombay, Including Notices of the Provinces and Tribes in Which the Practice Has Prevailed' *The Edinburgh Review*, Vol. 119, No. 244, April 1, 1869, pp. 389–412; D. Grey, 'Creating the 'Problem Hindu': Sati, Thuggee and Female Infanticide in India 1800–60' *Gender and History*, Vol. 25, No. 3, 2013, pp. 498–510; D. Grey, 'Gender, Religion and Infanticide in Colonial India, 1870–1906' *Victorian Review*, Vol. 37, No. 2, 2011, pp. 107–120.
110 Zedner (1991) op. cit.: 29.
111 H. Roberts, 'Marriage, Redundancy or Sin' in M. Vicinus (ed.) *Suffer and Be Still, Women in the Victorian Age*. London: Indiana University Press, 1972: 63.
112 Malcolmson (1977) op. cit.: 192.
113 Zedner (1991) op. cit.: 29.
114 Goc (2013) op. cit.: 21.
115 M. Finn, M. Lobban, and J. Bourne Taylor, 'Introduction: Spurious Issues' in M. Finn, M. Lobban, and J. Bourne Taylor (eds.) *Legitimacy and Illegitimacy in Nineteenth-Century Law, Literature and History*. Basingstoke: Palgrave Macmillan, 2010: 5; see also A. Levene, T. Nutt, and S. Williams (eds.) *Illegitimacy in Britain 1700–1920*. Basingstoke: Palgrave Macmillan, 2005; G. Frost, *Illegitimacy in English Law and Society 1860–1930*. Manchester: Manchester University Press, 2016.
116 Finn, et al. (2010) op. cit.: 5.
117 R. H. Helmholz, *The Oxford History of the Laws of England, Vol. I: The Canon Law and Ecclesiastical Jurisdiction from 597 to the 1640s*. Oxford: Oxford University Press, 2004: 560.
118 Finn, et al. (2010) op. cit.: 5.
119 F. Trollope, *Jessie Phillips: A Tale of the Present Day*. Stroud: Nonsuch, 2006.
120 E. Hansen, 'Overlaying in 19th-Century England: Infant Mortality or Infanticide?' *Human Ecology*, Vol. 7, No. 4, December 1979, pp. 333–352.
121 J. Pierson, *Understanding Social Work, History and Context*. Maidenhead: Open University Press, 2011: 95.
122 Children Act 1908, Part II, Section 13 'suffocation.'
123 Hansen (1979) op. cit.: 335; see also E. Ross, *Love and Toil, Motherhood in Outcast London 1870–1918*. Oxford: Oxford University Press, 1993: 189; S. Kingsley Kent, *Gender and Power in Britain 1640–1990*. London: Routledge, 1999: 239.
124 Kilday (2013) op. cit.: 86.
125 G. Eliot, *Adam Bede*. Oxford: Oxford University Press, 1996.
126 Ibid.: chapter 59.
127 'Imprisonment of Mary Voce' at: www.bl.uk/collection-items/imprisonment-of-mary-voce [Last accessed May 8, 2017].
128 G. Eliot (1996) op. cit.: 85.
129 'Offences Against the Person Act 1861, clause 27' at: www.legislation.gov.uk/ukpga/1861/100/pdfs/ukpga18610100 en.pdf: 823 [Last accessed March 11, 2014].

130 Higginbotham (1989) op. cit.: 326.
131 Ibid.
132 T. Ward (1999) op. cit.: 176; see also Higginbotham (1989) op. cit.: 319–337.
133 M. Jackson (1996) op. cit.: 114.
134 T. Hitchcock and R. Shoemaker, *London Lives: Poverty, Crime and the Making of a Modern City, 1690–1800*. Cambridge: Cambridge University Press, 2015: 259.
135 F. Miley and A. Read, 'Go Gentle Babe: Accounting and the London Foundling Hospital, 1757–97' *Accounting History*, Vol. 21, No. 2–3, 2016, pp. 167–184: 172.
136 Smart (1992) op. cit.: 22.
137 A. Ballinger, A. *Dead Woman Walking: Executed Women in England and Wales 1900–1955*. Aldershot: Ashgate Publishing Ltd, 2000: 65: see also '*British Medical Journal*, 'Baby Farming and Baby Murder' Saturday March 28th, 1868: 301–302.
138 Cossins (2015) op. cit.: 92.
139 Ballinger (2000) op. cit.: 65.
140 'Baby Farming and Baby Murder' (1868) op. cit.: 301–302.
141 For discussion on the 'Medical Campaign against Baby Farming' see D. Grey, '"What Woman is Safe … ?": Coerced Medical Examinations, Suspected Infanticide, and the Response of the Women's Movement in Britain, 1871–1881' *Women's History Review*, Vol. 21, No. 3, 2013, pp. 403–421: 404.
142 'Baby Farming and Baby Murder' (1868) op. cit.: 301–302.
143 See D. Grey, '"More Ignorant and Stupid than Wilfully Cruel": Homicide Trials and "Baby Farming" in England and Wales in the Wake of the Children Act 1908' *Crimes and Misdemeanours: Deviance and the Law in Historical Perspective*, Vol. 3, No. 2, 2009, pp. 60–77.
144 *York Herald*, 'Triple Execution at Newgate' Wednesday June 10, 1868. British Newspaper Archive (www.britishnewspaperarchive.co.uk); The British Library Board; Image © the British Library Board. All rights reserved.
145 *Wells Journal*, 'Discovery of Parents through Birth Certificates' Thursday 23rd April, 1896.
146 Ballinger (2000) op. cit.: 66.
147 Ibid; see also *York Herald*, 'Triple Execution at Newgate' Wednesday 10th June, 1868; *London Daily News*, 'Execution of Mrs Dyer' Thursday June 11, 1868. British Newspaper Archive (www.britishnewspaperarchive.co.uk); The British Library Board; Image © the British Library Board. All rights reserved.
148 Kilday (2013) op. cit.: see also T. Ward (1999) op. cit.: 165.
149 Kilday (2013) op. cit.: 214.
150 Ibid.: 8.
151 Ibid.: 15.
152 Ibid.
153 Ibid.: 16.
154 D. Grey, 'Women's Policy Networks and the Infanticide Act 1922' *Twentieth Century British History*, Vol. 21, No. 4, 2010, pp. 441–463.
155 J. Baker, 'Female Lunatics: A Sketch' *British Journal of Psychiatry*, Vol. 48, No. 200, January 1902, pp. 13–28: 19; Grammar and spelling are original.
156 Grey (2010) op. cit.: 442.
157 Ibid.: 441.
158 *R v McNaughtan* (1843) 10 Clark and F. 200, 8 Eng. Rep. 718.
159 *Northampton Mercury*, 'What the Maid Found' Friday March 14, 1924. British Newspaper Archive (www.britishnewspaperarchive.co.uk); The British Library Board; Image © the British Library Board. All rights reserved.
160 D. Cooper Graves, '" … In a Frenzy While Raving Mad": Physicians and Parliamentarians Define Infanticide in Victorian England"' in B. Bechtold and D. Cooper Graves (eds.) *Killing Infants: Studies in the Worldwide Practice of Infanticide*. New York: Edwin Mellen Press, 2006: 111.
161 Grey (2010) op. cit.: 441; T. Ward (1999) op. cit.: 163.

162 H. Allen, *Justice Unbalanced, Gender, Psychiatry and Judicial Decisions*. Milton Keynes: Open University Press, 1987: 27.
163 Ibid.
164 Ibid.
165 T. Ward (1999) op. cit.: 164.
166 J. Baker (1902) op. cit.: 19.
167 *R v O'Donoghue* (1928) 20 Cr. App. R. 132.
168 T. Ward (1999) op. cit.: 173.
169 Ibid.
170 Loughnan (2012) op. cit.: 217.
171 Infanticide Act 1938 c.36 S1 (1), available at: www.legislation.gov.uk/ukpga/Geo6/12/36/section/1 [Last accessed June 15, 2015].
172 H. Allen (1987) op. cit.: 27.
173 Ibid.
174 M. Marks and R. Kumar, 'Infanticide in England and Wales' *Medicine, Science and the Law*, Vol. 33, 1993, pp. 329–339.
175 T. Ward (2002) op. cit.: 250.
176 Ibid.
177 Ibid.
178 It was stated in the 1554 case of Buckley v Thomas in Frederick Pollock, ed., *English Reports*, 75:182 that *if matters arise in our law which concern other sciences or faculties, we commonly apply for the aid of that science or faculty which it concerns*. Golan (2004) op. cit.: 18.
179 C. Jones *Expert Witnesses, Science, Medicine and the Practice of Law*. Oxford: Clarendon Press, 1994: 23; See also L. Hand, 'Historical and Practical Considerations Regarding Expert Testimony' *Harvard Law Review*, Vol. 15, 1901, pp. 40–58; J. R. Spencer, 'The Role of Experts in the Common Law: A Comparison' in S. Ceci and H. Hembrooke (eds.) *Expert Witnesses in Child Abuse Cases*. Washington, DC: American Psychological Association, 1998.
180 C. Jones (1994) op. cit.: 23.
181 A. Adam, *A History of Forensic Science: British Beginnings in the Twentieth Century*. Abingdon: Routledge, 2016: 21.
182 Golan (2004) op. cit.: 18.
183 T. Ward, 'Law, Common Sense and the Authority of Science: Expert Witnesses and Criminal Insanity in England, CA, 1840–1940' *Social and Legal Studies*, Vol. 6, No. 3, 1997, pp. 343–362: 344.
184 Adam (2016) op. cit.: 13.
185 (1782) 3 Doug KB 157.
186 Golan (2004) op. cit.: 6.
187 C. Jones (1994) op. cit.: 58.
188 Ibid.: 23.
189 Ibid.: 59.
190 Golan (2004) op. cit.: 51.
191 Ibid.
192 (1782) 3 Doug KB 157.
193 [1975] 1 ALL ER 70.
194 *R v Turner* (1975) 60 Cr App R 80.
195 T. Ward, 'An Honourable Regime of Truth? Foucault, Psychiatry and English Criminal Justice' in H. Johnston (ed.) *Punishment and Control in Historical Perspective*. Basingstoke: Macmillan, 2008: 57.
196 See M. Redmayne, *Expert Evidence and Criminal Justice*. Oxford: Oxford University Press, 2001: chapter 6.
197 M. Jackson (1996) op. cit.: especially chapter 4.
198 Ibid.: 86.

199 Ibid.: 15.
200 Ibid.
201 C. Jones (1994) op. cit.: 5.
202 Ibid.: 10.
203 T. Ward (1997) op. cit.: 345.
204 J. Jackson, 'Expert Witnesses. Science, Medicine and the Practice of Law by C. Jones' *Journal of Law and Society*, Vol. 22, No. 2, June 1995, pp. 274–279: 274.
205 This was the case until the Criminal Procedure Rules were introduced in 2005, available at: www.legislation.gov.uk/uksi/2005/384/contents/made [Last accessed September 15, 2016].

Part 24 sets out the requirement to disclose expert evidence, but it was in the Criminal Procedure Rules 2014, Part 33.2 (1) where the expert's duty to the court is set out. Available at: www.justice.gov.uk/courts/procedure-rules/criminal/docs/crim-proc-rules-2014-part-33.pdf [Last accessed 1st August 2016]. Medical evidence may also be required, under Section 4 of the Criminal Procedure (Insanity) Act 1964 (a), Section 11 of the Powers of Criminal Courts (Sentencing) Act 2000(b), under Part III of the Mental Health Act 1983 (c) or under the Criminal Justice Act 2003 (d). These particular Acts also contain requirements about the qualifications of medical experts.

206 C. Jones (1994) op. cit.: 269.
207 Ibid.
208 Ibid.: 270.
209 Ibid.
210 Ibid.
211 M. P. Cosman, 'Medieval Medical Malpractice' in S. Jarcho (ed.) *Essays on the History of Medicine*. New York: New York Academy of Medicine, Neale Watson Publications, 1976: 288.
212 C. Jones (1994) op. cit.: 96.
213 Ibid.: 270.
214 Ibid.: 6.
215 Ibid.
216 L. Dufraimont, 'New Challenges for the Gatekeeper: The Evolving Law on Expert Evidence in Criminal Cases' *Criminal Law Quarterly*, Vol. 58, 2012, pp. 531–558.
217 T. Ward (1997) op. cit.: 345.
218 Ibid.
219 I. Burney, *Bodies of Evidence, Medicine and Politics of the English Inquest 1830–1926*. Baltimore: The John Hopkins University Press, 2000: 11.
220 C. Jones (1994) op. cit.: 100.
221 Ibid.
222 Clayton (2009) op. cit.
223 Ibid.: 337.
224 Ibid.: 348.
225 Ibid.: 349; *OBP* trials of: April 1729, Sarah Harwood (t17290416-67); October 1737, Sarah Allen (t17371012-2); May 1757, Mary Mussen (t17570526-22); September 1765, Maria Jenkins (t17650918-40).
226 See the case of *OBP*, March 2004, Louisa Lunn, t19040321-332.
227 Clayton (2009) op. cit.: 347; grammar and spelling are original.
228 Rabin (2002) op. cit.: 74; M. Hale, *History of the Pleas of the Crown Ede. Sollom Emlyn*, 2 Vols. London: Printed by E. and R. Nutt, and R. Gosling, (assigns of Edward Sayer, Esq.) for F. Gyles, 1736.
229 Cited in Rabin (2002) op. cit.: 75.
230 Ibid.
231 A. Norrie, *Crime, Reason and History: A Critical Introduction to Criminal Law*. London: Weidenfeld and Nicolson, 1993: 188.
232 R. Smith (1981) op. cit.: 145 in A. Norrie (1993) op. cit.: 188.

233 Norrie (1993) op. cit.: 188.
234 R. Smith (1981) op. cit.: 148.
235 J. Eigen, *Mad-Doctors in the Dock, Defending the Diagnosis, 1760–1913*. Baltimore: John Hopkins University Press, 2016: 2.
236 M. Foucault, *Abnormal*. London: Verso, 2003: 31.
237 Ibid.: 32.
238 Ibid.
239 Ibid.
240 Ibid.: xix.
241 Ibid.
242 Ibid.
243 T. Ward (2008) op. cit.: 58.
244 Foucault (2003) op. cit.: 15.
245 Ibid.: 18–22.
246 Ibid.
247 H. Marland, 'Getting Away with Murder' in M. Jackson (ed.) *Infanticide, Historical Perspectives on Child Murder and Concealment, 1550–2000*. Aldershot: Ashgate, 2002: 171; see also H. Marland, 'Under the Shadow of Maternity: Birth, Death and Puerperal Insanity in Victorian Britain' *History of Psychiatry*, Vol. 23, No. 1, 2012, pp. 78–90.
248 T. Ward (2008) op. cit.: 59.
249 Zedner (1991) op. cit.: 90.
250 A. Loughnan (2012) *Manifest Madness*, op. cit.: 3; see also A. Loughnan (2012) 'The Strange Case' op. cit.: 685–711.
251 Loughnan (2012) *Manifest Madness*, op. cit.: 4.
252 R. Smith (1981) op. cit.: 77.
253 Ibid.: vii.
254 Ibid.: 9.
255 Ibid.: 146.
256 W. B. Ryan, *Infanticide: Its Law, Prevalence, Prevention and History*. London: Churchill, 1862, cited in Ibid.: 145.
257 T. Ward (2002) op. cit.: 250.
258 R. Smith (1981) op. cit.: 147.
259 Ibid.
260 Ibid.
261 T. Ward (1999) op. cit.: 164.
262 Ibid.: 176.
263 Loughnan (2012) op. cit.
264 Ibid.: 211.
265 Ibid.
266 Ibid.
267 Ibid.: 212.
268 Ibid.
269 Ibid.: 212.
270 T. Ward, 'The Sad Subject of Infanticide: Law, Medicine and Child Murder' *Social and Legal Studies*, Vol. 8, No. 2, 1999, pp. 163–180.
271 'Oxford English Dictionary' at: www.oed.com/view/Entry/250011?redirectedFrom=autopoiesis#eid [Last accessed July 21, 2016].
272 G. Teubner, *Law as an Autopoietic System*. Oxford: Blackwell, 1993: 1; see also G. Teubner, 'How the Law Thinks: Towards a Constructivist Epistemology of Law' *Law and Society Review*, Vol. 23, 1989, pp. 727–757.
273 T. Ward (1999) op. cit.: 175.
274 T. Ward (1997) op. cit.: 343–362.

2 Midwifery evidence in infanticide cases

During the seventeenth century, the female midwife was considered to be the leading expert in childbirth as the:

> art of midwifery is doubtless one of the most useful and necessary of all arts, for the being and wellbeing of mankind, and therefore it is extremely requisite that a midwife, be both fearing God, faithful, and exceedingly well experienced in that profession.[1]

The art or skill of midwifery to which the seventeenth-century midwife, Jane Sharp, refers in her book *The Midwives Book*, not only depicts her perceptions of her profession, but arguably reflects the view of wider society towards midwifery during this period. In particular, this point could be considered in respect of the view held by the court, and the number of infanticide cases midwives were called upon to provide testimony, because until the eighteenth century the "midwife was the undisputed expert in infanticide trials."[2]

This chapter is devoted to the midwife, a term which refers to the female midwife (as opposed to the man-midwife), and will begin with an introduction to the midwife as an expert of childbirth, and midwifery as a profession. It will then examine broader changes in the history of midwifery, and in particular external influences that impacted on the midwife's role in the delivery room. Influences which in turn affected the role of the midwife as an expert witness in the courtroom and in infanticide cases in particular.

The remainder of this chapter will then present the research findings from three periods: 1688–1738, 1788–1838, and 1883–1913. The first period, 1688–1738, is 64 years following the implementation of the 1624 Act, "An Act to prevent the Destroying and Murthering of Bastard Children," to allow for the establishment of the Act. The second period, 1788–1838, aims to encompass the implementation of the 1803 Lord Ellenborough Act, and the final 40-year period, 1883–1913, consists of cases up until the discontinuation of the Old Bailey online records in 1913. By comparing the results from each timeframe, it has been possible to determine how the midwife's testimony was lacking in justifiable certainty within infanticide cases. However, due to a lack of newspaper articles reporting midwives as

DOI: 10.4324/9781003006299-2

expert witnesses in infanticide cases in Hull and the surrounding area, the research in this chapter will focus solely on cases recorded at the Old Bailey.

The cases will demonstrate how the seventeenth- and eighteenth-century courts relied on the midwife as an expert witness, giving weight to her opinion as she drew on her experience and training, however rudimentary, to perform her role. As the testimony given by midwives regarding the infant body as a source of evidence remained unsupported by scientific experiments, or testing, it could be described as raw. This chapter will therefore act as a useful starting point or baseline against which male medical experts studied in the remainder of this research can be measured.

As this research begins by exploring the role of the female midwife as an expert witness in the seventeenth century, it is fundamentally important to establish the extent of her authority as expert during this time. The term expert first appeared in English as an "adjective in the 14th century at the same time as the closely related experience";[3] then, in the seventeenth century, the Latin phrase "expertus sum"[4] was used when describing one's experience, in particular in the context of experiencing something routinely and often.[5] It could be argued that the concept of experience during the seventeenth century was considered to be inseparable "from the notion of expertise."[6] A notion which allowed all women who described themselves as midwives to be considered experts, however rudimentary their skills, regardless of level of education, and in the absence of any formal training or qualification.

The work carried out by English midwives in the seventeenth century varied across the country.[7] Some midwives attended births occasionally in the form of female bonding or neighbourly support, the majority of these women being elderly and untrained;[8] midwifery for these women tended to be considered as an additional part-time job on top of other work, such as that of washerwomen.[9] In many cases their midwifery knowledge was acquired informally through trial and error, with the use of antiquated practices, arguing "this was the way they had always been done,"[10] without necessarily understanding why. As a result of this, their ability to handle emergency situations tended to be poor, and they were likely to be at a loss when faced with difficult procedures or major obstetric problems.[11]

On the other hand, midwifery in other parts of the country was considered to be an occupation, with midwives using their skills to earn a regular income from their practice, and it has been noted by Willughby that "London midwives, as a group, were more competent and better trained than most country midwives."[12] These midwives were subjected to the close discipline of other women within a professional setting, and generally had the social status of minor city officials.[13] Therefore, midwifery was an opportunity for women to either show neighbourly support, or in other areas it was a form of employment, generating enough money for the midwife to be her family's breadwinner.[14] For poor women the midwife was an affordable option to the fees of the apothecary or surgeon; she was also easily accessible and of the same social class.[15] Deliveries without the presence of a midwife were rare, and as a result of this the presence of a midwife came to be considered a universal norm.[16]

In light of this, and in an attempt to close ranks to male competition, female midwives made several attempts to gain professional status throughout the seventeenth century, at a time when basic regulation of midwives in England began to evolve.[17] In 1616, midwives practising in London petitioned James I for a charter to create a society for the development of midwifery. The incorporation of midwives with the objective of the charter being to regulate the practice of midwifery and to enhance their skills with formal training. Although the petition was received with some interest by the king, it was opposed by the Royal College of Physicians, who blocked the professionalisation of midwifery with a number of counter proposals. A further attempt in 1663 was once again rejected and, as a result of this, the male control of midwifery throughout the eighteenth century became increasingly obvious within English medical practice.[18] Turner suggests that the professional strategy of male practitioners was to, "confine the midwife to the role of mere attendant at the birth and to encourage midwives to leave all abnormal births to the intervention of men equipped with the new instruments of medicine especially forceps."[19]

The introduction of forceps from 1720 was a significant landmark between medicine and midwifery,[20] as this advancement in obstetrics put female practitioners at a disadvantage. Owing to midwifery custom, the female practitioners were forbidden to use the instrument in their practice,[21] nor did they have access to the new academic or anatomical studies, as the prestige of these advances belonged to men. This combination of factors contributed to the increasing number of men entering the midwifery profession, and from the beginning of the sixteenth century, the term man-midwife became increasingly recognised within the English language in respect of their association with, and their ability to deal with, difficult or emergency situations.[22] Some men qualified as surgeons and physicians, others were surgeon-apothecaries or apothecary-surgeons; there were also men qualified as apothecaries, and in most cases non-medical men were also permitted to practice as midwives; however, they were all considered able to practise as man-midwives.[23] Regardless of qualification or professional title, men were considered to be superior to female midwives on the grounds of their "gender and education, which endowed them with a higher social status."[24] A transformation that led Wilson to argue that the whole concept of transferring childbirth from a female domain into a part of medicine cannot be "assimilated to wider medical change; it has its own distinctive history."[25]

Towards the late eighteenth century, the increasing presence of men in the lying-in room to attend women experiencing normal deliveries was received with scepticism. Women had held a natural authority over men in respect of reproductive matters, which stemmed from their gender and experience. The increased presence of men therefore attracted animosity and resistance from both midwives and labouring women. To hide his presence in the room, the man-midwife was expected to crawl into the room on all fours to reduce further distress to the labouring woman. Once in the delivery room, he may have been requested to work with his hands covered by a sheet to maintain the woman's dignity, a practice which undoubtedly led to error.[26]

By the end of the nineteenth century, male medical practitioners had successfully imposed professional control over female midwifery, and in preventing the emergence of a competitive professional group dominated by women, so that "within a broader perspective, we can see the development of male management of midwifery as part of the medicalization of motherhood."[27] A process that Oakley argues consisted of two main stages:[28] the first included the incorporation of motherhood into medical discourse in the seventeenth and eighteenth centuries as a natural state. The second is its gradual redefinition of pathology as a medical phenomenon akin to illness. It is a process which has developed along with the clinical antenatal care movement itself;[29] there is no conceptual differentiation of normal from abnormal pregnancy, in respect of the kind that has become central to obstetric discourse in the first quarter of the twenty-first century. The encroachment of male practitioners into the delivery or laying-in room clearly had a significant impact on the work of the female midwife, and in turn had an effect on the midwife's role as a witness in the courtroom, where midwives had historically been regarded as experts in childbirth and reproductive matters.

Midwives and the criminal justice system

The involvement of midwives within the criminal justice system dates back as far as the Middle Ages when childbirth was treated as a physiological process, dominated by norms and traditions and firmly rooted in the female culture.[30] During this time midwives could be called upon to provide testimony in court[31] or take part in exclusive female special purpose juries. Midwives were therefore regarded as "uniquely qualified to comment on irregularities in the female genitals."[32]

Ackerknecht has argued that midwives were called to testify on a number of issues concerning the female reproduction system, including female impotence, the absence or presence of virginity, and pregnancy, a "role of expert in court both reveals and bestows a relatively high status for the midwife."[33] In particular midwives were called to provide their opinion in cases such as infanticide, rape, and witchcraft.[34] In cases of witchcraft, for example, midwives were requested to search the suspect's body for a witches' mark,[35] a crucial role as the witches' mark was considered pivotal in establishing the guilt of the accused.[36]

Midwives were also called upon to examine women who had made allegations of rape, and present their findings to the court.[37] Owing to the intimate violation of rape and the reluctance of people to discuss personal sexual matters, at the risk of feeling embarrassed and humiliated, it was a crime that was notoriously difficult to prove.[38] Initially the girl needed to truly understand that a crime had been committed against her, and that the assailant needed to be punished; it was this combination of factors that made the midwife's evidence crucial for securing a conviction.[39]

Wiener has identified that rape indictments were rare in English courts between the mid-sixteenth century and the late eighteenth century: a fact that is reflected in the 203 cases recorded at the Old Bailey between 1730 and 1800.[40] It was generally believed that "common forms of illicit sexuality, adultery or prostitution were viewed as religious as opposed to criminal offences and were not tried at the Old Bailey."[41] During the limited occasions that proceedings did take place in court, it proved extremely difficult to establish that penetration had taken place; this resulted in many men who were initially accused of rape being instead charged with assault with intent to rape.[42]

The expertise of women in court was also relied on by courts through the appointment to serve on exclusive female juries, also known as a jury of matrons. The requirement to sit on such a jury was to be a "married woman, regarded as staid or dignified, especially a middle-aged woman with children" or "an old or elderly woman,"[43] excluding young women, as well as spinsters of any age.

The purpose of the exclusively female jury was usually to establish whether a female party to litigation was pregnant, especially in cases where women condemned to death had become pregnant whilst awaiting trial. In such cases, the accused would "plead her belly,"[44] a plea that initiated an investigation involving the jury of matrons, whose authority stemmed from the "crucial evidence of their special knowledge."[45] This special knowledge stemmed from their experience of childbirth, and so they were considered to be experts in the art of assisting childbirth.[46] The jury of matrons were required to establish whether the accused was "quick with child of a quick child,"[47] a phrase used to describe the first signs of movement of the foetus in the uterus, at three to four months gestation. This crucial notion of quickening became a key responsibility of the panel of jurors because, until the late eighteenth century, it was generally believed that this was not merely a sign of pregnancy, but the sign of the beginning of human life.[48] In the case of Margery Townley, who was found guilty of High Treason at the Old Bailey on February 21, 1694, and sentenced to death,[49] "she pleaded her belly, and a jury of matrons brought her in, that she was with child."[50] This use of juries of matrons was clearly remarkable, during an era when women were forbidden from serving as magistrates or jurors.[51] The use of juries of matrons was also lengthy, as Oldham has identified, for at least "seven centuries in English law, women served on exclusively female special purpose juries."[52]

The knowledge women acquired of the physiological signs of pregnancy was also relied upon during the Early Modern period for the recognition of illegitimate pregnancy. In the absence of a reliable method of confirming pregnancy, in some cases it was difficult to establish[53] and distinguish it from other medical conditions such as dropsy.[54] In many cases women's knowledge and suspicions became an invaluable tool as they watched for signs of pregnancy, such as the "shortness of the coats or the fullness of the hips and who peered into chamber pots to see what they could tell from the water in them."[55] It was women who, after acting on suspicions, confronted the accused and carried out physical searches of the women to determine if she had recently delivered,[56] bringing many cases of infanticide to light.[57] For example, when a young woman delivered her child alone and hid the corpse in her trunk, she became very ill; "the woman, (in whose house she lay) upon some suspicions sent for the midwife, who declared that she had had a child."[58] The corpse was discovered, and so the woman confessed, insisting that the child was stillborn. In the absence of marks of violence upon the body, she was found not guilty at the Old Bailey on September 6, 1677.[59]

Midwives tended to be called upon soon after suspicions were raised, attending the woman soon after the delivery. Assigned with a two-fold role, she was expected to examine the woman's body to determine whether she had recently delivered a child; after establishing this fact, she would then search for the infant cadaver.[60] As communities were small and closely knit, the midwife often knew the accused and the local community, a fact she may have benefited from if the court should ask her questions regarding the character and integrity of the accused.[61] Gowing has suggested that:

> The official, legal role of midwives in investigating pregnancy gave one group of women a stake in the legal process that was based on both professional qualifications and personal experience. But the experience that authorised their participation in legal structures was based most of all on their status as respectable married women and mothers in the community.[62]

Once the infant cadaver had been recovered, the greatest challenge was establishing if the child had been born alive.[63] On the basis of concern for evidence, it was imperative that the midwife was absolutely certain of the circumstances surrounding the child's mortality. By observing the growth of the hair on the child's head and the development of the finger and toenails, the midwife was able to use her experience and knowledge to determine the gestation of the child; in doing so she could determine premature delivery. In the case of Deborah Greening, for example, who was indicted for the murder of her female infant bastard by wilful strangulation, at her trial at the Old Bailey on February 24, 1725, the midwife deposed that "the prisoner did not go her full time, for the toenails of the infant were not perfect."[64] In the absence of any signs of violence upon the child it was impossible to prove that the child was not stillborn; Deborah produced some bedlinen in court in attempt to prove her good intentions towards the birth of the child.[65] It is unclear whether the acquittal of Deborah by the jury was attributed to the midwife's evidence or the bedlinen defence, but the midwife played a significant role.

The following cases, held at the Old Bailey during the seventeenth and early eighteenth century, also demonstrate that the midwife proved to be a key witness following an alleged infanticide. Once all the evidence had been heard, it was then for the jury to draw inferences from the evidence and agree on a verdict; if the jury found the woman guilty, then using his discretion, the judge could determine whether to recommend the woman for mercy and receive a royal pardon.[66]

Infanticide cases of the Old Bailey, 1688–1738

During the period 1688–1738, 76 infanticide cases were recorded at the Old Bailey, 54 involved evidence given by a midwife; 38 of these women were found not guilty. There were 16 women who were found guilty and sentenced to death, and only one of these women was respited for pregnancy.[67] In 3 of the

54 cases a surgeon also gave evidence, and in each of these cases the women were found guilty and sentenced to death. It is interesting to note that in the 22 cases where a midwife was absent from court, 17 women were acquitted, and in only 2 of these cases a surgeon gave evidence. In the remaining five cases, in the absence of midwifery evidence, the women were found guilty and sentenced to death.

A number of interesting points can be noted from the 54 infanticide cases recorded at the Old Bailey containing midwifery evidence. Due to the rapid, speedy turnover of criminal trials in the seventeenth and eighteenth century, the reporting of many cases tended to be brief, with very few facts recorded.[68] The condensing of the trial reports has been recognised as a shortcoming of these documents; by endeavouring to condense the trials into pamphlets containing 8 to 12 pages, reports had to be brief.[69] During the 1730 mayoral year, the OBSP underwent a change of format and an enhancement of detail.[70] There appears to be a number of inconsistent verdicts in some infanticide cases involving similar facts, and the cause of the infant's death was viewed by degrees of seriousness, an issue which may have related to intent.

There was not a universal concern as to whether the woman had made provision for the birth or not, but instead guilt or innocence depended on other predisposing factors of the case. For example, in cases where the accused claimed "my senses went from me," thus presenting with symptoms of insanity, juries were harsher with their verdict, possibly because they believed that women fell back on insanity when their guilt was otherwise obvious. It also seemed that juries were harsher with their verdicts in cases where the surgeon gave evidence, which could stem from developments in medical discourse, placing greater weight on his evidence. The most consistent point in the cases is the strength of the relationship between the midwife and the court, a factor evident from the weight placed on the opinion of the midwife as an expert witness: demonstrating a high level of respect to the midwife as an expert witness by the courts. Arguably, a point that is demonstrated in the case of Mary Campion,[71] on December 11, 1689, who was accused of killing her new-born infant by throwing it into a house of office,[72] it was reported that there was:

> no appearance of hurt on the child's body evidenced by the midwife. The prisoner said she was not near her time and there was no proof the baby was born alive – provision had been made for the birth, but the court believed that she was out of the statute and so she was acquitted.[73]

There is no explanation as to why Mary was considered to be out of the statute; however, it could be assumed that, because no evidence had been provided to prove the child had been born alive, the court was unable to proceed with an indictment for murder. The midwife's testimony of no "appearance of hurt on the child's body"[74] may have contributed to Mary's acquittal, as it was consistent with Mary's claim the child was stillborn. There is also no description of the appearance of the child with regard to birthweight, appearance, or gestational development to indicate the child was premature, but as Mary was acquitted this is of little matter.[75]

On the other hand, in the case of Elinor Hunt,[76] who on July 7, 1697, was also accused of killing her new-born infant by throwing it into a house of office, Elinor believed her infant to be eight weeks premature and stillborn, and yet she was found guilty. The midwife examined the child, and Elinor confessed to her that she had given birth to the child. Elinor believed there to be eight weeks remaining of her pregnancy and she believed the child to be stillborn, which no one could either corroborate or disprove, but all seemed to carry little weight in the decision of the jury. Elinor was found guilty and sentenced to death; she was executed on July 16, 1697.[77]

Both Mary and Elinor were accused of killing their new-born infants by throwing the child into a house of office, and both infants were premature, although the gestation of Mary's child is unclear. It is unlikely that Elinor's infant would have been born alive if it was indeed eight weeks premature, a fact which seemed to carry little weight with the jury, as they found her guilty and she was executed, whilst Mary on the other hand was acquitted.

In the case of Jane Bostock[78] on February 26, 1729, the possibility of a surprise delivery was acknowledged by the court. A woman lodging in the house in which Jane was a servant grew suspicious of her behaviour, and suspected her of having recently delivered a child. She informed a neighbour and together they searched the necessary (toilet) and found the child. She washed the child and it did not appear to have any marks of cruelty upon its body; Jane appeared to have gone to her full time, a fact confirmed by the midwife.

Jane had given birth to the baby in the house of office as she claimed she could not help it falling down, a fact the midwife confirmed to be possible. The OBSP provide little of the midwife's testimony, merely stating that the midwife confirmed the testimony given by the other women who had discovered the body. Jane was found not guilty; however, it might be possible to conclude that, in confirming the evidence provided by the other witnesses, the jury relied heavily on the opinion of the midwife to shape their verdict: it was possible for Jane to have experienced a precipitous delivery, resulting in the rapid birth of the infant.

Once the jury appear to accept the surprise delivery defence towards the latter years of this 50-year period it seems that evidence of violence did become increasingly important, possibly in an attempt to distinguish between those deaths which could be considered to be accidental and those that were intentional. The location of the delivery also became important, and this is evident in the verdict and punishment the women received. For example, a woman who was accused of killing her baby by throwing it into a privy, house of office, or house of easement was more likely to be found not guilty, than a woman accused of throwing her baby out of a window or other method involving brutality, which could result from mental incapacity. In many cases the midwife was asked if it is possible for a woman to be taken by surprise by the onset of delivery, resulting in a rapid delivery, with the child found in the vault or house of casement. When asked this question by the court the midwife's reply was "yes," which in many cases may have exonerated the woman's behaviour and contributed to her acquittal.

This is evident in the case of Mary Dixon,[79] September 11, 1735, who was indicted for the murder of her male infant by suffocation as a result of throwing the child into a house of office:

> on Tuesday Mary Dixon committed to Newgate for murdering her new-born son, by throwing it into a privy and then sinking the soil. She had been two years from her husband and returning in May left from Ireland to him, committing this barbarous act to hide her shame from her said husband.[80]

The landlord discovered the child alive in the vault; however, it died later that day and when the landlord asked Mary, how she could be so barbarous? She replied, "because she was wicked."[81] She said she had "got the gripes and went into the vault."[82] Mary had a husband and a four-year-old child and she claimed her "senses went from me and I did not recover myself I did not know what I did or said."[83] The midwife, Phoebe Webster testified that "I have known children come away perfectly involuntary and without any assistance, and by what I observed at the vault, I found she might have been delivered there, and I observed no sign in any other place." As the jury acquitted Mary in this case, it could be inferred that Webster's evidence assisted in shaping the verdict of the jury. By drawing on her previous experience she stated how it was not unusual for women to experience surprise deliveries in the vault, and by testifying there was no evidence to suggest Mary had delivered elsewhere and then thrown the child into the vault to hide her shame, she advocated Mary's innocence. This last piece of evidence indicates that the midwife did look for evidence of childbirth elsewhere, and did not merely take Mary's word for the fact she had delivered in the vault; on this basis, the midwife's evidence in this case is clearly significant.

It has been suggested by Rabin that Mary's testimony addressed the question of intention directly as she informed the court that "I was under no temptation for being so barbarous, for I had a good husband who was able to maintain the child."[84] It is interesting to note that the witnesses did not speak of any previous peculiar behaviour Mary might have displayed, when in fact, whilst in the witness box, Mary spoke at length about both her crime and her state of mind.[85] Owing to the fact that Mary was married, she would not have been indicted under the 1624 Act, instead she was indicted for murder; however, the jury acquitted her. The *Newcastle Courant* reported the verdict as "Mary Dixon the wine cooper's wife was tried for the murder of her male infant, by stifling it in the privy; but the evidence not being full, she was acquitted."[86]

Similarly, Jane Plintoff[87] was indicted for murdering her male infant bastard, on July 9, 1718, after the child was discovered in the house of office and brought up by a bucket. An examination of the child revealed a broken skull, an injury that might have been caused by the bucket. The midwife, Mrs Beecham, deposed that "as far as she could see, to the best of her judgement the child did appear to be at its full time; but it was so wasted by lying so long in the vault, she could say nothing to its having been born alive or not."[88] Jane believed the child to be early and to have been stillborn; however, it was impossible for the midwife to either prove or disprove her testimony. Jane confessed to the child being hers and to putting it into the vault, a fact she explained by being poor and not having the financial means to bury the child; she had made provision for the birth, and so she was acquitted by the jury.

Equally in the case of Francis Bolanson[89] on October 15, 1718, who was indicted for murdering her male bastard infant by throwing it in a house of office. After being suspected of recently delivering a child, the midwife carried out a search and the child was discovered in the vault. Francis duly confessed to the midwife, "but nothing could be seen on it whether it had been hurt or not, nor whether it came at its full time, it having lay'n there for 5 or 6 weeks."[90] The midwife was unable to deduce very much from the state of the corpse, and so gave limited evidence at the trial. Francis claimed to have been frightened by thunder and lightning, and had fallen ill with the measles; she believed her fright and illness occasioned the death of the child within her, as she had not felt it move for some time before the birth; she therefore claimed the child was premature and stillborn. Francis brought proof of both her illness and provision she had made for the birth; she was acquitted by the jury. As the burden of proof lay with the woman under the 1624 Act, this case demonstrates that the stronger the evidence a woman could produce to support her claims regarding the birth, the greater the chance of the court believing her. These cases also indicate that the court viewed the throwing of a child out the window as more serious than throwing into a house of office or vault, which may have occurred accidentally.

On the other hand, Jane Cooper was indicted for the murder of her female bastard infant on December 8, 1736, by wrapping it in a cloth; she was accused of choking and strangling her to death. When questioned, Jane said the child had not been born alive, that she had made no preparation for the birth, and nobody knew anything regarding the birth except herself. Elizabeth Hutchins, the midwife, deposed:

> it was at its full growth full nail'd, and had hair on its head; it was very much maul'd, the arm and skull were broke; and as to the face it had none; no eyes nor nose, and the skull was clasped one part over the other; I cannot say whether that might happen without violence or not, but the arm was broke between the shoulder and the elbow; perhaps the clasping of the skull one part over the other, might be occasioned by her wrapping it up so close together.[91]

Jane's defence was that the child was stillborn, and was never alive in this world, stating that she, "called for help but nobody heard her and so it was all over, and the child was dead, I did not think of telling anything about it."[92] It is difficult to ascertain in this case how much influence the midwife had in shaping the jury's verdict, it is possible that either the extent of the injuries the midwife described may have been a contributing factor, or the fact that Jane appeared ill-prepared for the birth, because the jury found her guilty and she was sentenced to death.

It is written in the Ordinary's Account (the chaplain of Newgate prison)[93] dated March 3, 1737, that Jane informed him that she had been:

> married but her husband dying, she went to service … with good reputation to herself. She owned she had her self-wrapped up the child in the manner it was found, but she professed she never discerned it had life in it. She was very sick during her confinement and so poor and naked, that at last she lost her sight. She seemed not to be of a compassionate temper but hard-hearted and was not to be made sensible of her crimes; yet she professed herself at peace with all the world, and on Thursday Feb. 3, about 4 in the afternoon she died.[94]

A contrasting case is that of Mary Tate,[95] who was indicted for the murder of her male bastard child on June 30, 1714, after she was found lying in a field in a languishing condition. She claimed she left the child wrapped in straw by the side of a pond, but later confessed to wrapping it in straw and then placing it in a hole of a kiln, whilst it was still burning, accusations she denied at her trial, whilst talking in a rambling manner. Although a midwife was involved in the case, her testimony is missing from the OBSP. This case, however, demonstrates the significance of lay evidence of insanity; several witnesses appeared at Mary's trial on her behalf, claiming she was a person not well in her senses, and had not been for some years; the jury acquitted Mary.

It is possible that the witness in Mary's trial who gave an account of her being "looked upon as a person not well in her senses for some years,"[96] might have contributed to the shaping of the jury's verdict. In the study of eighteenth-century courts carried out by Beattie,[97] it is indicated that strong character witnesses for defendants could result in an acquittal. Character witness testimony was used either in an attempt to suggest that the defendant was not the sort of person who was likely to have committed the alleged offence, or to prove that witnesses called on behalf of the prosecution may not have a reputation for veracity.[98] This is evident in the case of Sarah Hanesley,[99] held on August 30, 1721, who was indicted for the murder of her male infant by wrapping and smothering him in a linen cloth. Mrs Scott gave a character witness statement, stating "the prisoner had been her servant for 10 years and had behaved herself well."[100] Sarah also called several witnesses to testify as to her reputation, those witnesses gave her a good character and, therefore, after considering the facts, the jury acquitted her. It would seem that character witnesses whose testimony might support or undermine other testimony given under oath were often deployed as a means of shaping the jury's verdict. Shapiro has suggested that judges often encouraged the use of character witnesses on behalf of the defendant to "testify to the accused's habits of life and trustworthiness."[101]

It seems possible to conclude that the court considered the cause of death by throwing the child out of an open window as intentional and therefore murderous as opposed to the throwing of a child into a house of office or vault, which may be accidental. The cases of Jane Cooper and Mary Tate demonstrate that the court viewed the death of a child by wrapping it into a cloth and choking it as more serious than wrapping it in straw and burning it alive, and burning alive seemed consistent with insanity. It is therefore clear that the verdicts in these cases demonstrate a lack of consistency in eighteenth-century infanticide cases.

The cases provide a useful insight into the relationship between the midwife and the courts, particularly in cases where a surgeon also provides testimony. In the case of Mary Gough, for example, the surgeon gave his opinion by stating that he believed the child to be "at its full growth and was of the opinion that it might be born alive."[102] The midwife Elizabeth Stoner also gave her opinion, stating "the child was at full growth, but believed it to be still-born, and that it might be lost for want of help."[103] Mary had made provision for the birth of the child, and the jury acquitted her.[104] It is interesting to note a contradiction in opinion between the midwife and the surgeon; it is not possible to conclude that the acquittal of Mary stemmed solely from the opinion of the midwife, as she had made provision for the pending birth; however, it does appear that the midwife's opinion carried more weight than that of the surgeon, despite his medical knowledge and expertise, as Mary was acquitted. It could be argued that, by acquitting Mary, and potentially placing greater weight on the opinion of the midwife, the jury demonstrated a degree of humanitarian sympathy towards her.

In most of the infanticide cases recorded at the Old Bailey during this period, it seems that the midwife drew on her experience to state her observations and draw her conclusions. In the case of Christian Russel, held on January 14, 1702, for example, the midwife deposed that it was very likely that the child had been "born alive by reason it was a very large child and came to its full time"; she also said that she "found no marks about it, only that the arm was broke," as a result of this, the jury found her guilty and she was sentenced to death.[105] The midwife giving her observations stated that it was very likely that the child had been born alive due to its size alone, making the assumption that, because the child was at full term, it would naturally follow that it was born alive. It is possible that the jury in Christian's case placed a great deal of weight on the testimony given by the midwife, and as a result of this they found her guilty and she was sentenced to death. It is interesting to note the court's rejection of lay evidence regarding a fall: the witness deposed that "she had a great fall about a fortnight before, which hurt her very much, and she never felt the child stir."[106]

In the Ordinary's Account of Paul Lorrain, he stated that Christian confessed to him that the:

> child was born alive, and that she did cast him away. At first she seemed very little concerned with what she had done; she confessing her sins without apparent signs of true sorrow for them. But this might, in some measure, be attributed to her dullness and slowness of capacity, she being very stupid and ignorant and a poor simple creature … she declared that the young man that had got her with child had promised to marry her, but he kept not his promise to her and as it proves commonly so when he had made a whore of her he would not make her his wife.[107]

It is therefore possible to conclude that the midwife was right to state at the trial that she believed the child was born alive. Whereas, in the case of Ann Hasle, July 17, 1717,[108] the midwife deposed that the child was at its full time. She also testified that:

> there was no marks upon the child of its having been hurt anywhere, except that there was a blackish circle about the child's mouth (which a midwife likewise deposed was usual to such infants through dying by a natural death).[109]

It is possible that the jury placed a great deal of weight on the fact that the midwife drew on her previous experience by giving an explanation for the black circle around the child's mouth as resulting from natural causes, because Ann was acquitted.

In the case of Hannah Bradford, on April 19, 1732,[110] there becomes a distinct difference in the questioning of the witnesses, or indeed a difference in the reporting of the cases. There is evidence of detailed questioning and there are specific questions directed at the midwife, particularly requiring her to draw on her previous experience. The court questions the midwife, Elizabeth Taylor, in the following way, "is it usual for women to have such hasty labours?" to which the midwife replied, "tis not common, but I have known 2 or 3 instances that have been under my care."[111] They then asked, "did she tell you that she had a child?" to which the midwife replied, "yes; and I asked her whose child it was? she said her husband's."[112] The court then asked, "was this before or after you had examined her?" The midwife deposed, "it was after; for she was swooning away and dying, and not able to speak before."[113] She was then asked, "do you think it was likely the child should come from her in such a manner?" The midwife replied, "yes; I took the child up and washed it."[114] The midwife was then asked, "did you see any marks or bruises?" The midwife replied, "no; it was clear." The midwife also stated that the child was fully grown.[115]

This case demonstrates how the midwife drew on her previous experience to answer the questions put to her by the court. As the court report does not specify who in particular is asking the questions, it can be assumed that the court means the judge. In particular, the midwife describes how she has known previous hasty labours and surprise deliveries, explaining it could be possible for a child to be found in the vault. The court asks, "do you think it was likely the child should come from her in such a manner," to which she replies "yes."[116] The jury appears to have drawn inferences from the evidence given by the midwife and accepted the surprise delivery defence, as Hannah was acquitted.

The case of Mercy Hornby, on April 24, 1734, who was indicted for the murder of her female bastard infant by throwing her alive into the privy, is an example of a case in which the accused questions the witnesses herself. The midwife, Mary Fauks, who was sent for by the prisoner to:

> free her of the afterbirth, and I made her a free woman and left her safe. I was sent for on the Friday, but could not go, I saw the child, it was as fine a

> female as ever I set my eyes on, and I don't question but it was full grown; for I believe it was 3 quarters (of a yard long) and I believe it was born alive, for I can't think so large a dead child could make its own way. There was a great bruise on this side of the head.[117]

Mercy then asked:

> might not that come by a fall at its birth?" Fauks replied, "I can't say that." Mercy then asked Fauks "did not you take some child-bed-linen out of my trunk?" and she said "yes; a shirt, a blanket, and a night-cap, a biggin, and a long stay; but these I did not see till Monday, and it's much to be feared, that you did not put them there; for indeed I was informed they were borrowed of a neighbour.[118]

The court told the midwife "that's no evidence – you must not swear what you heard, but only what you know,"[119] referring to the hearsay principle that the witness should only speak of "what hath fallen under his senses," a point that became a fundamental principle in modern law.[120] It is unclear as to when the hearsay principle became a settled principle of law, but Langbein has identified cases that were held at the Old Bailey in which hearsay evidence was accepted in the absence of objection in the eighteenth century.[121]

It seems that the midwife in this case draws on her experience to testify that the child was full grown, and is yet another case in which the midwife draws the inference that, because of the size of the child, it must have been born alive. The midwife used conjecture to testify that the preparation for the birth had been staged, or planted, and so the court reprimanded her for this comment, stating it was hearsay and not her own knowledge. In her defence, Mercy stated that when she became unwell she called for help; however, next door was an ale house, and due to the fact that considerable noise emanated from there, no one heard and so no one came. She said she was:

> violent ill and in great extremity of pain, I was delivered in the kitchen. I never saw the child move … but it got that big bruise from falling from me … and then in a fright I took it up and carried it to the vault.[122]

The jury found her guilty and she was sentenced to death.[123]

It is interesting to note that a study carried out by Klein indicates that, even in cases of precipitous delivery, when the child is forcibly expelled and falls head first to the floor, fractures of the skull are rare occurrences. In Klein's study consisting of 183 cases of rapid delivery with the child falling onto the ground or floor there was in fact only one instance in which a child was killed.[124]

Hannah Butler[125] was indicted for the murder of her female bastard infant, on December 8, 1736, by choking and strangling her. The midwife carried out an examination of the child and also asked Hannah if she had made any preparation for the child, to which she replied, "no."[126] Hannah claimed the child had been stillborn and she intended to keep the birth a secret, hiding the body in a box until she was able to go into the country again, where she presumably would bury the box. As no evidence was provided at the trial either by the midwife or any other witness that supported the indictment, mainly due to the lack of visible signs of violence, the jury acquitted Hannah.[127] This case demonstrates that the evidence given by the midwife was significant, due to the examination made by the midwife of the child, demonstrating a strong relationship between the midwife and the court.

In the case of Mary Shrewsbury, on February 16, 1737, who was indicted for the murder of her male bastard child "by giving it a mortal wound with a knife to the throat."[128] Ann Palmer (midwife) gave evidence, providing an account of discovering the child locked in a trunk and hidden in a nook behind the chimney, the midwife was asked, "was the child's throat cut very much?" To which Palmer replied, "it could not be cut worse, unless its head had been cut quite off."[129] A further female witness believed the child to be full grown, the midwife appears to volunteer her opinion stating, "twas at its full growth: it had hair and nails perfect, and was a larger child than is common."[130] The midwife rules out premature delivery by stating the child was full grown, and she also emphasises the extent of the knife wound. In her defence Mary stated, "it was dark when I deliver'd, and the child was dead"; it is therefore possible that this case is an example of death through lack of assistance.[131] Mary attempted to cut the umbilical cord herself, inadvertently cutting the child's throat, and, as the room was dark, she was unable to see.[132] The jury found her guilty, and she was sentenced to death.

In the Ordinary's Account, James Gutherie, stated that:

> I represented to her the atrociousness of such a horrid cruelty, which she did not disown, but acknowledged that she was punished most deservedly and justly. While under sentence she behaved very well, and to outward appearance was penitent, and on several occasions, particularly when she received the sacrament, wept and cried most bitterly. She declared that she hoped for salvation thro' the merits of Christ's blood and sufferings; was sincerely penitent for all her sins, especially the heinous crime of murder and blood shedding, and in peace with all the world.[133]

On March 3, 1737, about 10:00 a.m., Mary was transported by cart from Newgate to Tyburn to be hanged.[134]

These cases collectively demonstrate the significance of the evidence given by the midwife in infanticide cases. Crucially, the number of cases in which a midwife alone is called to give evidence is significant; out of 76 infanticide cases recorded at the Old Bailey between 1688 and 1738, 54 included evidence given by a midwife. This point demonstrates that the midwife appeared to be the first choice as expert witness by the courts at this time, not only as an expert in childbirth, but as an expert witness in court. This also demonstrates the value the court placed on the opinion of midwives and in particular how her evidence could shape the verdict of the jury.

In respect of the high number of infanticide cases during the seventeenth century, Kilday believes this factor stems from the fact that women indicted for the capital offence of new-born child murder were more likely to be convicted in the immediate years following the enactment of the 1624 Act than in the subsequent periods, and the "strength of the evidence brought against her was largely irrelevant."[135] This point, she argues, rests largely with the fact that "statutes were more rigorously enforced in the initial decades following their ratification."[136] The robustness of the enforcement of the Act in the initial years following its implementation only contributes further to its unfairness and harshness, when considering there were two distinguishing factors that drove particular young women to commit infanticide. These were "social stigma from the lapse associated with illegitimacy and the economic misfortune that could result from such circumstances."[137]

Kilday also argues that the 1624 Act significantly impacted upon conviction not only in terms of the rate, as it increased notably, but also in respect of the intended targets of the legislation; lewd women were rarely convicted for the offence, a point that was raised in Chapter 1. Instead it tended to be women of good character who were charged with new-born child murder, in an attempt to protect and maintain their reputation.[138]

Similarly, Clayton's observation that during the latter years of the seventeenth century there were "desperate efforts of women who found themselves in a dire situation, attempting to circumvent the harshness of the 1624 statute, and thereby save their lives."[139] By 1803, several changes had been introduced, including developments in court proceedings, the increase of lawyer's participation in trials, and changes in the number and type of medical witnesses and evidence presented in court; she refers to these three strands as sensibilities.[140]

The manner in which the court questioned the midwife is also significant, as it requested her to draw on her previous experience when considering questions such as "have you seen hasty deliveries before?" "Were there any marks of violence upon the child's body?" These are questions that indicate the courts trust in the midwife's competence and experience, particularly when identifying anomalies. Questions such as whether the midwife believed the child to be full term, or if the child had been born alive, suggest that the court valued the midwife's previous experience to form an opinion. The extent of the midwife's previous experience may be relevant, as the lengthier her experience, the more weight they may have attached to her evidence. It does seem that the number of years' experience a midwife held was more important than how she had acquired her skills; most cases demonstrate that midwives were not questioned on how much training they had received, or by whom.

On this basis it is possible that the court relied heavily on the midwife's opinion to shape their verdict. In the years following 1732, it seems that the questioning of the midwife became more detailed, stemming from advancements in court procedure or advancements in medicine; as science gradually became more technical, the court responded with more technical questioning of the experts.[141] Alternatively the questioning of the midwife could represent the fact that cases began to evolve around the grading of evidence in terms of reliability and probable truth, a truth beyond reasonable doubt, as opposed to an absolute truth. This concept, although parochial in origin, was also evident within wider changes that were beginning to take place within the judicial system; changes that are now an accepted doctrine in law.

Infanticide cases recorded at the Old Bailey, 1788–1838

During the 50-year period 1788 to 1838, there were 49 cases of infanticide recorded at the Old Bailey, not only a distinct decrease in the number of cases from the previous 50-year period, but in only 7 cases (22%) a midwife gave evidence. In these seven cases medical men also gave evidence: in one case an apothecary, and in the remaining six cases a surgeon gave evidence in court. In total there were 32 cases in which the surgeon gave evidence, and in the remaining 10 cases there was no medical evidence given. These numbers alone suggest a change in the relationship between the law and the midwife; the lower numbers support the fact there was a strengthening relationship between science and the law, and it appears that the surgeon, apothecary, or man-midwife was beginning to replace the midwife in the delivery room, and as an expert witness in court.

In the seven cases where a midwife gave her opinion, five of the women were acquitted and the remaining two were found guilty of concealing the birth, a verdict which reflects the changing nature of the law on infanticide. Changes were also evident in the punishments these women received, as the length of the sentence differed from 14 days in 1 case to 2 years in another. In the 42 cases without midwife evidence, 11 women were found guilty of concealing a birth, 2 women were found guilty of murder, and in each of these cases the surgeon gave evidence in court; the remaining 29 women were acquitted.

In the case of Sarah Penny, on September 16, 1812,[142] the questioning of the midwife is thorough, demonstrating that the court may be looking for explicit answers. Lucy Bailey begins her evidence by stating that she was a midwife residing at Hackney. She is asked to "recollect and tell me whether before she said there was the child, you perceived anything?" To which she replied, "no I searched for the child and found it as she was sitting up, rather below her knees."[143] She was then asked, "was the child separated from the mother?" To which she stated, "no it was not, it was alive, and I separated the child."[144] Bailey was then asked how long had she been a midwife, to which she replied 25 years. She was then asked by the court:

> do you know that the bruises you saw were occasioned by impression at the time of the birth? I never saw such marks before in my life. I examined the inside of the mouth, I was not satisfied, and I went to Dr Reynolds.
>
> What appearances were there on it? I could not tell anything, the blood came, so it was a full-time child.
>
> Had you seen any child that had been delivered without assistance? Many without any person being present at the time of its birth.

> Supposing the birth to be difficult, can you say whether the marks were such as the child might have by the mother attempting to deliver herself? I couldn't say.[145]

In this case the jury found Sarah not guilty; however, the questioning in this case attempts to draw on Bailey's previous experience and knowledge as a midwife, whilst at the same time highlighting the limitations of her expertise as a whole, as she was unable to give definitive answers when questioned by the court.

The case of Susan Hyde, on June 6, 1821, demonstrates the difference in evidence provided by a midwife (Sarah Bowers) and an apothecary. The apothecary gives a lengthy testimony, and provides very little useful information: he begins by stating "I am an apothecary and have had a good deal of experience in the delivery room of women"; he continues by saying he is unable to determine whether the child was born alive or not, but says it is "rather unlikely that the child should drop from her." He stated that he found no marks of violence upon the child, but believed that a "surgeon of eminence should see it."[146] Although this evidence is confusing, on cross-examination he is asked "I believe a head presentation is usual at birth" to which the apothecary replies "yes, if born while she sat on the privy it would fall head foremost."[147]

The evidence provided by Bowers on the other hand is more succinct; she merely states:

> I first saw the prisoner about eight o'clock on Friday morning, she said she was delivered in the privy at one o'clock in the morning. I had a patient myself the other day who had liked to have dropped her child in the privy.[148]

The midwife in this case was not cross-examined, or at least it was not reported; it seems enough for the court to believe Bowers – that it is not unusual for a child to be born in a privy. The apothecary gave evidence first in this trial, and it is arguable as to whether or not this is significant. Bowers gave evidence towards the end of the trial; her evidence is brief, and she is not cross-examined. It is possible that the court is beginning to place greater weight on the evidence of the male practitioner over the midwife, regardless of the amount of experience or years of practice; the jury in this case acquitted Susan.

In the case of Catherine Weeks, on July 4, 1833,[149] whose infant was discovered in the privy, the midwife, Marian Allan, was cross-examined and asked to describe the state of the accused. She replied:

> she had the appearance of a woman who had been delivered 8 or 9 days ago, she was recovering from it, she was in a very weak state … I have every reason to believe this to be her first child, I have known several cases of women being involuntary delivered without knowing it.[150]

Catherine was found guilty of concealment, recommended to mercy, and confined for 14 days.

It is interesting to note that during this 50-year period a distinct shift occurs in the relationship between the midwife and the courtroom. The number of cases in which a midwife was called to give evidence is markedly reduced, and there are no cases in which the midwife was the sole expert. Significantly, as changes began to evolve within the nature of the criminal trial, and the ever-greater presence of male counsel, so too did changes evolve within the relationship between the midwife and the court. Once a strong relationship, it begins to disintegrate, a change that is congruent with the developing legal discourse, and the simultaneous development in medical discourse. During the eighteenth century, the Old Bailey began to require more certainty within infanticide cases, from evidence supported by post-mortem and scientific experiment. Techniques that could support testimony by providing certainty and enforce the argument of the surgeon, for example, the hydrostatic or lung test, which will be discussed in greater detail in Chapter 3.

Infanticide cases recorded at the Old Bailey, 1863–1913

During the period 1863–1913, there were 112 cases of infanticide recorded at the Old Bailey, none of which had any midwifery involvement. Five cases do have involvement from nurses or matrons who gave evidence regarding facts at the time of event, rather than opinion evidence that drew upon experience and expertise. In the case of Kate Marshall, on February 25, 1884, Kate Elizabeth Perry, Matron at the Infirmary of the Whitechapel Union, gave evidence.[151] It included a recollection of the treatment she administered to the child, on admission to the infirmary, and a later conversation she had with Marshall. She asked her "how she could ill use such a beautiful baby,"[152] to which she replied:

> she was very much intoxicated, and she had been drinking heavily for several days, she was taken ill and whilst passing through the yard the child was born and fell on the stones and she thought it was dead, she waited by it a short time and then laid it on the ash pit.[153]

The evidence given by the Matron is merely a factual statement, and there is no cross-examination or further questioning of her statement by the lawyers. Similarly, in the case of Florence Clark,[154] on May 3, 1897, Jessie Atkinson, a nurse in the Lambeth Infirmary gave evidence in court, founded on a conversation she had with Florence, who was of the opinion that the child couldn't be hers as she had only been four months pregnant. She said something had passed from her, and that it was blood clots, she could not recall what she had done with them; Jessie explained that Florence seemed confused at the time.[155] It seems that the tone of questioning towards the female witnesses had changed; the nurses were not asked to give their opinion, nor were they questioned on the extent of their experience, unlike the midwives as expert witnesses; they were merely asked to provide factual statements.

Arguably, the changing attitudes towards the midwives during the end of the nineteenth century and beginning of the twentieth century were reflected in the implementation of the Midwives Act 1902, an Act which introduced the registration of practising midwives.[156] The Act aimed to regulate the practice of midwifery and required midwives to be certified by a central governing body.[157] It did not, however, return the expertise of expert witness to the profession, a role previously possessed by eighteenth-century midwives, as this chapter has demonstrated.[158]

This chapter has demonstrated how the relationship between the courts and the midwife began to alter. As the art of midwifery gradually became more learned and skilful, particularly in the practice of abnormal deliveries, it was male medical experts who increasingly fulfilled this role. This transformation within the delivery room occurred simultaneously with changing attitudes within the courtroom, both in terms of the body as a source of evidence and medical jurisprudence.[159] Attitudes that were arguably founded on the increasing advances in scientific experiment, developments in medical discourse, and a greater understanding of human anatomy and physiology through dissection or post-mortem. It was this crucial development that led to a time in the eighteenth century when "midwives were no longer undisputed 'experts' in infanticide trials; male medical practitioners increasingly dominated court hearings."[160]

During the eighteenth century the courts demonstrated an increasing expectation of certainty from the medical evidence, particularly when a woman's life depended on the verdict. As the examination of the infant cadaver carried out by the midwife was restricted to an external examination, the midwives were not always in a position to provide definitive answers in court; midwives were not always able to meet the court's expectation of certainty. The courts during this time increasingly focused on the "expert testimony of medical witnesses, they eventually demanded a higher degree of certainty in that testimony,"[161] to the extent that "certainty was becoming the hallmark of influential medical testimony, its absence began to be treated as a serious defect."[162] This increasing expectation of certainty from medical witnesses in court is consistent with the replacing of the midwife as an expert witness. At the beginning of the century, midwives were considered to be the expert of choice by the courts to provide medico-legal evidence. From the middle of the eighteenth century, midwives began appearing in addition to a male medical witness, and were no longer called as the sole witness: midwives were gradually replaced by male medical witnesses. The following chapter will discuss the role of medical men in infanticide cases, beginning in the eighteenth century, a time when greater attentiveness was directed towards the body as a source of evidence.

Notes

1 J. Sharp, *The Midwives Book, or The Whole Art of Midwifry Discovered.* London: Printed for Simon Miller, at the Star at the West End of St. Pauls, 1671: 1.

2 D. Evenden, *The Midwives of Seventeenth-Century London.* Cambridge: Cambridge University Press, 2000: 186. See also D. Harley, 'Provincial Midwives in England: Lancashire and Cheshire, 1600–1760' in H. Marland (ed.) *The Art of Midwifery, Early Modern Midwives in Europe*. London: Routledge, 1993: M. Jackson, 'Developing Medical Expertise: Medical Practitioners and the Suspected Murders of New-Born Children' in R. Porter (ed.) *Medicine in the Enlightenment.* Amsterdam: Rodopi,

1995; E. Fife, 'Gender and Professionalism in Eighteenth-Century Midwifery' *Women's Writing*, Vol. 11, No. 2, 2004, pp. 185–200.

3 R. Williams, *Keywords, A Vocabulary of Culture and Society*. London: Fontana Press, 1983: 129.

4 P. Dear, 'Mysteries of State, Mysteries of Nature: Authority, Knowledge and Expertise in the Seventeenth Century' in S. Jasonoff (ed.) *States of Knowledge, The Co-Production of Science and Social Order*. London: Routledge, 2004: 206.

5 Ibid.

6 Ibid. From the nineteenth century, when England was becoming increasingly industrialised, more emphasis was placed on "specialization and qualification," and so the term continued to be used "over a wide range of activities at times with a certain vagueness" (R. Williams, 1983, op. cit.: 129).

7 E. Shorter, *Women's Bodies, A Social History of Women's Encounter with Health, Ill Health and Medicine*. New Brunswick: Transaction Publishers, 1991.

8 L. Rose, *Massacre of the Innocents, Infanticide in Britain 1880–1939*. London: Routledge and Kegan Paul, 1986: 86; E. Shorter (1991) op. cit.: 36.

9 Rose (1986) op. cit.: 86.

10 Shorter (1991) op. cit.: 36.

11 Ibid.; see also B. Turner, *Medical Power and Social Knowledge*. London: Sage Publications, 1987: 88.

12 The Casebook of Willughby cited in Evenden (2000) op. cit.: 4.

13 Turner (1987) op. cit.: 88.

14 H. Marland, 'Introduction' in H. Marland (ed.) *The Art of Midwifery, Early Modern Midwives in Europe*. London: Routledge, 1993: 2.

15 Rose (1986) op. cit.: 85.

16 A. Wilson, *The Making of Man-Midwifery: Childbirth in England, 1660–1770*. London: UCL Press, 1995: 26.

17 T. Forbes, 'The Regulation of English Midwives in the Sixteenth and Seventeenth Centuries' *Medical History*, Vol. 8, No. 3, July 1964, pp. 235–244.

18 Turner (1987) op. cit.: 87.

19 Ibid.: 88.

20 A. Wilson (1995) op. cit.: 3; see also See Section III – *General Rule for Using the Forceps* in W. Smellie, *A Treatise on the Theory and Practice of Midwifery*. London: Bailliere Tindall, 1974: 261–290.

21 J. Donnison, *Midwives and Medical Men, A History of the Struggle for the Control of Childbirth*. London: Historical Publications, 1988: 34.

22 Ibid.: 23.

23 Ibid.: 104.

24 Ibid.

25 A. Wilson (1995) op. cit.: 5.

26 Ibid.: 24.

27 Turner (1987) op. cit.: 88.

28 A. Oakley, *The Captured Womb: A History of the Medical Care of Pregnant Women*. Oxford: Basil Blackwell Publisher Ltd., 1984.

29 Ibid.: 12.

30 Marland (1993) op. cit.: 7.

31 E. Fife, 'Gender and Professionalism in Eighteenth-Century Midwifery' *Women's Writing*, Vol. 11, No. 2, 2004, pp. 185–200: 185.

32 Ibid.: 109.

33 E. Ackerknecht, 'Midwives as Expert Witnesses in Court' *Bulletin of the New York Academy of Medicine*, Vol. 52, 10th December 1976, pp. 1224–1228: 1225.

34 J. Sharpe, 'Women, Witchcraft and the Legal Process' in J. Kermode, and G. Walker (eds.) *Women, Crime and the Courts in Early Modern England*. London: UCL Press, 1994: 112.

35 The witches' mark was generally believed to be a "third teat in the woman's privy parts" from which it was thought that the witch's familiar sucked blood. (A witches' mark was discovered in the case of Joan Slater accused on the Isle of Ely. The midwife in this case stated that she had "not seen the like on any other woman.") Sharpe (1994) op. cit.: 110.
36 *The examination and confession of certain witches at Chelmsford in the counties of Essex before the Queens Majesties judges, the xxvi day of July ammo 1566* (London 1566) in Sharpe (1994) op. cit.: 110.
37 Harley (1993) op. cit.: 37.
38 K. Stevenson, 'Most Intimate Violations: Contextualising the Crime of Rape' in A. M. Kilday and D. Nash (eds.) *Histories of Crime, Britain 1600–2000*. Basingstoke: Palgrave Macmillan, 2010.
39 Sharpe (1999) op. cit.: Chapter Five.
40 M. Wiener, *Men of Blood, Violence, Manliness and Criminal Justice in Victorian England*. Cambridge: Cambridge University Press, 2004: 77–78.
41 C. Emsley, T. Hitchcock and R. Shoemaker, 'Crimes Tried at the Old Bailey', *Old Bailey Proceedings Online* (www.oldbaileyonline.org, version 6.0, 17 April 2011). [Last accessed June 10, 2014].
42 Ibid.
43 *Collins Concise English Dictionary*. Eighth Edition. Glasgow: HarperCollins Publishers, 2012: 1028; S. Johnson, *A Dictionary of Language*. Sixth Edition. London: Consortium, 1786.
44 Claim they are pregnant. In E. Fife, 'Gender and Professionalism in Eighteenth-Century Midwifery' *Women's Writing*, Vol. 11, No. 2, 2004, pp. 185–200: 185.
45 Sharpe (1994) op. cit.: 112.
46 Oldham (1985) op. cit.: 1.
47 Ibid.
48 Ibid.: 18.
49 *OBP*, February 1694, Margery Townley, t16940221-55.
50 *OBP* Punishment Summary, s16940221-1
51 Women were not permitted to serve as magistrates or jurors until the twentieth century. The first documented case of women carrying out jury service in England was in London on July 28, 1920. Available at: http://query.nytimes.com/mem/archive-free/pdf?res=9D06E1DA103DE533A2575AC2A9619C946195D6CF [Last accessed June 10, 2014].
52 Oldham (1985) op. cit.: 1.
53 Gowing (2001) op. cit.: 47.
54 "An Old Fashioned or Less Technical Term for Oedema" at: www.oxforddictionaries.com/defintion/english/dropsy [Last accessed October 12, 2015].
55 Gowing (2001) op. cit.: 47.
56 Policing existed in 1749 in the form of London's Bow Street Runners and it was not until the Metropolitan Police Act of 1829 when constables were introduced. See H. Johnston, *Crime in England 1815–1880, Experiencing the Criminal Justice System*. Oxford: Routledge, 2015: Chapter 3.
57 Gowing (2001) op. cit.: 47.
58 *OBP*, September 1677, (no name) t16770906-1.
59 Ibid.
60 Gowing (2001) op. cit.: 47.
61 Harley (1993) op. cit.: 37.
62 Gowing (2001) op. cit.: 49.
63 Harley (1993) op. cit.: 37.
64 *OBP*, February 1725, Deborah Greening, t17250224-9.
65 May (1995) op. cit.: 22.
66 Ibid.: 25.

67 Margaret Price was respited for pregnancy *OBP* t16960909-37.
68 'The Criminal Trial' at: www.londonlives.org/static/CriminalTrial.jsp [Last accessed September 20, 2016].
69 Shoemaker (2008) op. cit.: 560.
70 "Mayoral years began in December of the preceding year," therefore the change in detail and format became affective in December 1729. (Langbein, 2003, op. cit.: 235); see also Langbein, 1978, op. cit.: 263–316; J. Beattie, *Policing and Punishment in London 1660–1750: Urban Crime and the Limits of Terror*. Oxford: Oxford University Press, 2003.
71 *OBP*, December 1689, Mary Campion, t16891211-26.
72 Terms used to describe a "building or outhouse for some domestic purpose," or an outside toilet. Available at www.oed.com [Last accessed February 24, 2016].
73 *OBP*, December 1689, Mary Campion, t16891211-26.
74 Ibid.
75 Ibid.
76 *OBP*, July 1697, Elinor Hunt, t16970707-5.
77 'Executions at Tyburn 1695–1704' at: www.capitalpunishmentuk.org/tyburn1695.html [Last accessed October 6, 2015].
78 *OBP*, February 1729, Jane Bostock, t17290226-8.
79 *OBP*, September 1735, Mary Dixon, t17350911-88.
80 *Newcastle Courant*, 'From Several London Prints' Saturday, September 20, 1735. British Newspaper Archive (www.britishnewspaperarchive.co.uk); The British Library Board; © the British Library Board. All rights reserved.
81 *OBP*, September 1735, Mary Dixon, t17350911-88.
82 Ibid.
83 Ibid.
84 Rabin (2004) op. cit.: 98.
85 Ibid.
86 'From Several London Prints' (1735) op. cit.
87 *OBP*, July 1718, Jane Plintoff, t17180709-5.
88 Ibid.
89 *OBP*, October 1718, Francis Bolanson, t17181015-16.
90 Ibid.
91 *OBP*, December, 1736, Jane Cooper, t17361208-10.
92 Ibid.
93 C. Emsley, T. Hitchcock and R. Shoemaker, 'Ordinary of Newgate's Account', *Old Bailey Proceedings Online* (www.oldbaileyonline.org, version 6.0, 17 April 2011). [Last accessed, May 5, 2021].
94 *OBP, Ordinary's Account*, March 3 1737 (OA 17370303).
95 *OBP*, June, 1714, Mary Tate, t17140630-38.
96 Ibid.
97 Beattie (1986) op. cit.: 360–382.
98 B. Shapiro, 'Oaths, Credibility and the Legal Process in Early Modern England: Part Two' *Law and Humanities*, Vol. 7, No. 1, Summer 2013, pp. 19–54.
99 *OBP*, August 1721, Sarah Hanesley, t17210830-20.
100 Ibid.
101 Shapiro (2013) op. cit.: 31.
102 *OBP*, September 1719, Mary Gough, t17190903-32.
103 Ibid.
104 Ibid.
105 *OBP*, January 1702, Christian Russel, t17020114-7.
106 Ibid.
107 *OBP*, *Ordinary's Account*, January 28, 1702 (OA 17020128).
108 *OBP*, July 1717, Ann Hasle, t17170717-18.

109 Ibid.
110 *OBP*, April 1732, Hannah Bradford, t17320419-15.
111 Ibid.
112 Ibid.
113 Ibid.
114 Ibid.
115 Ibid.
116 Ibid.
117 *OBP*, April 1734, Mercy Hornby, t17340424-21.
118 Ibid.
119 Ibid.
120 C. J. Vaughan (1670) in Bushel's Trial, 6 How. St. Tr 999, 1003 cited in J. Wigmore, 'The History of the Hearsay Rule' *Harvard Law Review*, Vol. 17, No. 7, May 1904, pp. 437–458: 438.
121 Langbein (2003) op. cit.: 234. See also J. Langbein, 'The Historical Foundations of the Law of Evidence: A View from the Ryder Sources' *Columbia Law Review*, Vol. 96, 1996, pp. 1168–1202: 1186.
122 *OBP*, April 1734, Mercy Hornby, t17340424-21.
123 Ibid.
124 S. Smith and W. Cook (eds.) *Taylors Principles and Practices of Medical Jurisprudence,* Vol. II. Eighth Edition. London: J. & A. Churchill, 1928: 270.
125 *OBP*, December 1736, Hannah Butler, t17361208-40.
126 Ibid.
127 Ibid.
128 *OBP*, February 1737, Mary Shrewsbury, t17370216-21.
129 Ibid.
130 Ibid.
131 Ibid.
132 Ibid.
133 *OBP*, *Ordinary's Account*, March 3, 1737 (OA 17370303).
134 Ibid.
135 Kilday (2013) op. cit.: 41.
136 Ibid.
137 Ibid.: 37.
138 Ibid.
139 Clayton (2009) op. cit.: 338.
140 Ibid.
141 Golan (2004) op. cit.
142 *OBP*, September 1812, Sarah Penny, t18120916-44.
143 Ibid.
144 *OBP*, September 1812, Sarah Penny, t18120916-44.
145 Ibid.
146 *OBP*, June 1821, Susan Hyde, t18210606-36.
147 Ibid.
148 Ibid.
149 *OBP*, July 1833, Catherine Weeks, t18330704-33.
150 Ibid.
151 *OBP*, February 1884, Kate Marshall, t18840225-342.
152 Ibid.
153 Ibid.
154 *OBP*, May 1897, Florence Clark, t18970503-380.
155 Ibid.
156 R. Jenkins, *The Law and the Midwife*. Oxford: Blackwell Science, 1995: 21–24.
157 The Central Midwives Board.

158 Jenkins (1995) op. cit.: 21–24.
159 M. Jackson, 'Developing Medical Expertise: Medical Practitioners and the Suspected Murders of New-Born Children' in Porter, R. (ed.) *Medicine in the Enlightenment.* Amsterdam: Rodopi, 1995: 148.
160 D. Evenden, *The Midwives of Seventeenth-Century London.* Cambridge: Cambridge University Press, 2000: 186.
161 S. Landsman, 'One Hundred Years of Rectitude: Medical Witnesses at the Old Bailey, 1717–1817' *Law and History Review*, Vol. 16, No. 3, 1998, pp. 445–494: 456.
162 Ibid.: 457.

3 The role of medical men in infanticide cases

As the courts increasingly required certainty to ascertain a woman's culpability, there became a corresponding increase in the number of medical men who were called upon to provide evidence in court, thus replacing the midwife as the expert witness in infanticide cases. It is the role of medical men as expert witnesses, and the introduction of medical discourse into the courtroom and infanticide cases, which forms the focus of this chapter. In particular, this chapter will highlight that the medicalisation of infanticide has been overestimated by commentators, and instead medical men also failed to carry scientific weight in the shaping of the jury's verdict as expected. The manner in which the surgeon succeeded the midwife in this role, with their medical expertise, in the form of both post-mortem and, more specifically, the lung test, seemed to create a promise of certainty. But this chapter will demonstrate that there was little difference in the testimony of the raw evidence provided by the midwife and the medical man. The law required certainty in response to crucial questions, such as: was the child born alive? Did the child have a separate existence? What was the cause of the child's death? Questions that the midwives had been unable to answer definitively, and so the courts turned to medical men to provide certain answers to these questions.

Rather than offering certainty, this chapter will demonstrate that the introduction of the surgeon as an expert witness in infanticide cases generated uncertainty despite the assistance of science. This was not necessarily of detrimental value to infanticide cases, as this crucial anomaly could be viewed as an advantage for an uncertain jury who were reluctant to find a young woman guilty. Uncertain medical opinion allowed an uncertain jury to reach a verdict of not guilty, shielding the accused from capital punishment.[1]

The chapter is divided into three sections and will begin by exploring the origins of the medical profession. It will explain how the advancement of anatomical knowledge through dissection and a medico-legal relationship was established in cases of unexplained new-born child death. It will then focus on significant developments in a scientific experiment in cases of infanticide, namely the lung or hydrostatic test, by drawing on cases held at the York Assizes and reported in the provincial newspapers. The second section examines medical evidence at coroner's inquests into suspected infanticide cases, by drawing on inquests held in Hull and the surrounding area during the nineteenth century. The final section

DOI: 10.4324/9781003006299-3

examines medical evidence in cases recorded at the Old Bailey, in two 50-year periods, 1763–1813 and 1863–1913.

The origins of the medical profession

Prior to 1540, two separate organisations were in existence in London concerned with the practice of surgery and dissection: the Company of Barbers and the Fellowship or Guild of Surgeons, with the former becoming more commonly referred to as the Barber-Surgeons Company, due to their predominate involvement in surgery.[2] During the sixteenth century the boundary between the practice of surgery and medicine became increasingly blurred, provoking conflict between the barber-surgeons and the physicians. As a result of this, a charter came into force in 1617, enabling physicians to take proceedings against anyone who administered internal medicine, and not a member of the College of Physicians. A protest ensued from the barber-surgeons in response to this, resulting in a separate charter in 1629, confirming the powers of the surgeons. The physicians retaliated by obtaining an order in council in 1632, preventing the surgeons from performing any minor operations except in the presence of a member of the College of Physicians.[3] The conflict between the barber-surgeons and the physicians concerning exclusivity to medical and surgical procedures during this period may have also impacted the rejection of the Midwifery Charter in 1616, noted in Chapter 2.

There was also a growing interest in medicine by a third branch of the Medical Corporation in the form of the Apothecaries, whose work was limited to the preparation and dispensing of medicine. Following the landmark *Rose Case* in 1704, apothecaries successfully expanded the scope of their work to include medical as well as pharmaceutical practice, on condition that their charges were limited to the cost of the medication;[4] however, in respect of social status, apothecaries were considered to be the lowest ranking.[5]

As the diverse professions considered themselves to have differing rankings, they also differentiated aspects of their work. This was evident amongst the surgeons and physicians, who viewed those members of their association who chose to practice midwifery or pharmacy with a degree of contempt. This resulted in the Council of Surgeons electing to exclude from the council those members who participated in such practices. Physicians enjoyed the status of learned and cultured gentlemen, as they possessed a university degree and confined their practice to internal medicine, using their heads rather than their hands, advising rather than practising. Thus, midwifery and pharmacy were banned for physicians, as they were deemed to be too manual in nature. It was therefore believed that physicians who practised midwifery should be refused admittance to the fellowship, with surgeons adopting a similar stance on matters of midwifery, as it was generally believed that practitioners who practised midwifery had little time to devote to specialising in surgery.[6]

Thus, during the eighteenth and nineteenth century three separate medical associations existed, the Royal College of Physicians, the Company of Surgeons (from 1800, the Royal College of Surgeons), and the Worshipful Society of

Apothecaries, each with its own charter and bye laws. Being a professional medical practitioner was now defined by membership of a professional body of practitioners who held the authority to licence and discipline their members.[7] The passing of the Medical Act of 1858 allowed a consolidation of the laws relating to physicians, surgeons, and apothecaries, as well as introducing a general concept of qualified or registered general practitioner (GP), a role which by the 1830s included medicine, surgery, pharmacy and midwifery.[8]

Until the late nineteenth century, entry into the medical profession was restricted to men. It was only following the implementation of the Enabling Act 1875 that women were permitted to enter medical schools in the United Kingdom.[9] Although the 1875 Act permitted universities to grant medical licences to women, the admittance of women remained at the discretion of each individual university.[10] It was not until the early twentieth century that a small number of London hospitals began to train women, and it was not until 1944 that the government actively encouraged medical schools to recruit women through the use of the financial incentive.[11]

The restrictions within the profession demonstrate a gender division within medicine. As a result of the restriction on females entering the profession, there is no indication of a female medically trained professional, such as surgeon, pathologist, or psychiatrist, giving expert evidence in the infanticide cases included within this book.

The body as a source of evidence

In the search for the truth in cases of suspected infanticide, the examination of the cadaver was pivotal to the determination of the facts, as the "pathology of the cadaver itself was the main evidence presented to the court."[12] Dating back to at least Medieval Britain, it was the "cruentation or bier test"[13] of the infant corpse, which played a crucial role in the trial. It was believed that if the accused approached the corpse, called the child by its name, and then proceeded to walk round it two or three times whilst stroking its wounds, "evidence of guilt was revealed if during the procedure fresh bleeding occurred, the body twitched or foam appeared at the mouth."[14] The purpose of this cruentation test was twofold: it provided a "form of proof to legal officials who did not have recourse to the continental procedures of torture, and formal medico-legal investigation to provide evidence against suspects."[15] It also provoked a response from the suspect, for if the suspect believed that the corpse would twitch as she entered the room, there was a strong possibility that the suspect would concede with an admission of guilt.

During the eighteenth century, as the need for the body as a source of evidence strengthened, the knowledge of medical men progressed, and an increased understanding of morphology, pathology, and therapeutics became increasingly evident, sparking a sense of superiority in anatomy on an unprecedented level.[16] Anatomists were eager to publicly demonstrate their newly found skills and share their newly acquired knowledge with interested parties and junior colleagues at gatherings held at both private teaching hospitals and the hospitals of London.[17] Such scenes were encapsulated in the paintings by Thomas Rowlandson, particularly in works such as *The Dissection*, a watercolour of William Hunter in his anatomy school painted in 1776–1778, and the *Lancett Club at Thurtell Feast*, the dissection of the infamous murderer John Thurtell, carried out at St. Bartholomew's Hospital, under the direction of the surgeon John Abernethy in 1824.[18]

Trainee surgeons were required to pay an admission fee to attend a dissection amounting to five guineas to observe and seven guineas to perform, so that "by the end of the 1740's empirical experience in the dissection of corpses had become a conventional practice in surgical training,"[19] making dissection an integral practical stage of medical training and hospital sites for anatomical demonstrations and research.[20] Foucault refers to this form of dissection as "pathological anatomy," which he argues resulted from the "methods of analysis, the clinical examination, even the reorganization of the schools and hospitals seemed to derive their significance from pathological anatomy."[21] In his book the *Birth of the Clinic*, Foucault explores the development of the medical profession and the development of the clinic (teaching hospitals), focusing in particular on the medical gaze and the abrupt re-organisation of knowledge towards the end of the eighteenth century.[22] Traditionally medicine and medical treatment had ignored the patient, perceiving the patient as the "raw material, the unwitting bearer of a disease or lesion."[23] The concept of the medical gaze, Foucault argues, consists of the separation of the patient's body from the patient's identity or person, a dehumanising process that allows the medical practitioner, through observation, conversation, and training, to establish the onset of disease. By observing and examining the patient's body, for example, and through conversing with the patient, he is able to determine a medical history of the patient; by drawing on his own knowledge and experience, he can establish a cause of the disease. The process allowed medical men to create a field of knowledge of the body that, Foucault argued, in turn allowed the body to enter into a field of power, making it a possible target for manipulation. This re-organisation of knowledge towards the end of the eighteenth century, Foucault argued, led to the belief in the nineteenth century that medical men could eradicate all disease and therefore alleviate human suffering.[24]

Throughout the eighteenth century, as the public interest in dissection increased, the requirement of space became a necessity, the combination of the need for greater capacity to allow audience admission and a demand for space to perform the procedure. This awakening of public interest in dissection is reflected in Foucault's argument that "the need to know the dead must already have existed when the concern to understand the living appeared,"[25] a need that Foucault believed led to the clinic being founded on pathological anatomy.[26] In response to the increasing interest in pathological anatomy, universities across Europe began to build anatomical theatres, and used anatomy as a link between natural philosophy and moral philosophy.[27] An element of medicalisation that became a key concept in the social history of medicine, an element in the sense that surgeons were casting a shadow of doubt on infanticide cases through discourse and status, offering historians a means to explore the ways in which behaviours became defined medically, or pathologically, through fundamental links between the body and political power.[28] Owing to the fact that, during this time it was generally believed that "death was the end of life and if it was in its nature to be fatal, it was also the end of the disease,"[29] Foucault argued that medical thought in the eighteenth century centred on death as the "absolute fact and the most relative of phenomenon."[30] If the nature of the disease was thought to be fatal it would be the end of life; the end of life would therefore be the end of the disease, with the disease becoming a mere memory.[31]

As the demand for anatomical knowledge grew, the increase in demand for corpses also grew; the annual fixed number of corpses (hanged felons) available for anatomical dissection since the reign of Henry VIII in 1491[32] was simply inadequate to fulfil the demand. Therefore, owing to this rapid progression in medical training during the eighteenth century, the greater demand for corpses forced hospitals to resort to either "rob graves or compete with physicians and surgeons for bodies of hanged malefactors."[33] During this period, Burney has argued that the law "passed judgement in sable garments, and executed sentence with the red towel of the dissecting room."[34] The growing need for corpses led to the passing of the Murder Act 1751, which allowed judges to select the bodies of those hanged for murder for dissection.[35] Two women who fell victim to this Act were Jane Cornforth, May 18, 1774,[36] a case discussed in further detail later in this chapter, and Sarah Reynolds, December 6, 1775.[37] The women were found guilty of murdering their infants at the Old Bailey and sentenced to death. Their corpses were to be dissected and anatomised, a decision feared by many, more than the death itself, due to the humiliation associated with public anatomisation and the subsequent lack of a Christian burial.[38] From the surgeons' point of view, Foucault argued that it was anatomically advantageous for the surgeon to perform an autopsy immediately after death, as it reduced the latency period between death and the autopsy, making it possible for the "last stage of pathological time and the first stage of cadaveric time almost to coincide, the effects of organic decomposition were vertically suppressed."[39] The carrying out of an autopsy soon after death therefore allowed the results of the autopsy to be free from contamination and putrefaction, where asphyxiation was the cause of death as a result of hanging, the process of putrefaction or decomposition had a rapid onset.[40] In the bodies of new-born infants who had not been fed, the process of decomposition was slow, as their bodies were sterile, whereas with infants and new-borns who had been fed prior to death, or those who had suffered external injury, the onset of putrefaction was rapid.[41]

As the Murder Act 1751 only applied to those offences considered to be criminal as opposed to immoral, the

> legal status of a corpse was such that it could not be regarded as goods. It was not property, so it could not technically be owned, bought, sold or stolen which is why body snatchers took care to leave the shroud as legally no offence had been committed.[42]

This resulted in the passing of the Anatomy Act 1832, allowing the automatic donation of unclaimed bodies in pauper institutes to schools of anatomy, an Act that contributed significantly to the number of cadavers lawfully available for scholarly or educational dissection purposes.[43]

In infanticide cases, as the courts were unable to gain sufficient evidence from the woman as the sole witness, it was generally believed that the infant corpse could provide the answers they required. As Kilday specifies, from the eighteenth century onwards the "focus of judicial attention shifted from the interest in the medical condition of the accused to interest in the forensic pathology of the victim."[44] In spite of the fact that in many cases the evidence given by male medical experts was no more conclusive than evidence given by female midwives, the use of scientific and medical discourse allowed medical men, in theory, an "aura of authority and helped to lessen at least the semblance of uncertainty which plagued these trials";[45] in practice, however, uncertainty remained. This discourse also allowed medical experts to imply a correlation between the fact that their skills permitted them internal access through dissection, and post-mortem, and their ability to interpret the psychology of the mother's mind at the time she committed the act.[46]

In spite of the fact that dissections tended to be inconclusive, the "medical evidence became crucial to these trials for reasons other than its ability to offer reliable scientific determinations";[47] they were inclined to "validate new defences of non-responsibility,"[48] which proved vital to the woman to demonstrate her innocence. At the same time, this inconclusive medical evidence also instigated a shift in public opinion, a shift which saw the sympathy the dead child had once received, being transferred to compassion for the mother.[49]

Challenges faced by the court

The court faced a number of challenges in infanticide cases. One particular challenge the prosecution faced was the difficulty in proving intention; the injuries the child received in many cases could have been sustained as a result of the birth. As many women delivered alone, the injuries could be explained as a result of a difficult unassisted delivery; the cutting of a child's throat in an attempt to cut the umbilical cord or cranial damage that could result from the impact of the head hitting a hard floor if the woman adopted a standing or squatting position. In the case of Rebecca Beaumont, who was indicted for the murder of her male bastard child at the Castle of York, in July 1803, John Scholes, a surgeon, disposed that he

> was sent for to examine the child, that there was a contusion on the fore and back part of the head and a great neglect in the treatment of the child immediately after delivery, which might occasion it to bleed to death. That there were other circumstances attending the birth of the child (as the woman was delivered at that time of night without assistance which might occasion the aforesaid fractions and contusions).[50]

The judge, after summing up the evidence, claimed:

> there were many circumstances in favour of the prisoner. In the first place she lived in a house by herself, was delivered at a time of night that rendered it impossible to get any assistance. That had caused the death of the child. The jury immediately returned a verdict of not guilty.[51]

Smith has identified other difficulties in determining cases of infanticide that also arose. He noted that the law makes the "question of criminality to depend upon the period at which the injuries prove fatal and not upon the time at which they are inflicted on the body of a child";[52] thus if the accused had killed the child before it was born, she would not be guilty of a crime. This notion stems from the definition of murder that the victim must be a reasonable creature "in the king's peace,"[53] and so the killing of a child in the womb or during the birth would not be deemed as murder.[54]

The court also struggled with physiological questions, such as at which point during a delivery is a child considered to be born alive? A number of cases have addressed this important issue and directed the jury accordingly. In *R v Brain*, for example, Mr Justice Park, when summing up stated that a child must be:

> actually wholly in the world in a living state to be the subject of a murder charge, but if it is wholly born and alive it is not essential that it should have breathed at the time it was killed, as many children are born alive and do not breathe for some time after their birth – but you must be satisfied that the child was wholly born into the world at the time it was killed or you ought to find the prisoner guilty of murder.[55]

Eliza Brain was found guilty of concealment. The approach taken by Mr Justice Park was a view held by the courts in a number of cases.[56]

The difficulty in answering these physiological questions placed the surgeons under enormous pressure, a point which William Hunter anatomist, physician, surgeon, and man-midwife raised in his 1818 paper.[57] A paper described as an "extraordinarily compassionate defence of women accused of murdering their infant children."[58] Written in the style of a letter, in response to a magistrate requesting his expert opinion regarding an infanticide case, Hunter sets out his defence of infanticidal women in the form of a number of claims. The magistrate believed the accused woman to be innocent, and yet she had been found guilty; he sought Hunters' medical opinion to substantiate his view.[59] Hunter claimed that there was a growing pressure on medical men to give accurate evidence in court. Leading many medical men to concur with his opinion that "danger may arise from the evidence and opinions given by physical people who are called to settle questions of science which judges and jurymen are supposed not to know with accuracy."[60] He believed that too much responsibility had been left to the decision of medical witnesses. In answering the important physiological questions, the court asked them to:

> form a solid judgement about the birth of a new-born child from the examination of its body, a professional man should have seen many new-born children both still born and such as had outlived their birth a short time only and he should have dissected or attended the dissections of a number of bodies in the different stages of advancing putrefaction.[61]

Hunter also believed that, in a number of suspected infanticide cases, many injuries sustained by the child could be explained as a result of natural childbirth, once again conveying uncertainty. For example:

> when a child's head or face looks swollen and is very red or black, the vulgar because hanged people look so, are apt to conclude that it must have been strangled. But those who are in the practice of midwifery know that nothing is more common in natural births and that the swelling and deep colour gradually go off, if the child lives but a few days.[62]

He believed this to be a common occurrence, particularly in cases where the navel string had been coiled tightly around the neck of the foetus in-utero, or in situations where the head is delivered several minutes before the rest of the body. On this basis it would seem the injuries evident on the corpse of the infant could be mistaken for signs of violence, resulting in the mother being accused of murder.

The following two cases, held at the same York Assizes in July 1803, support the argument made by William Hunter to a certain degree; the injuries evident on each child could have been the result of childbirth, whilst they also demonstrate inconsistencies in verdict. The case of Rebecca Beaumont, which has been previously discussed, regardless of evidence of bruising and other external wounds on the body of the child, and the death was alleged to have been caused by suffocation, but the surgeon was unable to provide evidence to support these causes. Rebecca was found not guilty of murder but was confined for two years in the house of correction for concealment of birth.[63]

Whereas in the case of Martha Chapel of Ackworth, who was also charged on the coroner's inquest with the wilful murder of a new-born female bastard child, she repeatedly denied being with child throughout her labour, arguing instead the pain and discomfort was related to a urinary tract infection. Following the discovery of a blood stain on the floor between two beds in her room, a search began for the child; the child was discovered wrapped in a cloth in an empty bed, with its throat torn from ear to ear and the jaw torn off. Upon hearing footsteps approaching her bedroom, Martha shouted, "hush, hush, the Doctor is coming cover up the child and say nothing about it."[64] Martha was charged with murder. She said if she had "done anything she was not to blame, for she had done it in assisting herself."[65] Mr Robert Smith, surgeon and man-midwife of Pontefract, was sent for and found Martha "labouring under a retained placenta, after assisting her to that complaint he inquired for the child."[66] He examined the child and described the direction of the wound which:

extended from both sides of the mouth entirely down to the neck. The cheek bones had been broken and the great arteries of the throat torn asunder so as to occasion the immediate death of the child, the jaw bone had been torn away.[67]

Mr Smith asked the prisoner, "what had been the cause of the mischief?" She replied that "what she had done, had been done in assisting herself."[68]

Mr Smith stated that he:

> doubted at first whether an instrument had been made use of by the prisoner and asked if any had been found near her, he searched the sheets and upon shaking them part of the jaw bone fell out, he said that no instrument had been found and so he believed that no instrument had been used to form the lacerated appearance of the wound but it had probably been caused by the fingers.[69]

Mr Smith was then asked by Mr Raine whether he had knowledge of instances of delirium or frenzy during painful labour, particularly in a first pregnancy, Mr Smith replied:

> no, he had attended in many very difficult cases and where the pains of labour had lasted for some days, but never knew of a case of delirium or phrenzy at the time of delivery though he had frequently known it take place a few hours after.[70]

He was then asked to describe the probable effect of a painful and difficult labour where no medical assistance was on hand and asked to describe the agonies of pain (which he if present would be able to mitigate might not be so acute as to produce phrenzy), to which he replied, "the case was not impossible but, in his opinion, highly improbable."[71]

The judge then asked Mr Smith if he "supported the present situation to have been a difficult labour and whether the prisoner might not have occasioned the death of the child in attempting to assist herself?"[72] He replied that he was "afraid not, the child was a fine full grown one and there was no bad conformation of the bones of the mother so that in his opinion there would have been little difficulty in the birth."[73] The judge then "distinctly stated the evidence to the jury and in less than quarter of an hour returned and found the prisoner guilty, the judge was so much affected in passing the sentence as to be scarcely able to proceed."[74] Martha was sentenced to death, and her body to be dissected and anatomised.[75] The author of the *York Herald* article who witnessed the trial described Martha as a victim rather than a criminal. In doing so, he placed the blame firmly on her seducer, an opinion that may have been a broader reflection of public interest at this time:

> this unfortunate girl was seduced by the person while in service she lived a few months before she went to Colonel Surtees (current employer). That she

> still retained a strong sense of female honour, appears from both the dreadful act she committed and from the whole of the subsequent deportment. Though the seducer of this poor girl now looks with cruel indifference on the ruin he has occasioned because he is not punishable by human laws, he will one day be arraigned before another tribunal and found guilty of the double murder of his child and its ill-fated mother.[76]

After receiving her sentence, she was in a "state of stupor and on recovering from it she appeared overpowered by a sense of her dreadful situation and the terror of death seemed the predominant sensation of her mind to the very last moment."[77] She claimed that the:

> agony of child birth had deprived her of her reason and that being wholly inexperienced the child was mangled in the delivery though she never meant to destroy it. She did not acknowledge her guilt but to the last declared that she must have committed the crime in a momentary delirium.[78]

Regardless of this fact, she "died without a struggle amid the multiple sobs of the multitude."[79] The cases of both Rebecca and Martha raise some interesting points: each appeared before the same Assizes, similar facts were evident, and they both delivered their infants alone, although Martha was offered assistance. Both infants presented with external injuries, or marks of violence, which could have been sustained during unassisted delivery, and yet each received different sentences.

The medical expert at Martha's trial contributed greatly to the shaping of the jury's verdict; by ruling out the possibility of delirium or frenzy, he implied her sensibilities had not escaped her and declared her sane. By stating that Martha's bone conformation was satisfactory, he also dismissed the fact that the birth had been difficult, apparently overlooking the fact that she delivered her child unassisted and alone. One particular argument put forward by Gatrell may go some way to explaining why Martha received the death sentence, and failed to receive a pardon. He identifies that well into the "nineteenth century the atrociously criminal woman was still deemed a monster";[80] infanticidal women in particular continued to be sentenced to death as a deterrence to others.[81] For the women whose crimes resulted from the villous behaviour of men, a degree of sympathy was evident, a sympathy that created an "anxiety about executing women tended to be activated by the sense that even at their worst, women were creatures to be pitied and protected from themselves."[82]

Ackerknecht argues that the transition to replace midwives was a result of many attacks made by surgeons and physicians over a long duration "in order to replace and subdue them."[83] Attacks which began in the sixteenth century eventually succeeded in the eighteenth century; however, now with the surgeon as the key trial witness, it was generally believed that "the truth of these cases was increasingly sought through the dissection performed on the infant's corpse."[84] This has led Sommers to argue that the hydrostatic or lung test was the only piece of evidence that separated the findings of male practitioners from those of the midwife, and "dissections rarely offered any other substantial evidence as to whether the child had been born alive."[85]

The hydrostatic test

As medical men became increasingly pressurised by the courts to provide certainty within their testimony, they in turn became increasingly pressurised to rely on science as a source of evidence. In 1653, the English Physician, William Harvey, revealed it was possible for changes in lung colour at birth to be evident. Regardless of the fact that the infant may have died immediately after taking its first breath, he believed by applying this simple test it might be possible to determine whether a child was born alive or stillborn.[86] Fourteen years later Jan Swammerdam carried out a series of physiological studies of respiration. Such tests revealed that if an infant had breathed after birth its air-filled lungs would float in water; alternatively, if the lungs had not been inflated with air, the lungs would sink; this was referred to as the "docimasia pulmonum hydrostatica, or the hydrostatic, floatation or lung test."[87]

The application of the test, to simply insert the lungs into water together, separately or in sections, would indicate if the lungs had inflated through inspiration (inhaling) as they would "contain enough air to reduce their specific gravity and float, in this case floatation was taken as evidence that respiration had occurred and that the infant has been born alive."[88]

It was the anatomist from Bratislava Karl Rayger (1641–1701) who believed that the lung test could be used in cases of infanticide to prove live birth.[89] The first physician to introduce the hydrostatic test into medico-legal practice was Johann Schreyer of Zeitz in Silesia, in 1682, wherein a 15-year-old peasant girl was accused of murdering her new-born baby. Schreyer carried out a post-mortem, part of which included a lung test; the lungs sank, leading Schreyer to conclude that the child had been stillborn. The peasant girl was acquitted; however, as a result of his testimony, Schreyer himself was faced with a lengthy law suit.[90] The hydrostatic test as a form of scientific evidence has been described by Brittain as the greatest advance of the seventeenth century, and as "important as being one of the earliest applications of medical observation in a way designed solely to help in the administration of justice."[91]

During the middle decades of the eighteenth century, the English courts increasingly required substantial conformation that the child had been born alive before being murdered by the suspect, thus placing greater demand on the medical practitioner to produce convincing evidence to the court, because "English law did require that a child be born viable that is with a capacity to survive in order for its slayer to stand accountable for murder."[92] In an attempt to produce evidence that the child had lived, the medical practitioner performed a lung test on the corpse of the child to determine initial signs of life. The test, initially aimed at supporting the findings of the surgeon, did in fact attract a great deal of attention through discussion and questioning by the courts, especially in respect of its reliability and accuracy. Jackson claimed the hydrostatic test attracted the most attention by the courts during this period as a woman's life depended upon the outcome.[93] A subsequent test or examination was therefore usually performed by the medical practitioner, consisting of a physical examination of the child to observe for signs of violence. Whether violence was the result of labour or intentionally caused was now an issue that surgeons were equally unable to substantively prove. For example, in the case of Sarah Harwood at the Old Bailey on April 16, 1729,[94] who was indicted for the murder of her male bastard son by suffocation, as a result of throwing him into a house of office, the surgeon examined the child which he claimed to have been born alive. He believed it to be born at full time, and no marks of violence were evident; he performed a hydrostatic test where the lungs failed to sink. Owing to the fact that the lungs floated, the surgeon concluded that the child had been born alive; however, he was unable to provide a cause of death.

Sarah said she did not realise she was so near her time, and when she swooned, she was not aware of the child dropping from her; she said that she never laid a finger upon the child and she could not remember how she got up the stairs. Sarah was found guilty and sentenced to death; however, after pleading her belly a jury of two matrons found her to be "not with quick child";[95] as there is no record of Sarah's death, it is possible her sentence was reduced to transportation.

As medical men were facing increasing pressure from the courts to provide certainty, doubts were beginning to be raised regarding the reliability of the lung test.[96] It was a widely held belief by some in the medical profession that the lungs may be filled with air as a result of putrefaction, resulting from attempts to resuscitate the child or possibly in cases where infants are born in a weakened condition, breathing for several minutes independently, thus producing a false positive reading. Any of these pre-disposing factors would produce unreliable results in the hydrostatic test risking an unsafe conviction. Even in cases where doctors could declare with confidence that respiration had occurred, it did not naturally follow that this was conclusive in proving live birth; regardless of this, however, Behlmer believed that "English doctors stood by the hydrostatic test long after it had fallen into disrepute among continental experts."[97]

Concerns regarding the lung test were also raised by Hunter, when he stated that if a child's lungs floated during the hydrostatic test, and conclusions were drawn that the child was born alive,

> the most dangerous and most common error into which we are apt to fall is this viz, supposing the experiment to have been fairly made … we may rashly conclude that the child was born alive and therefore must probably have been murdered, especially in a case where the mother has taken great pains to conceal the birth … it cannot amount to more than a ground of suspicion and therefore should not determine the question otherwise doubtful between an acquittal or an ignominious death.[98]

Notwithstanding the extent of uncertainty the hydrostatic test produced, it was used as a source of scientific evidence to support the surgeon's evidence in infanticide cases. The midwife's inability to provide definitive testimony had raised the element of uncertainty in infanticide cases, and the surgeon's testimony was equally as uncertain, as it was supported by an unreliable scientific test.

The coroner's inquest and medical evidence

The office of coroner dates back to September 1194, when the "justices in Eyre were required to see that three knights and one clerk were elected in every county as keepers of the pleas of the crown,"[99] when his fundamental responsibility included to view and hold an inquest. The inquest was held upon the bodies of all those who died unnaturally, suddenly, or in prison, or any death in suspicious circumstances, in the presence of the jury, and it was forbidden for the body to be buried until the inquest had ended.[100] Towards the end of the eighteenth century, however, there grew a general census that coroners' inquests should be restricted to sudden deaths with manifest violence, and that the need for medical evidence at such inquests was fruitless.[101] This view stemmed from the belief that if marks of violence were evident, a medically untrained person would be able to determine the cause of death using their own common sense, and by drawing inferences from the evidence; in the absence of marks of violence, an inquest was considered to be unnecessary.[102] In addition to this, a lack of substantive medical jurisprudence on forensic skill and knowledge prior to the nineteenth century reduced the credibility of medical evidence given by medical men at both coroner inquests and trial courts.[103] Notwithstanding this shortcoming, Jackson has argued that coroners were not "deterred from holding inquests, and medical opinion in respect of cause of death was by no means disregarded during the seventeenth and eighteenth centuries."[104]

The inquest process has been described as one of the most "anciently constituted tribunals in English law whose primary responsibility was to conduct inquiries into a range of unspecified types of death."[105] As coroners were forbidden from initiating their own enquiries inquests were instigated by members of the public who passed information onto them by reporting a "fact of death,"[106] thereby requesting an investigation, a process investigative in nature, as opposed to adversarial. Once a body had been discovered, the coroner had to be summoned, and it was the duty of the first finder to raise the "hue and cry."[107] After receiving notification that sudden death had occurred, coroners were required to visit the crime scene with the specific purpose of holding an inquest there.[108] As the inquest was held around the body, wherever it had been found, the corpse took centre stage; the intention and aim was clear – to focus on the cadaver.[109] Once the body had been viewed the proceedings continued in greater comfort indoors,[110] and up to the twentieth century coroners regularly held inquests in public houses amidst the "several implements of conviviality, the odour of gin and the smell of tobacco smoke."[111] A typical scene that is depicted in Charles Dickens' *Bleak House*,[112] where an inquest was held at the Sol's Arms Tavern, or in the more recent novel, *Death Comes to Pemberley*,[113] set at the beginning of the nineteenth century by P. D. James, in which an inquest was held into the death of Denny in the Kings Arms, in a large room at the back of the inn.[114] A similar scene is described in an article from the *Hull Packet and East Riding Times*, which reads:

> suspected child murder near Hull, on Saturday morning of a female child was found on a heap of ashes on the farm of Mr Smith Thearne. Immediately after the discovery of the body information was given to the East Riding police at Beverley. The man who was collecting the soil never saw the body and does not know how it got there, possibility that the corpse was hidden amongst the ashes after placed on the farmstead. An inquest was held at the Dixon Arms Woodmansy near Beverley on Monday before Mr Wigmore Deputy Coroner. C. Le Gay Bereton of Beverley deposed that he made a full examination of the body and was of the opinion that the child had lived for some days and died about a week ago. There was a fracture of the skull caused by a hammer or similar instrument and a fracture of the jaw, in other respects the child was quite sound and in a healthy condition. He made a post-mortem examination of the child and found nothing internally to indicate the cause of death. Death had been occasioned by the injuries described. The inquest was adjourned by a week in order that the police might inquire into the affair.[115]

The following Monday evening an adjourned inquest was held and "Detective Sergeant Smith of Hull stated that no evidence had been obtained which was likely to lead to the crimination of any parties. A verdict of wilful murder against some person or persons unknown was then returned,"[116] the mother in this case remained unknown. The pub-based inquiry served as a place to form a relationship between the lay person and the medical expert, "the dead and the living, the purposeful and the prurient, the sentimental and the instrumental."[117] A fact reflected in the following newspaper article when it reads:

> the enquiry opened on Tuesday afternoon before Mr R. B. Porter coroner for Howdenshire the house of Mr Barker, the Anchor Inn, Booth. The jury viewed the body of the deceased which was that of a fine healthy child and afterwards inspected the pigsty in which the body was found. Medical evidence was to the effect that death had been produced by suffocation.[118]

Throughout the nineteenth century as jurors increasingly found the "view of the body" to be a disagreeable, revolting duty and a burden that was a waste of time.[119] It was a duty, however, that, if it were to be abolished, an increase in the reliance on medical evidence would follow, because the jury would lack crucial observations of their own, making it "all the more desirous of hearing the doctor."[120] A parliamentary Bill proposing the abolition of the view was withdrawn in 1888, as it was claimed that many of its modifications were considered to be unfavourable at the time. One of which stated that in all:

> cases where a view of the body has been dispensed with it shall be obligatory on the coroner to order a medical man to examine it, with or without a post-mortem examination and give evidence thereon at the inquest.[121]

Another recommendation of the withdrawn parliamentary Bill in 1888 proposed that if the coroner was himself a medical man,

> a casual inspection of the body by the trained eye of an experienced coroner especially if he is a medical man, helps him immensely in his interrogation of the medial witness, suggesting the line to take, enabling him to go straight to the point and void many useless irrelevant questions.[122]

A strong advocate of this recommendation was Thomas Wakley, founder of *The Lancet* and one of England's first medically qualified coroners. This debate surrounding the issue of legal and medical coroner's sparked controversy, particularly when coroners such as Wakley asked questions such as "why should lawyers be of necessity the persons whose duty it should be to inquire into matters of common sense and justice?"[123] He believed that coroners should be medically trained rather than originate from the legal practice,[124] as a medical coroner "alone could be capable of interpreting the value of medical evidence to a jury, on such points as the proper interpretation of the physical signs of death or of a separate existence."[125] A number of inquests held by Wakley were reported in *The Lancet*, in particular when medical interest arose from evidence. Wakley was, therefore, a "medical coroner and firmly convinced that a good coroner without medical evidence could not be."[126] From his long-term study of infant suffocation, for example, he concluded that only a small proportion of children supposedly overlain in bed had actually been killed by the pressure of a person sleeping with them.[127]

It was the coroner's duty to issue a warrant directed at the constable to return a "competent number of good and lawful men,"[128] consisting of between 12 and 24 local men, who could serve on the basis of locality and lawfulness. Summoned to serve on a rotational basis, as it was generally believed, "every man should feel that he has an interest in the coroner's court being held in as much respect as possible and in-its duties being rightly and thoroughly fulfilled."[129] After being sworn in, the jury viewed the body and listened to the testimony given upon oath by witnesses, namely the person who had detected the body, along with other interested parties such as the police and medical witnesses. Once the jury had declared their verdict on the cause of death, a record was made of both the circumstances surrounding the death and the final verdict, in an official document referred to as an inquest or inquisition.[130]

Legislation during the sixteenth century empowered coroners to take written statements from both witnesses and suspects coming before them. Any such documentation acquired during the inquest was then returned to the Assizes or other relevant courts. In respect of the suspected criminal, coroners had the legal power to commit suspected killers to prison or bind them over along with other witnesses to appear in court for trial.[131]

In Victorian England there were three types of coroner:

> county coroners elected by freeholder and comprising two-thirds of all coroners, borough coroners appointed by the town councils and franchise coroners appointed in the manner provided by the charter creating the franchise usually the lord of the manor. No coronial qualifications whether medical or legal were laid down beyond being a freeholder.[132]

The majority of coroners, however, were lawyers with no medical training; the cause of death was established by jury verdict and carried out in the presence of a public audience and press.[133] It was not until the twentieth century, with the implementation of the Coroners (Amendment) Act 1926, that requirements were set out for the need for coroners to have professional qualifications in either law or medicine.

There were three coroners during the nineteenth century who fought for both political and social reform and, in particular, were renowned for their contributions to suspected infanticide inquests: Dr Thomas Wakley, as noted above, founder of *The Lancet* and campaigner for medical coronership.[134] Athelstan Braxton Hicks, Barrister at Law and Coroner of Kennington District and County of Surrey, and son of John Braxton Hicks, nineteenth-century surgeon and contributor to obstetrics and midwifery with his research of the latter stages of pregnancy, and the description of practice contractions now widely known as "Braxton Hicks" contractions. Thirdly, Edwin Lankester, successor to Wakley as coroner of Central Middlesex, contributing as his predecessor had done before him to the awareness and study of infanticide.[135] In Hull during the nineteenth century, the coroners were members of the same family, John Thorney solicitor and Superintendent Registrar, who was succeeded by his son John Joseph in 1853, who was then succeeded by his son Alfred, who was coroner and Superintendent Registrar until 1925.[136]

The nature of the inquest was significant in establishing the truth behind unexplained deaths, as it was held speedily after the discovery of the body in a lay, localised manner. Burney has described the inquest as "perhaps the most prominent point of regular contact between expert and lay knowledge in the formal structure of English civil order."[137] The body was viewed by the jury, who were observing for marks of violence and then delivering their verdict using their own judgement, as medical evidence was only heard at the coroner's discretion.

The involvement of medical experts at inquests increasingly grew during the nineteenth century and the requirement for medical experts to be present at inquiries into unexplained death became enshrined in the Medical Witnesses Act 1836.[138] This Act allowed medical men to receive remuneration for their services; carrying out the post-mortem and giving evidence at inquests, it also made the involvement of ordinary practitioners into inquiries into death a statutory obligation, placing them at the heart of the English legal system of inquiries into fatalities.[139] The Act therefore made "obedience to a coroners summon a statutory obligation based on normal professional involvement with a fatal case, the

Medical Witnesses Act placed the ordinary practitioner at the very centre of the English system of death inquiry."[140]

One fundamental problem with this principle was that it created an assumption that all medical men were equally competent in both carrying out a post-mortem and giving evidence in court. Kilday has argued that the experience of forensic pathology of medical experts in the eighteenth and early nineteenth century was varied; this resulted in problematic forensic testimony and the dismissal of some infanticide trials.[141] In the inquest into the death of the child of Mary Watson, for example, held at the house of Mr James Dixon, the Unicorn Inn without Monks Bar, the surgeon, Mr William Matterson, begins his evidence:

> I examined the child, but saw no marks of violence whatever. The navel string was about four inches long, but with no ligature to it. It had been cut with some sharp instrument. After the different experiments on the lungs and the heart I could not say that the child was born alive, the child might have been born alive or it might have bled to death in consequence of the navel string being cut, two small parts of the lungs swam, the other parts sank. The left lung had not been filled with air, I tried two lobes of the lungs of the left side alone and they sank, the other three lobes of the right side also sank. The lungs were afterwards cut in pieces and tried. We squeezed them under water to see if there were any bubbles from the air within but there were none. If the child had breathed considerably, I should have expected the lungs to have swam.[142]

It is therefore unsurprising that the jury in this case returned a verdict of "found dead, no satisfactory evidence being given of the child having been born alive or dead,"[143] with the surgeon conveying uncertainty.

Glasgow has suggested that the transformation of the Victorian inquest to meet the demands of both the law and medicine had different interpretations.[144] One interpretation of this transformation merely meant the implementation of the Medical Witnesses Act 1836; to others, however, it meant "not the provision of objective medical evidence, but the establishment of medical coronership."[145] It was generally believed that medical experts should play a more dominant role in a medicalised system of an inquiry into death, and in particular it was argued that a medically qualified coroner would understand the autopsy and be able to identify shortcomings made by inexperienced medical men. From the mid-nineteenth century there became a growing demand for an "expert orientated reform," the argument from coroners being that "medical expertise and scientific legitimacy and not legal knowledge should play a key role in distinguishing a natural, from an unnatural death."[146] In many respects the underlying fundamental aim of the proposals for reform consisted of the respectful treatment of the body, and more specifically the prevention of mistreatment, triggering demands in the late nineteenth century for a specialised forensic pathologist; the coroner John Troutbeck, Coroner of Westminster, particularly argued that this should be the case.[147] Glasgow states these arguments were "campaigns based on local circumstances and not on national strategy, the reasons behind it differed according to localities."[148]

At the inquest into the unexplained death of a new-born child, at Hull Town Hall before Mr J. Thorney Esq. Borough Coroner, Mr Ross, surgeon to the police, deposed that he carried out a post-mortem examination of the body which left him with "no doubt that it had been born alive," and the child's skull was also fractured in three places. Although the mother in this case remained undiscovered, Mr Thorney in addressing the jury referred to Mr Ross's opinion that the child had met with its death unfairly; as a result of this, the jury returned a verdict of wilful murder against some person or persons unknown.[149] This case raises two important issues: firstly, although the surgeon failed to disclose his methods in reaching his conclusion that the child had been born alive, he appeared to be adamant of his conclusion, and secondly the reference and emphasis placed on the surgeon's evidence by Mr Thorney when addressing the jury.

The appearance of a witness to give evidence in courts of justice was considered to be a duty imposed on by all citizens and in particular on medical men.[150] It is believed that "from the time he takes on the duties of a hospital appointments he is ever liable to be called on to prove material facts or speak as to the extent of the injuries sustained in criminal cases by the prosecutor,"[151] the liberty of the accused being the important factor. The importance of medical evidence at a coroner's inquest has been highlighted by Smith when he states that "as much care should be taken by a medical practitioner as if he were giving evidence before a judge at the Assizes."[152] The attendance of medical witnesses before the coroner is provided for by the Coroners Act 1887, which states that "after authorising coroners to order medical witnesses to attend inquests (section xxi) a legally medically qualified practitioner who has attended an inquest in obedience to a summons may claim remuneration" (section xxii).[153]

In the inquest into the death of child of Sarah Kilvington, in August 1858, in Hull, the *York Herald* reports that:

> an investigation of a very painful nature was made the Town Hall before the borough coroner Mr Thorney on Monday evening respecting the body of a new-born female child, which had been discovered the day before in an ash pit behind a house on Beverley Road, and which is subsequently ascertained to be the child of Sarah Kilvington.[154]

Two surgeons carried out a post-mortem, Mr Hardey and Mr Gibson. Producing the body of the child before the coroner, Mr Hardey deposes that they found the child to be female of mature growth, as it had gone to its full term:

> externally there was a slight blackness on the right temple and some very faint marks of compression on the neck, they were very slight and required a good light to discern them. Upon opening the child's chest, they found it to be fully expanded. As fully as in the case of any child that has been born alive and the lungs have fully inflated, the right lung especially. The left lung was not quite

> so fully inflated, generally they have both inflated. There was not the slightest sign of decomposition, he applied another test – a hydrostatic test. We separated the lungs from the heart and placed them into water, they floated lightly on the water, we then took each lung and divided it into two-three parts, squeezed out all of the air we could and then threw them into the water again, and they floated as before. This child would bleed to death and also after death. We examined the head and found the crown of the head had been seriously fractured and blood effaced on the brain. It is difficult to say whether that had happened after death. I should say whether the effusion was the result of the blow, whether the blow was from the fall of the child or otherwise. I believe that the child was born alive, I think the cause of death was injury to the brain arising partly from the pressure on the throat from those two cases conjointly, but whether the fracture has been caused wilfully or accidently, I cannot say. It is possible that the fracture may have been accidental.[155]

The article continues to reveal background details of the foreman of the jury and surgeons:

> the very full inquiry made by the coroner of this borough and an intelligent jury of tradesmen of whom Mr Balk chemist and druggist was foreman and the very clear evidence given by two medical gentlemen one of whom Mr Hardey was for many years lecturer on midwifery in the Hull and East Riding School of medicine and anatomy and the other Mr H. Gibson fills that office at present – leaves we regret to say a very strong case of circumstantial evidence, upon which the jury came to the unanimous verdict that Sarah Kilvington had wilfully murdered her new-born infant.[156]

The coroner at the inquest empathised the extent of Mr Hardey's expertise and years of practice and then accentuates the fact that clear evidence was given by the medical men. On this basis it would appear that the jury relied heavily on the medical evidence to shape their verdict.

Similarly, in the inquest of the child of Emma Horsefield of Beverley, in September 1868, the surgeon, Mr William Stephenson, gave evidence. He conducted a post-mortem examination of the child, stating that the "child was particularly healthy and that it had breathed. The evidence was to the effect, that the child had been born alive."[157] The jury returned a verdict, that the child died from suffocation, and described how that was produced, but there was no evidence to show this. "The girl who resided in a low part of town, although only 19 year of age has had three illegitimate children, the eldest of which (the only one living) is 5 years old."[158] This is yet another example in which the jury is uncertain as to the cause of the asphyxiation, and in the absence of certainty the woman was shielded from both prosecution and punishment.

Jackson has argued that, by the end of the eighteenth century, as the coroner's inquest became an integral pre-trial inquiry, both medical evidence and the inquest became "essential components of investigation into suspected murders of new-born children."[159] The initial hearing of medical evidence during this pre-trial stage presented the opportunity to discuss the "validity of medical evidence and assisted in the dissemination of medico-legal knowledge."[160]

Infanticide cases at the Old Bailey, 1763–1813

Landsman has suggested that, during the hundred years between 1717 and 1817, there was a subtle but perceptible increase in the authority ascribed to medical evidence given by medical men at the Old Bailey, which has been linked to a demand that medical witnesses provide opinions articulated with a degree of certainty.[161] It was expected that the medical expert would "satisfy a growing demand for forensic certainty,"[162] an increasing demand that, Landsman has argued, is evident in cases of murder, rape, and infanticide.[163] This growing desire for certainty is documented in the changing behaviour of judges towards medical witnesses, along with the increasingly sophisticated use of experimental and symptom-based evidence.[164]

Landsman also believed that by 1800 the importance of certainty is evident by the pressing of medical witnesses in court on the question of certainty, scrutinising each answer they gave for uncertainty.[165] In the case of Joanna M'Carthy, for example, who was indicted for the murder of her female bastard child, on September 18, 1802, the apothecary Robert Barnett was cross-examined by the defence in the following manner, he was asked:

> the child found, was a female child? – Yes. Do you mean to swear positively that the child you examined was born alive? No, I do not, but to the best of my knowledge it was. Do you mean to be understood, that you have always said you believed the child was born alive? Yes, I do, it was. Have you always said so, clear as you are now? I don't know anything to the contrary. Upon your oath, did you not before the Magistrate, entertaining a doubt whether the child was born alive or not? No. You never entertained any doubt? No. It is my duty to warn you a little of what you have said; you said it was impossible for you to say it was born alive? I was asked whether, by opening the body, I could, or not, then say, it was born alive; I said, if it was opened, and I had the lungs of the child, and they floated; I said, that even from that, no gentleman of the faculty could swear it was born alive. Do you mean to say now, positively, that you believe it was born alive? I have every reason to believe it was; the question put to me before the Magistrate was, whether I could not swear positively; I said, no, it was out of the power of any gentleman to swear it; a child coming into the world may fetch a gasp that will expand the lungs equally the same as though it lived twelve hours, with regard to the appearance of the child, it appeared not to have been born above ten or twelve hours. From the appearance of the woman, are you enabled to form any opinion whether they had been delivered more than that time, or about that time? No; I can form no opinion of that. I want to know what it is you do mean; when I read your deposition before the Alderman, I was led to suppose that it amounted to your idea, and to the best of your opinion; I understand

> you will not now swear it as a positive fact? I cannot swear it as a positive fact, though I believe it.[166]

Joanna was found not guilty by the jury; however, the case demonstrates an increasingly growing demand for substantive evidence that in turn increased the "burden prosecutors had to meet in order to convict."[167]

Between the period 1763 and 1813, there were 39 cases of infanticide recorded at the Old Bailey, 19 (49%) of which included the evidence of a surgeon. In 3 of the remaining 20 cases without surgeon evidence, a midwife gave evidence, and in 4 cases both a surgeon and midwife gave evidence. There were also three cases in which the man-midwife gave evidence and one case in which a surgeon/apothecary gave evidence, and a further case in which a surgeon/man-midwife gave evidence. There was also one case in which both a nurse and a surgeon gave evidence and another in which a midwife gave evidence with a surgeon/apothecary/man-midwife. In six cases there was an absence of medical evidence and in each case all of the women were acquitted except for one, who was found guilty of a misdemeanour and confined for one year (found guilty of concealment), which raises the question, how necessary was medical testimony in infanticide cases?

At the trial of Maria Jenkins, who was indicted for the wilful murder of her male bastard child following the discovery of the child's body in the necessary (toilet), on September 18, 1765, William Complin (surgeon and man-midwife) was sent for and ordered by the coroner to perform a post-mortem on the corpse, in the presence of a second surgeon. Complin stated that they:

> tried the usual experiment to know whether the child had been born alive, that is upon the lungs, if the lungs had imbided the air, if the child has breathed, they will swim upon the surface of the water, if not they will sink, we gave it as our opinion, that the child had breathed.[168]

The questioning of Complin continued in the following manner:

> how do you apprehend it was killed? It appeared to me it was stifled in the necessary. Do not you think such a child as that might make a great noise, in being brought downstairs, if it was born alive? I think it might.[169]

On cross-examination, he was asked:

> then this experiment is entirely from the inflation of the lungs? It is. Suppose the child's head was to come into the open air, don't you think the child's lungs would be instantly inflated? Yes, if it gives but two gasps; if it cries, the child was born alive.[170]

It would seem that the court sentenced Maria on the evidence of the lung test alone; it is interesting to note Complin's answer to the final question, and, in particular, how he reached this conclusion, as he does not appear to be legally correct. This point appears to go unnoticed by the judge, and Complin overstepped his authority in this instance, with the judge allowing him to do so. The decision in this case was a surprising one when compared to other decisions during this 50-year period, as Maria was found guilty and sentenced to death, she was executed at Tyburn, on September 23, 1765.[171] The *Derby Mercury* describes her punishment as a result of "the wilful murder of her male bastard child, born in the Minories, by suffocation in the necessary house."[172]

In the case of Mary Robinson, held on February 24, 1768, Mr Patch, the surgeon was questioned on the certainty of the lung test; he was asked if he made the "usual experiment upon the lungs."[173] He was then asked, "is it held to be a certain evidence of the child having drawn breath?" to which he replied, "I should consider it as very inconclusive evidence; there were no marks of violence upon it; I observed that the navel string was not tied, the child might have bled to death from thence."[174] Mary was acquitted by the jury; however, this case is yet another example of the surgeon providing a restrained opinion that conveyed uncertainty.

Both a surgeon and a midwife gave evidence in the case of Elizabeth Warner,[175] who was indicted for the wilful murder of her female bastard child on October 24, 1770, by strangulation. She claimed that the child dropped from her as she sat on the vault, and it was later found by the midwife in a box wrapped in a petticoat; she was acquitted by the jury. In this case both the midwife and surgeon were called to give evidence. The midwife was questioned on the membrane which covered the child's body, stating that "it was owing to a very quick labour," she was then asked if she thought the child to be full time, to which she replied, "I think it was, it was a very fine child."[176] She was also questioned as to whether she thought that the child had been born dead or alive, to which she replied, "I could not tell that."[177] When the surgeon, Dr Underwood, was asked the same question, he replied, "I cannot say."[178] He was also questioned on the membrane covering the child to which he replied that it was owing to the fact that the "labour must have been exceedingly quick; a great many children are lost by exceedingly quick labours."[179] There is little difference in the evidence given by the midwife and the surgeon; Dr Underwood is unable to confirm that the child was born alive and reaffirms the opinion and evidence given by Mrs Smith, the midwife; the jury acquitted Elizabeth.[180]

It seems that, for a time, surgeons generally held a great deal of confidence in the lung test; in the case of Elizabeth Wood[181] on July 2, 1766, for example, the questioning of the surgeon Ferdinando Gellio began:

> I am pupil to a surgeon. On Monday June the 9th, I was sent for on the Coroner's inquest, and was desired to open the body of a female infant, in order to inform them whether it was still-born; I did, and tried the usual experiment; I took the lungs out, and put them into a bowl of water; they swam.[182]

He was then asked, "what do you infer from that?" to which he replied "the inference I infer from that is, that the child had breathed. Did it appear to have been at its full time? It did."[183] On cross-examination he was asked:

> have you seen this experiment tried? I have frequently and have tried it myself; the lungs are specifically lighter upon the water by having been inflated. Will they swim when they are putrid? They will. Whether, in your opinion and judgment, the unfortunate woman at the bar might be delivered of this child as she sat on the vault? I believe there is a possibility of that. Do you believe the child might have dropped from her as she sat on the vault? I do.[184]

Elizabeth was acquitted; the jury concluded that the child may have died as a result of an accident. As surgeons were beginning to question the infallibility of the lung test, by demonstrating an increasing reluctance to present the findings from such tests as evidence, and with an absence of medical guidelines for procedure and interpretation of results, there became increasing inconsistency in the performance of the lung test. Surgeons were carrying out the test in different ways and therefore reporting different results, and there continued to be an absence of a standard procedure for medical practitioners.[185] Although the necessity of applying a degree of caution to such results in infanticide cases was raised, medical men continued to be employed by both coroners and trial courts to carry out the lung test and present the findings.[186]

In the case of Sarah Hunter,[187] on June 28, 1769, the man-midwife, Mr Abel, stated that the lung test he performed during the autopsy upon the child was not mentioned as an infallible rule:

> it was a full-grown male child, with a considerable wound on its neck. It was cut straight down the neck, and afterwards across the neck. The first began about two inches or an inch and a half below the right ear and came down right about two inches or an inch and a half long. It reached to the first bone of the neck. It penetrated quite to the bone, about an inch and a half deep. The other cut across was full two inches long, and full two inches deep. It appeared to have been washed when I saw it. I did not see any blood.[188]

He was then asked:

> is anything to be inferred from its fresh bleeding, as Mrs. Steers has given an account that it was born alive? No. If it had been born dead, it might have bled. On the Monday the coroner sent to me and asked if it was necessary to open the child, to find out whether it was born dead or alive. I told him it was a received opinion, if it had been born dead, the lungs would sink, but did not know it was an infallible sign. I took out the lungs and put them in water, and they swam. I don't mention this as an infallible rule.[189]

Finally, he was asked: "what is your judgment, upon the whole, of the appearance of this child, or can you form any judgment upon it, whether it was born dead or alive? I would rather think it was born alive."[190] It is interesting to note Abel's statement, "I don't mention this as an infallible rule," as if he is openly admitting that the test is uncertain; however, regardless of the fact that the child in this case had visible external marks of violence around the neck; Sarah was acquitted.

In the case of Ann Spinton[191] on September 11, 1771, who was accused of the wilful murder of her female bastard child, Hugh Penfold attended Ann when he was sent for by the prisoner. He discovered the child concealed within a bundle laid upon the bed, stating that "in appearance at its maturity," and upon closer inspection of the child, on the:

> head lay a large pin, flat the point stuck in the skull, it did not go into the cavity of the head. The prisoner said she did not do that. The skull was not penetrated, it might have been an accident. I lifted up the child's head, and I saw three large stabs in its throat; the wound divided the right internal jugular; that of course must have occasioned a great effusion of blood. That wound was certainly mortal. I opened the body, the lungs appeared in a sound state and on throwing them into water, they swam.[192]

The court responded by saying, "I think that it is the modern theory that the experiment is not decisive," to which Penfold replies, "it is held that this experiment is not decisive";[193] Ann leaves her defence to her counsel, and she was acquitted by the jury.

In the case of Ann Arbour,[194] who was indicted for the wilful murder of her female bastard child, on December 4, 1793, the surgeon, Robert Bradford, was asked:

> did you observe any symptoms about this child or mark? I observed no marks of violence whatever it was a very fair body, there was a slight bruise on the top lip, but of no consequence whatever, I observed the navel string was broke, and not tied, it was a fully grown child.[195]

Mr Bradford was then asked, "from your medical knowledge, can you take on yourself to say whether the child was born alive or not? No, I cannot."[196] He was then asked by the court "you did not open the body or make any experiments on the lungs? I did not because those experiments have failed me many a time."[197] The jury asked Mr Bradford whether in his opinion, she went to her proper time, to which he replied, "in all human probability she went her proper time," Ann was found not guilty by the jury.[198]

The case of Ann Spinton raises the element of doubt in the lung test, creating uncertainty in turn, and in the case of Ann Arbour, it is interesting to note that the surgeon refrains from using the lung test completely, thus making his evidence indistinguishable from that of the midwife in Chapter 2.

The case of Elizabeth Parkins,[199] who was indicted for the wilful murder of her male bastard child on April 10, 1771, raises some interesting issues surrounding external marks of violence. Mr Wathen, surgeon, gave evidence to the effect that the child had a wound on the:

> fore part of its neck in which was divided the windpipe, the gullet or throat the large arteries which we call the carotas on both sides of the jugular veins and the lateral muscles of the neck on both sides also; the wound was so deep as also partly to separate the spine of the neck.[200]

Wathen was asked if the wound was fresh. To which he replied, "yes", he was then asked if the child had bled, to which he replied, "it had no appearance of blood."[201] The questioning then continued in the following manner:

> did it appear to have bled? it must certainly have bled, if it had been born alive. Tell us the reasons of your judgment that it had bled. Only the vessels being divided, and the child being full grown, therefore I suppose it to have been alive … did you make any observations of any kind by which you could say the child had been once alive? Certainly, it had been so. Was it after it was born? I cannot say. I did make an experiment on the lungs, which was formally thought decisive; but now that opinion is exploded, that a child had been stillborn had not the lungs inflated with air.[202]

Wathen was then asked whether it was possible for the umbilical cord to become entangled around the infant's neck during delivery, to which he replied, "there are instances of it, and strangulation very possibly may arise there from";[203] Elizabeth was acquitted by the jury.

Whereas in the case of Jane Cornforth, on May 18, 1774, the surgeon, Thomas Oliver, was called to examine the child that was initially found alive:

> a considerable parcel of the small intestines came through a small wound about three quarters of an inch above the navel; I could not return them into the abdomen till I had dilated the wound; when I had cleaned and returned them, and stitched up the wound, the child was then alive. I had a good deal of difficulty in reducing these intestines into the place; some few ashes or cinders were upon them; they were not wounded: the wound appeared as if it had been made with a sharpish instrument, though not a knife; it was rather too irregular to be made by a knife; I saw no other particular marks; I think the wound could not be made by a blunt stick; it might be by meeting some sharp thing in the soil, or in throwing the child down, or by a nail in taking it up. I believe the wound and the intestines being so long exposed to the cold air were the occasion of the child's death; when the child was dead I opened it before the coroner, and could plainly discover, which were, the intestines that had been exposed to the cold air, because they were discoloured. The child lived seven or eight hours; I opened it to see if the wound had been done with a knife, because I think if it had, it was almost impossible, but some of the intestines must have been wounded; upon the whole I have no doubt but the child's life was lost by this wound and the intestines coming so out of its body.[204]

Ann Hooker, midwife, also gave evidence in court, she stated that Jane did not realise she was in labour, "only she said she had the head ache," upon examining the child Hooker stated:

> the child was at its full growth; had its hair and nails; I asked her how she came to cut it; I told her there was a cut a-cross the belly above the navel; the bowels were out; there was a mark on the shoulder, and contusions in the face, but not such as to kill, only bruise; upon this the prisoner said if it was done, it was with the stick she poked it down the vault with; I asked her how she came to throw ashes in upon the child; she said because she thought the soil was not deep enough to cover it.[205]

In this case it could have been the evidence of the midwife that largely shaped the verdict of the jury, and in particular Jane's admission that she used a stick to push the child down into the vault. In her defence, Jane said she "apprehended it to be born dead: she had a very good character, for her good nature and love to children in general."[206] Despite her defence, she was found guilty and sentenced to death, she was hanged on May 23, 1774,[207] and after her "body had hung the usual time, her body was sent to surgeon's hall for dissection."[208]

In the case of Jane Lyall[209] on April 2, 1800, the surgeon claimed that "from the most strict examination, it is not in my power to say the child was born alive,"[210] and so Jane was found not guilty by the jury. This case raises important issues regarding the competence of the surgeon and the reliability of science; regardless of the fact that a strict examination had been carried out, the surgeon admitted it was beyond his power to confirm the child had been born alive. It may therefore have been possible for a more competent surgeon to determine this factor, as without proof the child was born alive it would have been impossible to proceed with the indictment for murder; once again there is little difference in the evidence given by the surgeon in this case and the evidence of the midwife in Chapter 2.

Towards the latter part of the eighteenth century, a growing attitude towards the humane treatment of infanticidal mothers became increasingly evident. Arguably, this attitude became enshrined in the Lord Ellenborough's Act of 1803 (43 Geo. III, c.58) and is encapsulated in the opinion of Andrew Wynter when he states:

> the dislike of inflicting the extreme penalty of the law in cases of this kind is so great, that practically as far as capital convictions are concerned the law is wholly inoperative. The jury is often swayed towards the side of mercy in these cases often to the prejudice of justice.[211]

Members of parliament, as well as writers advocating reform in criminal law during this period, believed that the aim of the penal system was predominately to deter rather than punish. As the practice of destroying children was seen as a detriment to society, especially to the growth of the population, the legislation was predominately justified when the argument for reform arose. Regardless of this fact, prominent individuals were arguing for reform, individuals such as Burke, Fox, Harbord, and Sir William Meredith. However, it was Mr Lockhart who raised the issue in the House of Commons in his "Bastard Children Act to Repeal" Bill, a Bill that was twice rejected by the House of Lords.[212] Their general consensus for advocating reform stemmed from two observations: that the concealment of the birth of a bastard might originate from the best motives, from real modesty and virtue, and secondly the non-use of the statute by the courts.[213]

Notwithstanding the fact that the 1803 statute repealed the 1624 law, Jackson has argued that it failed to recognise humanitarian concerns; it was still possible for an unmarried woman to be sentenced to death if found guilty of murdering her baby.[214] The 1803 Act also gave the courts the power to indict a woman for one offence and yet punish her for another. Although it has been argued that "a woman could not be punished for another offence" since, strictly speaking, "concealment was not a substantive crime. Women were in reality, punished simply for a pattern of behaviour deemed punishable although not technically criminal."[215] It could be argued that the 1803 Act was a reflection of the wider interest in the "profound changes in society in relation to pain and cruelty that emerged in the eighteenth and nineteenth centuries."[216] Profound changes that Halttunen has described more broadly as a "culture of sensibility"[217] which increased humanitarian feeling to encompass, "previously despised persons including slaves, criminals and the insane."[218]

The cases in the period 1763–1813 demonstrate a number of interesting points; the surgeons repeatedly not knowing is both an interesting point and one that is crucial to this research. The midwives, with their limited clinical skills in answering crucial questions the court sought definitive answers to, had been replaced with surgeons, and with this replacement came an increased expectation of certainty, removing the element of doubt. However, a number of surgeons repeatedly testified they did not know the answers – in particular, not knowing answers to key questions such as whether the child was born alive. Did the child have a separate existence? What was the cause of death? Fundamental questions the midwife had previously been unable to answer with certainty. The expectation that the hydrostatic test would support the opinion of the surgeon resulted instead with surgeons revealing results of the lung test with restrained opinion and scepticism. The introduction of the lung test therefore brought a sense of certainty with the support of science to the opinion of the surgeon, but very quickly the surgeons doubted the results, verbally raising concerns under oath regarding its fallibility or reliability. The results of the infanticide cases recorded at the Old Bailey 1763–1813 indicate that, whilst the medico-legal relationship between medical men and courts began to develop, it was also beginning to fail in terms of public perception and the expectation of the court surrounding the principle of certainty. The court required specific answers to key questions to ensure certainty in the crucial decision of a capital offence. In many cases, as medical men produced uncertainty and doubt, they provided little expert opinion to the jury who through common sense, and their own suspicions drew their own inferences.

Infanticide cases at the Old Bailey, 1863–1913

In the 50-year period 1863–1913, there were 112 cases of infanticide recorded at the Old Bailey, interestingly, in many of these cases there was an absence of any medical expert evidence. Out of the 112 cases, only 29 involve medical witnesses' evidence, therefore the remaining 82 infanticide cases make no mention of a medical witness in court. These figures depict a further shift in the relationship between the courts and medical experts. It was highlighted in Chapter 2 that there was no midwifery involvement in the cases during this period, and the expectation was that the surgeon had taken this role. However, the majority of cases do not make any reference to evidence given by either surgeon, apothecary, or man-midwife in court, which is yet a further interesting change in the medico-legal relationship.

Out of the 82 cases in which there was an absence of medical men in court, only six make reference to the fact that there was not enough medical evidence to confirm that the child had had a separate existence from the mother, suggesting some degree of involvement of a medical man prior to the court case; however, the remaining 76 cases make no reference to medical involvement.

There were 28 cases of infanticide recorded at the Old Bailey in the final decade of this 50-year period between 1903 and 1913, 15 of which involve the use of a medical witness and therefore medical evidence. This would suggest that, whilst there were only 29 cases in total throughout the 50-year period which involved the use of medical experts, 52% of them occurred within the final decade of this period. It is possible to ascertain from these figures that the relationship between the court and medical expert was once again beginning to shift. Regardless of this fact, there remains a high number of cases wherein there was no medical evidence (13/28 [46%] of cases). In many of these cases it would seem that the prosecution could not produce sufficient evidence to confirm that the child had had a separate existence from the mother, and therefore a lack of sufficient evidence that a crime had been committed.

It is interesting to note that surgeons were continuing to carry out the lung test on infants in cases of suspected infanticide during this period. In the case of Elizabeth Strangeway, on December 12, 1864,[219] for example, who was indicted for the wilful murder of her new-born male infant, a discussion arose surrounding the effectiveness of the lung or hydrostatic test. The surgeon, Walter Munday, gave evidence, stating that the lungs floated when placed in water, and when placed in water both with and without the heart. He then cut the lungs into 12 or 14 pieces, pressing each piece to ensure they were free from air, yet still they floated, leading him to conclude that the child had breathed, albeit in the act of being born, "there is nothing to assist my opinion as to whether it breathed in a state of existence separate from the mother – the body was completely drained of blood, every organ."[220] On cross-examination the surgeon was asked whether it was possible for the child to breathe before passing into the world, to which the surgeon replied "yes there is a great difference of opinion about whether the hydrostatic test can safely be relied upon."[221] Elizabeth was found guilty of "endeavouring to conceal the birth, recommended to mercy by the jury on account of her youth – confined for twelve months."[222]

The case of Minnie Edwards,[223] on December 14, 1868, is interesting, as her child was not a new-born; she had resided in the Islington Workhouse for three weeks following the birth of her child, William, who was estimated to be two or three weeks old. George Maccliestine, physician, examined the child, who believed the child had died from suffocation. On cross-examination he was asked:

> I presume you have seen a very great deal of children? Yes, they are apt to take into their mouth anything that is placed near it and on that account, they should not be covered over the mouth. Looking at the quantity of bed gown that was in the mouth of this child, in your judgement, is it possible that it could have been sucked in? I think not.[224]

Notwithstanding the physician's answer, Minnie was found not guilty, and although she was charged on an alternative indictment of wilfully deserting the said child, no evidence was offered. This case is interesting for two reasons: firstly, it is not the usual infanticide case which could lead to a lesser indictment of endeavouring to conceal the birth; the birth had not been concealed; William's birth had been registered on October 12, 1868; and secondly, the physician's opinion that the child could not have placed the bed gown in his own mouth suggests that someone else did. This case is an example of a physician ruling out a possible defence.

Elizabeth Harvey was indicted for the wilful murder of her newly born child on July 13, 1863. Thomas Dickenson believed that respiration was fully established:

> respiration might have been accomplished before the child was entirely produced I should say that the wound had been inflicted before death, the flesh would present a different appearance if the wound was inflicted after death, the umbilical cord was broken, I cannot say whether the wound was inflicted before or after the umbilical cord was broken.[225]

Yet again the surgeon could not be certain and so Elizabeth was found guilty of endeavouring to conceal the birth and sentenced to nine months' imprisonment.

In the case of Mary Rainbow, on August 5, 1879, the domestic servant of James Dilley was accused together with Dilley of the wilful murder of a female child.[226] They had travelled to London as Mr and Mrs Hull, and although they were not married to each other, James Dilley was a married man with three legitimate children, so he feared his wife would discover his indiscretion. The child was four to six weeks old and presented with a head injury, but the contents of the stomach during the post-mortem revealed the presence of laudanum. The surgeon, Matthew West Berry, stated: "in my opinion the cause of death was injury to the brain whilst under the action of narcotics."[227] The jury found both defendants guilty, but believing Mary to be under the influence of the male prisoner, they recommended her to mercy. On passing the death sentence, "the female prisoner fainted and was carried insensible from the dock. The man did not exhibit the slightest emotion."[228] The case demonstrates that although the surgeon gave his opinion as to the cause of the child's death, the jury, using their own judgement, drew inferences from the witness testimony and recommended Mary to mercy, a recommendation that was successful. The *New York Times* stated that:

> the prisoners continue in a very depressed condition, especially the woman Rainbow who takes but little food. She has made a statement respecting the murder, in which she avers that she was most fond of the child and that Dilley took the infant from her and went away with it. When he returned he said he had got rid of it.[229]

Mary received a reprieve merely two days before the planned execution, but James was hanged[230] within the walls of Newgate.[231] It is recorded on the 1861 consensus that Mary had returned home and continued to work in service; she died at the end of 1934, aged 83, and was buried on January 1, 1935.[232]

The manner in which the surgeon succeeded the midwife as an expert witness in infanticide cases, with both medical expertise and scientific experiment, seemed to spark a high expectation regarding the certainty of infant death. This related in particular to the combination of the surgeon's newly developed skills in dissection and in-depth knowledge of anatomy and medical discourse. An expectation that he would be able to definitively answer key questions to infanticide, thus creating certainty. Notwithstanding this expectation, the cases in this chapter have demonstrated that this was simply not the case, and instead there was little difference in the answers provided by the midwife and the surgeon. It was recognised by Sommers that the lung test was the only piece of evidence which separated the findings of male practitioners from that of female midwives,[233] a test which, this research has demonstrated, created an element of uncertainty relating its reliability, raising the possibility of unsafe convictions.

Throughout the nineteenth century, as the hydrostatic test continued to create uncertainty as to whether a child had had a separate existence or not, it became apparent that "nineteenth century textbooks of forensic medicine were in general agreement that if it was properly done, it could offer good evidence of respiration, but not of live birth, or separate existence from the mother."[234] The combination of uncertain medical evidence and the softer approach adopted by the courts suggested that, over time, there was less emphasis placed on live birth and therefore the significance of the hydrostatic test; juries tended to find women guilty of concealment of birth as opposed to murder, an offence which carried a short prison sentence and for which the evidence was substantive.

This chapter has demonstrated an initial decline in the number of medical men being called upon to provide evidence in infanticide cases; instead, it seems that the jury interpreted the evidence by drawing inferences, using their own judgement and common sense to reach a verdict. The declining use of medical men as expert witnesses may go some way to explaining how the medicalisation of infanticide has been overestimated by the commentators, as the opinion of medical men failed to carry as much scientific weight in the shaping of the jury's verdict as expected. This decline in the use of medical men stems from the lack of certainty generated by the lung test, the persistent restrained opinion of medical experts, and the repeatedly "not knowing" answers to the key questions in infanticide cases. Their evidence failed to confirm certainty for the jury and instead confirmed uncertainty, a fact that resulted in very little difference between the testimony of the raw evidence provided by the midwife, and the medical man's scientific investigation. The final decade of this period, 1903–1913, demonstrates an increase in the number of medical men called to give evidence on the infant cadaver. This increase could be explained as a result of developments within science and advancements in pathology generally or related to broader calls for changes within infanticide legislation during the beginning of the twentieth century.

This research will now turn away from the body as a source of evidence, with the following chapter focusing on the mental state of the accused woman; it will begin with mental state expert involvement in infanticide cases leading up to the 1922 Infanticide Act.

Notes

1 See C. Krueger, 'Literary Defences and Medical Prosecutions: Representing Infanticide in Nineteenth-Century Britain' *Victorian Studies*, Vol. 40, No. 2, Winter 1997, pp. 271–294.

2 J. Dobson and R. Milnes Walker, *Barbers and Barber-Surgeons of London: A History of the Barbers and Barber-Surgeons Companies*. Oxford: Blackwell Scientific Press, 1979: 55. Also, for a discussion on the College of Physicians, see M. Pelling, *Medical Conflicts in Early Modern London, Patronage, Physicians and Irregular Practitioners 1550–1640*. Oxford: Clarendon Press, 2003: Especially chapter 1.

3 Dobson and Milnes Walker (1979) op. cit.: 55.

4 H. Cook, 'The Rose Case Reconsidered: Physician, Apothecaries and the Law in Augustan England' *Journal of the History of Medicine and Allied Science*, Vol. 45, October 1990, pp. 527–555: 527.

5 I. Waddington, *The Medical Profession in the Industrial Revolution*. Dublin: Gill and Macmillan Ltd, 1984: 4; see also T. Whittet, 'The Apothecary in Provincial Gilds' *Medical History*, Vol. 8, No. 3, July 1964, pp. 245–273.

6 I. Waddington (1984) op. cit.: 40.

7 Watson. (2011) op. cit.: 6.

8 I. Waddington (1984) op. cit.: 6.

9 L. Jefferson, K Bloor, and A. Maynard, 'Women in Medicine: Historical Perspectives and Recent Trends' *British Medical Bulletin*, Vol. 115, No. 5, 2015, pp. 5–15: 6; see also K. Campbell Hurd-Mead, *A History of Women in Medicine, from the Earliest Times to the Beginning of the Nineteenth-Century*. Haddam, Conn: The Haddam Press, 1938; M. A. Elston, 'Women Doctors in a Changing Profession: The Case of Britain' in E. Riska and K. Wegar (eds.) *Gender, Work and Medicine: Women and the Medical Division of Labour*. London: Sage, 1993.

10 Jefferson et al. (2015) op. cit.: 6.

11 Ibid.

12 Kilday (2013) op. cit.: 101; see also S. Jarcho, 'Problems of the Autopsy in 1670 AD.' *Bulletin of the New York Academy of Medicine*, Vol. 47, No. 7, July 1971, pp. 792–796.

13 Kilday (2013) op. cit.: 104.

14 Ibid.
15 Watson (2011) op. cit.: 31.
16 For background reading on this subject see R. Richardson, *Death, Dissection and the Destitute*. London: Routledge & Kegan Paul, 1987.
17 P. Linebaugh, 'The Tyburn Riot against the Surgeon' in D. Hay, P. Linebaugh, J. Rule, E. Thompson, and C. Winslow (eds.) *Albion's Fatal Tree: Crime and Society in Eighteenth-Century England*. London: Verso, 1977: 70.
18 S. Wheeler, 'Medicine in Art: "The Lancett Club at Thurtell Feast" by Thomas Rowlandson' *Journal of the History of Medicine and Allied Sciences*, Vol. 57, No. 3, July 2002, pp. 330–332: 330.
19 P. Linebaugh (1977) op. cit.: 70.
20 K. Waddington (2011) op. cit.: 105.
21 M. Foucault, *The Birth of the Clinic, An Archaeology of Medical Perspective*. London: Tavistock, 1973: 152.
22 Ibid.
23 R. Porter, 'Introduction' in R. Porter (ed.) *Patients and Practitioners: Law Perceptions of Medicine in Pre-Industrial Society*. Cambridge: Cambridge University Press, 1985: 2.
24 Foucault (1973) op. cit.
25 Ibid.: 154.
26 Ibid.
27 K. Waddington (2011) op. cit.: 105.
28 Ibid.: 7.
29 Foucault (1973) op. cit.: 173.
30 Ibid.: 172.
31 Ibid.
32 Burney (2000) op. cit.: 55.
33 Ibid.: 71.
34 Ibid.: 69.
35 D. Burch, *Digging Up the Dead, Uncovering the Life and Times of Astley Cooper, an Extraordinary Surgeon*. London: Vintage Books, 2007: 56.
36 *OBP*, May 1774, Jane Cornforth, t17740518-23.
37 *OBP*, December 1775, Sarah Reynolds, t17751206-82.
38 Burch (2007) op. cit.: 56.
39 Foucault (1973) op. cit.: 173.
40 'Putrefaction' at: www.forensicpathologyonline.com/e-book/post-mortem-changes/putrefaction [Last accessed 18th October 2016]; see also 'Hanging' at: www.forensicpathologyonline.com/e-book/asphyxia/hanging [Last accessed October 24, 2016].
41 'Putrefaction' op. cit.
42 Burch (2007) op. cit.: 55. A view which remains today, see S4 of the Theft Act 1968; *Sharpe* (1857) D & B 160; A. T. H. Smith, 'Stealing the Body and Its Parts' *Criminal Law Review*, Vol. 623, 1976; H. Conway, *The Law and the Dead*. Oxford: Routledge, 2017, chapter 1.
43 Burney (2000) op. cit.: 55.
44 Kilday (2013) op. cit.: 101.
45 S. Sommers, 'Remapping Maternity in the Courtroom, Female Defences and Medical Witnesses in Eighteenth-Century Infanticide Proceedings' in E. Klaver (ed.) *The Body in Medical Culture*. Albany: State University of New York Press, 2009: 47.
46 Ibid.
47 Ibid.: 37.
48 Ibid.
49 McDonagh (2003) op. cit.: 32–35.
50 *York Herald*, 'Trial of Rebecca Beaumont, for the Murder of Her Male Bastard Child, at the Castle of York, Friday July 25th' Saturday August 1, 1803. British Newspaper

Archive (www.britishnewspaperarchive.co.uk); The British Library Board; Image © the British Library Board. All rights reserved.
51 Ibid.
52 S. Smith (ed.) (1928) op. cit.: 223.
53 Ibid.
54 Ibid.
55 (1834) 6 C. & P. 349.
56 *R. v Poulton* (1832), 5 C. & P. 329; *R. v Sellis* (1837) 7 C. & P. 850; *R v Crutchley* (1837) 7 C. & P 814; *R. v Trilloe* (1842) 2 Moody, 260.
57 W. Hunter, *On the Uncertainty on the Signs of Murder: In the Case of Bastard Children.* London: Callow, 1818. This paper was read to the Medical Society on July 14, 1783, and posthumously published in 1818. Available at: https://books.google.co.uk [Last accessed January 7, 2015].
58 Laqueur (1989) op. cit.: 185.
59 Ibid.
60 Hunter (1818) op. cit.: 18.
61 Ibid.: 19.
62 Ibid.: 21.
63 *York Herald*, 'Trial of Rebecca Beaumont' Saturday August 1, 1803, op. cit.
64 *York Herald*, 'Trial of Martha Chapel' Saturday August 6, 1803. British Newspaper Archive (www.britishnewspaperarchive.co.uk); The British Library Board; Image © the British Library Board. All rights reserved.
65 Ibid.
66 Ibid.
67 Ibid.
68 Ibid.
69 Ibid.
70 Ibid.
71 Ibid.
72 Ibid.
73 Ibid.
74 Ibid.
75 'Criminals and Executions in York' at: http://pastsearch-archaeo-history.co.uk/wp-content/uploads/2012/01/Criminals-and-Executions-Jan12.pdf: 47 [Last accessed March 2, 2015].
76 'Trial of Martha Chapel' (1803), op. cit.
77 Ibid.
78 L. Rede, *York Castle in the Nineteenth-Century, Being an Account of All the Principle Offences Committed in Yorkshire from the Year 1800 to the Present Period with the Lives of the Capital Offenders*. London: John Bennett, 1831: 292. Available at: https://books:google.co.uk [Last accessed February 27, 2015].
79 Ibid.: 293.
80 V. Gatrell, *'The Hanging Tree' – Executions and the English People 1770–1868*. Oxford: Oxford University Press, 1994: 336.
81 Ibid.
82 Ibid.
83 Ackerknecht (1976) op. cit.: 1227.
84 Sommers (2009) op. cit.: 37.
85 Ibid.: 50.
86 Watson (2011) op. cit.: 107.
87 *OBP*, September 1765, Maria Jenkins, t17650918-40.
88 Watson (2011) op. cit.: 107.
89 Ibid; for a Victorian discussion of viability and the onset of life see, A. Taylor, A. Lacassagne, and J. Casper, *A Handbook of the Practice of Forensic Medicine*. Vol. 3,

Third Edition, trans. W. Balfour. London: The New Sydenham Society, 1861: 7–10. Available at: https://archive.org/details/handbookofpracti01casp [Last accessed March 2, 2017].

90 R. Brittain, 'The Hydrostatic and Similar Test of Live Birth: A Historical Review' *Medico-Legal Journal*, Vol. 31, 1963, pp. 189–194: 190.

91 Ibid.: 189.

92 G. Behlmer, 'Deadly Motherhood: Infanticide and Medical Opinion in Mid-Victorian England' *Journal of the History of Medicine and Allied Sciences*, Vol. 34, No. 4, 1979, pp. 403–427: 411.

93 M. Jackson (1995) op. cit.: 152.

94 *OBP*, April 1729, Sarah Harwood, t17290416-67.

95 Ibid.

96 Watson (2011) op. cit.: 107.

97 Behlmer (1979) op. cit.: 410.

98 Hunter (1818) op. cit.: 23.

99 R. Hunnisett, *The Medieval Coroner*. Cambridge: Cambridge University Press, 1961: 1.

100 Ibid.: 20.

101 Hale (1736) op. cit.: 222.

102 M. Jackson, 'Suspicious Infant Deaths: The Statute of 1624 and Medical Evidence at Coroners' Inquests' in M. Clark and C. Crawford (eds.) *Legal Medicine in History*. Cambridge: Cambridge University Press, 1994: 64.

103 Ibid.: 65.

104 Ibid.

105 E. Hurren, 'Whose Body Is It Anyway?: Trading the Dead Poor, Coroners Disputes and the Business of Anatomy at Oxford University 1885–1929' *Bulletin of the History of Medicine*, Vol. 82, No. 4, Winter 2008, pp. 775–818: 803.

106 Ibid.

107 Hunnisett (1961) op. cit.: 10.

108 As stated under the Coroners Act 1887; See also E. Hussey, *Miscellanea Medico-Chirurgica: 3rd Part, Occasional Papers and Remarks*. Oxford: Horace Hart, 1894: 25.

109 Burney (2000) op. cit.: 82.

110 Hunnisett (1961) op. cit.: 20.

111 Burney (2000) op. cit.: 83.

112 C. Dickens, *Bleak House*. London: Low Chapman and Hall, 1891.

113 P. D. James, *Death Comes to Pemberley*. London: Faber, 2012.

114 Ibid.: especially chapter 6.

115 *Hull Packet and East Riding Times*, 'Local Intelligence' Friday June 15, 1866. British Newspaper Archive (www.britishnewspaperarchive.co.uk); The British Library Board; Image © the British Library Board. All rights reserved.

116 *Hull Packet and East Riding Times*, 'Local Intelligence' Friday June 22, 1866. British Newspaper Archive (www.britishnewspaperarchive.co.uk); The British Library Board; Image © the British Library Board. All rights reserved.

117 Burney (2000) op. cit.: 82.

118 *Hull Packet and East Riding Times*, 'Child Murder near Howden' Friday November 18, 1864. British Newspaper Archive (www.britishnewspaperarchive.co.uk); The British Library Board; Image © the British Library Board. All rights reserved.

119 *The British Medical Journal*, 'The Abolition of "The View" at Inquests' Vol. 2, No. 1970 (October 1, 1898), pp. 995–996.

120 Ibid.

121 Ibid.

122 Ibid.

123 S. Sprigge, *The Life and Times of Thomas Wakley*. London: Longmans, Green and Co, 1897: 320.
124 Ibid.: 369.
125 Ibid.: 421.
126 Ibid.: 400.
127 Behlmer (1979) op. cit.: 409.
128 J. Sharpe and J. Dickinson, 'Coroners Inquests in an English County, 1600–1800: A Preliminary Survey' *Northern History*, Vol. XLVII, No. 2, September 2011, pp. 253–269: 254.
129 J. Toulmin Smith, *The Parish: Its Powers and Obligations at Law*. Second Edition. London: H Sweet, 1857: 379. Available at: https://archive.org/streat/parishitspowers00smitgoog#page/n398/mode/2up [Last accessed November 7, 2014].
130 Sharpe and Dickinson (2011) op. cit.; see also Hurren (2008) op. cit.: 803.
131 Sharpe and Dickinson (2011) op. cit.: 254.
132 G. Glasgow, 'The Campaign for Medical Coroners in Nineteenth-Century England and Its Aftermath: A Lancashire Focus on Failure (Part I)' *Mortality*, Vol. 9, No. 2, May 2004, pp. 150–167: 151.
133 I. Burney, 'Viewing Bodies: Medicine, Public Order and English Inquest Practice' *Configurations, Society for Literature and Science*, Vol. 2, No. 1, Winter 1994, pp. 33–46: 33.
134 See Glasgow (2004) op. cit.; G. Glasgow, 'The Campaign for Medical Coroners in Nineteenth-Century England and Its Aftermath: A Lancashire Focus on Failure (Part II)' *Mortality*, Vol. 9, No. 3, August 2004, pp. 223–234; Burney (1994) op. cit.
135 R. Kellett, 'Infanticide and Child Destruction – The Historical, Legal and Pathological Aspects' *Forensic Science International*, Vol. 53, 1992, pp. 1–28; Rose (1986) op. cit.
136 'A Short History of the Hull Register Office' at: http://www.paul-gibson.com/social-history/hull-register-office.php [Last accessed August 18, 2015].
137 Burney (1994) op. cit.: 33.
138 6 and 7 Will. IV. C89. An Act to provide for the Attendance and Remuneration of Medical Witnesses at Coroners Inquests [17th August 1836]. A second piece of legislation The Births, Deaths and Registration Act 1836 (6 and 7 Will. IV. C86. An Act for registering Births, Deaths and Marriages in England [17th August 1836]) was also introduced during this year, making it a legal requirement to register all births and deaths and generated the need for a medical certification to be obtained stating the cause of death; see Burney (2000) op. cit.: 108.
139 This is in contrast to the Coroners Act 1887, which states that in cases where a person died in hospital the medical officer had to give evidence but could not claim a fee (*The British Medical Journal*, 'Medical Witnesses and Their Fees' Vol. 1, No. 1945, April 9, 1898, pp. 966–967).
140 Burney (2000) op. cit.: 109.
141 Kilday (2013) op. cit.: 101.
142 *York Herald*, 'Supposed Child Murder in York' Saturday August 3, 1839. British Newspaper Archive (www.britishnewspaperarchive.co.uk); The British Library Board; Image © the British Library Board. All rights reserved.
143 *York Herald*, 'Supposed Child Murder in York' Saturday August 10, 1839. British Newspaper Archive (www.britishnewspaperarchive.co.uk); The British Library Board; Image © the British Library Board. All rights reserved.
144 Glasgow (2004) (Part I) op. cit.: 151.
145 Ibid.
146 Burney (1994) op. cit.: 34; Glasgow (2004) (Part I) op. cit.: 152.
147 Glasgow (2004) (Part I) op. cit.: 153.
148 Ibid.

149 *Hull Packet and East Riding Times*, 'Local Intelligence' Friday April 11, 1845. British Newspaper Archive (www.britishnewspaperarchive.co.uk); The British Library Board; Image © the British Library Board. All rights reserved.
150 *The British Medical Journal*, 'Medical Men as Witnesses', Vol. 2, No. 2020, September 16, 1899, pp. 741–743: 741.
151 Ibid.
152 S. Smith (ed.) (1928) op. cit.: 225.
153 'Medical Men as Witnesses' (1899) op. cit.: 741.
154 *York Herald*, 'Child Murder and Attempted Concealment of Birth at Hull' Saturday August 7, 1858. British Newspaper Archive (www.britishnewspaperarchive.co.uk); The British Library Board; Image © the British Library Board. All rights reserved.
155 *Hull Packet and East Riding Times*, 'Child Murder by a Mother in Hull' Friday August 6, 1858. British Newspaper Archive (www.britishnewspaperarchive.co.uk); The British Library Board; Image © the British Library Board. All rights reserved.
156 Ibid.
157 *York Herald*, 'Beverley' Saturday 26th September 1868. British Newspaper Archive (www.britishnewspaperarchive.co.uk); The British Library Board; Image © the British Library Board. All rights reserved.
158 Ibid.
159 M. Jackson (1994) op. cit.: 81.
160 Ibid.
161 S. Landsman, 'One Hundred Years of Rectitude: Medical Witnesses at the Old Bailey, 1717–1817' *Law and History Review*, Vol. 16, No. 3, Autumn 1998, pp. 445–494: 449.
162 Ibid.
163 Ibid.
164 Ibid.
165 Ibid.
166 *OBP*, September 1802, Joanna M'Carthy, t18020918-134.
167 Landsman (1998) op. cit.: 459.
168 *OBP*, September 1765, Maria Jenkins, t17650918-40.
169 Ibid.
170 Ibid.
171 'Female Executions, 1735–1799' at: http://www.capitalpunishmentuk.org/fem1735.html [Last accessed August 17, 2017].
172 *Derby Mercury*, 'London, September 24' Friday September 27, 1765. British Newspaper Archive (www.britishnewspaperarchive.co.uk); The British Library Board; Image © the British Library Board. All rights reserved.
173 *OBP*, February 1768, Mary Robinson, t17680224-42.
174 Ibid.
175 *OBP*, October 1770, Elizabeth Warner, t17701024-51.
176 Ibid.
177 Ibid.
178 Ibid.
179 Ibid.
180 Ibid.
181 *OBP*, July 1766, Elizabeth Wood, t17660702-36.
182 Ibid.
183 Ibid.
184 Ibid.
185 M. Jackson (1994) op. cit.: 81.
186 Ibid.: 80.
187 *OBP*, June 1769, Sarah Hunter, t17690628-27.
188 Ibid.
189 Ibid.

190 Ibid.
191 *OBP*, September, 1771, Ann Spinton, t17710911-63.
192 Ibid.
193 Ibid.
194 *OBP*, December 1793, Ann Arbor, t17931204-31.
195 Ibid.
196 Ibid.
197 Ibid.
198 Ibid.
199 *OBP*, April 1771, Elizabeth Parkins, t17710410-35.
200 Ibid.
201 Ibid.
202 Ibid.
203 Ibid.
204 *OBP*, May 1774, Jane Cornforth, t17740518-23.
205 Ibid.
206 *Kentish Gazette*, 'London' Wednesday May 25, 1774. British Newspaper Archive (www.britishnewspaperarchive.co.uk); The British Library Board; Image © the British Library Board. All rights reserved.
207 'Executions at Tyburn 1765–1774' at: www.capitalpunishmentuk.org/tyburn65.html [Last accessed February 1, 2016].
208 *Shrewsbury Chronicle*, 'Thursdays Post' Saturday May 28, 1774. British Newspaper Archive (www.britishnewspaperarchive.co.uk); The British Library Board; Image © the British Library Board. All rights reserved.
209 *OBP*, April 1800, Jane Lyall, t18000402-36.
210 Ibid.
211 A. Wynter, 'The Massacre of the Innocents' *Fortnightly Review*, April 15, 1866, pp. 607–612: 611.
212 *Journals of the House of Lords (1770–1773)*, Vol. 23, June 1, 1772, p. 445 and *Journals of the House of Lords (1770–1773)*, June 28, 1773, p. 692. Available at: http://parlipapers.chadwyck.co.uk [Last accessed January 26, 2015].
213 Radzinowicz (1948) op. cit.: 435.
214 M. Jackson (1996) op. cit.: 173.
215 Ibid.: 180.
216 R. McGowen, 'Cruel Inflictions and the Claims of Humanity in Early Nineteenth-Century *England*' in Watson, K. (ed.) *Assaulting the Past Violence and Civilization in Historical Context*. Newcastle: Cambridge Scholars Publishing, 2007: 38.
217 K. Halttunen, 'Humanitarianism and the Pornography of Pain in Anglo-American Culture' *The American Historical Review*, Vol. 100, No. 2, April 1995, pp. 303–334: 303.
218 Ibid.
219 *OBP*, December 1864, Elizabeth Strangeway, t18641212-140.
220 Ibid.
221 Ibid.
222 Ibid.
223 *OBP*, December 1868, Minnie Edwards, t18681214-147.
224 Ibid.
225 *OBP*, July 1863, Elizabeth Harvey, t18630713-886.
226 *OBP*, August 1879, Mary Rainbow, t18790805-698.
227 Ibid.
228 *Reynolds Newspaper*, 'Central Criminal Court' Sunday August 10, 1879. British Newspaper Archive (www.britishnewspaperarchive.co.uk); The British Library Board; Image © the British Library Board. All rights reserved.
229 *New York Times*, at: http://query.nytimes.com/mem/archive-free/pdf?res=9804E1DB1738E23ABC4153DFBF668382669FDE [Last accessed February 1, 2016].

230 'British Executions' at: http://www.britishexecutions.co.uk/execution-content.php?key=1233 [Last accessed April 10, 2015].
231 *Staffordshire Sentinel*, 'Executions Yesterday' Tuesday 26th August 1879. British Newspaper Archive (www.britishnewspaperarchive.co.uk); The British Library Board; Image © the British Library Board. All rights reserved.
232 'The Shefford Murders' at: http://www.bedfordshire.gov.uk/CommunityAndLiving/ArchivesAnd RecordOffice/CommunityArchives/Shefford/TheSheffordMurderers.aspx [Last accessed April 10, 2015].
233 Sommers, (2009) op. cit.: 50.
234 Watson (2011) op. cit.: 108.

4 Medical evidence and mental state of the infanticidal woman

The medical experts in infanticide cases so far in this book have given evidence in court that centred upon the cadaver as a source of evidence. As medical men were unable to provide definitive proof of the facts in issue, which in turn created uncertainty in their testimony, and with juries reluctant to find a woman guilty of infanticide, it could be argued that this reflected a shared attitude of jurors and medics; thus, the courts began to adopt a softer approach towards infanticidal women. The passing of the Lord Ellenborough's 1803 Act allowed an unmarried woman who was acquitted of murder to be charged with concealment of birth, an offence that carried a maximum sentence of two years' imprisonment, regardless, in some cases of evidence of murder.[1] This appears to have led to a general rule that, where uncertainty remained, the woman should be given the benefit of the doubt. In contrast to the general rule, in cases where certainty prevailed and there was little doubt of culpability, the punishment was severe. This is reflected in the case of Rebecca Smith, the last woman to hang for infanticide in 1849.[2] Rebecca was suspected of murdering more than one infant, but as poison had been her modus operandi, and this implied intention, she did not receive a pardon. Therefore, the law generally held a "legally exculpatory attitude towards infanticidal women."[3]

An alternative defence, however, was to plead insanity. Prior to the nineteenth century, defendants who were found to be mentally deranged were found "not guilty, by reason of insanity." The Victorians began to question this verdict and in particular its consequences, which led to criminals instead being found "guilty, but insane" – guilty of the act, but not responsible in law[4] – a verdict introduced by the case of Daniel McNaughtan,[5] and a case which will be discussed further within this chapter.

In cases of infanticide, Ward has argued that very few women pleaded insanity or argued that their actions were the result of fleeting, temporary frenzy; instead, he maintains that insanity defences appeared more frequently in infanticide cases involving married women,[6] or, as Watson has highlighted, in cases involving the death of an infant up to the age of 12 months.[7] It is this defence which forms the basis of this chapter, arguing that, during the nineteenth century, courts were reluctant to find infanticidal women "guilty but insane." This could be attributed to either the uncertainty created by the surgeon's testimony regarding the body,

DOI: 10.4324/9781003006299-4

the softer approach towards women in court, or the harsh indefinite Victorian detention that an insane verdict would carry.

This chapter will therefore focus on the essential element of the guilty mind of the accused. Beginning with an introduction discussing puerperal insanity, and in particular its onset, and signs and symptoms, this chapter will focus initially on the nineteenth century, a period during which puerperal insanity first arose as a medical entity in the medical and legal arena. The chapter will then move onto the criminal justice process, discussing puerperal insanity as a defence to new-born child murder, and cases in which a verdict of "guilty but insane" was given, and also cases where a defendant may be found "unfit to plead." The establishment of mental state experts within the criminal justice process will then be examined, including the assessment of the mental state of infanticidal women within institutions such as Holloway Prison, where women were held on remand, prior to trial. The chapter will then discuss verdicts at the Old Bailey and in Hull and the surrounding areas (between 1863 and 1913) in infanticide cases of "not guilty on the grounds of insanity," after 1800, and "guilty of the act but not responsible at the time,"[8] after 1883. Following an introduction of twentieth-century legislation, this chapter will conclude with a discussion of the few cases held at the Old Bailey, and in Hull and the surrounding area where a verdict of "guilty but insane" was given during the 1914–1955 period.

Puerperal insanity

During the eighteenth century, a radical transition occurred in the history of madness, a disease of the mind that is as old as mankind.[9] In response to an increasing awareness of mental illness and the establishment of madness in the medical arena, a number of institutions or asylums specialising in the care of mental patients began to emerge, and an increasing number of alienists or physicians choosing to specialise in madness. Alienists began to increase their expertise and knowledge of the mental illness, particularly through the study of the brain, leading to such publications as William Battie's *The Treatise of Madness*.[10] This increased medical knowledge of madness undoubtedly filtered through to the criminal justice system and the courtroom, albeit slowly. Eigen has identified that "medical witnesses in the late 1700s were by far the exception, appearing in no more than ten per cent of insanity trials."[11]

When questions concerning the sanity of a criminal arose within the eighteenth century and the first half of the nineteenth century, it lay with the English juries to provide the answers. They were expected to base their judgement on personal knowledge and experience, and it was they who determined the sanity of a defendant – a rule that Foucault refers to as the "rule of the common truth,"[12] the drawing of "inferences from evidence that any rational subject can understand and assess."[13] It is therefore no coincidence that, during the eighteenth century, infanticide trials began to include testimonies concerning the mental state, and, more specifically, two types of insanity were raised as mitigation for infanticide: idiocy, present since childbirth, and a form of frenzy or temporary insanity.[14]

With no impartial witness present at the death of the infant, diagnosing a woman's mental state at the time of the act proved difficult and was inconsistent. Quinn found that, during the late Victorian period, some cases of infanticide relied on diagnosis by merely observing a photograph of the woman.[15] It was generally believed that "insanity was rooted in biology and could therefore be read on the body, especially the face."[16] On this basis, it was thought to be unnecessary to meet a patient, as a diagnosis could be made through a study of the face of the patient in a photograph.[17] Through the use of photography, it was possible to capture the patient's recovery from the mental state in a series of photographs.[18] It was also thought that by showing a photograph to the patient of their face, which depicted their heightened state of derangement, it would stimulate a swift recovery.[19]

In other cases, mental state witnesses gave evidence at trials by drawing on their knowledge from similar cases in the past, personal knowledge of the woman's history of mental illness, or traits of lunacy in the history of the woman's family, which led to the conclusion that lunacy was genetic.

In the case of Elizabeth Wrath, who appeared before the Yorkshire Summer Assizes on July 10, 1834, indicted for the murder of her new-born infant in Hatfield West Riding, the surgeon attested to her insanity as he knew her; he had attended her before, and following her confinement:

> this morning the jury proceeded to try whether Elizabeth Wrath charged with the murder of her infant child was of sound mind or not. The insanity of the prisoner was clearly proved by the surgeon who attended her before and since her confinement and also by two or three witnesses who lived near her, one of whom detailed the circumstances of the murder, which were that on the nurse going to take the child out of the bed for the purposes of washing it, she found that it had been strangled.[20]

Elizabeth had also attempted to take her own life shortly after the event:

> the poor woman it appears after her confinement which was attended with serious illness became subject to temporary aberrations of intellect, under the influence of which, she not only deprived her infant of its life, but also lacerated her own arm with a large pin, as to render her recovery almost hopeless, nor is she yet considered perfectly out of danger.[21]

When Elizabeth was confronted about her actions, she stated, "she had hanged it with her bed gown and that the devil had instructed her to do it"; after a short deliberation, the jury returned a verdict of not sane.[22]

The question of insanity also arose in the case of a male suspect, indicted for the wilful murder of his infant. James Hayes, tried on January 11, 1875, at the Old Bailey, had been ill and confined to bedrest since the birth of the child.[23] A neighbour who lived above described him as a "kind hearted, hardworking man, a good father and a good husband; he always lived on affectionate terms with his wife and children."[24] A second neighbour, Jane Peters, who lived in an adjoining house, entered the property upon hearing children's shouts of "murder." She said he was stood with his:

> right hand stretched out towards his wife, trying to get at her. I ran in between them and laid hold of him; the baby was lying on the ground at the foot of the bed. He said, "I will kill her as well, she detains me, four men is ready to execute me," there were no men there at that time; he was under that impression for days that four men were going to execute him; he had said it before.[25]

William Squire, surgeon, and a licentiate of the apothecaries' company, also gave evidence, stating that Hayes had been diagnosed with bronchitis but had later presented with additional symptoms. As a result of this, he changed the medication, which resulted in:

> symptoms of delirium, tremens setting in. He complained of things crawling about him, which is a very strong symptom of delirium tremens and he had all the other symptoms of it, there was no fever about him—his hand was moist and quite clammy—when I first attended him I had not the slightest idea it arose from drinking, I did not find it out till the Wednesday.[26]

A further witness testified that James was "not in the habit of being occasionally intoxicated, I never saw any symptoms of it, at Christmas he might have some with his mates but nothing to speak of."[27] James was found "not guilty on the grounds of insanity" and ordered to be detained at Her Majesty's Pleasure. As Smith has identified, "as with criminals generally, the majority of criminal lunatics were men … occasionally women were at the centre of attention, but there are reasons for dealing with them separately … because of their association with infanticide."[28]

In 1820, Gooch published his essay *Observations on Puerperal Insanity*,[29] identifying a specific condition prevalent in childbearing women. He described puerperal insanity as a "nervous irritation that is very common after delivery … other women are thoroughly mad"[30] and identified two distinct periods when women were most at risk:

> during the long process or rather succession of processes, in which the sexual organs of human female are employed in forming, lodging, expelling and lastly feeding the offspring, there is no time at which the mind may not become disordered, but there are two periods at which this is chiefly liable to occur, the one soon after delivery when the body is sustaining the effects of labour, the other several months afterwards when the body is straining the effects of nursing.[31]

On this basis it would appear that there was a lack of prescribed time for the onset of puerperal insanity to appear. Instead, its broad time frame could include any time from birth until the woman ceased to breastfeed, and sometimes beyond. The link between puerperal insanity and childbirth could therefore be described as tenuous: it could be years following the birth of a child before the illness was diagnosed.[32]

The broad time frame and varied signs and symptoms led asylum practice to divide puerperal insanity into two categories: melancholy and mania.[33] Recognised by its sudden onset and symptoms, which included overexcitement, deviance, and violent behaviour, mania became a more frequently diagnosed condition. Marland describes it as a "moral usually temporary insanity, which was usually manic, often severe and occasionally fatal,"[34] whereas Jones argued that puerperal mania was characterised by "gibberish nonsense, immodest conduct and bad behaviour" of the women.[35] Puerperal mania was a form of insanity that was "dangerous and difficult to manage, carrying with it the risk of death from exhaustion."[36] Baker observed that a woman experiencing a temporary frenzy or mania such as this was more likely to direct her anger towards her husband than attack her child.[37]

Melancholia, on the other hand, was typically slow to develop and difficult to diagnose; often by the time it had been identified, it was "entrenched and difficult to cure."[38] Melancholia was more likely to be diagnosed in the late puerperal period, when women may experience "delusions of unworthiness, and in these cases ideas of suicide, and homicide are more common."[39] It is during this period of lactational insanity that "child murder occurs more frequently,"[40] and in many cases the "mental causes are insidiously at work for weeks and months of pregnancy and continue for weeks and months afterwards, finally culminating in a tragedy during the lactational period."[41]

A study carried out in 1927, by Stanley Hopwood, at The State Criminal Lunatic Asylum, Broadmoor, demonstrated that the women experiencing lactational insanity or exhaustive psychosis were experiencing extreme forms of sleep deprivation, eating very little, causing malnutrition, usually anaemic, and in a very poor state of general health.[42] These factors extrinsically linked mental state to general health and wellbeing, which could also be associated with living conditions, hygiene, and poverty. The link between lactation, exhaustion, and mental state has also been highlighted by Ward, who noted that women nursed their infants for a couple of years postpartum,[43] both as a form of free nutrition and as a dubious form of contraception, facts that undoubtedly contributed to the mother's prolonged poor state of health. Marland has highlighted differing causal links to puerperal insanity made by different practitioners. For example, midwifery practitioners, who treated wealthier women with puerperal insanity at home, linked the condition to the stress and trauma of childbirth, whereas those treating poorer women with puerperal insanity within an asylum tended to associate the condition with economic factors such as poverty and poor health.[44]

By the mid-nineteenth century puerperal insanity had "established a firm place in the insanity discourse."[45] In time, insanity of pregnancy and of lactation were attributed separate labels, and together the "three disorders accounted for increasing numbers of female asylum admissions."[46]

Two years following the publication of Gooch's essay, the first case of puerperal insanity as a defence to murder was recorded at the Old Bailey.[47] Ann Mountford, a married mother of ten children, was indicted for the wilful murder of her youngest, a nine-month-old child, on May 22, 1822. The Old Bailey was "crowded to excess to witness the trial,"[48] with curious members of the public. As she was placed at the bar, Ann was described as "mild and becoming, but her countenance bore a wild sort of smile."[49] The first witness was Mary Ireland, a neighbour, whom Ann had visited after the alleged crime had taken place. She gave a detailed account of Ann's confession and behaviour and was asked on cross-examination, "have you the least doubt of her being insane at the time?" to which Mary replied, "I am positive she must be insane."[50] Charles Leagow, who had known the prisoner for many years, was also asked, "you have no doubt of her derangement?" He replied, "I am positive she could not be in her right mind: she was a kind and humane mother as ever lived and has nine children now. I believe every sense of recollection had left her."[51]

Patrick Tuft, the defendant's brother, explained that when Ann was ten years old, he was involved in an accident, and when she saw him, he said she "went out of her mind, and was deranged for nearly a month. My mother was deranged in her younger days, and in the latter part of her life, at different intervals."[52] He encountered Ann in the street about eight months ago but had not seen her since. He claimed that he saw her, "twisting and looking back in a deranged manner, I asked what the matter was, she said she was very poorly and did not know where she was going; it struck me that she was a little deranged."[53]

The final witness, surgeon Joseph Dalton, who had treated the defendant two and a half years previously for a bodily disorder, stated that Ann was a woman of:

> melancholy temper. She had symptoms which indicate a predisposition to insanity, it was a species of insanity which is at times hereditary in families, and it is very susceptible to break out at particular intervals. I have known an attempt to wean a child and not accomplishing it, produce insanity; if it was lurking in the habit it would be more likely to break out at that time. When I attended her in 1819, she repeatedly made use of the words, "I have no peace at all," I was not at all surprised when I heard she was the subject of insanity.[54]

In her defence, Ann claimed that "in a moment of phrenzy, I seized a knife and severed the little innocent's head from its body."[55] So following the examination of these witnesses:

> who described various acts of incoherency in her conduct which united, constituted a train of circumstances that left little doubt of her being out of her senses, or labouring under some temporary mental attack at the time she committed the murder.[56]

The jury reached a verdict of "not guilty, being insane".

With the increased awareness of puerperal insanity, there was also corresponding recognition by experts that this type of insanity was a form of consequential madness,[57] and "puerperal insanity was a condition that could be cured or alternatively could kill."[58] Despite its strong association with death, suicide, and some cases infanticide, asylum superintendents argued for the removal of such women from their family home to the asylum, where they could be treated away from the cause of their insanity. Such a strong assertion made by the asylum superintendents not only aimed to assist women suffering from puerperal insanity but also demonstrated that, when it came to puerperal insanity, they were superior over medical men specialising in obstetrics.[59]

Following the case of Mountford, medical experts began to construct a diagnosis of puerperal insanity as a defence for a woman accused of murdering her infant and began to present themselves as experts on the condition which:

> led to more refined descriptions of its causality and was increasingly used as a defence plea in cases of infanticide or concealment and this in turn increased the position of doctors presenting themselves as experts on the disorder.[60]

The varying degrees of puerperal insanity in terms of its onset, signs, and symptoms have raised the question of its existence as a clinical entity. Loudon suggested that some cases belong to "manic depressive illnesses, some to dementia and others to toxic confusional or neurotic states."[61] He argues that although different terms were used to refer to the same condition, "puerperal insanity, puerperal mania or puerperal melancholia," it was puerperal mania that was the cause of many women being admitted to the asylum.[62] Notwithstanding this observation, it is interesting to note that even when a woman was diagnosed with suffering puerperal insanity at the time she killed her infant, she could still be acquitted. In the trial of Maxwell Rae, on January 30, 1888, at the Old Bailey, the surgeon, Mr Holland Hodgson Wright, deposed that at the time she "committed the offence she appeared to be suffering from puerperal mania and was not accountable for her actions, and in addition to this the injuries might not have been inflicted until after the death of the child"; she was found not guilty.[63]

Victorian textbooks implied that the madness of women was intrinsically linked to either disorders of the reproductive system or the side effects associated with puberty, pregnancy, or the menopause.[64] Zedner has identified that Victorian women tended to be recognised as experiencing mental weaknesses: weaknesses present in every female and exacerbated by childbirth. In particular by the "stresses of labour that were seen to be increased if there was evidence of poverty, insanitary or miserable surroundings, or cruelty or neglect by the husband."[65]

Insanity and the criminal justice process

The insane were therefore beginning to be considered a unique group, both within the medical discourse and the law, a fact that stemmed from the implementation of the Criminal Lunatics Act 1800: an Act that ordered the detention of criminal lunatics "during His Majesty's Pleasure."

The 1800 Act came into force following the decision in *R v Hadfield*, where James Hadfield was accused of attempting to assassinate King George III.[66] As Hadfield had planned the attack, his defence counsel, Thomas Erskine, argued that the normal test of insanity was insufficient and instead successfully argued that Hadfield's insanity at the time of the act should be taken into consideration. The jury returned a verdict of "not guilty by reason of insanity."[67] This verdict raised concerns among politicians, who believed it would set a precedent, allowing similar criminals to go free. In response, the Criminal Lunatics Act 1800 was implemented, "defendants acquitted were given the new verdict of 'not guilty on the grounds of insanity'"[68] and remanded in custody until receiving a royal pardon. This led many magistrates to question the rationality behind "acquitting someone of a criminal charge on grounds of insanity, and then imprisoning him anyway."[69]

From 1843, any "guilty but insane" verdicts given were founded on the decision in the case of *R v McNaughtan*[70] and the subsequent *McNaughtan Rules*;[71] the judges cleverly provided the clarification that the public and the law required by applying a minor amendment. Smith claims that the judge's answers added very little to the existing law, merely restating the right–wrong test "a man was not responsible for his criminal deed if at the time of committing it, he was unable to know that the deed was wrong."[72] The *McNaughtan Rules* therefore, whilst incorporating the right–wrong test at the same time rejected the notion of impulsive behaviour. The case of *R v McNaughtan* has been described as the "most famous trial featuring in the development of criminal responsibility"[73] and remains influential today. Eigen has argued that the rules "conspicuously omitted any mention of a host insanity diagnosis (moral insanity, lesion of the will, irresistible impulse) that medical witnesses had introduced into courtroom testimony"[74] before 1843, electing instead to reposition insanity as a matter of cognitive defect alone.[75]

Issues relating to the sanity of the accused could occur at any stage throughout the criminal justice process,[76] although one particular stage in which a prisoner's mental state might be questioned was during the arraignment. Once the indictments had been established, the prisoner would be "arraigned before the court,"[77] a process that involved the reading of the indictment, to which the prisoner would be expected to enter a plea. In cases where the prisoner omitted to enter a plea by remaining silent, the mental capacity of the prisoner was questioned. For example, the question of mental state arose in the case of *R v Dyson*, where the jury were asked to consider the sanity of a deaf and dumb woman accused of infanticide.[78] Esther Dyson was a 26-year-old deaf and dumb woman who was charged with the wilful murder of her female bastard child at Ecclesfield (near Rotherham). The child was found in a mill pond with her head severed, and the jury were asked to consider Esther's ability to understand and whether this weakness that affected her ability to respond to the charge related to disability or mental capacity. In cases involving deafness it was essential that the court distinguished between those defendants who were considered to be "mute of malice," through wilful silence, and those who were mute by a "visitation by God": deaf mutes, or were insane.[79] Esther's form of deafness intrigued the public, and the case attracted a great deal of interest, with many attending to witness the proceedings:

> in consequence of the prisoner labouring under the infirmity of having been born deaf and dumb, the greatest interest was excited, and the galleries were crowded on the opening of court. The prisoner was 26 years of age, but does not appear so old, she is rather tall and of slender make. She has light hair and complexion, and of rather a pleasant and pensive cast of feature. She was dressed in a coloured silk bonnet, a light calico print dress and a red cloth cloak. She had the appearance of a respectable female in the lower walks of life.[80]

At the coroner's inquest Esther had effectively communicated to the jury through the aid of an interpreter or signer her account of events leading up to the alleged infanticide, claiming that during the night that labour commenced, she made several unsuccessful attempts to awaken her deaf brother who

> slept but a foot from her. That in the agony of parturition, she pulled off the head of the child, then placed it gently and nicely in the water. To the truth of these assertions, she appealed to judgement of heaven and called from imprecations on a person when she was charged with the crime of the seduction, in a manner most distressing to many of the jurymen who were intelligent farmers living in neighbouring townships.[81]

Mr Jackson and Mr Campsall, the medical men who performed the autopsy, stated that the child "was born alive and exhibited unusual signs of strength and fullness of maturity."[82] Whilst they omitted details of how they had reached this conclusion, they continued with the fact "that its head had been severed from its body with a knife or some cutlery instrument with a blunted or dull edge,"[83] thus contradicting Esther's account of the events.

Mr Justice Parke asked the jury to determine whether she was insane in the legal sense; the two signers determined that she was "sufficiently intelligent enough to understand common matters of daily occurrence,"[84] stating that, "if they were satisfied that the prisoner had not then, from the defect of her faculties, intelligence enough to understand the nature of the proceedings against her, they ought to find her not sane."[85] The jury "returned a verdict that the prisoner was not sane"[86] in the legal sense, a verdict that allowed Esther to escape the death penalty, only to be detained under the Criminal Lunatics Act 1800. This verdict baffled Esther's neighbours, as they had always found her to be "both sane and in sign, comprehensible."[87] Esther spent the following ten years in the West Riding Pauper Asylum where "removed from her community, she became violent and depressed."[88]

It prima facie appears that the decision in *R v Dyson* is nonsensical; the judge takes the view that just because the interpreter could not make her understand her rights, she should be considered to be insane, completely disregarding that she could communicate the facts of the case. The case was therefore decided on her level of understanding rather than her ability to communicate. An issue that was further raised in 1836, in *R v Pritchard*, a deaf mute who was accused of bestiality, where Baron Alderson stated that the:

> jury must be satisfied that the prisoner was of sufficient intellect to comprehend the course of the proceedings on the trial so as to make a proper defence, to challenge a juror to whom he might object, and to understand the details of the evidence.[89]

On this basis, in order for the prisoner to be able to make a proper defence, he must have the ability to either cross-examine the witnesses if he is defending himself or be able to instruct his defence counsel to do so on his behalf; in either case he must have a reasonable comprehension of the legal process. Maurice Hamblin Smith argued that, if this rule were to be applied strictly it would result in a large number of prisoners declaring unfit to plead.[90] The right to object, or challenge a juror, Hamblin Smith argued, was not widely known by the prisoners.[91] The rule in *Pritchard* did not exclude all deaf mutes from their trial, particularly if the accused had the ability to communicate through sign language; *Pritchard* does however remain the leading case on unfitness to plead today.[92] In the case of Mary Ann Hathway, April 25, 1887, following *Pritchard*, the OBSP states that "upon the evidence of Mr Philip Francis Gilbert, surgeon to her Majesty's Prison of Holloway,[93] the jury found that the prisoner was insane and unfit to plead, and ordered her to be detained until Her Majesty's Pleasure be known."[94] Mary was indicted for the wilful murder of her child, Frances Mary Hathway, the age of the child was undisclosed.[95]

For those criminals who were found either unfit to plead or "guilty but insane," they were ordered to be detained until His Majesty's Pleasure be known or a long-term committal.[96] Until 1863, this was often in a local county asylum or occasionally Bethlem; however, when Broadmoor opened in 1863, most criminal lunatics were committed there.[97] Whilst awaiting sentencing, women were held on remand in prisons like Holloway, then a city prison used for mental state assessment. Walker and McCabe have identified Holloway as being a place for assessing mentally disturbed suspects from at least 1873.[98] Ward also observed that, by the late nineteenth century, magistrates were "remanding defendants to prison for observation of their mental condition,"[99] a practice that notably increased within some prisons particularly Holloway where numbers increased from 4 to 401 in 1886.[100] In the case of Emily Moir, on March 10, 1902, who was indicted for the wilful murder of her newly born male infant, the OBSP state that "upon the evidence of Doctor Scott, the medical officer at Holloway Gaol, the jury found the prisoner of unsound mind and unable to plead, she was to be detained during His Majesty's Pleasure,"[101] implying that Emily was assessed on admission to the gaol and possibly at regular intervals thereafter, a fact consistent with the increasing use of Holloway for pre-trial observation which increased greatly in the 1890s.[102]

This practice was discouraged by the Home Office, however,[103] who argued that evidence of insanity should be produced pre-trial, before cases were heard before the magistrate.[104]

Mental state assessment

The process of assessing the mental state of suspects on remand stems back to at least the eighteenth century when medical men were employed to assess prisoners and when prison psychiatry was born. Although a "surgeon had been appointed at Newgate since 1692 and some Houses of Correction since their earliest days,"[105] the enactment of The Health of the Prisoners Act 1774 (An Act for Preserving the Health of Prisoners in Gaol and Preventing the Gaol Distemper) established the requirement of the "appointment of an experienced surgeon or apothecary to attend each local gaol."[106] Following a period of "prison reform" and campaigning by reformers such as John Howard, the Gaols Act 1823 was implemented. This aimed to improve the health and mental wellbeing of prisoners by reasserting the need to appoint surgeons, prohibiting the use of irons and shackles, permitting visits by a chaplain, allowing female wardens to guard the female prisoners and payment of gaolers.[107] In the absence of regulation, the 1823 Act had varying effects across the country, until the implementation of the Prisons Act 1835, an Act that introduced the prison inspectorate. The further implementation of the Prisons Act 1877 ensured the centralisation of the running of prisons and the creation of a medical inspector of prisons.[108]

The creation of the role of an experienced surgeon attending each local gaol, a role of observation, arguably gave rise to contemporary forensic psychiatrists; Sir William Norwood East, Prison Commissioner and Director of the Prison Medical Service in 1930s, was one of the "first prison medical officers to show a complete command of the technical aspects of forensic psychiatry which he gained from the practical application of a wide reading in theory."[109] Within Holloway Prison, the remand prisoners who were diagnosed as psychotic by mental state experts were assessed pre-sentence,[110] though "prison commissioners were saying that prisons were not a proper place for persons such as these."[111] This process of mental state assessment established the role of the mental state expert during the nineteenth century, with two distinct categories of expert: asylum superintendents and superintendents of workhouse infirmaries, and private practitioners such as Henry Maudsley.

A distinctive function for prison surgeons and placing them firmly within the heart of the institution became a crucial factor within Foucault's theory. At the heart of his analysis were the processes of "discipline, surveillance, individualization and normalisation,"[112] which were crucial in the rise of the medical profession both within and outside institutions towards the end of the eighteenth century.[113] As "medical discourse was part of a disciplinary strategy which extended 'control over minutiae of the conditions of life and conduct'. Within this discourse the doctor became 'the great advisor and expert.'"[114] He argues that by putting doctors in charge of mentally assessing prisoners or patients within the asylum, medical men developed into the role of experts on madness as opposed to being placed into the role of assessing mentally ill criminals because they were experts.[115] The 1865 Prisons Act included the provision for surgeons to assess prisoners weekly, allowing them access to many more conditions that could potentially be diagnosed under the genre of mental health. Similarly, Eigen has argued that "prisons and jails afforded medical men numerous opportunities to observe and converse with the putative mad, there was little doubt that asylum superintendents afforded the most sustained contact with the mentally troubled."[116] This allowed medical men to be placed within "prisons, jails, and most important of all, police stations,"[117] and in the absence of prior knowledge of the accused, the surgeon made his assessment and diagnosis following the crime; it was the crime that generated the encounter.[118]

By the 1880s, London saw a well-organised system for assessing individual mental states, within both medical and criminal institutions, such as Holloway,[119] where practitioners functioned in factory-like environments diagnosing mental states. The objects of such assessment, the criminal lunatics, have been described by Smith as experiencing "an uneasy existence between prison and asylum, between discourses of guilty and disease."[120] This process led experts to be called upon during criminal insanity trials, medical experts such as Dr Bastian,[121] who were instructed by the Treasury to assess mental states, but would invariably be called by the defence when his evidence was favourable to them.

Across the rest of England and Wales, the role and responsibilities of the prison doctor became enshrined in the rules governing prisons derived from those promulgated in 1794;[122] their primary duty was to examine each prisoner upon admission, then weekly, to assess the state of both body and mind, and to report.[123] Some convicted prisoners deemed to be insane were transferred to county asylums; however, many remained in, or were transferred to, prisons such as Millbank in London, where a medical superintendent was in attendance.[124] In 1863, Broadmoor Hospital[125] opened under the control of the Home Office for the criminally insane; this was in response to concerns regarding the treatment of the criminally insane within county lunatic asylums.[126] Broadmoor Hospital was the first criminal lunatic asylum in England and Wales to admit criminals who were found to be insane at the time of committing an offence and those who developed insanity whilst serving a prison sentence.[127] One of the first patients to be admitted, Martha Bacon, was found "guilty but insane" at the Old Bailey on May 11, 1857, for murdering her 2-year-old son and 11-month-old baby, by cutting their throats.[128] Broadmoor had a capacity for 100 women and 400 male criminals.[129] Not all women found "guilty but insane" were sent to Broadmoor; in some cases, upon request to the Home Office, they were sent to a county asylum. Dr Matheson, Governor and Medical Officer to Holloway Prison, stated that:

> he did not think there was much difference in the time they spent under restraint. If they went to Broadmoor, they did not necessarily stay a long time. Sometimes they get out of Broadmoor more quickly than out of the

county hospitals. Cases are continually reviewed and if they are found to be fit, they are discharged.[130]

Thus, by the middle of the nineteenth century, medical men were involved in assessing mental states by carrying out initial assessments on the insane, compiling expert opinions on abnormal behaviour, using eye witness statements and their own short meetings, and reporting anomalies to the prison governor. This opinion was then presented to the jury to determine whether the defendant was insane, and, in doing so, Freemon suggests, the "medical witness was taking over the function of the jury."[131]

Infanticide cases at the Old Bailey, 1863–1913

There were 152 cases of infanticide recorded at the Old Bailey between 1863 and 1913; 27 of which included a verdict of "guilty but insane," less than 20% of infanticide cases during this period. Twenty-seven is a fair number, although when considering that the existing literature indicates a high level of mental state involvement in infanticide cases, one might have expected this number to be considerably higher. There were three cases in which the question of mental state was fleetingly raised, but the defendant in each case was found to be sane. Eliza Colley was indicted for the wilful murder of her female child on January 27, 1868. Eliza abandoned the child in a field in Hornsey; it was found deceased the following morning, having died from exposure. Emma Colley, her sister, gave evidence. On cross-examination she was asked if her sister was a nervous person; she replied, "yes, so much so that she is subject to fainting fits, and hysterical too."[132] At the inquest Emma had previously stated, "she used to be subject to fainting fits and was at times somewhat strange, but she was never insane."[133] Following her arrest Eliza stated, "I am very sorry: I did not think the child would die";[134] Eliza was found guilty of manslaughter and sentenced to ten years' penal servitude.

In the case of Dinah Cohen, held on March 23, 1896, at the Old Bailey, Dinah was indicted for the wilful murder of her female infant, Maud Cohen. Dinah was found crying in the basement of 82 Cleveland Street by a policeman, where she admitted to killing her infant which was wrapped in a parcel at her feet. The infant was cold and dead and appeared to be three weeks old. The surgeon, Robert Murdoch McClellan, who carried out the post-mortem, deposed that cause of death was asphyxiation, caused by a lump of cotton wool in the mouth. He also stated that:

> just after childbirth, in a girl of a nervous temperament great depression may be caused; it is not unusual to find them not altogether responsible for their actions; they might be described as of unstable equilibrium, a mental shock or strain would upset them, in such a case the suppression of lactation is frequent, but not necessarily; it is a symptom; sometimes it occurs within a week, and may occur again up to the third or fourth week, dilatation of the eyes would be one of the symptoms, the two main reasons of temporary

> distress of mind are mental distress and bodily weakness from defective nourishment; if both those conditions existed in the same woman, that would certainly tend to upset her, I said before the Magistrate that walking about from twelve to six, with mental trouble and insufficient nourishment, might temporarily upset the mind; that is still my opinion.[135]

George Edward Walker, medical officer of H. M. Prison Holloway, also gave evidence deposing that whilst under his observation:

> she has not said or done anything leading me to suppose her not to be of sound mind; she conversed with me in a perfectly rational manner, she seemed to have a perfect recollection of all the facts on the 18th, and referring to her intention at the time, supposing her to be insane at the time this was done, she might afterwards have some recollection of it, but confused, not a perfect recollection, she had given no evidence of insanity while under my observation.[136]

On cross-examination he stated that "I have never been of the opinion that she was insane in the ordinary sense of the word."[137] Dinah was found guilty of manslaughter and recommended to mercy by the jury; she was sentenced to seven years' penal servitude.[138]

Discussion of the mental state of the accused also arose in the case of Eleanor Eslick, accused of the wilful murder of her newly born male infant on March 19, 1912. A witness, Georgina Pegg, stated that Eleanor "looked very ill and she was very excited; she talked a good deal to herself and rather frightened me. It was that that roused my suspicions."[139] Eleanor admitted to Dr Brown, who was subsequently sent for, that she had delivered the child that morning and that when the child was born it was alive, and she subsequently tied a tape around its throat. The post-mortem confirmed that the tape caused asphyxiation, causing the death of the child.

At the trial, Dr Harry Brown, gave the following evidence:

> when confinement comes on women frequently suffer from temporary insanity and they have been known to suffer from delusions; if a woman were having her first confinement by herself, I think those circumstances might send to make her do things without realizing what she was doing.[140]

"Mr. Oliver for the defence urged in mitigation of the sentence that the prisoner did not know what she was doing in concealing the body as she did."[141] So the medical practitioner was recalled by the court, and Dr Brown stated that the "prisoner appeared to him when he saw her to be in a healthy condition mentally, but she did not seem to realize the seriousness of her position, although she certainly knew that what she was doing was wrong."[142] Eleanor pleaded guilty to concealment of birth, and the jury returned a verdict to that effect; she was sentenced to four months' imprisonment.[143] It appears that the reason for Eleanor's acquittal of murder stemmed from uncertain mental state evidence.

The following cases are examples of those 27 recorded at the Old Bailey during this period, with a "guilty but insane" verdict, and focus in particular on the testimony given by mental state experts. In the case of Harriet Goodliffe, for instance, a discussion arose surrounding the disease of her mind. Harriet, a married woman, was indicted for the wilful murder of her eight- or nine-month-old infant, the youngest of her three children, on May 11, 1863. The first witness who lived below the accused stated that:

> I went up and saw her standing near the window with the child in her arms, her husband was with her, she was hallowing out in a very senseless state, so that people were coming around to see what was going on, I stopped there till she was quiet, and then went down, about half past 1. I was called up again by the little boy and girl, I found the prisoner standing in the doorway I caught hold of her, and she dropped the child to the ground I thought she was out of her mind the little boy, ten years old, took the child from the ground the husband came and took her on his knee, and I went down again; between 3 and 4 o'clock I went up again, hearing a noise, the poor woman was screaming I saw her standing near the window the upper part of the child was then gone I stayed and took care of the prisoner till the policeman came and took her in charge, I afterwards saw the child outside the house, the window was down, and she had her hands raised like, hanging onto it the child was then gone, I stayed and took care of the prisoner till the policeman came and took her in charge, I afterwards saw the child outside the house.[144]

On cross-examination, Christian Kahler stated that he believed her to be "quite out of her senses."[145] Granger Tandy, a surgeon, who examined the child, deposed that:

> it was very much injured, as if from a fall, there was a fracture at the base of the skull, those injuries were the cause of death, I did not see the prisoner then, I had seen her two days before, I then believed her to be of unsound mind, from her general incoherence of manner and demeanor, I think she was then in a condition to know the difference between right and wrong; but her state was such that it was in progress to a condition in which she would not know what was right and what was wrong.[146]

The surgeon of Newgate Gaol, John Rowland Gibson, stated that "the prisoner has been about ten days under my care in the gaol, I consider her to be of unsound mind."[147] On cross-examination he was asked, "I believe you have had a great deal of experience in cases of homicidal mania?" He replied:

> I have, it is not at all an uncommon thing, after the act of homicide has been committed, for the mind partially to recover itself, I do not consider that she has completely recovered her mind yet, she is still of unsound mind.[148]

He was then asked, "when she came under your care was the disease of her mind to such an extent that she might mistake right for wrong?" To which he replied, "I think it was."[149] Harriet was found "not guilty on the ground of insanity and ordered to be detained during Her Majesty's Pleasure";[150] she was committed to Broadmoor, where she remained until her death.[151]

In contrast to the case of Harriet is the case of Adelaide Freedman where the potential link between melancholy and acts of violence was discussed. Adelaide was indicted for the wilful murder of her month-old daughter on November 22, 1869; she also attempted suicide. Her husband had left her five years ago, for Peru; in his absence, Adelaide had formed a relationship with another man, as a result of which this child was born. Upon hearing that her husband was returning she became "despondent … and administered poison to the child and took a portion herself."[152]

At the Old Bailey, the prisoner's sister testified that Adelaide:

> always had a vacant look, both before and after the birth of the child, I saw her three times a week after the birth of the child, and observed on those occasions a strangeness about her appearance and manner when I attempted to speak to her, she was always melancholy, and used to complain dreadfully of her head – she always behaved to the child with kindness and affection.[153]

She continued by stating that other family members had been confined due to mental illness; their mother and brother had a history of mental disease, and two aunts were committed to a lunatic asylum. After Adelaide had poisoned her child, the landlady testified that Adelaide said, "my head is so bad I shall go mad, my troubles are so great" – she seemed quite unconscious of what she was doing."[154] As Adelaide had not only administered salts of lemon to her daughter, she had also ingested the poison herself, and she was treated by Mr Morrison, surgeon, who described her as having:

> a wild vacant look which made him suspicious of her sanity—the peculiar look of puerperal mania, which is a well-recognized form of insanity with women about the period of their confinement—it affects them when they are not able to give milk to a child, and is the consequence of it. This form of puerperal mania develops itself sometimes by acts of violence to the nearest and dearest, and to the offspring of the woman—there is no fixed period at which it arrives at insanity, sometimes one and sometimes two weeks after confinement—there are two forms, the acute, wild, raving, and the other is the melancholy sort, with which there are no delusions.[155]

On cross-examination, he was asked to reaffirm that:

> melancholy, is without delusions—they both lead to acts of violence—the second form is the melancholy type, and is what the prisoner's symptoms indicated—the second form is a recognized form of insanity; there are no

> delusions, but it leads to acts of violence—I do not believe that persons who have that melancholy form have sufficient control over themselves to prevent them committing crime.[156]

Mr Morrison was then asked, was it his opinion that:

> in a person labouring under puerperal mania the killing of a child may be the result of an uncontrollable impulse seizing her at the time the act is done; but it may be done with a knowledge on the part of the mother that the act she is doing will cause death? Knowing that the act of giving poison or cutting a child's throat would cause death, might she still be under that uncontrollable mania which would cause her to do it?[157]

Mr Morrison replied, "yes." He was then asked, "where you find melancholy puerperal mania, do you often find acts of violence?"[158] to which he replied:

> in both sorts of puerperal mania you may have infanticide—more kill their children than kill themselves—I draw a distinction between puerperal mania and homicidal mania—I did not observe these symptoms before she was confined, not till about a fortnight after, and then they did not appear to be at all alarming; there was a peculiar expression of the eyes, but no other symptom—there was only sufficient for me to warn the friends; my assistant warned the sister, and I spoke to her myself—puerperal mania may come on as long as six weeks after a confinement.[159]

John Rowland Gibson, prison surgeon, concurred with the evidence, testifying that "she has been in a melancholy condition the whole time she has been in Newgate, I have not been able to enter into any conversation with her-my opinion is that she is in a peculiar condition, amounting to a form of insanity."[160]

Following Mr Gibson's testimony, the judge stated that he had "witnesses present to prove the insanity of the prisoner's mother, grandmother, and great-grandmother."[161] The jury stated that they were of the unanimous opinion that on the "9th October, the prisoner was in such a mental condition as to be incapable of distinguishing right from wrong";[162] Adelaide was therefore found not guilty on the grounds of insanity. The interesting issue this case presents is the way the jury apparently spontaneously translates an "irresistible impulse" defence, strictly outside McNaughtan into a "right from wrong defence."[163] It therefore seems that in this case they were "linking the effects of puerperal mania to lay testimony describing the prisoner as "quite unconscious of what she was doing" and melancholy's ability to impaired knowledge that the act was wrong."[164] Adelaide Freedman was also committed to Broadmoor Lunatic Asylum, where she remained until her death in 1912, aged 72.[165]

Inaccuracies surrounding diagnosis are also reflected in the cases. In the case of Sarah Norman, for example, her GP's original diagnosis was one of temporary malady, a diagnosis which was clearly incorrect. Sarah, a married woman, was indicted for the wilful murder of her female child, on January 10, 1881, by stabbing the child in the head and then throwing her into the fire.[166] The child had been delivered by midwife, Mary Ann Morley, on December 14, 1880. On December 17, the midwife was called to see Sarah, where she found her to be:

> looking very wild and strange about the eyes. I saw blood on the floor, and asked her how it came there, she said it was "where I cut the baby with the scissors." She said that she took the scissors from a nail over her sister's portrait, and had put them on the mantelshelf, I saw them there covered with blood … I saw the child dead and lying on a pillow, I saw that it was quite dead, I waited till the sergeant came, and then I removed it to the back room, Mr. Kelsey, the doctor, came with the sergeant.[167]

On cross-examination, the midwife stated that:

> I had not noticed anything strange about her till this occurrence, not the slightest, I went in and found her in that strange wild state, and when I spoke to her she was a long while before she answered; she answered fairly clear, but still there was an amount of strangeness about her, when I asked her the reason she had done it, she said that the baby was so tiresome and wanted to keep sucking so, she had not complained of her breasts to me; she was to let me know if anything was the matter, I have attended many cases of confinement, and have seen cases of puerperal mania before; it comes on suddenly.[168]

Arthur Kelsey, GP, who also attended Sarah Norman following the murder, asked her why she had done it, and repeating the question several times she replied:

> "Because it cried" I asked her if that was the only reason, she said "Two nights ago I thought I should kill it"—I asked her if something told her she must get out of bed and kill the child—she said "No; I got out of bed because it cried, and I put the scissors into its brain"—she also said that while speaking to her I was noticing the condition she was in; she seemed not to be able to collect her ideas, in fact she seemed to have no ideas at all; she did not seem to be all affected by the crime she had done—it did not seem to make the slightest impression upon her—having had that conversation with her I came to the conclusion that she was suffering from puerperal mania—that is frequently attendant upon confinements; it generally comes on from twenty-four hours to a fortnight after the confinement, and very suddenly, without any warning—there are no premonitory symptoms at all—I have attended her since, and saw her on various occasions—I was examined at the police-court, and said "I am of opinion that the prisoner is still suffering from puerperal insanity"—I saw the child immediately after I put those questions to the mother—it was then lying in a corner of the room on a pillow covered up with some sheets; it was burnt; nearly the whole of the skin of the body was

> charred and blackened, and its head had a wound on the top penetrating the whole depth of the brain; that was the cause of instantaneous death.[169]

On cross-examination he believed Sarah to be experiencing a temporary malady, stating that he did have:

> reason to hope she will get right again, it is only a temporary malady—she is a great deal better than when I last saw her, and I hope she will be perfectly well in a short time, and in a perfectly sound state of mind—she was not accountable for her actions when she committed this crime, I do not think she knew that what she was doing was wrong, as when she did it she was not of sound mind.[170]

Sarah was found "not guilty on the grounds of insanity" and ordered to be detained under Her Majesty's Pleasure. Notwithstanding the fact that the GP believed Sarah to be experiencing a mere temporary malady, she too was committed to Broadmoor, where she remained until her death.[171]

In contrast to the case of Sarah Norman is the case of Mary Ann Reynolds, who lived with her husband, and was indicted for the wilful murder of her five-month-old infant. During the trial at the Old Bailey on September 17, 1888, Dr Sidney Lloyd Smith, GP, gave evidence, stating that he was called upon to visit Mary, where she stated, "I clutched the baby round the neck and found it was dead."[172] Regarding Mary's state of mind he went onto state that:

> the prisoner had called upon me about a month previous, about the vaccination of this very baby; she appeared most anxious about it; she would not allow me to vaccinate it from another child, but from the calf—that arose from her extreme consideration for the child—I arranged to get some calf lymph, but meanwhile this happened-from what I saw of her, I formed the opinion that at that time she was insane—I came to that conclusion from her previous history that I got from her husband, also from the fact of this coming on during the time of suckling—there is a well—recognized form of insanity which comes on then, it is a form of puerperal mama—this was about five months after her confinement, her milk had not been flowing quite freely just before this, and she had a lot of trouble, she had three broken ribs, followed by inflammation of the lungs, and six days after her confinement her husband lost his situation, she was suffering from a great deal of trouble.[173]

Philip Francis Gilbert, surgeon to Her Majesty's Gaol, Holloway, who also gave evidence during the trial, deposed that:

> the prisoner was under my constant observation there from the 11th August—she was suffering from delusions when she came, and in my opinion was of unsound mind—she was not in a condition to know the nature of the act she had committed, after some time the delusions passed away, she was brought

> to me with a letter stating that she was violent in the hospital; that drew my attention to her, she was under the delusion that her husband was then in the ward—she was sleepless and restless, and complaining very much of her head, she improved, and is perfectly rational now, so as to know the nature of the present proceedings.[174]

The jury found Mary "guilty of the act, being insane at the time, and was ordered to be detained as a criminal lunatic until Her Majesty's Pleasure be known."[175]

Asneth Cohen was indicted for the wilful murder of her new-born female infant on March 7, 1898, by throwing the child out of an open window, three stories above ground level. On searching her room, "traces of the woman's pain and trouble were evident in the bloodstains found on articles of clothing."[176] Shortly after the incident, Asneth wandered out of the house without outdoor clothing and was missing for several hours. She finally visited some friends who described her to be "wandering in her mind and strange in her manner, besides without either coat or hat."[177]

At the Whitechapel's Coroners Court, Asneth was "present in court in custody and appeared to feel her position acutely."[178] She was:

> about 22 years of age and a little over 5 foot in height, she is of a pronounced Jewish type, dark skinned, dark eyed, lips rather thick and prominent and a profusion of jetty black hair, being thick set and inclined to stoutness, her condition seems to have escaped even the keener eyed amongst her neighbours.[179]

The jury returned a verdict of guilty of wilful murder:

> but desired to add that she was not responsible for her action but were told by the coroner that that was beyond their province. The jury replied that they were unanimous on the point and added a rider suggesting that the young woman's mind should be inquired into.[180]

Mr Myers, Asneth's solicitor, said the prisoner was "very ill and had been wandering the streets for two days."[181] The police did not discuss the charge with her immediately, but when confronted and the charge read to her, she replied, "Yes I threw the baby out of the window, it was on a Sunday night, I don't want them to kill me."[182]

Upon Asneth's admittance to Whitechapel Infirmary, she was seen by Herbert Larder, medical superintendent. In his testimony he claimed that she did not seem to understand him; he believed this was because she spoke and understood little English, as opposed to lack of understanding due to her mental state, her first language being Yiddish. He examined her and found her to have recently delivered a child, but he also found her to be "very weak and of a high nervous temperament and very likely under the circumstances might be subject to puerperal mania."[183] She was found "guilty, but insane" and ordered to be detained in Holloway Prison during Her Majesty's Pleasure. *The Lloyds Weekly London Newspaper* reported that the jury found the accused "guilty, but that she was not accountable for her actions when she committed the deed, an order for her detention as a criminal lunatic was made."[184]

The cases from the Old Bailey have demonstrated how few "insanity trials" there were between 1863 and 1913, both in terms of those with a guilty but insane verdict, but more broadly trials in which evidence was entered suggesting mental impairment or derangement at the time of the offence. Whilst women might or might not have experienced puerperal mania at the time of the offence, the criminal justice process showed great reluctance in pursuing this defence and a punishment which resulted in indeterminate detention. The wiser approach for infanticidal women would have been to plead guilty to concealment of birth and receive a short prison sentence; 66 women during this period were found guilty of concealment of birth and given varying lengths of prison sentences, of up to 2 years, and a further 48 accused women were found not guilty. The remaining number of women were found either guilty of murder and received a reprieve or were found guilty of manslaughter.

The cases also indicate that the women who received "guilty but insane" verdicts were often accused of killing older infants, an element which appears inconsistent with the other cases of infanticide in this thesis. This could relate to the fact that there was less room for uncertainty as to the cause of death or live birth. A further inconsistency rests with the fact that the majority of women in these cases were married, and, in many cases, they were multiparas; the murdered child was not their first born. The link between insanity and lactation is also reflected in many of the cases, highlighting in particular the contextual factors associated with nursing mothers, such as poverty, exhaustion, anaemia, dehydration, and stress.

Infanticide cases in Hull and the surrounding area, 1863–1913

In Hull and the surrounding area there were four infanticide cases involving an "insanity trial" reported in the newspapers. The first case was Jane Crompton, accused of the wilful murder of her four-month-old child in May 1873 by severing the head with a kitchen knife. At the inquest, held before Mr J. J. Thorney at Mr Charles Kirk's, at Tynemouth Castle Inn, in Osbourne Street, Hull, the coroner thought it unnecessary to call any medical evidence:

> the law provided that if any person took the life of another after great provocation the crime was reduced to manslaughter. There could not possibly however be any provocation in this instance. The whole facts lay in a nutshell. The question as to the state of the woman's mind whether she was sane or otherwise would have to be dealt with by another court and that need not engage the attention of the jury at all. The jury without hesitation returned a verdict of wilful murder against Jane Crompton.[185]

The *York Herald* reported that at the inquest it was stated, "that the prisoner's mind has of late wandered and that she had taken a dislike to the child."[186]

At the Assizes Court, before Mr Baron Pollock, in his charge to the grand jury, he stated that:

> when the case came to be fully inquired into hereafter by the common jury, that some explanation might be given as to how so fearful and horrible a thing came to be committed, but he need not tell them that whatever might be the state of the mind of the prisoner it would be no part of their duty to inquire into that. It would be their job merely to inquire into the facts proved as to the commission of the deed.[187]

Mr Tempest Anderson, deputy surgeon, at York Castle, gave evidence at the trial. He stated that he had:

> seen the prisoner many times whilst a prisoner in York Castle. She was suffering from melancholia which often led to suicide and murder. It might lead to a state of mind that the patient would not be alive to the nature of the action she was committing and might lead to the commission of an action which the patient might not be able to stop. When he was re-examined, he said that it was possible that a person suffering from melancholia might be able to distinguish between right and wrong, and yet not be able to prevent themselves from the commission of an act.[188]

The surgeon stated that Jane was insane and that in his "dealings with her she knew the difference between right and wrong, but probably didn't at the time the murder took place."[189] He had investigated and discovered a letter from a "surgeon at a lunatic asylum stating that Jane had numerous psychological problems, she also had a brother and a cousin who were classed as insane and incarcerated in an asylum."[190] As a result, the jury delivered a verdict of not guilty on the ground of insanity and "the prisoner was ordered to be detained during Her Majesty's Pleasure."[191] When asked why she had performed such a terrible thing, she replied that she would never have done so "if the neighbours had treated me properly."[192]

Catherine Hutton, in March 1876, a scullery maid at Everingham Park, near Pocklington, was charged with attempting to murder her new-born child by throwing it down a privy; at the trial she held the child in her arms. The defence urged:

> she could not have been conscious of what she was doing at the time, she put the child into the privy and that the kind of manner in which she attended to it afterwards proved that she never would have had a malicious intention to take its life away.[193]

The article does not state who was called to give evidence; however, as she could not have been conscious of her actions at the time of the incident, the jury accepted the evidence and found her not guilty: she was subsequently discharged.

The inquest into the death of Mrs Wiles in August 1891, who took her own life and that of her child, demonstrates how serious melancholia could be; her body was found by a lamp lighter who was in the process of extinguishing gas lamps in a line with the Timber Pond, at the east end of the Victoria Dock. He noticed the body of a female floating on the surface of the pond, her arms outstretched. Whilst attempting to retrieve the body he also noticed the body of an infant, and both bodies were removed and transferred to Castle Street Mortuary, later identified by George Wiles as his 19-year-old wife and their 6-month-old child. Mr Wiles had taken work on the Keel Guiding Star, as a purchase-man, and had left Hull a month previously, not returning until Saturday night when he discovered them missing.[194]

At the coroner's court before Mr Alfred Thorney, it was stated that:

> all she had in her pocket when Mr Wiles left her was a shilling, he never sent her any remittance or even a letter which led to her feeling so despondent that there was no doubt she made away herself and the child. A neighbour saw the deceased standing with the child in her arms at the top of Maisters Entry between eight and nine o'clock on Saturday night. She was crying, so she asked her what the matter was, but she did not reply, she offered to take the child and nurse it, but Mrs Wiles walked away. On her body was a note saying "Goody-bye mother don't weep for me but love my child for my sake. Good-bye all, yours truly." It is believed she jumped into the Timber Pond. The jury returned a verdict of committed suicide, whilst in a state of temporary insanity.[195]

The following passage from a *Driffield Times* article, implies that the crowd witnessing the proceedings, blamed Mr Wiles for the deaths of his wife and her child:

> throughout Monday, Salthouse Lane bore an unusually crowded appearance and any stranger casually passing through would at once have recognized that something out of the common had occurred, whenever Mr Wiles the husband of the dead woman appeared to be met with a very hostile reception and in the morning a scene of great excitement was witnessed. Many people were not satisfied with relieving their feelings by shouting and hooting at him, but went so far as to aim any handy missile at him and but for the assistance of PC Murray, it is highly probable that he would have received severe ill treatment at the hands of the crowd. Towards evening the crowd increased and when about eight o'clock the hearse arrived for the mortuary, containing the bodies the street was literally packed, women as usual predominating. Mr Wiles was hustled by the crowd as he left the inquest.[196]

The case of Mrs Wiles epitomises the link between infanticide, abandonment, and poverty, and as Chadwick has identified and argued, the courts were more likely to accept poverty as an excuse for a woman to kill her infant than a man who killed his infant.[197]

Frances Bryan, in September 1910, was a young married woman residing in Hull, who was charged with the murder of her infant and attempted suicide:

> from the police evidence it appeared that the prisoner and her child were found by neighbours suffering from the effects of poison. The child died but the mother recovered and was discharged as cured. A neighbour stated that Mrs Bryan told her she had bought a packet of rat poison and shared it with her baby. Dr Lilley was called to attend the child and he asked a police witness if the prisoner knew what she was saying, when she said she had poisoned her child. Detective Burton said I thought she did.[198]

Interestingly, in this case, the doctor appears to base his assessment of Frances on a statement made by the police witness rather than assessing the prisoner himself.

In conclusion, these cases demonstrate inconsistencies with the general perception that there were a large number of "guilty but insane" verdicts in infanticide cases, and they do so on two levels. The first is there were few cases in which mental state evidence was given, despite the evolving profession of the mental state expert and their increasing involvement within murder cases; there are a surprisingly low number of "guilty but insane" verdicts. Secondly, despite the growing legal and medical discourse on puerperal insanity, there are a surprisingly low number of cases in which puerperal insanity is referred to.

The beginning of the twentieth century was a period in history which experienced a significant shift towards a greater interest in child welfare and a deeper concern for motherhood, a shift that began following the Boer War when both the health of the nation and the dwindling numbers of the population were raised, a concern which continued following World War I. Concerns were so great that a steady number of pieces of legislation were implemented aimed at the welfare of infants and the improvements in maternity care;[199] broader changes within England and Wales, which arguably influenced significant legislative changes in infanticide in the 1920s and 1930s.

The twentieth century continued to see evidence of common factors in cases of infanticide; infanticide was an enduring crime strongly associated with mothers and continued to be difficult to prove. Public reaction to new-born child murder also continued to be unpredictable, "as attitudes towards perpetrators flit between sympathy and condemnation."[200] The implementation of the Infanticide Act 1922 not only brought a significant change to the way women were prosecuted, but it created the new offence of "infanticide."[201] Notwithstanding the fact that commentators argued that women who killed their new-born infants were least likely to have killed their child as a result of an "imbalanced mind,"[202] the Act created a partial defence for women who killed their new-born infant if they could prove that the balance of their mind was disturbed as a result of giving birth. They argued that women who killed their older infants were more likely to have experienced an imbalance of mind at the time of the killing, but, as these infants were not considered to be new-born, these women fell outside the statute.

This section will now concentrate on the twentieth century, arguing that, despite the implementation of the Infanticide Act 1922 and Infanticide Act 1938, women accused of killing their babies were rarely found insane.[203] This section will begin with the Infanticide Act 1922, drawing on cases from across the United Kingdom, and continue with the Infanticide Act 1938, drawing on cases between the period 1914 and 1955, held at the Old Bailey and Hull and surrounding area.

Twentieth-century legislation

As highlighted in Chapter 1, the passing of the 1922 Infanticide Act was a milestone for infanticidal women, as it created a partial defence to murder. Grey has argued that the reason for not passing the Infanticide Act 1922 before this time related to the difficulty in reaching "any consensus among critics, about the most appropriate way of dealing with this special offence."[204]

The long-awaited 1922 Infanticide Bill, according to Ward, was triggered by "humanitarian sentiment,"[205] which Grey has argued emanated from a "focused campaign in Leicester after the 1921 conviction for new-born child murder of Edith Mary Roberts."[206] The infant was discovered in a box with an item of clothing tied tightly around its mouth; Edith had concealed both her pregnancy and delivery, and no one had suspected her of either, until the body of the infant was discovered. Edith was found guilty of murder by an all-male jury and sentenced to death, with strong recommendations for mercy; her sentence was later commuted to penal servitude for life. This decision provoked a strong reaction from the Women's Freedom League, and in particular referring to the defence counsel, who wished to exclude women from the jury as he "wanted a fair jury and he did not think that women were fair to their own sex."[207] The secretary of the League argued that the unfairness lay in the fact that the father of the child was not present in court to take responsibility; Edith had taken sole responsibility. The League were also offended when the judge, in summing up, told the jury "to steel their hearts against being led away by sympathy for a woman," along with the fact that Edith's counsel was a man and not a woman.[208] Crucially, this trial came at a time when a number of significant changes in sex equality were taking place regarding women's rights in general and within the law; the Sex Disqualification (Removal) Act 1919 and the Law of Property Act 1922 are two such examples, allowing women access to the legal profession, and permitting husband and wife to inherit equally respectively.

The first case to be held at the Lincolnshire Assizes, at Lincoln Castle, following the Infanticide Act 1922, was that of Emma Temple, in October 1922, where Mr Justice Lush described the provisions as a "new, wise and merciful Act."[209] Emma pleaded guilty to infanticide, stating, "I plead guilty, but at the time I did not know what I was doing."[210] Mr Justice Lush went onto state, "I do not know what that plea may be. It is not very definite. You plead guilty to taking the life of the child, but owing to the fact, you having just given birth to it, your mind was off its balance?"[211] To which Emma replied, "yes my lord."[212] His lordship said the prisoner had:

> acted quite rightly in pleading guilty to the offence of infanticide. He was most thankful that under the Act of Parliament which in his opinion, and was sure in the opinion of many, was a most wise and humane piece of legislation, it was not necessary to put her on trial for the indictment of murder.[213]

Emma was sentenced to four months' imprisonment. Mr Justice Lush, in summing up, described the Infanticide Act 1922 as being a

> fresh step in the improvement of criminal law and his lordship was glad to avail himself of its provisions. He felt great pity for the prisoner, and if one consulted one's own feelings, one would be glad to have said she had suffered punishment enough. He must however take care that the way he dealt with her should be a deterrent to others. A young woman about to become a mother must make proper provision for her child.[214]

The Infanticide Act 1922 gave rise to a number of sentiments and perceptions of the underlying intentions of the Act. Resnick believed that if a woman was found to be insane at the time of the crime and therefore not responsible, she should not then be subsequently convicted of a lesser crime,[215] whereas Mr Justice Sankey, in passing sentence on Maggie Page from Rotherham, in May 1923, at the West Riding Assizes, stated,

> it was important that people understood what the law of infanticide meant. The 1922 Act was not passed to make people who committed offences of this nature not guilty, but in order that they should be dealt with more mercifully.[216]

Maggie's child was found drowned in a bucket, and Maggie was discovered with a cut to her right breast; a charge of attempted suicide was not proceeded with, and she received a three-month prison sentence.

Merciful sentencing is reflected in the opinion of Mr Justice Sankey's, in the case of Nellie Lister; Nellie was employed in a public house in Doncaster, where she gave birth to a child in April 1923; she placed the body of the child in a tin box and then concealed the box in a drawer. The body was discovered with tape around the neck, and the post-mortem reported that the child had had a separate existence. "In a statement to the jury Lister said she did not know what she was doing at the time. She had been ill for three days before it happened and had had much pain."[217] A young miner wanted to marry her, and as she had a friend who was prepared to take care of her until the ceremony could be performed, the judge stated she was to be spared prison;[218] the marriage took place on July 14, 1923.[219]

Initially, it appears the Infanticide Act 1922 was accepted by the courts without fault, as it was considered to be favourable towards infanticidal women. For example:

> the new provision brings legal into line with moral justice. A mother so distracted as to consider killing her child is not likely to be deterred by any penalty and in any case, for the last 15 years the harsh provision of the law has been got round either by the refusal of the juries to convict, or by the clemency of the home office, yet infanticide has not increased. The reduction of the law to the part of fiction, nevertheless tended to lessen the force and dignity of the courts at the same time proved the need for reform.[220]

Despite being initially welcomed by the courts, the Act was criticised by medical professionals who believed it did not go far enough in providing protection for women who were at risk of lactational disturbances.[221] These women may have experienced both physical and emotional related disturbances associated with lack of sleep, exhaustion, and emotional stress, factors that collectively might have affected the mother's state of mind.[222] A further shortcoming of the 1922 Act was its exclusion of a definition of the term "new-born," a point raised in the case of Mary O'Donoghue. Mary was in great distress during the weeks following the birth, as a consequence of poverty and malnutrition; she was accused of killing her 35-day-old child, a crime she freely admitted. She was sentenced to death, a sentence later commuted to penal servitude for life. It was argued at her trial that she had not fully recovered from the effects of giving birth, and at the time of the act her mind was disturbed. The court discussed what constitutes "newly born," and it was held that it was for the "jury in every case to decide whether the child was newly born or not."[223] Ward argues that the decision in O'Donoghue faced criticism from both medical and legal commentators for

> perpetuating the solemn and almost blasphemous farce of sentencing a woman to death with all the accessories of the black cap etc, when everyone in court, except perhaps the unhappy victim, was well aware there was no prospect of the sentence being carried into effect.[224]

McIlroy argued that, since Mr Justice Avory confirmed that a child aged three weeks did not fall into the definition of new-born, the circumstances of Mary O'Donoghue were not covered by the 1922 Act, and as a result it is unclear "what constitutes in a law a newly born child."[225] She claimed that in medicine the definition of a new-born is contradictory, "obstetricians look upon the newly born or neo-natal infant as under ten days old, but for purposes of mortality statistics and diseases, this period is extended to one month."[226] She called for the term newly born to be erased from the 1922 Act, replacing it with an age limit ranging between six and nine months from the day of the child's birth.[227] McIlroy also called for an extension of the definition of puerperal insanity to include lactational insanity, arguing that in criminal asylums there are many women "incarcerated because of homicidal acts towards their infants or children due to lactational insanity."[228] These women are not "fully recovered from the effects of giving birth and so should be entitled to the benefits of the Infanticide Act's provisions."[229] Grey argues that the term new-born was left intentionally ambiguous and undefined, as it assisted the:

> civil service and politicians to try and help ease through a measure that had been repeatedly rejected in previous years, and where in any case it was felt that setting an age limit for the potential victim was ultimately arbitrary.[230]

In the case of Mrs Brenda Hale, the Infanticide Act 1922 was also criticised; Brenda was a 24-year-old farmer's wife and was charged with both the murder of her 3-week-old son before attempting suicide; both were discovered with wounds to their throats. Brenda was admitted initially to Holloway Prison, as she was presenting with signs of mental confusion and fatigue. During an initial examination of her, it was reported that "she could not remember killing the baby, the first thing she could remember of the incidents of that morning, was seeing herself with her throat cut in front of a mirror."[231]

During the trial Mr Justice Humphreys criticised the Infanticide Act 1922 for its ambiguity towards the term "new-born," leaving the courts to interpret its meaning in each individual case. Mr Justice Humphreys did not deem the child to be new-born; however, the depression Brenda was experiencing through lactational exhaustion meant her mind was clearly disturbed. Shortly after the case of Brenda Hale, arguments were made for both a specific definition of the term "newly born," and the time limit for puerperal insanity to be extended, encompassing the effects of lactational insanity on the mother's state of mind as a mitigating factor.[232] In his address to the jury, Mr Justice Humphreys stated:

> if you return the verdict which I think you will return, that this woman was not responsible for her actions, that relieves me from the necessity for having to sentence a person whom you may think ought not be sentenced for any offence, but has done an act for which she was not responsible by reason of her insanity.[233]

Brenda was found guilty of murder but insane; she attempted suicide and was ordered to be detained during His Majesty's Pleasure.[234] In passing the sentence, Mr Justice Humphreys said he believed the statement "guilty but insane unfortunate, as it suggested that a person was guilty of murder, but it did not mean that it was acquittal."[235]

The term "newly born" was also discussed in the case of Ivy Toulson, who was accused of the wilful murder of her six-week-old child by throwing it into a boating lake in a Sheffield public park. If a child ceases to be a new-born at the age of four weeks, for example, would a mother be guilty of infanticide before this time and guilty of wilful murder after four weeks?[236] The defence in this case argued that the child was lively and it sprang out of the mother's arms and fell into the water, and as there was no evidence to contradict this point, Ivy was found not guilty and discharged.[237]

In 1938 the Infanticide Act was passed, which addressed and clarified the two fundamental shortcomings of the 1922 Act. Clarification of the age of the infant – infanticide should include all infants under the age of 12 months, and the effects of lactation on the state of mind of the mother, in addition to the effect of the birth alone. Section 1 (1) of the Infanticide Act 1938 reads:

> where a woman by any wilful act or omission causes the death of her child being under the age of twelve months, but at the time of the act or omission the balance of her mind was disturbed by reason of her not having fully recovered from the effect of giving birth to the child, or by reason of the effect of lactation consequent upon the birth of the child, the [if] the circumstances were such that but for this Act the offence would have amounted to murder [or manslaughter], she shall be guilty of felony, to wit of infanticide, and for such offence be dealt with and punished as if she had been guilty of the offence of manslaughter of the child.[238]

The 1938 Act was also criticised for stressing the weakness of motherhood associated with childbirth and lactation, an issue that has been regarded as a "male chauvinistic sentiment"[239] and exclusive.[240] The exclusivity towards the age of the child in general and to the mother in particular; if a woman should kill her older child or someone else's child she would fall outside the statute.

Infanticide cases at the Old Bailey, 1914–1955

The period 1914–1955 adds a new element to the historiography of infanticide; evidence continues to be prevalent of the common motivations behind infanticide; women murdering their illegitimate infants to protect their reputations, and hide their shame; however, married women were also committing infanticide. Married women who became pregnant whilst their husbands were away from home fighting in the war were also desperate to hide the evidence of their adulterous behaviour. The women in Hull were just as mentally and physically affected by warfare as the women in London; during World War II, Hull was the second most-bombed city in England after London with "ninety-five per cent of houses either destroyed or damaged."[241]

In the 40-year period 1914–1955, there were at least 39 cases of infanticide tried at the Old Bailey reported in the British newspapers, although the first of these was not reported until 1922. It is possible that not all cases were reported in the press; the numbers, therefore, may not be an accurate reflection of the number of trials during this time; however, the cases reported will provide a general trend.

Of the 39 cases reported at the Old Bailey, in 21 cases, women were bound over: 9 women were discharged, 2 were ordered to go into a home, 3 were sent to prison, and 4 were detained during His Majesty's Pleasure. Six of these women were found guilty but insane, and were either detained during His Majesty's Pleasure or bound over to be cared for by family members. This final section will examine some of the most detailed expert testimony from the newspaper evidence.

Mrs Jennie Margaret Dormer, November 1938, was described as almost insane at her trial. Her infant was found dead in the gas oven; she said she was troubled by the recent crisis and worried she could not get gas masks for her two young children. Mr Christmas Humphreys, prosecuting, stated that "Mrs Dormer had not recovered from the birth of her second child when the crisis came. It had such an effect on her mind that she became almost insane. She put the child in the gas oven and it died from gas poisoning."[242] The Governor and Medical Officer of Holloway Prison, Dr Matheson, stated that "Mrs Dormer had steadily improved in prison and was now comparatively well."[243] She was to stay with a friend in the country until she was fully recovered and so she was bound over for two years.[244]

Dr Matheson also gave evidence in the case of Agnes Maud Hope in July 1939. Agnes, who worked as a chambermaid in a hotel, pleaded guilty to infanticide and attempting to conceal the birth of her newly born child by the secret disposal of the child's body.[245] The body was discovered in a cupboard in her room with several injuries, including a fractured skull. Dr Matheson said she was:

> certifiable as a feeble-minded person under the Mental Deficiency Act. There was a escort in Court to take the woman to a hospital in Essex, where she would be detained under the order and treated as a feeble-minded person.[246]

Mr Justice Humphreys confirmed that:

> on the medical evidence I am satisfied she is a mental defective, and I make an order to that effect. The result of it will be that she will be taken away and detained as a mental defective.[247]

Towards the end of the nineteenth century, "feeblemindedness" was identified as a category of mental defectiveness. The "feebleminded" occupied a "critical and social space" between the "educationally and socially normal and the pathological."[248] Individuals diagnosed with feeblemindedness were argued to be "blighted by mental incapacity for making correct moral judgements, and therefore as incurable inadequates."[249] When a diagnosis was made, the label of "criminal" was removed and replaced with the label "irresponsible." On this basis conventional forms of penal punishment or detention were abandoned as ineffective for such a condition and were replaced with life-long detention; individuals were segregated in special institutions.[250] Mary Dendy (1855–1933), an advocate of residential schools for the mentally handicapped, became a promoter of the "feebleminded." She believed in segregating such people to prevent them from committing a crime and to prevent them from passing such problems onto their children; in other words, the social problems these people experienced were seen as intrinsically linked to their feeblemindedness.[251]

At the trial of Freda Lydia Wray, November 1938, it was found that she was in a distressed condition in her living room with her four-month-old infant dead in the perambulator; Freda also had a history of mental illness.[252] It was determined by the marks of discolouration and bruising around the child's neck that death was caused by asphyxiation due to strangulation. Freda had bathed and dressed the child; however, she began to feel unwell, her head was aching, and the room was spinning, and the child would not stop crying. Following the birth of her first child in 1934, she experienced a nervous breakdown in 1936, and following the birth of this child, her mental condition was reportedly becoming "alarming." Dr Hearn found her "mentally distressed and showing signs of abnormal depression,"[253] and Dr Matheson, described her as being "mentally upset when she went to the prison, but she was very much better now";[254] he believed that Freda would benefit from care and attention in an institution.[255] It was considered that she may best be cared for by her parents with her sister as a companion, as a "satisfactory form of treatment, than any which could be obtained in an institution."[256] Mr Justice Asquith stated that "he was perfectly satisfied that when Mrs Wray did what she had done, her state of mind was disturbed by the state of her health."[257]

Whereas Mrs Patricia Waller was described as "weeping silently as she entered the dock at the Old Bailey"[258] in July 1942, as she pleaded guilty to infanticide. Mr Christmas Humphreys, prosecuting, stated that this was a

> pathetic story of a young woman, happily married, who deliberately killed her first-born child, whom she undoubtedly loved. Since her confinement she had been feeling very queer and tired, and when she heard that her husband's ship had been sunk she became so bad that she felt life was not worth living, and she decided her husband was drowned she would do away with herself and the child.[259]

She described how she was walking beside the lake and a terrible urge came over her to pick the child up, kiss it, and drop it into the water; she meant to go with him, but she was a coward. Mr Curtis Bennett (defending) stated, "since the passing of the 1938 Infanticide Act, never had there been a case more clearly within its provisions than that pathetic case."[260] She was bound over for two years to reside with her sister in Colchester until her husband returned from sea, when she would be in his care.[261]

Infanticide cases in Hull and the surrounding area, 1914–1955

During the period 1915–1955, there were at least 14 cases of infanticide reported in the British Newspaper Archive in Hull and the surrounding area, 6 of which include a verdict of "guilty but insane." The first is the case of Clara Minnie Stathers in February 1923, who had a history of mental illness and was already consulting a doctor in Spring Bank for her condition. The case received detailed coverage in the *Hull Daily Mail*, including her history of mental illness and mental state following the birth of her child, Earnest.[262] The newspaper follows the case throughout, and an article ten years later also described how the family was hoping for her discharge from Broadmoor. Clara was accused of murdering her ten-month-old infant son Earnest by drowning him in a zinc bath; she had been in "indifferent health since his birth and had lately been suffering from neurasthenia."[263] Her brother-in-law, who lived with the family, described Clara as being in weak health for a long time, and that weakness and depression had grown increasingly worse since the birth of her baby. She had been treated in several institutions for this condition,[264] and on the morning of the alleged infanticide, the two eldest boys went to school, leaving Clara alone with the two younger children, Earnest and a toddler, when it was claimed she "yielded to a mad impulse that surged through her brain."[265] Her brother-in-law was visiting Clara's mother and had been there around ten minutes when Clara flew open the door in a distraught manner:

> her eyes were wild looking and her hair dishevelled she said, "I have drowned the baby," "why have you done it?" he asked as he rushed to see what had occurred. When he arrived at the house in front of the fireplace stood a small zinc bath, about half full of warm water, the baby lay face downwards dead.[266]

Clara remained in her mother's house, when asked why she had committed the terrible crime she replied, "wringing her hands and weeping, I did it mother because I loved him so."[267] Her neighbours expressed their sympathy as they knew she had been suffering depression recently, at times "appearing so depressed that she hardly knew what she was doing";[268] she had been treated in an institution before the birth of Earnest for neurasthenia.[269]

After receiving treatment at Hull Royal Infirmary, Clara was charged with the wilful murder of the child. At Hull Police Court, she was described as a "frail looking woman, in a much distressed condition, crying bitterly and apparently not taking much interest in the proceedings."[270] Mr Lavine, Senior Medical Officer, at the hospital, described her on admission as being in a "dazed condition";[271] she had been kept under observation, and he concluded, she came under the "category of a person of unsound mind, she was suffering from a form of depressive insanity."[272] Dr Parker, of Spring Bank, had been treating Clara for the previous two months and had diagnosed her with axillary abscesses and experiencing a neurasthenic state, which he believed to be a chronic condition; he stated that over the duration of their acquaintance she had become increasingly "mentally worn."[273]

Clara told her brother-in-law she had been experiencing bad dreams. One particularly affected her; she dreamt her wedding ring had broken in two, and she asked him to take care of her husband and children as she believed she was going to die. Shortly after this conversation Mr Stathers found a note written by Clara which read, "Dear Husband, I love you. I am not here for long. I love little Ernie and he is going with me: forgive me John, the nurse said he will take a lot of bringing up. Kisses for bairns."[274] In his concluding remarks, the coroner stated that the evidence suggested there was no doubt of Clara's state of mind at the time of the offence. She was committed to York Assizes, where it was concluded she was unfit to plead or to understand what she had done; she was admitted to Broadmoor as insane. Ten years later, Councillor William Fox of the Hull branch of the British Legion began campaigning for Clara's release from Broadmoor, as it seemed that "Broadmoor has helped Clara to regain her health" she sent her family gifts with the money she earned in the asylum laundry and had written regularly to her husband and children, who now only seem to have dim memories of their mother.[275] Sadly, there is no record of Clara ever being reunited with her family.

In October 1944, Rose Marion Bontempo, "looking dazed and ill was charged at Hull Police Court as she was charged with the wilful murder of her 19-day old child."[276] Dr Philip Science stated the child had died from shock and haemorrhage due to a wound to the throat. The grandmother, who identified the body, was asked for an explanation of why Rose may have committed such an offence; she said she could not say, but her "granddaughter worshiped the kiddie," but "she had been much run down and in a nervous condition."[277] She was committed for trial at York Assizes, but she was unfit to plead. Mr Justice Charles stated that she should be kept under strict custody during His Majesty's Pleasure. Dr Derry, prison medical officer of Hull Prison, had had Rose under observation since October 5, and in his opinion she was insane.[278]

Whereas Dorothy Dickinson, in March 1948, a 21-year-old shop assistant from Hull, was arrested at Hull Royal Infirmary, appearing later the same day in Hull Court; she was charged with murdering her newly born child by stabbing it in the neck with a pair of scissors.[279] Three doctors gave evidence, two of whom gave their opinion as to her state of mind at the time of the offence: a house surgeon from Hull Royal Infirmary and a doctor called to the scene shortly after the incident. Dr Ferens stated that he was called to the house soon after the birth of the child. He found her to be unnaturally calm, when he would have expected weeping and hysteria; in his opinion this showed Dorothy's mental imbalance at the time. On the floor he found a bundle; inside was the body of the child with an incised wound in the neck and Dorothy told him she used the scissors. Dr Merson, house surgeon, at Hull Royal Infirmary, stated he was also of the opinion that, at the time of the birth, Dorothy was probably of unstable mentality. Dr Philip Science, police surgeon, said the cause of the death was the loss of blood from a stab wound in the neck and other sources. All three doctors were shown a pair of scissors which they agreed could have caused the wound.[280]

At Leeds Assizes, Dorothy pleaded guilty and said she had been let down by a man who had promised to marry her. Regardless of the fact she was in a wild mental state at the time of the offence, Dorothy received a custodial sentence. Mr Justice Atkinson, whilst sentencing her to prison for nine months, stated,

> you have one child already, you must have been aware of your condition, yet made no preparation for the birth of this child. Women must not think they can produce children they do not want and kill them with impunity.[281]

In light of the evidence by two doctors that her mind was unbalanced at the time of the act, the sentence Dorothy received appears harsh.

During the case of Ann Josephine Willey, in November 1948, the term psychiatrist is used for the first time in a Hull case. Ann was found unconscious by her husband on the bathroom floor with a bottle of ammonia beside her and her four-month-old infant daughter, dead in the cot with a throat wound. Dr Philip Science said that the child died from shock and haemorrhage following a stab wound to the neck.[282] The *Hull Daily Mail* reported that she had killed her child while her mind was unbalanced following its birth.[283] Her husband told the coroner that "before they were married he believed that she suffered from nervous trouble, she was very weak when she came out of a nursing home following the birth of their daughter."[284] Dr John Mackay, the city psychiatrist, said her memory of events on the afternoon of October 14 when the baby died were completely blank:

> he saw her on the 19th October at Beverley Road Hospital, questioned her, and obtained replies by means of writing, because she was unable to speak. He found her suffering from mild depression. She showed a "curious apathy" towards the death of the child … she was rational in her replies, but the apathy continued during subsequent examinations.[285]

He therefore used hypnosis, which showed that she was "prone to dissociation, that is to say, she could find herself in such a state for the time being she would perform acts of which she had no knowledge, or memory when she regained her normal self."[286] She was committed for trial at York Assizes on a charge of infanticide and attempted suicide, where she was found "guilty but insane" and ordered to be detained during His Majesty's Pleasure.[287] Although the Infanticide Act 1938 was in force at the time, the jury found Ann "guilty but insane," as opposed to "guilty of infanticide." It is difficult to ascertain whether this verdict related to poor defence counsel or whether the prosecution pressed for a "guilty but insane" verdict.

It appears that women continued to receive "guilty but insane" verdicts in the Hull area in the years following the Infanticide Act 1938 and also continued to receive custodial sentences despite the evidence being produced to prove an imbalance of the mind.

It is evident from both the cases recorded at the Old Bailey and Hull and the surrounding area that, whilst some women were found "guilty but insane," there remained a substantial number of women who were not. This could have arisen from a number of variables; the uncertainty created by the surgeon's testimony regarding the body as a source of evidence, the softer approach the courts were adopting towards women, the indefinite Victorian detention such a verdict would carry, or a combination of these. In other murder cases, pleading insanity may have saved the life of the criminal; however, in cases of infanticide it seemed to be the worst thing to do. For women accused of this "special crime,"[288] evidence suggests that it was wiser to plead guilty to concealment of birth and receive a short prison sentence than to plead insanity and receive an indefinite detention. Notwithstanding this, Dr Matheson argued that, upon the question of whether it is better to be "put into a criminal lunatic asylum or was it better to serve a sentence and be finished with it?"[289] He replied that "from the individual's point of view he thought it was better to go into a county hospital, because one might get discharged fairly soon, whereas a sentence had to be served."[290]

The cases within this chapter have also indicated that the sentences women received varied; some were sent to prison, regardless of the evidence stating they were not responsible for their actions, and yet others were detained during Her Majesty's Pleasure or bound over to be cared for by family members. Notwithstanding this fact, it is a complete transformation from historical capital punishment women received which, by the twentieth century, was perceived with the fact that:

> no man can fail to be shocked at the alacrity with sentence of death was pronounced, often on prisoners of tender years, for offences which at the present day would be regarded as trifling, meriting at most imprisonment for a short period. Such sentences are viewed now as the evidence of savagery of the times.[291]

The change in punishment of infanticidal women merely reflected wider public opinion towards infanticide. Once perceived as a crime that warranted the death penalty, the twentieth century sought an alternative treatment for these women. On this basis it could be argued that it is difficult to explain modern infanticide; Wheelwright has argued that it is no longer fitting to associate the infanticidal woman with traditional stereotypes associated with the infanticidal woman of the past, as "economic, class and social profile of victims are no longer adequate to explain modern infanticide."[292] Similarly, nor do these women fall into a typical category of mental illness, as they "appear to be functional both before and after pregnancy."[293] With the introduction of the Infanticide Acts, as argued by Ward, there became a "reconstruction of medical concepts to fit the needs of the law,"[294] achieving a balance between the avoidance of a large number of "concealment of birth" verdicts and the prevention of farcical cases whereby a few number of women who were given the death sentence, received a reprieve.[295] Whilst, at the same time, the legislation also established a place within the law "for a subject who is neither mad nor bad, but sad, a social casualty driven by overwhelming stress."[296]

This difficulty in explaining modern infanticide is reflected in the cases in this chapter; the problem appears to stem from the difficulty of diagnosing the mental state of the woman; the cases collectively demonstrate that insanity was both difficult to identify and to gauge in terms of the degree of severity. It was only through the passage of time that an assessment could be made, and the extent of a woman's insanity revealed. Whilst some women experienced a "temporary malady" and recovered relatively quickly from an episode of insanity, others did not; their insanity was more deep-rooted. This is evident in the cases of Harriet Goodliffe, Adelaide Freedman, Sarah Norman, and Clara Stathers, who all spent the rest of their lives in Broadmoor. In the case of Sarah Norman, the mental state diagnosis was misleading; the registered medical practitioner Arthur Kelsey believed her insanity to be temporary, but she spent the rest of her life in Broadmoor, a case that could be argued contributed to uncertainty in medical testimony.

Watson has argued that insanity could be:

> made to fit many different scenarios, from the young unmarried mother who gave birth in secret and immediately destroyed her child to the older married mother who gave birth and then, exhausted by breastfeeding a few weeks or months later (lactational insanity) killed one or more of her children.[297]

This chapter has demonstrated that this was not necessarily the case; young unmarried women who gave birth in secret were less likely to be found "guilty but insane" and more likely to be found guilty of concealment or acquitted.

The following chapter will return to the body as a source of evidence by examining the testimony of the pathologist. However, as the introduction of the Infanticide Act 1938 shifted the focus of the medical evidence to the mental imbalance of the woman, it will argue that the testimony provided by the pathologist was largely disregarded as it became overshadowed by evidence of the woman's state of mind.

Notes

1 Loughnan, (2012) op. cit.; see also A. Loughnan, "In a Kind of Mad Way': A Historical Perspective on Evidence and Proof of Mental Incapacity' *Melbourne University Law Review*, Vol. 35, No. 3, 2011, pp. 1049–1070.
2 Grey (2010) op. cit.
3 R. Smith (1981) op. cit.: 147.
4 Ibid.: 1. See also The Trial of Lunatics Act 1883.
5 J. Eigen, *Mad-Doctors in the Dock, Defending the Diagnosis, 1760–1913*. Baltimore: John Hopkins University Press, 2016: 4.
6 T. Ward, 'Psychiatry and Criminal Responsibility in England, 1843–1939' PhD Thesis De Montfort University, 1996: 168; see also F. McLynn, *Crime and Punishment in Eighteenth-Century England*. Oxford: Oxford University Press, 1991.
7 K. Watson, *Medicine and Justice, Medico-Legal Practice in England and Wales, 1700–1914*. Oxford: Routledge, 2020, p. 188.
8 Eigen (2016) op. cit.: 23; also the Trial of Lunatics Act 1883.
9 R. Porter, *Madness: A Brief History*. Oxford: Oxford University Press, 2002: 10.
10 London: J. Whiston and B. White, 1758.
11 J. Eigen, 'Partial Insanity in Early Forensic Testimony' *Medical History*, Vol. 35, 1991, pp. 25–49: 28.
12 Foucault (1977) op. cit.: 47–57.
13 T. Ward, 'Standing Mute' *Law and Literature*, Vol. 24, No. 1, 2012, pp. 3–20: 13.
14 Rabin (2004) op. cit.: 104.
15 See C. Quinn, 'Images and Impulses: Representations of Puerperal Insanity and Infanticide in Late Victorian England' in M. Jackson (ed.) *Infanticide, Historical Perspective on Child Murder and Concealment, 1550–2000*. Aldershot: Ashgate, 2002.
16 Ibid.: 203.
17 Ibid.: 204.
18 Ibid.
19 Ibid.: See also S. Gilman, *The Face of Madness: Hugh W. Diamond and the Origin of Psychiatric Photography*. New York: Brunner/Mazel, 1976.
20 *Bradford Observer*, 'Yorkshire Summer Assizes, Crown Court at the Castle, Thursday' Thursday July 24, 1834. British Newspaper Archive (www.britishnewspaperarchive.co.uk); The British Library Board; Image © the British Library Board. All rights reserved.

21 *York Herald*, 'Murder and Attempt at Suicide' Saturday 12th July 1834. British Newspaper Archive (www.britishnewspaperarchive.co.uk); The British Library Board; Image © the British Library Board. All rights reserved.
22 *Bradford Observer*, 'Yorkshire Summer Assizes' Thursday 24th July 1834, op. cit.
23 *OBP*, January 1875, James Hayes, t18750111-145.
24 *OBP*, January 1875, James Hayes, t18750111-145; see also J. Shepherd, 'One of the Best Fathers until He Went Out of His Mind': Paternal Child Murder, 1864–1900' *Journal of Victorian Culture*, Vol. 18, No. 1, 2013, pp. 17–35.
25 Ibid.
26 Ibid.
27 Ibid.
28 R. Smith (1981) op. cit.: 143.
29 R. Gooch, *A Practical Compendium of Midwifery; Being a Course on Lectures on Midwifery and on the Diseases of Women and Infants, Delivered at St Bartholomew's Hospital by the Late Robert Gooch, M. D.* London: Longman, Rees, Orme, Brown and Green, 1831.
30 Ibid.: 290.
31 R. Gooch, *An Account of Some of the Most Important Diseases Peculiar to Women.* London: John Murray, 1829: 108. Available at: https://books.google.co.uk/books [Last accessed May 11, 2015]
32 I. Loudon, 'Puerperal Insanity in the 19th Century' *Journal of Royal Society of Medicine*, Vol. 81, February 1988, pp. 76–79: 76. For a case ten weeks post-delivery, see M. Brown, 'Puerperal Mania' *Medical and Surgical Reporter*, Vol. 26, 1872, pp. 92–94. Available at: https://archive.org/details/medicalsurgicalr26philuoft [Last accessed April 26, 2016].
33 H. Marland, 'At Home with Puerperal Mania: The Domestic Treatment of the Insanity of Childbirth in the Nineteenth Century' in P. Bartlett and D. Wright (eds.) *Outside the Walls of the Asylum, the History of Care in the Community 1750–2000*. London: The Athlone Press, 1999: 45.
34 Ibid.: 48; see also C. Hallett, 'The Attempts to Understand Puerperal Fever in the Eighteenth and Early Nineteenth Centuries: The Influence of Inflammatory Theory' *Medical History*, Vol. 49, 2005, pp. 1–28; M. DeLacy, 'Puerperal Fever in Eighteenth-Century Britain' *Bulletin of the History of Medicine*, Vol. 63, No. 4, 1989, pp. 521–556.
35 R. Jones, 'Puerperal Insanity' *British Medical Journal*, Vol. 1, 1902, pp. 579–586, 646–651: 583.
36 H. Marland, 'Under the Shadow of Maternity: Birth, Death and Puerperal Insanity in Victorian Britain' *History of Psychiatry*, Vol. 23, No. 1, 2012, pp. 78–90: 79.
37 J. Baker (1902) op. cit.: 16.
38 Marland (2012) op. cit.: 80.
39 S. Hopwood, *Child Murder and Insanity British Journal of Psychiatry*, Vol. 73, January 1927, pp. 95–108: 96.
40 Ibid.: 97.
41 J. Baker (1902) op. cit.: 18.
42 Hopwood (1927) op. cit.: 97.
43 T. Ward (1996) op. cit.: 167; see also J. Baker (1902) op. cit.: 21.
44 Marland (2004) op. cit.
45 Loughnan (2012) op. cit.: 210.
46 Marland (2012) op. cit.: 80.
47 See J. Eigen, *Witnessing Insanity: Madness and Mad-Doctors in the English Court*. New Haven and London: Yale University Press, 1995: Especially page 142; Marland (2004) op. cit.: Especially from page 173.
48 *Morning Post*, 'Old Bailey' Saturday May 25, 1822. British Newspaper Archive (www.britishnewspaperarchive.co.uk); The British Library Board; Image © the British Library Board. All rights reserved.
49 Ibid.

50 *OBP*, May 1822, Ann Mountford, t18220522-45.
51 Ibid.
52 Ibid.
53 Ibid.
54 Ibid.
55 *Glasgow Herald*, 'London May 24th' Monday May 27, 1822. British Newspaper Archive (www.britishnewspaperarchive.co.uk); The British Library Board; Image © the British Library Board. All rights reserved.
56 *Cambridge Chronicle and Journal*, 'Old Bailey Sessions' Friday May 31, 1822.
57 In *The Treatise of Madness*, William Battie identifies two categories of madness: "original madness," an incurable madness resulting from a defect from birth and "consequential madness," a madness resulting from an external influence on the individual's mind and therefore imagination. Battie believed that consequential madness could be cured, but only if the patient retreated from the environment that had caused the initial onset of madness: in other words, confinement was the prerequisite to cure. (W. Battie, *A Treatise on Madness*. London: J. Whiston and B. White, 1758. Available online at: https://books.google.nl/books?id=F6JbAAAAQAAJ&printsec=frontcover&hl=nl&source=gbs_ge_summary_r&cad=0#v=onepage&q&f=false [Last accessed March 30, 2016]).
58 Marland (2012) op. cit.: 80.
59 Ibid.
60 H. Marland, 'Getting Away with Murder? Puerperal Insanity, Infanticide and the Defence Plea' in M. Jackson (ed.) *Infanticide: Historical Perspectives on Child Murder and Concealment 1550–2000*. Aldershot: Ashgate Publishing, 2002: 173.
61 Loudon (1988) op. cit.: 76.
62 Ibid.
63 *OBP*, January 1888, Maxwell Rae, t18880130-282.
64 E. Showalter, *The Female Malady: Women, Madness and English Culture 1830–1980*. New York: Pantheon Books, 1985: 55.
65 Zedner (1992) op. cit.: 89.
66 *R v Hadfield* (1800) 27 St Tr 1281.
67 Ibid.
68 Eigen (2016) op. cit.: 21.
69 A. Scull, *Museums of Madness, The Social Organisation of Insanity in Nineteenth Century England*. London: Penguin, 1979: 55.
70 *R v McNaughtan* (1843) 10 Clark and F. 200, 8 Eng. Rep. 718.
71 *R v McNaughtan* (1843) 10 Clark and F. 200, 8 Eng. Rep. 718. 722–723.
72 R. Smith (1981) op. cit.: 15.
73 A. Loughnan and T. Ward, 'Emergent Authority and Expert Knowledge: Psychiatry and Criminal Responsibility in the UK' *International Journal of Law and Psychiatry*, Vol. 37, 2014, pp. 25–36: 27.
74 Eigen (2016) op. cit.: 4.
75 Ibid.
76 P. Bartlett. 'Legal Madness in the Nineteenth Century' *Social History of Medicine*, Vol. 14, No. 1, 2001, pp. 107–131: 13.
77 J. H. Baker (1986) op. cit.: 282.
78 *R v Dyson* (1831) 7 C & P 305.
79 W. Hawkins, *Pleas of the Crown*. London: Professional Books, 1973, [1716]: 124; See also F. Woodbridge, 'Some Unusual Aspects of Mental Irresponsibility in the Criminal Law' *Journal of Criminal Law and Criminology* (1931–1951), Vol. 29, No. 6, March–April 1939, pp. 822–847; T. Ward (2012) op. cit.; M. Hamblin Smith, 'Unfitness to Plead in Criminal Trials' *Journal of Mental Sciences*, Vol. 62, No. 259, 1916, pp. 763–774: 765; P. Brown, 'Unfitness to Plead in England and Wales: Historical Development and Contemporary Dilemmas' *Medicine, Science and the Law*, Vol. 59, No. 3, 2019, pp. 187–196.

80 *York Herald and General Advertiser*, 'Friday March 25th, Charge of Murder' Saturday March 26, 1831. British Newspaper Archive (www.britishnewspaperarchive.co.uk); The British Library Board; Image © the British Library Board. All rights reserved.

81 *The Sheffield Independent and Yorkshire and Derbyshire Advertiser*, 'Shocking Case of Infanticide and Commitment for Murder at Ecclesfield' Saturday October 2, 1830. British Newspaper Archive (www.britishnewspaperarchive.co.uk); The British Library Board; Image © the British Library Board. All rights reserved.

82 Ibid.

83 Ibid.

84 T. Ward (2012) op. cit.: 13; *R v Dyson* (1831) 7 C & P 305.

85 *R v Dyson* (1831) 7 C & P 305.

86 *York Herald and General Advertiser* 'Friday March 25th' Saturday March 26, 1831, op. cit. British Newspaper Archive (www.britishnewspaperarchive.co.uk); The British Library Board; Image © the British Library Board. All rights reserved.

87 E. Cleall, "Deaf to the Word': Gender, Deafness and Protestantism in Nineteenth Century Britain and Ireland' in J. De Groot and S. Morgan (eds.) *Sex, Gender and the Sacred: Reconfiguring Religion in Gender History*. Chichester: Wiley Blackwell, 2014: 201.

88 Ibid.

89 *R v Pritchard* [1836] 7 C & P 303; Hamblin Smith (1916) op. cit.: 767.

90 Hamblin Smith (1916) op. cit.: 767.

91 Ibid.

92 T. Ward (2012) op. cit.: 12.

93 Holloway was a House of Correction in London, opening in 1852 to both male and female convicts. In 1903 it became a female only prison and closed in July 2016 when the land was sold for housing. 'A Woman's Place?' at: www.theguardian.com/society/2015/nov/28/closure-of-holloway-womens-prison-revolution [Last accessed January 3, 2017].

94 *OBP*, January 1887, Mary Ann Hathway, t18870425-543.

95 Ibid.

96 Bartlett (2001) op. cit.: 13.

97 Ibid.

98 N. Walker and S. McCabe, *Crime and Insanity in England*. Edinburgh: Edinburgh University Press, 1973.

99 T. Ward (1996) op. cit.: 53.

100 Ibid.

101 *OBP*, March 1902, Emily Moir, t19020310-239.

102 See T. Ward (1996) op. cit.: 53.

103 Home Office (1889) Circulars *Justice of the Peace* 53: 793–794.

104 T. Ward (1996) op. cit.: 53.

105 J. Sim, *Medical Power in Prisons, The Prisons Medical Service in England 1774–1989*. Milton Keynes: Open University Press, 1990: 11.

106 S. Wilson and I. Cumming, 'Introduction – The History of Psychiatry' in S. Wilson and I. Cumming (eds.) *Psychiatry in Prisons, A Comprehensive Handbook*. London: Jessica Kingsley Publishers, 2010: 10. See also J. Sim (1990) op. cit.: 11.

107 S. Wilson and I. Cunning (2010) op. cit.: 11.

108 Sim (1990) op. cit.; S. Wilson and I. Cunning (2010) op. cit.: 11.

109 'William Norwood (Sir) East' at: http://munksroll.rcplondon.ac.uk/Biography/Details/1385 [Last accessed March 24, 2016].

110 S. Dell, et al., 'Remands and Psychiatric Assessment in Holloway Prison I: The Psychotic Population' *British Journal of Psychiatry,* Vol. 163, No. 5, 1993, pp. 634–640.

111 Walker and McCabe (1973) op. cit, cited in Dell, et al. (1993) op. cit.: 634.

112 Sim (1990) op. cit.: 9.

113 Ibid.

114 Ibid.

115 Foucault (1977) op. cit.: especially page 249.
116 Eigen (2016) op. cit.: 57.
117 Ibid.: 51.
118 Ibid.
119 Opened as a mixed prison in 1853 and became a female only prison in 1903.
120 R. Smith (1981) op. cit.: 34.
121 See Loughnan and Ward (2014) op. cit.: 29.
122 D. Chiswick and E. Dooley, *Psychiatry in Prisons*. Available at: http://www.rcpsych.ac.uk/pdf/PracForenPsych_09.pdf [Last accessed June 29, 2015].
123 Ibid.
124 Ibid.
125 Under the Criminal Lunatic Asylum Act 1860.
126 J. Shepherd, '"I Am Very Glad and Cheered When I Hear the Flute:" The Treatment of Criminal Lunatics in Late Victorian Broadmoor' *Medical History*, Vol. 60, No. 4, October 2016, pp. 473–491.
127 Shepherd (2016) op. cit.
128 *OBP*, May 1857, Martha Bacon, t18570511-649.
129 Shepherd (2016) op. cit.
130 J. Matheson, 'Infanticide' *Medico-Legal and Criminology Review*, Vol. 9, 1941, pp. 135–152: 151.
131 F. Freemon, 'The Origin of the Medical Expert Witness: The Insanity of Edward Oxford' *The Journal of Legal Medicine*, Vol. 22, 2001, pp. 349–373: 349.
132 *OBP*, January 1868, Eliza Colley, t18680127-181.
133 *South London Chronicle*, 'Extraordinary Case of Alleged Child Murder at Harrow' Saturday January 18, 1868. British Newspaper Archive (www.britishnewspaper-archive.co.uk); The British Library Board; Image © the British Library Board. All rights reserved.
134 Ibid.
135 *OBP*, March 1896, Dinah Cohen, t18960323-300.
136 Ibid.
137 Ibid.
138 Ibid; for a discussion on Dinah Cohen's ethnic background, see D. Grey, 'Almost Unknown Amongst the Jews': Jewish Women and Infanticide in London, 1890–1918' *The London Journal*, Vol. 37, No. 2, July 2012, pp. 122–135.
139 *OBP*, March 1912, Eleanor Eslick, t19120319-13.
140 Ibid.
141 Ibid.
142 Ibid.
143 Ibid.
144 *OBP*, May 1863, Harriet Goodliffe, t18630511-716.
145 Ibid.
146 Ibid.
147 Ibid.
148 Ibid.
149 Ibid.
150 Ibid.
151 J. A. Hatfield, 'An Irresistible Impulse: Puerperal Insanity and Infanticide in Nineteenth-Century England' MA Dissertation, 2014. Available at: http://julieannhatfield.co.uk/ma-in-english-and-american-literature-dissertation-an-irresistible-impulse-puerperal-insanity-and-infanticide-in-nineteenth-century-england/ [Last accessed January 5, 2017].
152 *The Daily Telegraph*, 'Police Intelligence' Friday October 15, 1869. British Newspaper Archive (www.britishnewspaperarchive.co.uk); The British Library Board; Image © the British Library Board. All rights reserved.

153 *OBP*, November 1869, Adelaide Freedman, t18691122-36.
154 Ibid.
155 Ibid.
156 Ibid.
157 Ibid.
158 Ibid.
159 Ibid.
160 Ibid.
161 Ibid.
162 Ibid.
163 This was common in murder cases generally, as demonstrated in the research of Ward (1996) op. cit.
164 J. Eigen, *Unconscious Crime, Mental Absence and Criminal Responsibly in Victorian London*. London: The John Hopkins University Press, 2003: 78.
165 'Hannah Samuel' at: www.geocities.ws/lzbthjoachim/Hannah_Samuel.html [Last accessed January 4 2017].
166 *OBP*, January 1881, Sarah Norman, t18810110-201.
167 Ibid.
168 Ibid.
169 Ibid. Captalisation, grammar, and punctuation are original.
170 Ibid.
171 Hatfield (2014) op. cit.
172 *OBP*, September 1888, Mary Ann Reynolds, t18880917-824.
173 Ibid.
174 Ibid.
175 Ibid.
176 *Lloyds Weekly Newspaper*, 'Ghastly Affair at Whitechapel' Sunday January 30, 1898. British Newspaper Archive (www.britishnewspaperarchive.co.uk); The British Library Board; Image © the British Library Board. All rights reserved.
177 Ibid.
178 *Lloyds Weekly Newspaper*, 'Jewess Charged with Murder, Child Thrown Out of Window' Sunday February 20, 1898. British Newspaper Archive (www.britishnewspaperarchive.co.uk); The British Library Board; Image © the British Library Board. All rights reserved.
179 'Ghastly Affair at Whitechapel,' (1898) op. cit.
180 'Jewess Charged with Murder,' (1898) op. cit.
181 Ibid.
182 Ibid.
183 *OBP*, March 1898, Asneth Cohen, t18980307-232.
184 *Lloyds Weekly Newspaper*, 'Old Bailey Trials' Sunday March 13, 1898. British Newspaper Archive (www.britishnewspaperarchive.co.uk); The British Library Board; Image © the British Library Board. All rights reserved.
185 *Hull and East Riding Times*, 'Horrible Child Murder in Hull Yesterday' Friday May 16, 1873. British Newspaper Archive (www.britishnewspaperarchive.co.uk); The British Library Board; Image © the British Library Board. All rights reserved.
186 *York Herald*, 'Horrible Murder by a Mother at Hull' Saturday May 17, 1873. British Newspaper Archive (www.britishnewspaperarchive.co.uk); The British Library Board; Image © the British Library Board. All rights reserved.
187 *Hull Packet and East Riding Times*, 'Yorkshire Summer Assizes' Friday August 1, 1873. British Newspaper Archive (www.britishnewspaperarchive.co.uk); The British Library Board; Image © the British Library Board. All rights reserved.
188 D. Goodman, *Foul Deeds and Suspicious Deaths in Hull*. Barnsley: Wharncliffe Books, 2005: 62.
189 Ibid.

190 Ibid.
191 'Yorkshire Summer Assizes,' (1873) op. cit.
192 S. Wade, *Yorkshire Murderous Women, Two Centuries of Killings*. Barnsley: Wharncliffe Books, 2007: 55. Available at https://books.google.co.uk/books [Last accessed June 4, 2015].
193 *Yorkshire Gazette*, 'Yorkshire Spring Assizes' Saturday March 30, 1867. British Newspaper Archive (www.britishnewspaperarchive.co.uk); The British Library Board; Image © the British Library Board. All rights reserved.
194 *Hull Daily Mail*, 'Another Murder in Hull' Monday August 24, 1891. British Newspaper Archive (www.britishnewspaperarchive.co.uk); The British Library Board; Image © the British Library Board. All rights reserved.
195 *Driffield Times*, 'A Fearful Death' Saturday August 29, 1891. British Newspaper Archive (www.britishnewspaperarchive.co.uk); The British Library Board; Image © the British Library Board. All rights reserved.
196 Ibid.
197 R. Chadwick, *Bureaucratic Mercy: The Home Office and the Treatment of Capital Cases in Victorian England*. New York and London: Garland, 1992. Cited in T. Ward (1996) op. cit.: 310.
198 *Yorkshire Evening Post*, 'Alleged Infanticide' Monday September 12, 1910. British Newspaper Archive (www.britishnewspaperarchive.co.uk); The British Library Board; Image © the British Library Board. All rights reserved.
199 Children Act 1908; The Maternity and Child Welfare Act 1918, which gave local authorities the power to set up both maternity and child welfare clinics; Adoption of Children Act, 1926, An Act which allowed the adoption of Children: See also J. Lewis, *The Politics of Motherhood: Child and Maternal Welfare in England, 1900–1939*. London: Croom Helm and McGill-Queen's University Press, 1980.
200 Kilday (2013) op. cit.: 183.
201 Loughnan (2012) *Manifest Madness*. op. cit.: 216.
202 J. Baker (1902) op. cit.; McIlroy (1928) op. cit.; H. Allen (1987) op. cit.; T. Ward (1999) op. cit.; Grey (2010) op. cit.
203 See also Higginbotham (1992) op. cit.
204 D. Grey, 'Parenting, Infanticide and the State in England and Wales, 1870–1950' in H. Barron and C. Siebrecht (eds.) *Parenting and the State in Britain and Europe, Raising the Nation*. Cham, Switzerland: Springer Nature, 2017: 80.
205 T. Ward (1996) op. cit.: 183.
206 Grey (2010) op. cit.: 445.
207 *Nottingham Evening Post*, 'New Entente Trouble' Thursday July 28, 1921. British Newspaper Archive (www.britishnewspaperarchive.co.uk); The British Library Board; Image © the British Library Board. All rights reserved.
208 Ibid.
209 *Yorkshire Post and Leeds Intelligencer*, 'A Meteokic Career' Tuesday October 31, 1922. British Newspaper Archive (www.britishnewspaperarchive.co.uk); The British Library Board; Image © the British Library Board. All rights reserved.
210 Ibid.
211 Ibid.
212 Ibid.
213 Ibid.
214 *Aberdeen Journal*, 'Humane Legislation' Tuesday October 31, 1922. British Newspaper Archive (www.britishnewspaperarchive.co.uk); The British Library Board; Image © the British Library Board. All rights reserved.
215 P. Resnick, 'Murder of the New-Born: A Psychiatric Review of Neonaticide' *American Journal of Psychiatry*, Vol. 126, No. 10, 1970, pp. 1414–1420.
216 *Yorkshire Evening Post*, 'Judge and Infanticide' Saturday May 12, 1923. British Newspaper Archive (www.britishnewspaperarchive.co.uk); The British Library Board; Image © the British Library Board. All rights reserved.

217 *Yorkshire Evening Post*, 'Charge of Infanticide' Tuesday April 10, 1923. British Newspaper Archive (www.britishnewspaperarchive.co.uk); The British Library Board; Image © the British Library Board. All rights reserved.
218 *Yorkshire Post and Leeds Intelligencer*, 'Yorkshire Assizes' Saturday May 12, 1923. British Newspaper Archive (www.britishnewspaperarchive.co.uk); The British Library Board; Image © the British Library Board. All rights reserved.
219 *Yorkshire Post and Leeds Intelligencer*, 'A Romantic Leeds Wedding' Monday July 16, 1923. British Newspaper Archive (www.britishnewspaperarchive.co.uk); The British Library Board; Image © the British Library Board. All rights reserved.
220 *Aberdeen Journal*, 'Laws for Women' Thursday November 2, 1922. British Newspaper Archive (www.britishnewspaperarchive.co.uk); The British Library Board; Image © the British Library Board. All rights reserved.
221 Kilday (2013) Op. cit.: 188; see also D. Davies, 'Child-Killing in English Law Part I' *Modern Law Review*, Issue 3, December 1937, pp. 203–223: D. Davies, 'Child-Killing in English Law Part II' *Modern Law Review*, Issue 4, March 1938, pp. 269–287.
222 Kilday (2013) op. cit.: 188.
223 Ibid.
224 C. Mercer, 'Medico-Legal Notes' *Journal of Mental Science*, Vol. 74, 1928, pp. 98–102: 100 in T. Ward (1999) op. cit.: 172.
225 L. McIlroy, 'The Effects of Parturition upon Insanity and Crime' *The British Medical Journal*, Vol. 1, 1928, pp. 303–304: 304.
226 Ibid.
227 Ibid.
228 Ibid.
229 Ibid.
230 Grey (2017) op. cit.: 81.
231 Matheson (1941) op. cit.: 140.
232 Kilday (2013) op. cit.: 188.
233 *Nottingham Evening Post*, 'Guilty but Insane' Tuesday July 21, 1936. British Newspaper Archive (www.britishnewspaperarchive.co.uk); The British Library Board; Image © the British Library Board. All rights reserved.
234 *Western Daily Press*, 'Mother Charged with Murder' Tuesday July 7, 1936; *Nottingham Evening Post*, 'Guilty but Insane' Tuesday July 21, 1936. British Newspaper Archive (www.britishnewspaperarchive.co.uk); The British Library Board; Image © the British Library Board. All rights reserved.
235 'Guilty but Insane' (1936) op. cit.
236 *Western Daily Press*, 'What is a Newly Born Child?' Saturday December 5, 1931. British Newspaper Archive (www.britishnewspaperarchive.co.uk); The British Library Board; Image © the British Library Board. All rights reserved.
237 Ibid.
238 Infanticide Act 1938, 1 & 2 Geo 6 c 36, Section 1 (1).
239 Kilday (2013) op. cit.: 189.
240 T. Ward (1999) op. cit.: 176.
241 'The Hull Blitz' at: www.mylearning.org/the-hull-blitz/p-1805/ [Last accessed July 31, 2015].
242 *Sunderland Echo and Shipping Gazette*, 'Crisis Fears Made Mother Kill Baby' Thursday November 17, 1938. British Newspaper Archive (www.britishnewspaperarchive.co.uk); The British Library Board; Image © the British Library Board. All rights reserved.
243 Ibid.
244 *Yorkshire Evening Post*, 'Mother Bound over on Charge of Murder' Wednesday November 16, 1938. British Newspaper Archive (www.britishnewspaperarchive.co.uk); The British Library Board; Image © the British Library Board. All rights reserved.

245 *Chelmsford Chronicle*, 'Sad Braintree Case, Baby's Body in Cupboard' Friday July 21, 1939. British Newspaper Archive (www.britishnewspaperarchive.co.uk); The British Library Board; Image © the British Library Board. All rights reserved.
246 Ibid.
247 Ibid.
248 M. Jackson, *The Borderland of Imbecility: Medicine, Society and the Fabrication of the Feeble Minded in Late Victorian and Edwardian England.* Manchester: Manchester University Press, 2000: 12.
249 Zedner (1992) op. cit.: 264.
250 Ibid.
251 M. Jackson (2000) op. cit.: 11; see also D. Taylor, 'Beyond the Bounds of Respectable Society: "The Dangerous Classes" in Victorian and Edwardian England' in J. Rowbotham and K. Stevenson (eds.) *Criminal Conversations, Victorian Crimes, Social Panic, and Moral Outrage*. Columbus: The Ohio State University Press, 2005: 17; Diagnosis and treatment of feeblemindedness in children can be found at Royal Commission, 'Royal Commission on the Care and Control of the Feeble-Minded Vol II Minutes of Evidence' *Parliamentary Papers*. London: Wyman and Sons, 1908: 3.
252 *Bedfordshire Times*, 'Bedford Mother Bound Over' Friday November 18, 1938. British Newspaper Archive (www.britishnewspaperarchive.co.uk); The British Library Board; Image © the British Library Board. All rights reserved.
253 Ibid.
254 Ibid.
255 Ibid.
256 Ibid.
257 Ibid.
258 *Derby Daily Telegraph*, 'Killed First Born Baby Whom She Loved' Thursday July 16, 1942. British Newspaper Archive (www.britishnewspaperarchive.co.uk); The British Library Board; Image © the British Library Board. All rights reserved.
259 *Gloucestershire Echo*, 'Baby in Lake: Mother Bound Over' Thursday July 16, 1942. British Newspaper Archive (www.britishnewspaperarchive.co.uk); The British Library Board; Image © the British Library Board. All rights reserved.
260 Ibid.
261 Ibid.
262 *Hull Daily Mail*, 'Drowned in his Bath' Thursday February 15, 1923. British Newspaper Archive (www.britishnewspaperarchive.co.uk); The British Library Board; Image © the British Library Board. All rights reserved.
263 Ibid.; Neurasthenia is defined as a "*Vague Disorder, Characterised by Chronic Abnormal Fatigability, Depression, Inability to Concentrate, Loss of Appetite and Insomnia. Popularly Called Nervous Prostration.*" Available at: http://medical-dictionary.thefreedictionary.com/neurasthenia [Last accessed August 3, 2015].
264 'Drowned in his Bath,' (1923) op. cit.
265 Ibid.
266 Ibid.
267 Ibid.
268 Ibid.
269 Ibid.
270 *Hull Daily Mail*, 'West Parade Drowning Tragedy' Friday February 23, 1923. British Newspaper Archive (www.britishnewspaperarchive.co.uk); The British Library Board; Image © the British Library Board. All rights reserved.
271 Ibid.
272 Ibid.
273 Ibid.
274 *Hull Daily Mail*, 'I Want My Pet' Friday January 23, 1923. British Newspaper Archive (www.britishnewspaperarchive.co.uk); The British Library Board; Image © the British Library Board. All rights reserved.

275 *Hull Daily Mail*, 'Hull Man's Ten Years' Ordeal' Saturday March 18, 1933. British Newspaper Archive (www.britishnewspaperarchive.co.uk); The British Library Board; Image © the British Library Board. All rights reserved.

276 *Hull Daily Mail*, 'Hull Mother Charged with Murdering Her Baby' Thursday October 5, 1944. British Newspaper Archive (www.britishnewspaperarchive.co.uk); The British Library Board; Image © the British Library Board. All rights reserved.

277 Ibid.

278 *Hull Daily Mail*, 'Unfit to Plead' Tuesday November 14, 1944. British Newspaper Archive (www.britishnewspaperarchive.co.uk); The British Library Board; Image © the British Library Board. All rights reserved.

279 *Hull Daily Mail*, 'Girl Arrested at Infirmary' Tuesday March 2, 1948. British Newspaper Archive (www.britishnewspaperarchive.co.uk); The British Library Board; Image © the British Library Board. All rights reserved.

280 *Hull Daily Mail*, 'Hull Girl Accuse of Infanticide' Monday March 8, 1948. British Newspaper Archive (www.britishnewspaperarchive.co.uk); The British Library Board; Image © the British Library Board. All rights reserved.

281 *Hull Daily Mail*, 'Hull Girl Jailed' Wednesday April 28, 1948. British Newspaper Archive (www.britishnewspaperarchive.co.uk); The British Library Board; Image © the British Library Board. All rights reserved.

282 *Hull Daily Mail*, 'Baby Dead in Cot, Wife Unconscious with Ammonia Bottle Near' Thursday November 4, 1948. British Newspaper Archive (www.britishnewspaperarchive.co.uk); The British Library Board; Image © the British Library Board. All rights reserved.

283 *Hull Daily Mail*, 'Accused Mother not Recovered from Birth' Tuesday November 2, 1948. British Newspaper Archive (www.britishnewspaperarchive.co.uk); The British Library Board; Image © the British Library Board. All rights reserved.

284 Ibid.

285 *Hull Daily Mail*, 'Mothers Memory a Blank' Friday November 5, 1948. British Newspaper Archive (www.britishnewspaperarchive.co.uk); The British Library Board; Image © the British Library Board. All rights reserved.

286 Ibid.

287 Ibid.

288 Grey (2017) op. cit.: 79.

289 Matheson (1941) op. cit.: 152.

290 Ibid.

291 *Sheffield Evening Telegraph*, 'Infanticide and the Law' Friday March 8, 1901; British Newspaper Archive (www.britishnewspaperarchive.co.uk); The British Library Board; Image © the British Library Board. All rights reserved. Grammar and spelling are original.

292 J. Wheelwright, ''Nothing in between': Modern Cases of Infanticide' in M. Jackson (ed.) *Infanticide: Historical Perspectives on Child Murder and Concealment 1550–2000*. Aldershot: Ashgate, 2002: 274.

293 Ibid.: 275.

294 T. Ward (1999) op. cit.: 174.

295 Ibid.

296 T. Ward (1999) op. cit.: 176.

297 Watson (2011) op. cit.: 108.

5 The expert evidence of the pathologist in infanticide cases

As the courts began to adopt a softer approach towards infanticidal women, the application of a general rule became evident; where uncertainty remained in infanticide cases, the woman should be given the benefit of the doubt, unless substantive evidence could be produced of the mother's intention to murder her infant. The previous chapter identified how mental state evidence was gradually relied upon in cases during the nineteenth and twentieth centuries, where those considered not responsible for their actions in law were given a verdict of "guilty, but insane." In addition to mental state evidence, however, the court continued to rely upon medical experts for evidence relating to the body as a source of evidence – a role historically fulfilled by medical men: experts who predominately treated the living. However, during the nineteenth century a new role developed, the pathologist, a doctor specialising in the dead.[1]

Pathology has been characterised as "the body of medical and paramedical scientific knowledge which may be used for the purposes of administrative law,"[2] involving the investigative preparation and "preservation and presentation of evidence and medical opinion for the courts of law and administrative regulatory agencies."[3] In particular, forensic medical practitioners or pathologists who performed medico-legal autopsies were selected "not for their special skill in reading dead bodies as generic texts, but for their supposed capacity to provide evidence in relation to the specific circumstances of a specific death."[4] By drawing on their pathological skills, they acquired the ability to answer legal questions through their investigation of physiological analysis. It was this specialist medical expert with both the ability to perform autopsies and provide detailed medical evidence in court that nineteenth-century coroners demanded. It naturally followed that such experts would be able to determine with greater accuracy and certainty how a child had died. However, this chapter will argue that, contrary to this logic, in many cases of infanticide, the evidence provided by pathologists was largely overlooked. This anomaly may have arisen as either a result of the uncertainty created by the medical experts in general and their reliance on the lung test in particular, or from a shift in focus from the body of deceased, to the mind of the accused as a source of evidence.

This chapter will begin with a historical account of the development of the role of the pathologist in England. It will discuss the significance that the coroner

DOI: 10.4324/9781003006299-5

played in this development, resulting in a strong medico-legal undercurrent in the role of the pathologist. It will then briefly discuss the influential developments of cytology (the study of the structure and function of cells) and histopathology in pathology. This significant development in microscopic examination gave medical experts the means to study abnormal tissue and became fundamental in distinguishing between diseased and normal cells, thus aiding the interpretation of mortality. However, regardless of these developments, the pathologist continued to experience difficulties establishing certainty in many infanticide cases. Pathologists were often able to establish a child had been born alive, but there was not always sufficient evidence to establish the cause of death and, more crucially, to establish intention. Due to a lack of cases from Hull and the surrounding area, this chapter will draw on a number of Lincolnshire cases to demonstrate this issue. The pathologist also provided testimony in overlaying cases, and this will briefly be discussed, drawing on two cases from the Old Bailey. Finally, the chapter will concentrate on twentieth-century cases in which pathologists gave evidence, during the period 1914–1955, at the Old Bailey and in Hull and the surrounding area. It will demonstrate how evidence given by medical experts continued to remain uncertain, often appearing to carry little weight.

Historical account of the role of the pathologist

In England, the history of necropsy is long and established, carried out for medico-legal intentions, its ultimate primary purpose being to establish a cause of death in sudden or suspicious circumstances. It was a role that became more prominent during the twentieth century when the "encounter between the body and the pathologist became a high profile and personalised practice."[5] Prior to this, the procedure tended to be carried out by "faceless investigators often local practitioners with no claims to forensic expertise,"[6] who conducted the investigation and presented their findings to the court. Throughout the eighteenth and nineteenth centuries, as shown in Chapter 3, the surgeon, the barber surgeon, and occasionally the man-midwife performed necropsies in cases involving infanticide. The aim was to establish whether the child had had a separate existence and if it had died from natural causes. The objective was to provide answers to three pivotal medico-legal questions: whether the child had had a separate existence, the cause of the child's death, and if the mother had killed the child intentionally or by accident. He would present his findings to the court, and the jury could then draw inferences and decide a verdict beyond a reasonable doubt. As noted in Chapter 3, medical men often struggled to provide definitive answers to these questions, and by doing so inadvertently conveyed uncertainty rather than certainty in such cases. The medical men during the eighteenth and nineteenth centuries encountered two main problems associated with pathology. Firstly, pathology was in its infancy and very slow to evolve, and secondly there were a limited number of medical men with knowledge and expertise of pathology to effectively carry out forensic medicine, so, in many suspected infanticide cases, autopsies were superficial, carried out apathetically with "very little value or not held at all."[7]

Dr Scott expressed the difficulties medical men faced when providing testimony in infanticide cases during the nineteenth century, in an in-depth account of a post-mortem procedure and findings.[8] In 1826, a dead child was discovered lying on a table wrapped in a shawl in the same room as the mother; he removed the child to a neighbouring house in order to carry out the post-mortem.[9] He discovered substantive and circumstantial evidence to suggest the mother had murdered the child; however, in court this appears to be insignificant, as her defence counsel advised her to plead guilty to concealment of birth and subsequently the murder charge was dropped.[10] In response Scott stated:

> we do not pretend to penetrate the reason which induced the public prosecutor to abandon the capital charge, unless from the known uncertainty and insufficiently of medical testimony in the generality of cases of infanticide … but if medical testimony should be allowed to have any weight in a case of this nature – or if a woman shall be punished capitally for infanticide, which we very much doubt from the prevailing feeling of the law in regard to medical evidence – we think that this was certainly a case as strongly made out as it is almost possible to conceive.[11]

Scott implies the court's response in ceasing to punish women for infanticide rested with unreliable and uncertain medical evidence:

> it is a different thing when his opinion comes to be canvassed in a court of law; because their mere opinion will not suffice – it is the reasons for such opinion that are of avail … we think it is in a great measure, owing to the want of the habit of close reasoning on the part of many medical men, together with the uncommonness of their situation, that some of them have made so awkward appearance before the judge and jury.[12]

As he highlights, the nineteenth-century courts were no longer interested in the sole opinion of medical men; they were interested in scientifically based medical reasoning.

As the role of the pathologist developed during the nineteenth century, the Victorians were simultaneously developing a curiosity for detective fiction. Novels such as *The Moonstone* by Wilkie Collins[13] generated an interest for detective fiction, which developed into an interest in murder mystery, primarily incited by Sir Arthur Conan Doyle as the creator of the medico-investigative team of Sherlock Holmes and Doctor Watson. As a qualified doctor, Doyle took inspiration for creating Sherlock Holmes from the surgeon Joseph Bell, at Edinburgh University, who had a unique talent for recognising symptoms and diagnosis before the patient could disclose any details.[14] It is possible that this literature contributed to the change in the public mind-set towards forensic medicine, from the historical perception of the surgeon as a body snatcher to that of crime solver and public hero.

As a suspicious death arose it placed the pathologist at the centre of the investigation; with his skills and expertise he had the ability to uncover crucial facts concerning the victim's death. Through his ability to read the body he sought to piece together the last moments of the victim's life and cause of death, uncovering crucial clues as to the identity of the perpetrator. In many suspicious or unexplained deaths, the pathologist successfully fulfilled his role, and with the aid of advancements in science and developing medical discourse, there came the growing anticipation that the element of certainty would be evident in medical witness testimony in infanticide cases. However, in the absence of a succinct legal definition of the onset of life and increasing concerns over the accuracy of the lung test, infanticide verdicts continued to be inconsistent. In many cases, medical expert evidence continued to be based on opinion and individual professional experience, leading to partiality and subjection rather than scientifically based evidence.

During the twentieth century, the responsibility of forensic experts initially fell to the General Practitioner (GP), who tended to be called upon to carry out the autopsy. During this period there were arguments for the pathologist to become more specialised in this role. In particular, GPs were criticised for their unscientific approaches to autopsies, instead of relying upon the deceased medical history and knowledge of family and friends as opposed to science. However, GPs were also avoiding a potential conflict of interests, because, by probing into death, his career with the living may be affected through any smear on his reputation. As Alfred Swaine Taylor observed, in many cases there was:

> no post mortem examination of the dead body by a qualified medical man; in a small proportion even of those autopsies which are made the cause of violent death may be overlooked through lack of familiarity on the part of the investigator with (a) the signs of a violent death or (b) with the steps necessary to be taken in a medico-legal inquiry.[15]

He continues by stating that in many cases the "verdicts of coroner's juries are sometimes contrary to the medical evidence and it is by no means unknown for a coroner to call no medical evidence whatever."[16]

Concerns were increasingly being raised regarding the GP's lack of professional development, and current practising knowledge of autopsy. This led to one provincial GP, practising in Sunderland, to write:

> however well up in it he may have been when he left college, and although able to detect a gross lesion, such as a clot on the brain, the minuter microscopic appearances will prove elusive to him, and he will have no alternative left but to make the necropsy confirm his previous diagnosis.[17]

The need for assistance and emphasis on the importance of GPs giving evidence in the courtroom was provided in the form of Stanley Atkinson's *Golden Rules Of Medical Evidence*, where it states that "anatomical post mortem examinations should be carried out in medico-legal cases: they are essential in alleged criminal homicides."[18] It also specifies that all "legally qualified and registered general practitioner may be called to give evidence by the coroner"[19] in or near where a death has occurred, as determined in section 21, Coroner's Act 1887.

There was therefore an increasing argument for an independent expert in the form of the pathologist and a need for both practitioners to combine their resources – with the GP's knowledge of the deceased's life guiding the pathologist to determine the cause of death. This is evident at the trial of Louisa Lunn, on March 21, 1904, at the Old Bailey, both the GP and Pathologist gave evidence.[20] Louisa was a servant, indicted for the wilful murder of her newly born female infant. She was complaining of feeling unwell with dropsy; however, suspicions arose when bedlinen and clothing were found stained with blood. The doctor was sent for; he then carried out an examination of Louisa, determining that she had recently delivered a child, and she:

> admitted she had given birth to a child, and said she had been in pain the whole of the previous Saturday, and that the child was born about 6 a.m. on Sunday—I asked her if it had cried, and she said, "Yes"—I said, "What happened then?"—she said, "I killed the child and put it up the chimney."[21]

Louisa was engaged to one Alfred Smith who, when told of the child, denied being the father and "she was to get out of it the best way she could."[22] Louisa informed the GP that the child had lived for about 15 minutes. The GP carried out an external examination of the child and found marks around the child's neck.[23] He stated:

> I do not think the fingers could have caused it, because it was too regular, and it completely encircled the neck—I do not think it could have been done before the child was completely born, because the only way it could have been done then would be by the umbilical cord, and the mark did not correspond with that—the mark was not like what you get in an ordinary labour—if the violence was caused before the child was completely born there would not be distinct signs of a separate existence.[24]

The GP attending Louisa not only carried out a physical examination of the mother but also asked crucial questions which may have assisted in assessing her mental state.

The key developments within the coroner's court, discussed in Chapter 3, also had a profound effect on the developments of the pathologist. Coroners argued for a specialised forensic pathologist, who had the ability and skills to interpret scientific physiological investigation into legal answers, with the ultimate aim of determining the cause of a suspicious or sudden death. However, it could be argued that pathology is a questionable branch of medicine owing to its strong medico-legal undercurrent, an undercurrent that firmly established a link between forensic medicine and the law, as opposed to merely another branch of medicine.[25]

On the other hand, Jan Van Den Tweel and Clive Taylor have argued that, from the mid-nineteenth century onwards, rather than the contributions made by coroners or doctors, it was advances in technology that transformed pathology, particularly the increased optics of the microscope and its financial availability. The microscope became increasingly used in autopsy as medical men were able to analyse organs in detail, through the study of cell and tissue structure.[26] The pathologist who carried out the autopsy on the child of Louisa Lunn, Ludwig Freyberger, presented the autopsy findings and stated:

> there was a broad encircling mark of constriction running round the neck below the thyroid cartilage … under the skin covering the neck, above the constriction were numerous haemorrhages and others in the muscles surrounding the larynx and the back of the head … I found two haemorrhages on the back of the tongue, each the size of a lentil, and a number of smaller ones in the mucous membrane covering the tonsils.[27]

The detail in the findings made by Freyberger indicates that it was highly likely a microscope was used to observe the minute nature of the injuries he discovered. Freyberger believed the cause of death to be "suffocation by strangulation by some soft material being tightly, wound round the neck, and the reasons for his opinion are the width to the circling mark."[28] He also believed the child to be born fully before death had taken place, all factors that strongly pointed to the possibility of murder. However, the jury found Louisa guilty of manslaughter, with the strong recommendation of mercy; she was discharged on her own recognisances, as she was willing to go into a home for two years.[29]

Following the landmark case of Dr Crippen, pathology received recognition of a specific science.[30] Dr Crippen, a "Yale Tooth Specialist"[31] stood accused of murdering his wife and burying her corpse in the cellar. When police discovered "several of the bricks were loose, the officers decided to dig up the whole floor and after some time came across human remains."[32] The remains found by the police were described as a "headless, limbless de-sexed remains of a human body wrapped in pyjamas."[33] Dr Bernard Spilsbury (1877–1947), who through his interpretation of the evidence found at the crime scene, significantly contributed to the establishment of the profession. When giving evidence at the trial, he stated that

> on September 9th he made a microscopical examination of a piece of skin with a mark upon it. He formed the opinion that it was an old scar on subcutaneous tissue, the skin showed changes due to dissection and a very slight formation of adiopocere[34]

However, "he could find no putrefaction and no microorganisms were present."[35] He was of the opinion that the scar was evidence of surgery, consistent with the medical history of Cora Crippen, who had had an ovary removed. Although when asked if he could determine the gender of the deceased, he replied, "no he was unable to tell, nor could he tell which part of the body the skin had been attached."[36]

Throughout his career Spilsbury worked alone, an issue that resulted in the absence of confirmation of his findings or peer review. Spilsbury assembled a "story about the body from within the enclosed space of the mortuary and then emerged to defend it in public and contested space of the courtroom."[37] This attitude led to increasing concerns that Spilsbury was developing a celebrity status; with his overwhelming ability to present expert opinion in court he might distract the jury, who appeared persuaded by his eminence, as opposed to his scientific evidence.[38] Based on the evidence from Spilsbury, it took the jury at the Old Bailey 27 minutes to find Dr Crippen guilty of the murder of his wife; he was hanged at Pentonville Prison 1910.[39]

In infanticide cases, the developing profession of pathology was crucial. Infanticidal women had given birth alone, and with a lack of independent witness, it was difficult to determine whether a child had been born alive. As previously identified, the accusations of murder were stronger if the body of the child had been hidden away and the birth concealed. Accusations were stronger still if the child had sustained external marks of violence, such as knife or puncture wounds, strangulation, or throat injuries, many of which may have been caused during an unassisted delivery. In court, medical men had previously answered crucial legal questions with both vagueness and uncertainty. However, as juries demonstrated sympathy towards infanticidal women and a reluctance to find them guilty, arguably, science continued to produce uncertainty, a crucial element for the acquittal of these women.

This is depicted in the case of Maud Waines, a domestic servant in service at Bridlington, who was charged with the wilful murder of her infant child in August 1909. The body of the child had been found near a railway bridge just outside the town. Dr Forrest, Medical Officer for the Borough, carried out the post-mortem but struggled to provide a definitive answer to whether the child had had a separate existence. However, he appears to be certain the child was born alive; he testified that

> the body appeared to be fully developed and the examination of the lungs indicated that respiration had taken place. He concluded that the child had been born alive. He could not positively affirm that it had a separate existence, but he thought it probably had a short separate existence. There was an extensive contusion on the scalp. He also found an effusion of coagulated blood which pointed to the probability of violence having been inflicted either during life or immediately after death. The immediate cause of death in the witness's opinion was violence so inflicted causing concussion of the brain. A fall at birth might have caused the injuries the witness found.[40]

The child had been dead for seven days before the post-mortem took place, a fact that hindered the doctor's diagnosis, except it seems with regard to the lungs as he found "the separate existence of the child if at all was of very short duration, not more than five minutes. He based his opinion of the child having had a separate existence mainly on the lungs and other signs."[41] On cross-examination, Dr Forrest was asked:

> what tests did you apply to the lungs? I put them undivided into water and found they floated. I compressed them and they still floated. I cut the lung into pieces, compressed them and they still floated. Are those tests conclusive? Yes. Absolutely conclusive? I consider they are. Is it possible for a child to be partly born and breathe? Yes. Breathing is not the same as being born alive? No. A child may breathe and yet be born dead? Yes.[42]

This evidence highlights the inconsistencies in Dr Forrest's testimony; he states that it is possible for a child to breathe but be born dead. He also appears to have a great deal of confidence in the hydrostatic test, believing the test to be "absolutely conclusive," regardless of the concerns about its accuracy and reliability.

In respect of a precipitous birth, the questioning of Dr Forrest continued in the following manner:

> is it possible for the injuries to be caused by a fall on a brick floor? Yes, if the birth was precipitate. He was then asked, if the contusion was caused by a direct blow, should you have looked for abrasion of the skin and fracture of the skull? Yes, I should have looked for it, but it was possible to deliver such a blow without abrasion of the skin. Was a fall in this case as probable as a direct blow? I think it might be equally possible. The coagulated blood would be equally probable if the contusion was caused just before or just after death? Yes. Dr Forrest was then re-examined, stating that five minutes was the outside limit of the child's separate existence and assuming that it was alive for that length of time it would not be a case of the child making shallow respirations. Birth contusions did not usually cause death.[43]

When examining the witness Morris Sonnenfeld, a pawnbroker's assistant, who had known the prisoner for the past 12 months, he was asked to describe his relationship with the prisoner. The bench "intimated at this stage that all respectable women should leave the court, and every female left."[44]

The defence argued that Maud had been in:

> very great distress and in an anxious state of mind when she came too on the occasion of the birth, the child was dead on the bed. She did not like to part with the body, but she had to dispose of it somewhere. She had already suffered for what she had done, not only in mind but also in body. She had been in prison for the last four months and he suggested the most humane case would be to bind her over. The father went into the box and said he was prepared to take his daughter back and welcome her into his home.[45]

The judge was satisfied the contusion on the baby's head was caused by falling when she had no one to help her; she was bound over.

Lizzie Marsh was indicted with the wilful murder of her illegitimate infant at Lincoln Assizes in February 1901. The child was discovered in a pond, its mouth stuffed with rags:

> the medical evidence indicated that the child must have lived after it was born, but the doctor was unable to say positively that it had a separate existence. Lizzie pleaded guilty to concealment of birth and she was sentenced to twelve months hard labour.[46]

The judge stated that the evidence was not "sufficient to substantiate the charge of wilful murder, but there were circumstances in the case which rendered it one of very grave suspicion."[47]

The cases demonstrate how the courts adopted a softer approach towards women accused of infanticide, with the evidence given by medical men continuing to assist the jury in doing so. As the medical men before them, pathologists were also required to concentrate on providing answers to three key questions; did the child have a separate existence? Was the child born alive? And, if so, what was the cause of death?[48] However, the most important issue was establishing separate existence, as without this, no crime had taken place. The only clear sign indicating that separation had not been achieved was maceration, described as an "aseptic partial breakdown of the skin and body organs of the infant and signifies death in-utero, thus ruling out any possibility of separate existence."[49] In the absence of maceration, pathologists continued to rely heavily on the lung test, which did not specifically prove separate existence, but merely established that the child might have taken a breath. As Dr Forrest stated in the case of Maud Waines, the fact that the child might have taken a breath does not emphatically prove live birth, and therefore as a source of scientific evidence, this test is unreliable: he testified that it was possible for a child to breathe and yet be born dead.[50]

The issues of whether a child is born alive and the meaning of life in the legal sense were discussed in the civil case of *Brock v Kellock*,[51] a case that concerned the administration of property. In this case, two methods were identified for determining whether a child was live-born:

> the child may respire soon after delivery or the child may be, born the cord pulsating showing that it is alive, yet it may not respire. In this state, it may continue for some time, then die from natural causes or as a result of criminal interference before respiration has commenced.[52]

If a child is born in this condition in the absence of respiration, surviving only as a foetus in utero by means of circulation, supplied through the umbilical cord attached to the mother, and the child dies before the onset of respiration, "there are no changes which have taken place by which the previous vitality could be established. This view shows how impossible it would be to prove that a child has been born alive independently of respiration."[53] Such a situation clearly added to uncertainty in the findings of the pathologist. Two medical men at the trial regarded respiration as a significant element; however, others argued that "any one indication of vitality, whether respiration, pulsation or muscular action after birth was sufficient to testify to the existence of life."[54] Due to the fact that pulsation of the cord had been felt and yet respiration had not occurred, the court in this case held the latter opinion and declared the child had been born alive.[55]

The continuous struggle for medical men to provide definitive answers to the key questions in cases involving infanticide is also related to the fact that there is "no authorised definition of live birth in the theory of the law and the proof that this condition in conformity with any definition submitted is often not easy."[56] There is a very clear decisive answer to the medico-legal question, when does life end? The answer to which is when the heart ceases to beat;[57] however, the answer to the question, when does life begin? is not so explicit. This contributed to the uncertainty surrounding cases of infanticide over the centuries and continues to be a contentious issue today, specifically in debates surrounding the "right to life."[58] If the answer is based upon the unambiguous question of death, then it should naturally follow that life begins when the heart begins to beat; however, this would be shortly after conception at approximately two weeks' gestation. But the developing embryo at this stage would not be able to breathe independently and would therefore be incapable of a separate existence. The lungs of the embryo are growing and developing but only begin to respire when born, free of physiological or gestational complications. This question of live birth has historically been a complicated one; medical men were impeded by physiological facts and "judicial dicta, restricted by terms of the definition of murder."[59] Since 1803 and the introduction of the Lord Ellenborough Act, a definition of the precise moment at which a foetus became a living human being was required. Clarification was needed whether it was when the child was born wholly into the world, or when a separate existence had been achieved. The concept of being born must mean that the whole body is brought into the world, and it is not sufficient that the child respires in the progress of the birth. This pivotal change at birth, signifying the onset of life, is as follows: "respiration is the chief change at birth; and the appearance and condition of the lungs are proof of it";[60] hence, the heavy reliance on the hydrostatic test to prove the separate existence in cases involving infanticide. However, its lack of reliability led to a reluctance in the courtroom to attach significance to its results, and so throughout the late eighteenth and during the nineteenth century it began to receive much criticism by medical men such as William Hunter and Alfred Swain Taylor.[61]

An absence of independent witnesses to the majority of cases of infanticide left the only other "witness capable of stating whether the child achieved a separate existence is the pathologist who examines the body of the child post mortem."[62] The following twentieth-century Lincolnshire cases demonstrate the medical men who were certain the child was born alive and that death occurred following the live delivery of the child in each case; however, none of the women were found guilty of wilful murder.

Maria Smith was charged with the murder of her illegitimate child, before the Grimsby stipendiary magistrate, in December 1921. The body was discovered by her sister, Lydia, amongst refuse at the back of her house. Maria admitted giving birth to the child but claimed it was stillborn. Dr Wallace, who carried out an examination of the body, stated that

> the child's hair nostrils and mouth were filled with dust. There was a mark on the throat, which was due to considerable pressure. The mark had evidently been caused by human hand. The child was fully developed, and had evidently had a separate existence as dust, which proved to be cinder dust, extended into the windpipe, thus showing the child had breathed. Death was due to suffocation, either from the presence of foreign bodies in the wind pipe or by pressure on the larynx.[63]

Lyndia Ann Thurston, a witness, stated that she heard the cries of an infant. Both Maria and Lydia Smith were charged with wilful murder and committed for trial at Lincoln Assizes. However, the case collapsed when the "counsel for the defence submitted there was no evidence against Lydia Smith," and the judge said the case "could not go any further as there was no evidence to show which woman was implicated. He directed the jury to find a verdict of not guilty against them both," which they duly did, and they were both discharged.[64]

In the case of Ethel Rickells, in June 1925, her child was found wrapped and left under a hedge, near Ashby in Lincolnshire; she was indicted for infanticide. Medical tests proved that the child had had a separate existence, and in the "opinion of the doctor who carried out the tests, the child died from lack of attention and exposure."[65] Dr Bellamy said the child was a "fully developed male, weighing 8Ibs and had lived, the cause of death was a shock, exposure and general want of attention. He had also seen the accused and her condition was consistent with recently having given birth to a child."[66] The judge urged the jury to consider the fact there had been no criminal wilful negligence; the jury therefore returned a verdict of "guilty of concealment of birth and the prisoner was sentenced to six months imprisonment."[67]

At the inquest into the death of the child of Gladys May Barton, April 1932, the body of the child had been discovered in a garden at Corringham, in Lincolnshire. Dr Scorgie who carried out the post-mortem, stated:

> the child was well nourished and there were marks of violence on the body. There was a large compressed fracture of the right side of the head three inches in length and two inches in breadth, while the skull over this area was exposed the scalp having been torn off. There was a lacerated wound of the chest wall one and a half inches long. The legs were in their entirety charred and the skin of the back and abdomen was burned to a much lesser degree. The brain was severely mutilated, but the heart and lungs were normal. The possible cause of death was syncope[68] resulting from haemorrhage. He thought that the wounds on the chest and the fracture of the skull and the burning of the body occurred after death.[69]

The coroner asked, "the child must have been alive?" To which the doctor replied, "yes probably for an hour." The coroner then asked, "there was nothing to enable you to form the opinion there was any wilful act or omission?" "No," replied the doctor. In summing up, the coroner stated:

> the cause of death was syncope due to haemorrhage that could not be natural and therefore it must be accidental, there was no evidence said the coroner of murder or manslaughter or of infanticide, because there was no evidence of wilful murder neglect or omission.[70]

At the Lincoln Assizes, where Caroline Bingham in November 1931 had been charged with infanticide in the town of Brigg, Dr Lambert of Lincoln described how a towel had been tied around the child's neck, covering the child's head:

> it had evidently been tied by a person who had shown great determination, a post-mortem examination showed that the child had breathed and had had a separate existence, he could only come to the conclusion that death had been caused by strangulation.[71]

On cross-examination, he denied that the child might have breathed and yet not have had a separate existence. Mr Sandlands, defence lawyer, said that as Dr Lambert was unable to "assure the court beyond reasonable doubt that the towel had not been tied after the child had died, he submitted that there was no case for him to answer."[72] Without leaving the jury box, the jury returned a verdict of "not guilty" of infanticide, as there was insufficient evidence.[73]

In the case of Dora Whiter, who was charged with the murder of her newly born child, in November 1937, the body of her infant was discovered wrapped in paper in the River Witham in Lincolnshire. At the inquest, medical evidence revealed that "the child had been dead for some 10 or 14 days, but apparently it had only been in the water for a few hours. The doctor was definitely of the opinion that the child had had a separate existence."[74] Dr Lakes, who carried out the post-mortem, stated that the child had

> breathed and cried, its lungs were fully expanded, very well preserved and were pink and mottled. There was no evidence of decomposition. The body was that of a full-time male child weighing 7Ib 5oz. Externally there was considerable decomposition. On the right side of the skull was a bruise, the size of a 5s piece, which in itself was not sufficient to cause death.[75]

He continued by stating:

> there was no evidence to show how the child had died. He could no further than to say that had any determined effort had been made to keep the child alive, it would have been alive. It might have died through violence or it might have died through neglect. If the child had been wrapped up and placed in a cupboard for two or three weeks, he would expect to find conditions similar to those he had found in this case.[76]

It is apparent from Dr Lakes' evidence that the cause of death is unclear and uncertain, although he does appear certain the child breathed and had a separate existence prior to death. The jury found Dora "guilty" of concealment, and she was sentenced to three months' imprisonment.

These cases demonstrate the difficulty the pathologist might experience in determining whether the mother of the child had contributed to the death of her infant, whether through act or omission. The difficulty lay with the general perception that an autopsy would somehow reveal the mother's guilty mind, and, as this clearly was not the case, it merely added to the extent of uncertainty already present in the circumstances in each case. Once again, the uncertainty created by the pathologist's evidence proved to be advantageous to the jury, who were then able to find the woman not guilty or guilty of the lesser offence of concealment of birth.

Overlaying

Pathologists have also been involved in the controversial cases of overlaying where the courts have relied heavily on medical expert evidence to provide answers to significant questions of intent; such cases have been described as controversial as overlaying was interpreted by some as a method of infanticide. Historically, it was common practice for parents to place a nursing infant in their bed at night, consequently overlaying occurred when a parent rolled over onto the child smothering it and causing death, a practice which has been argued by Hanson in many cases as "intentional" with parents wishing to dispose of unwanted children.[77] However, there were in fact very few overlaid infants that were considered victims of infanticide, mainly due to the "lack of proof to contradict claims that the overlaying was accidental."[78]

The role of the nineteenth-century pathologist in such cases related to the determining of the cause of death, and crucially to ascertain whether the child's death was caused intentionally. The intoxication of the mother in many cases added to the already difficult factors of the case, calling into question whether the mother was capable of caring for the child at the time of its death or if she was sober enough to be in control of her actions.[79] The following cases from the Old Bailey demonstrate some of the difficulties the medical men faced: Susannah McKenzie, who was indicted for feloniously killing and slaying two-month-old Thomas McKenzie on July 2, 1855, was known to take to drinking for several days at a time. Dr Simpson, surgeon, gave evidence at the trial, stating that

> on Sunday evening, 24th June, I was called to go to the prisoner's mother's house, with Sergeant Roberts, about half past 8 o'clock—I saw the child; it had then been dead, I should say, three or four hours—from what I heard, I should fancy it died from suffocation—I found no blood on its person there was a mark completely round the loins; that was caused by pressure it might have been caused by overlaying the child—I made a post mortem examination, and was of the opinion that death was caused by suffocation; not by the hands of a person, but by overlaying—the bruise on the loins was not connected with the cause of death; alight pressure might cause that in so young a child—I saw the prisoner at the house; she was intoxicated, and I should say not capable of taking care of the child.[80]

He concludes that death was caused by suffocation, and "not by the hands of a person,"[81] implying that suffocation was not caused by a person's hands but possibly by their body; it is also possible that by stating suffocation was not caused by the hands of a person he is stating he believed the death to be accidental. Susannah was found not guilty by the jury.

Charlotte King was indicted for the wilful murder of her male infant child on January 7, 1867,[82] after the infant was found in a bundle on the muddy banks on a riverbank. At the trial two medical men were in disagreement: Henry John Thorpe, surgeon, who performed a post-mortem upon the child believed death occurred because of asphyxia:[83]

> on 4th December I was called by Drewitt and made an examination of the body of a male child—the whole surface was covered with livid patches, livid discolourations, but there were no marks of violence—the livid discolourations extended to the face—I then opened the head, and found the brain and its membranes perfectly healthy—I opened the chest and found the lungs pale and collapsed, and the right side of the heart full of clotted blood—the stomach contained a little milk, and the intestines a little fecal matter—every organ was perfectly healthy—the bladder was empty and the kidneys somewhat congested—my opinion is that the child died from *asphyxia*, that is suffocation—there was nothing whatever to indicate disease—the appearances I describe were consistent with the cause I assign.[84]

On cross-examination, he was asked:

> is suffocation the absence of air from the lungs from whatever cause? Yes—there was nothing to indicate what caused the asphyxia—I have no doubt that in children death sometimes occurs where a post-mortem examination shows no assignable cause for death—I should think that spasm of the glottis might cause a child's death. Do I understand you that you cannot tell whether the suffocation was by immersion or otherwise? The appearances were compatible with suffocation from drowning. Compatible with suffocation by being overlaid? Yes, or any other cause—it is the fact that healthy children are sometimes suffocated by being overlaid and are deprived of breath without any intention to destroy them—the symptoms I saw were consistent with death from that or any other cause.[85]

Fredrick James Gant, surgeon to the Royal Free Hospital and pathological anatomist, on the other hand claimed the colour of the lungs to be inconsistent with any kind of suffocation and that the child died suddenly because of natural causes:

> the pale colour of the lungs described by Mr. Thorpe is in my judgment inconsistent with sudden or forcible pressure on the lungs from any cause, and inconsistent with any kind of suffocation, and as regards the membranes of the brain, I should expect to find them congested from violent suffocation—I

> should not expect to find the lungs collapsed if the air had been excluded from them by forcible means, or by forcible pressure be made on the wind-pipe in any way.[86]

He concluded that death was caused by asphyxia but inconsistent with drowning or overlaying. The jury found Charlotte not guilty, and, arguably, by each doctor not knowing and contradicting each other's findings, they conveyed uncertainty.

Old Bailey cases, 1914–1955

The remaining sections of this chapter will concentrate on cases reported at the Old Bailey and in Hull during the period 1914–1955. There were 39 cases reported in newspapers during this period, a factor that undoubtedly highlighted that not all infanticide cases held may have been reported in the newspapers. A further shortcoming is the fact that the majority of newspapers publish a short report of the Old Bailey cases; in contrast to this, the local newspaper's reporting the provincial cases of Hull and the surrounding area are more detailed.

The Old Bailey cases highlight that during this period three pathologists in particular tended to be called upon: Dr Francis Camps, Dr Keith Simpson, and Dr Donald Teare. The developing role of the pathologist appears to have transpired into something of a celebrity status; it has been reported, for example, that Dr Teare travelled round London in a chauffeur-driven Rolls Royce along with his secretary and her typewriter.[87] Whereas in the mortuary, in many instances, the "attendant had opened up many of the bodies so that Dr Teare could complete the autopsy, with the suspicious deaths saved for Teares' inspection before any incisions."[88] The work carried out by pathologists on high-profile murder cases may also have placed them firmly in the public eye, in contrast to the nineteenth-century medical men, working in the background to determine the cause of death, carrying out post-mortems anonymously. This high-profile status also gave them the opportunity to provide recommendations for public health from their findings; at the inquest into the death of three-month-old Raymond Pearson, Home Office Pathologist, Dr Simpson, gave evidence to the effect that the child suffocated in his cot. He recommended the use of hard pillows which, he said, "may be uncomfortable but it is much safer."[89]

In July 1925, Emily Agnes Farthing pleaded guilty to infanticide; the doctor stated that the child had died from strangulation caused by lace tied around the neck. As there was no proof the child had had a separate existence, Emily was discharged. The case demonstrates that, regardless of advancements in scientific technology and forensic medicine, medical men continued to struggle to prove separate existence in suspected infanticide cases.[90]

Similarly, in the case of Olive Horton, who was accused of the wilful murder of her infant, the *Dundee Evening Telegraph* reported that "no evidence was offered at the Old Bailey, she was described as a factory hand, she was found not guilty and discharged."[91]

Kathleen Constance Blundell Hughes pleaded guilty to infanticide in June 1936; a post-mortem examination of the child revealed that the "child had lived and that the cause of death was asphyxia from pressure on the nose and throat."[92] Following the inquest, Kathleen had attended the police station and admitted the child was hers, stating, "It was my baby, I did it."[93] The defence stated that her father had been in the Royal Navy and had drowned at sea during the last war; her mother and grandmother had therefore raised her. The Lord Chief Justice bound her over for 12 months, stating, "no good purpose could be served by sending her to prison,"[94] despite the overwhelming medical evidence that the child was asphyxiated.

Mrs Lola Joan Heathcote pleaded guilty to infanticide in January 1944; she stated that she was unaware she was pregnant. At the time of the trial, Lola's husband was a prisoner in the hands of the Japanese. Lola had been staying with friends when the child was born;

> she tied a tape around its neck on one occasion. She had been to a party where there were many yanks; she had some drink and remembered nothing … she was sentenced to two days imprisonment, which meant her immediate release.[95]

Similarly in the case of Kathleen Betty Cross, March 1950, who pleaded guilty to infanticide, Dr Teare said the child who was between "two and four weeks premature had lived for five to ten minutes, and death was due to haemorrhage from fractures from the skull."[96] Kathleen was granted a conditional discharge from Mr Morris J., stating, "you have already suffered and I am not going to send you to prison, you are not likely to get into trouble again."[97]

The cases demonstrate that, despite substantive evidence proving the mother's guilt, the evidence provided by the pathologist was largely overlooked. This is evident in the verdict the women were given and the sentence they received. Statements such as "she is unlikely to get into trouble again" and "no good purpose could be served by sending her to prison" indicate not only a degree of sympathy towards these women but also that the judges did not necessarily regard these women as criminals.

Hull and the surrounding area cases, 1914–1955

In the period 1914–1955 there were 14 cases of infanticide in Hull, some of which have already been discussed in Chapter 4, as the women were found guilty but insane. The following section will discuss cases in which medical evidence was given by either a police surgeon or pathologist, highlighting in particular how the evidence continued to convey uncertainty. Some of the cases proceeded to the Assizes court; however, others were dealt with at the inquest stage, and whichever authority dealt with the charge, medical expert evidence was usually given.

At the inquest into the death of an unidentified child, discovered wrapped in paper in a public lavatory in Hulls West Park in April 1929, a crucial piece of evidence was presented by Dr Malcolm McLeod, who carried out a post-mortem examination on the body. He stated that "death was caused by asphyxiation due to strangulation; particularly important was the evidence to the severe restriction of the neck."[98] A band had been discovered which encircled the neck

> so many times, and was so securely fixed that there was no question as to an accidental cause. Therefore, it must have been done by some person with evil intent. From the age of the child and from the period that it had been dead, the doctor's evidence was that the mother would hardly have been in condition to take the body to the place where it was found. Therefore, even if she had had any active hand in the end of the child, someone else must have taken the parcel to the lavatory. There was also the possibility that the woman's condition might have been such that she knew nothing of what had happened. The jury therefore returned the verdict of murder against some person or persons unknown.[99]

Similarly, at the inquest into the death of a child found in a pond at Wawne, in East Yorkshire, despite the fact a piece of string had been tied around the child's neck, the medical witness said he was

> unable to ascertain whether the death was due to strangulation. He stated that it was quite impossible to tell whether the string around the neck was the cause of death, there being no means of telling how the child had died.[100]

As there was not sufficient evidence to determine the cause of death, the jury returned an open verdict of found dead.

At the inquest into the death of the child of Joan Davis, on October 1, 1931, Dr Mcleod gave evidence at the Hull Royal Infirmary. McLeod stated that the child had been born alive and had breathed freely, the death was caused by "asphyxia, it was due to strangulation or pressure of the windpipe."[101] He added, "I do not know what it was due to, but it was caused by something which excluded free access of air to the lungs. It might have been due to wrapping the child up in a cloth during life."[102] He found the child in a "receptacle with its mouth and nostrils and the rest of the body, with the exception of the head completely submerged, but it was not drowned. The child had probably been placed in the receptacle after it was dead."[103] The jury returned a verdict of inattention at birth.

At the inquest into the death of one of Florence Lee's twin infants, Dr McLeod examined the child, believing it to be fully developed. He stated that "there were no external marks of violence, but there was present a muddy fluid. In his opinion, the child had breathed freely and had lived; death was due to asphyxiation following drowning."[104] In her defence, Florence stated she was unaware of her condition, she did not anticipate the birth and had not prepared for the arrival of either child. The jury returned a verdict of inattention at birth.

An inquest was held at Londesborough Park in the East Riding in November 1931, looking into the death of Margery Cobner's newly born child, discovered in a shoebox under her bed. Dr Ashwin gave evidence, he explained how a sleeve from a blouse had been

> tied around the child's neck and a portion of cloth was in the child's mouth; the knot was sufficient to cause death. Death could have been caused by any form of suffocation, which was always a great danger at inattention at birth.[105]

However, Margery's defence team argued that the sleeve was not tied very tightly and the blouse could easily have been placed over the child's head in an attempt to dress the infant. The jury found that the "child had been born alive and was suffocated by the mother, by tying a piece of cloth round its neck, but that Cobner had not fully recovered and her mind was disturbed. A verdict of infanticide was returned."[106] At the York Assizes Dr Ashwin stated,

> the blouse was tied sufficiently tight to cause death. The child had had a separate existence. In his opinion, death was due to strangulation. He stated that the girl's condition was consistent with a collapse immediately after birth. The jury found the prisoner not guilty and she was discharged.[107]

At the inquest into the death of the infant of Elsie Lilley, in September 1944, Dr Philip Science, police surgeon, carried out an autopsy. He stated that

> the child had had a separate existence and had lived about one day. The body was so much burned that it was impossible to detect any signs of violence. It was also impossible to say whether the child was dead or alive when it was taken from the fire. In his opinion, the cause of death was shock following extensive burns. That is providing the child was alive when it was put on the fire, observed the coroner. Yes, replied Dr Science.[108]

Elsie's husband was away serving with the armed forces, and they had two children. In his absence Elsie had a relationship with another man and was expecting his baby. She had informed her neighbours that, as soon as the baby was born, it was to be adopted; this, however, was not the case.[109] The judge at the York Assizes postponed sentencing while he asked the authorities to find an establishment for her for not less than 12 months.[110]

At the inquest into the death of the child of Joan Marshall, in August 1950, Dr Arthur Shillitoe, pathologist, of Kingston General Hospital, stated that "he carried out a post-mortem and found that the girl was well nourished. The body was in a good state of preservation. There were no fractures. Dr Shillitoe said that in his opinion the cause of death was asphyxiation."[111] When Joan appeared before the East Riding Magistrates Court, she was indicted for the murder of her two-week-old infant, within two hours of returning from hospital and burying the body under a hedge. She confessed to suffocating and burying the child but continued by saying, "what made me do it, I don't know, I had a bad time in hospital." She said she "wanted to keep the child, but felt it was hard on my father. It was not my husband's baby."[112] Dr Shillitoe said Joan had been suffering from pyrexia. Anyone suffering from pyrexia would be abnormal.[113] Joan was committed to trial at York Assizes,[114] where the judge stated that the "prison doctor who has given great attention to your case does not give a favourable view of you, he describes you as skittish, emotionally unstable and inclined to throw herself at any man who looks at you."[115] She was placed under the supervision of the probation officer for two years.

The provincial cases and the cases held at the Old Bailey demonstrate how the medical evidence continued to produce uncertainty. The questions crucial to cases of infanticide particularly remain uncertain in many cases, and it seems that the

> simple and indubitable fact is that when a mother destroys her child's life a few minutes after birth and before any has seen it living, it is next to impossible – we should say quite impossible – for any medical practitioner to be sure that it has been fully born alive and it is only those who know little about the subject who will dare to swear that any post mortem signs are conclusive of complete living birth.[116]

A problem is created by the lack of a definition as to being wholly born, a separate existence and a definitive answer to the onset of life.

The uncertainty created by the medical experts during the period 1914–1955 allowed the jury to give a softer or more lenient verdict. However, in some cases lenient verdicts continued to be given, despite substantive evidence, proving the woman's guilt either through pathological evidence or confession. The lenient approach is also reflected in the sentences given to the women during this period; the courts were beginning to focus on care for these women as opposed to punishment. This raises the question – were infanticidal women regarded as a legal problem, or was infanticide now beginning to be perceived as a moral or medical problem?

Notes

1 Today the role of the pathologist includes histopathology and cytology and continues to include the performance of autopsy, either at the request of clinicians to establish or confirm cause of death or at the request of the coroner. Histopathology is the "study of abnormal tissue especially by means of microscopic examination" *The Oxford English Dictionary*, available at: www.oed.com/view/Entry/296270?redirectedFrom=histopathology#eid [Last accessed 16th February 2016]; Cytology is the "study of the structure and function of cells" *The Oxford English Dictionary*, available at: www.oed.com/view/Entry/46739?redirectedFrom=cytology#eid [Last accessed February 16, 2016].

2 S. Smith, 'The History and Development of Forensic Medicine' *The British Medical Journal*, Vol. 1, No. 4707, 1951, pp. 599–607: 599.

3 E. Sagall, 'Forensic Medicine, the Medicolegal History' *Journal of Law, Medicine and Ethics*, Vol. 8, No. 2, 1980, pp. 10–13: 10.

4 Burney (2000) op. cit.: 109.

5 I. Burney and N. Pemberton, 'The Rise and Fall of Celebrity Pathology' *British Medical Journal*, Vol. 34, No. 7786, 18–25 December 2010, pp. 1319–1321: 1319.

6 Ibid.

7 Kellett (1992) op. cit.: 3.
8 D. Scott, 'Case of Infanticide with Remarks' *Edinburgh Medical and Surgical Journal*, Vol. 26, 1829, pp. 62–73: 72. Available at: https://books.google.co.uk/books [Last accessed February 18, 2016].
9 Ibid.
10 Ibid.
11 Ibid.
12 Ibid.: 62.
13 W. Collins, *The Moonstone*. New York and London: Harper & Brothers Publishers, 1874.
14 'The Sherlock Holmes Society of London' at: www.sherlock-holmes.org.uk/conan-doyle/ [Last accessed September 16, 2015].
15 A. Taylor, *The Principles and Practice of Medical Jurisprudence*. Tenth Edition, 2 Vols. London: J. & A Churchill, 1928: Vol. 1: 15.
16 Ibid.: 16.
17 B. Strachan, 'Coroners' Necropsies' *British Medical Journal*, Vol. 2, No. 2168, 19th July 1902, p. 232. Spelling is original.
18 S. Atkinson, *Golden Rules of Medical Evidence*. Bristol: John Wright, 1902: 47. Available at: https://archive.org/details/b20443481 [Last accessed August 14, 2015].
19 Ibid.
20 *OBP*, March 1904, Louisa Lunn, t19040321-332.
21 Ibid.
22 Ibid.
23 Ibid.
24 Ibid.
25 For further insight into the historical developments of the relationship between science and the law, see A. Adam, *A History of Forensic Science, British Beginnings in the Twentieth Century*. Oxford: Routledge, 2016, Chapter 1.
26 J. Van den Tweel and C. Taylor, 'A Brief History of Pathology' *Virchows Arch*, Vol. 457, 2010, pp. 3–10: 7.
27 *OBP*, March 1904, Louisa Lunn, t19040321-332.
28 Ibid.
29 Ibid.
30 This case was not only a landmark case in pathology, but it was also the first case in which a "wanted person" had been captured with the use of wireless communication. Crippen had absconded with his 27-year-old mistress to Brussels and it was the captain of the ship SS Montrose, sailing from Antwerp to Quebec, who recognised the fugitives escaping to start in new life together in America.
31 *Sheffield Evening Telegraph*, 'The Discovery' Friday July 15, 1910. British Newspaper Archive (www.britishnewspaperarchive.co.uk); The British Library Board; Image © the British Library Board. All rights reserved.
32 Ibid.
33 G. Pierce, 'Homicide by Hyoscine: The Case of Dr Crippen' *Irish Medical Times*, Vol. 44, No. 23, June 4, 2010, pp. 24–25: 24.
34 *A Greyish or Yellowish-White Waxy or Cheesy Substance Formed in Dead Bodies as Part of the Process of Bacterial Decomposition*. Available at: www.oed.com/view/Entry/2394?redirectedFrom=adipocere#eid [Last accessed August 23, 2015].
35 *Hull Daily Mail*, 'Crippen and Miss Le Neve' Friday September 16, 1910. British Newspaper Archive (www.britishnewspaperarchive.co.uk); The British Library Board; Image © the British Library Board. All rights reserved.
36 Ibid.
37 Burney and Pemberton (2010) op. cit.: 1320.
38 See Adam (2016) op. cit.: 34–37.
39 D. Foran, et al., 'The Conviction of Dr. Crippen: New Forensic Findings in a Century Old Murder' *Journal of Forensics Sciences*, Vol. 56, No. 1, January 2011, pp. 233–

240; G. Pierce, 'Homicide by Hyocine: The Case of Dr. Crippen' *Irish Medical Times*, Vol. 44, No. 23, 4th June 2010, pp. 24–25.

40 *Hull Daily Mail*, 'Charge of Murder' Tuesday August 24, 1909. British Newspaper Archive (www.britishnewspaperarchive.co.uk); The British Library Board; Image © the British Library Board. All rights reserved.

41 Ibid.

42 Ibid.

43 Ibid.

44 Ibid.

45 *Hull Daily Mail*, 'Bridlington Case' Wednesday November 17, 1909. British Newspaper Archive (www.britishnewspaperarchive.co.uk); The British Library Board; Image © the British Library Board. All rights reserved.

46 *Sheffield Daily Telegraph*, 'The Alleged Child Murder at Frodingham' Tuesday February 19, 1901. British Newspaper Archive (www.britishnewspaperarchive.co.uk); The British Library Board; Image © the British Library Board. All rights reserved.

47 Ibid.

48 The three key questions however can be divided into a further detailed questions, see, G. M. Male, *An Epitome of Judicial or Forensic Medicine*. London: T and G Underwood, 1816: 93–94.

49 Kellett (1992) op. cit.: 14.

50 *Hull Daily Mail*, 'Charge of Murder' Tuesday August 24, 1909. British Newspaper Archive (www.britishnewspaperarchive.co.uk); The British Library Board; Image © the British Library Board. All rights reserved.

51 *Brock v Kellock* (1861). 3 Giff. 58.

52 Ibid.

53 Ibid.

54 *Illustrated Times*, 'Law and Crime' Saturday May 4, 1861. British Newspaper Archive (www.britishnewspaperarchive.co.uk); The British Library Board; Image © the British Library Board. All rights reserved.

55 1861 30 L. J. Ch., 498.

56 S. Atkinson, 'Life, Death and Live-Birth' *Law Quarterly Review*, Vol. 20, 1904, pp. 134–159: 134.

57 T. Clark, 'The Law of Infanticide' *Journal of Jurisprudence*, Vol. 3, No. 25, 1859, pp. 1–9: 1.

58 See M. Rendel, 'Abortion and Human Rights: The European Convention on Human Rights Safeguards the Right to Life' *New Law Journal*, Vol. 141, No. 6520, 1991, pp. 1270; F. Kamm, *Creation and Abortion: A Study in Moral and Legal Philosophy*. New York: Oxford University Press, 1992; R. Gillon, 'Is There a 'New ethics of abortion'?' *Journal of Medical Ethics*, Vol. 27 supl II: ii5–ii9, 2001; K. Jones and C. Chaloner, 'Ethics and Abortion: The Arguments for and against' *The Nursing Standard*, Vol. 27, No. 47, 2007: 45–48.

59 Atkinson (1904) op. cit.: 141.

60 Clark (1859) op. cit.: 2.

61 Kellett (1992) op. cit.: 14.

62 Ibid.

63 *Lincolnshire Echo*, 'Alleged Child Murder' Thursday December 8, 1921. British Newspaper Archive (www.britishnewspaperarchive.co.uk); The British Library Board; Image © the British Library Board. All rights reserved.

64 *Nottingham Evening Post*, 'Case Collapses' Thursday February 2, 1922. British Newspaper Archive (www.britishnewspaperarchive.co.uk); The British Library Board; Image © the British Library Board. All rights reserved.

65 *Lincolnshire Echo*, 'Alleged Infanticide' Thursday June 18, 1925. British Newspaper Archive (www.britishnewspaperarchive.co.uk); The British Library Board; Image © the British Library Board. All rights reserved.

66 Ibid.
67 Ibid.
68 '*A Temporary Loss of Consciousness Caused by a Fall in Blood Pressure*' at: www.oxforddictionaries.com/definition/english/syncope [Last accessed September 1, 2015].
69 *Lincolnshire Echo*, 'Childs Body in Garden' Monday April 11, 1932. British Newspaper Archive (www.britishnewspaperarchive.co.uk); The British Library Board; Image © the British Library Board. All rights reserved.
70 Ibid.
71 *Lincolnshire Echo*, 'Found Not Guilty' Friday November 6, 1931. British Newspaper Archive (www.britishnewspaperarchive.co.uk); The British Library Board; Image © the British Library Board. All rights reserved.
72 Ibid.
73 Ibid.
74 *Nottingham Evening Post*, 'Charged with Murder' Thursday November 25, 1937. British Newspaper Archive (www.britishnewspaperarchive.co.uk); The British Library Board; Image © the British Library Board. All rights reserved.
75 Ibid.
76 *Lincolnshire Echo*, 'Lincoln Murder Charge' Thursday December 2, 1937. British Newspaper Archive (www.britishnewspaperarchive.co.uk); The British Library Board; Image © the British Library Board. All rights reserved.
77 Hanson (1979) op. cit.: 335.
78 R. Sauer, 'Infanticide and Abortion in Nineteenth-Century Britain' *Population Studies*, Vol. 32, No. 1, March 1978, pp. 81–93: 81.
79 Lancet, 'Is "Overlaying" Infanticide?' *Portsmouth Evening News*, Monday March 23, 1885. British Newspaper Archive (www.britishnewspaperarchive.co.uk); The British Library Board; Image © the British Library Board. All rights reserved.
80 *OBP*, July 1855, Susannah McKenzie t18550702-723.
81 Ibid.
82 *OBP*, January 1867, Charlotte King, t18670107-45.
83 Ibid.
84 Ibid.
85 Ibid.
86 Ibid.
87 T. Hedley-Whyte, 'On Being a Pathologist: How Does One Plan a Career, or Does One?' *Human Pathology*, Vol. 39, No. 9, 2008, pp. 1269–1974.
88 Ibid.: 1269.
89 *Dundee Evening Telegraph*, 'Hard Pillows Urged for Babies' Saturday August 27, 1949. British Newspaper Archive (www.britishnewspaperarchive.co.uk); The British Library Board; Image © the British Library Board. All rights reserved.
90 *Gloucester Citizen*, 'Mothers Acquittal of Child Murder' Tuesday July 21, 1925. British Newspaper Archive (www.britishnewspaperarchive.co.uk); The British Library Board; Image © the British Library Board. All rights reserved.
91 *Dundee Evening Telegraph*, 'Woman Acquitted of Infanticide' Thursday December 10, 1931. British Newspaper Archive (www.britishnewspaperarchive.co.uk); The British Library Board; Image © the British Library Board. All rights reserved.
92 *Gloucester Citizen*, 'Infanticide Admitted' Thursday June 25, 1936. British Newspaper Archive (www.britishnewspaperarchive.co.uk); The British Library Board; Image © the British Library Board. All rights reserved.
93 Ibid.
94 Ibid.
95 *Derby Daily Telegraph*, 'Woman Did Not Know She Was Expecting Child' Wednesday January 12, 1944. British Newspaper Archive (www.britishnewspaperarchive.co.uk); The British Library Board; Image © the British Library Board. All rights reserved.

96 *Western Daily Press*, 'Melksham Wray's Betrayal' Thursday March 23, 1950. British Newspaper Archive (www.britishnewspaperarchive.co.uk); The British Library Board; Image © the British Library Board. All rights reserved.
97 Ibid.
98 *Hull Daily Mail*, 'Hull Park Mystery' Wednesday April 10, 1929. British Newspaper Archive (www.britishnewspaperarchive.co.uk); The British Library Board; Image © the British Library Board. All rights reserved.
99 Ibid.
100 *Hull Daily Mail*, 'Baby in Pond' Tuesday June 25, 1929. British Newspaper Archive (www.britishnewspaperarchive.co.uk); The British Library Board; Image © the British Library Board. All rights reserved.
101 *Hull Daily Mail*, 'Mystery of Newly Born Baby' Thursday October 1, 1931. British Newspaper Archive (www.britishnewspaperarchive.co.uk); The British Library Board; Image © the British Library Board. All rights reserved.
102 Ibid.
103 Ibid.
104 *Hull Daily Mail*, 'Hulls Childs Death Verdict of Inattention at Birth' Thursday May 14, 1931. British Newspaper Archive (www.britishnewspaperarchive.co.uk); The British Library Board; Image © the British Library Board. All rights reserved.
105 *Hull Daily Mail*, 'Infants Body in Box', Wednesday June 24, 1931. British Newspaper Archive (www.britishnewspaperarchive.co.uk); The British Library Board; Image © the British Library Board. All rights reserved.
106 Ibid.
107 *Yorkshire Post and Leeds Intelligencer*, 'York Assizes, Londesborough Woman Acquitted' Thursday 26th November 1931. British Newspaper Archive (www.britishnewspaperarchive.co.uk); The British Library Board; Image © the British Library Board. All rights reserved.
108 *Hull Daily Mail*, 'Day-Old Baby Alleged Placed on Fire' Wednesday September 27, 1944. British Newspaper Archive (www.britishnewspaperarchive.co.uk); The British Library Board; Image © the British Library Board. All rights reserved.
109 *Hull Daily Mail*, 'Sentence Postponed' Saturday November 18, 1944. British Newspaper Archive (www.britishnewspaperarchive.co.uk); The British Library Board; Image © the British Library Board. All rights reserved.
110 Ibid.
111 *Hull Daily Mail*, 'Inquest on Baby Found in Hedge' Tuesday August 22, 1950. British Newspaper Archive (www.britishnewspaperarchive.co.uk); The British Library Board; Image © the British Library Board. All rights reserved.
112 *Hull Daily Mail*, 'Alleged to Have Buried Her Baby under a Hedge' Wednesday August 16, 1950. British Newspaper Archive (www.britishnewspaperarchive.co.uk); The British Library Board; Image © the British Library Board. All rights reserved.
113 *Yorkshire Evening Post*, 'She Murdered Baby Then' Wednesday August 16, 1950. British Newspaper Archive (www.britishnewspaperarchive.co.uk); The British Library Board; Image © the British Library Board. All rights reserved.
114 *Hull Daily Mail*, 'This Miserable Woman is Entitled to Be Spared any Anguish' Thursday August 17, 1950. British Newspaper Archive (www.britishnewspaperarchive.co.uk); The British Library Board; Image © the British Library Board. All rights reserved.
115 *Hull Daily Mail*, 'Infanticide of Melton Woman' Wednesday November 1, 1950. British Newspaper Archive (www.britishnewspaperarchive.co.uk); The British Library Board; Image © the British Library Board. All rights reserved.
116 Clark (1859) op. cit.: 7.

6 Conclusion

This book has demonstrated how uncertainty surrounding crucial answers arose from anatomical examination and scientific experiments. This in turn contributed to a significant shift of opinion towards infanticidal women in terms of how they were perceived and the treatment of these women by the courts and their punishment. Over time, the effect of changing moral perceptions made courts receptive to uncertainty as infanticidal women were perceived as not wicked enough for the death sentence; then, progressively during the twentieth century, infanticidal women were not perceived as wicked enough for a prison sentence. Throughout the passage of time, as the number of women acquitted of new-born child murder increased, two elements became essential in the acquittal of infanticidal women: the courts and their sympathy towards infanticidal women, and uncertain medical evidence. Focusing on these two elements, this conclusion will begin by identifying the key reasons why juries were reluctant to convict infanticidal women, before summarising the chapters within this book, and how each medical witness in turn contributed towards the uncertainty argument in infanticide cases.

During the eighteenth century, a period when a "litany of multiple offences carried the death penalty,"[1] jurors began to scale down the number of executions given, and avoided finding the prisoner guilty of an offence that carried the death sentence.[2] Jurors turned to mitigating circumstances such as the character of the prisoner or the nature of the offence.[3] Langbein has noted one juror's remark made to a parliamentary committee investigating capital punishment as being, "the majority of juries in cases not marked with any peculiar atrocity are desirous of discovering some circumstances in favour of the prisoner; are desirous of availing themselves of the least favourable circumstance or shadow of doubt,"[4] a principle that not only led to the sparing of many innocent lives but also many culpable lives. The process of contextualising the crime in this manner made jurors more receptive to the element of doubt; it therefore becomes increasingly transparent how important uncertainty became for infanticidal women to avoid the death sentence. Medical expert evidence, and particularly uncertain medical expert evidence supported by science, proved that uncertainty became crucial to the courts, as it allowed jurors to find the women not guilty of murder. As long as the capital offence existed, it seemed that a source of uncertainty was needed to avoid the death sentence in cases of infanticide.

DOI: 10.4324/9781003006299-6

The changes within the criminal justice process throughout the eighteenth century also contributed towards the acquittal of women of new-born child murder. Throughout the passage of time, there was less emphasis on the search for the truth and the dispute surrounding the questions of fact; instead, the courts turned to the motive or intention behind the killing. It was this intention that was difficult to establish, and it becomes apparent that the courts held the expectation that a post-mortem would reveal the woman's intention. Arguably, the development of the adversarial criminal trial assisted in the increasing number of acquittals of many infanticidal women and the gradual emergence of defence counsel towards the end of the eighteenth century.[5] Defence counsel had been permitted in felony trials at the Old Bailey from the 1730s however, very few defendants were represented.[6] Between 1784 and 1803, for example, "named defence counsel was employed in just under a third of trials,"[7] as the questioning of the defendants tended to be carried out by the judge.[8]

The issue of culpability is evident from some of the cases within this research, as the courts gradually came to recognise that the real perpetrator, her seducer, was not on trial. The fact that an infanticidal woman concealed the corpse of her illegitimate child suggests that the act was carried out in the hope of concealing her shame. The reluctance of the jury to convict women of infanticide was criticised by Martin, who states that the "prosecution takes no pains to convict, and judges and juries are determined not to believe that a child has been murdered, unless they find it with their throat cut, or its brains dashed out on the pavement,"[9] arguably, a reluctance that stems in part from uncertainty, created by medical evidence.

As the courts began to adopt a softer approach towards infanticidal women, the application of the general rule became established – that where uncertainty remained in infanticide cases, the woman should be given the benefit of the doubt, unless substantive evidence could be produced of the mother's intention to murder her infant.[10] As previously highlighted, women were found guilty of concealment of birth, an offence that carried a short prison sentence, and a sentence which may have been given in light of the fact they could have contributed to the death of the child. The reason for this increase in convictions of concealment, and the giving of shorter sentences, might lie with either uncertainty or the gendered construction of penal responses. Zedner has argued that during the nineteenth-century "penal responses to criminality and deviance were shaped by constructions of femininity."[11] She argues that criminal women were compared to a "highly artificial notion of ideal woman – an exemplary moral being,"[12] and so the women had not only committed a crime but had also committed an act that went against the grain of femininity – the women who were sent to prison for acts that contravened accepted norms, for example, sexual promiscuity and drunkenness,[13] were considered to be doubly deviant as they were considered guilty of both "breaking the law and conventions of appropriate female behaviour."[14] Penal responses therefore focused on the failings of these women by remoulding women into characters acceptable to both society and feminine ideology.[15] In respect of infanticide, it could be argued that the motive for the killing of her infant lay primarily with the desire to protect her reputation and economic situation. A fact that suggests that she understood and conformed to Victorian ideology, so there would be no need for reform in the prison system; she already understood it.

The issue that many infanticidal women received a short prison sentence for concealment of birth raises a further important issue: infanticide was not considered a crime that contravened accepted norms like crime associated with prostitution, such as drunkenness or soliciting. Arguably, if this had been the case, a greater number of women would have been found guilty. On the other hand, it could be argued that it did contravene accepted norms to at least the same extent as soliciting and drunkenness, but the penalty was seen as disproportionate. By punishing the woman for concealment and not for murder, did the courts truly consider the concealing of the corpse to be a greater crime than the killing of the infant? Arguably, the answer to this lies firmly in the concept of certainty: the courts were certain that the woman had not disclosed the birth of the infant by hiding the corpse, so the jury were able to draw inferences from conclusive evidence; the facts were axiomatic. Juries were uncertain as to whether the child had a separate existence or died because of an act or omission attributably by the mother, an issue that is intrinsically related to medical experts and scientific experiments.

Throughout the eighteenth and nineteenth centuries, the courts adopted a softer approach towards infanticidal women,[16] and science contributed towards this softer approach. Arguably, at the beginning of the eighteenth century, the prosecution sought medical evidence to secure convictions in infanticide cases, yet through the passage of time, the courts began to seek medical evidence to assist in the acquittal of these women. The uncertainty surrounding separate existence and cause of death was confirmed by science; therefore, science confirmed doubt in respect of the woman's culpability. The reliance upon science assisted medical experts in providing indefinite answers in court that lacked both clarity and certainty and assisted juries in finding women not guilty; it was a positive contribution. By understanding the woman's situation – the prospect of a child born out of wedlock in a harsh Victorian system founded on moral codes and the subsequent loss of employment and homelessness – the courts began to demonstrate sympathy towards infanticidal women. The uncertainty created by science therefore allowed the jury's consciences to be absolved in the acquittal of these women.

Medical witnesses have attempted to provide definitive proof in court that determined whether the woman had delivered a live child and the cause of the child's death. In the late seventeenth and early eighteenth century, the midwife gave evidence in court, drawing her conclusions from an external examination of the new-born cadaver and her experience and knowledge. As her testimony was based on supposition, lacking anatomical or physiological reasoning, the courts began to draw on medical evidence based on scientific experiments and medical reasoning to provide substantive evidence of separate existence.

As an increasing presence of male experts became evident within the delivery room, such as the man-midwife and surgeon, midwives were gradually attending fewer and fewer deliveries, a significant change during the eighteenth century that became increasingly evident in the courtroom. Male practitioners were carrying out the examinations of the infant cadaver, and so the same male practitioners were also called to give evidence in court. The courts therefore called an increasingly large number of male expert witnesses during the eighteenth century to give evidence. Jackson saw this replacing of the female midwife as largely related to professional ambition, stating that:

> part of wider enlightenment attempts to establish the supremacy of male reason over female irrationality and superstition, both in the replacement of female midwives as witnesses by male medical practitioners, and in the adoption of an explanatory framework of female behaviour that not only emphasized female passivity and instability but also carried professional benefits for male medical practitioners.[17]

The medical man's increasing knowledge of science became evident in his examination of the infant cadaver and medical discourse. Not only did he perform an external examination of the cadaver as the midwife had previously performed, but he also acquired the skill to carry out an internal dissection. Part of the post-mortem included a lung test, an experiment that became a widely used practice for determining whether the child had breathed and had a separate existence. The unreliability of such a test became increasingly clear, and, as Chapter 3 suggests, courts were reluctant to attach weight to such a dubious test, particularly when the woman's life was at risk. The answers provided by the medical experts in court became restrained and unscientific, allowing similarities to be drawn between those of the medical men and those of the midwife.

Foucault argued for the importance of dead bodies for the purposes of dissection and medical advancement, an advancement, he argued, which led to the medical gaze and an increasing anatomical knowledge of the body. As medical men developed techniques of observation, the surgeons refined their medical gaze, and, in turn, they gained power. However, in most cases of infanticide post-mortem results proved inconclusive, which in turn led to a lack of medical reasoning and the creation of uncertainty. In this light, it seems that the uncertainty argument is inconsistent with Foucault's perspective, a concept that Ward raises when he argues that it is "fair to ask how far Foucault's analysis applies to England."[18]

Ward argued that:

> Foucault maintained that courts and other institutions routinely accepted statements as true merely on the basis of the status of their maker, even in matters of life and death, because this was a practical necessity for the working of the machinery of power.[19]

In this respect, many of the cases within this research appear to be anti-Foucauldian, unless the grounds of uncertainty were provided by the expert themselves. In cases where there appeared to be substantive evidence proving the woman's guilt, the jury continued to demonstrate a reluctance to deliver a "guilty of murder" verdict, favouring instead a verdict of concealment of birth, even in cases where there was evidence of violence, for example, the cutting of the child's throat.[20]

The fact that it became increasingly noticeable towards the end of the nineteenth century that the Old Bailey in particular refrained from calling medical experts in cases of infanticide also appears to be anti-Foucauldian. The court may have considered that, in the absence of medical evidence based on medical reasoning, juries were capable of determining the facts of the case by drawing on common sense and judgement; the facts of the cases became axiomatic.

Pathologists also encountered issues stemming from uncertain evidence, which led to uncertain scientific findings, issues that resulted from the lack of a definition of the onset of life. In the absence of a clear, succinct definition in respect of the onset of life, it was almost impossible for a medical expert to interpret accurately the preciseness of death. Once again, in the absence of definitive answers, uncertainty remained, resulting in the jury reaching a verdict of inattention at birth or insufficient evidence. This resulted in many women appearing to be treated with leniency by the courts, particularly when the evidence against them was substantive.

During the nineteenth century a shift occurred within murder trials and other indictable offences. Prisoners indicted for murder were beginning to rely on the insanity defence, a plea that would save their life, because where a prisoner was found to be "guilty, but insane," a death sentence was reduced to "detention during Her Majesty's Pleasure," and yet, in cases of infanticide, this was a plea that would have been to the woman's detriment. If a woman was found guilty of concealment of birth, she would receive a maximum of two years' imprisonment; however, if she was found "guilty but insane," she could be detained indefinitely during Her Majesty's Pleasure. Unless there was substantive evidence of puerperal or lactational insanity, it would have been to the woman's detriment to enter an insanity plea.

Where suspicions of puerperal insanity were great, the remanding of women in custody allowed medical men to assess her mental state and compile evidence that would be crucial in court. Chapter 4 demonstrated that the mental state evidence provided in court appears to have varied in respect of both certainty and quality between the GPs who were being called to give evidence and medical superintendents. The lack of understanding of puerperal insanity is evident, with confusion arising surrounding whether a woman was experiencing a temporary malady or a chronic mental illness. Chapter 4 has demonstrated that the link between mental state experts and the uncertainty argument is tenuous; in many cases it is unquestionable that the woman caused the infant's death. Instead, the question for the court was one of responsibility.

The principle of uncertainty is strongest where doubt exists regarding newborn infants. Where the questions that arose were: had the child been born alive? What caused the death? Was it intentional or accidental? Whereas in cases involving the death of an older child, many women either confessed or carried out the act in the presence of a witness. The answers the court sought in cases such as these stemmed from the woman's responsibility for her actions in law, and it is in these cases that the link between the uncertainty argument and mental state expert evidence becomes tenuous.

By drawing on cases from Hull and the surrounding area, the uncertainty argument has been tested outside London, from which it is possible to conclude that, although cases were few, there were similarities between London and Hull. One would particularly expect that during the nineteenth century, with an increase in emigration to London, the spiralling metropolis and its advancement of ideas, the innovation of medical practice, and the desire to learn or teach medicine would be very different to Hull. However, the same level of doubt over whether a child had a separate existence, and if the child was born alive, existed in both London and Hull. Parallels can also be drawn between medical evidence and the use of science; science created the same element of uncertainty in cases held in Hull and London. Police surgeons, and GPs, were more commonly called expert witnesses in Hull, as opposed to the specialists who were called in London. The motives for committing infanticide, such as poverty and destitution, shame and reputation, remain the same, and there are also parallels between the cases during World War II, when married women were committing infanticide to hide their shame from adultery.

Fundamentally, the cases have demonstrated that the element of certainty did not increase in infanticide trials with the passage of time, the introduction of scientific experiment, or medical discourse, and, rather than producing certainty, medical experts conveyed uncertainty. Nevertheless, rather than being a sign of professional failure, the uncertainty created by medical experts made a positive contribution to the legal process that was arguably welcomed by the courts.

Notes

1 D. Cox, *Crime in England, 1688–1815.* Oxford: Routledge, 2014: 107; see also L. Radzinowicz (1948) op. cit. Vol. 1: 4; Hay (1977) op. cit.
2 For an understanding of the number of executions following the 'Bloody Assizes' see E. De Beer, 'Executions Following the Bloody Assizes' *Historical Research,* Vol. 4, No. 10, 1926, pp. 36–39.
3 C. Emsley, T. Hitchcock and R. Shoemaker, 'Punishments at the Old Bailey', *Old Bailey Proceedings Online* (www.oldbaileyonline.org, version 6.0, 17 April 2011). [Last accessed January 26, 2017]; see also Beattie (1986) op. cit.: 420; M. Wiener, 'Judges v Jurors: Courtroom Tensions in Murder Trials and the Law of Criminal Responsibility in Nineteenth-Century Britain' *Law and History Review,* Vol. 17, 1999, pp. 467–506.
4 *Report from the Select Committee to Consider so Much of the Criminal Law as Relates to Capital Punishment in Felonies* (London 1819) (8 Parliamentary Papers) cited in Langbein (2003) op. cit.: 335.
5 Langbein (2003) op. cit.: 333.
6 J. M. Beattie, 'Scales of Justice: Defence Counsel and the English Criminal Trial in the Eighteenth and Nineteenth Centuries' *Law and History Review*, Vol. 9, No. 2, 1991, pp. 221–267; Clayton (2009) op. cit.: 344; J. H. Langbein, 'The Criminal Trial before the Lawyers' *The University of Chicago Law Review*, Vol. 45, 1978, pp. 307–314.
7 Clayton (2009) op. cit.: 345.
8 Ibid.: 344.

9 P. Martin, 'Observation on Some of the Accidents of Infanticide' *Edinburgh Medical and Surgical Journal,* Vol. 26, July 1826, p. 36.
10 See R. Smith (1981) op. cit.: 147.
11 Zedner (1994) op. cit. cited in H. Johnston, 'Gendered Prison Work: Female Prison Officers in the Local Prison System, 1877–1939' *The Howard Journal,* Vol. 53, No. 2, 2014, pp. 193–212: 193.
12 L. Zedner, 'Women, Crime, and Penal Responses: A Historical Account' *Crime and Justice,* Vol. 14, 1991, pp. 307–362: 308.
13 H. Johnston, *Crime in England 1815–1880.* Hoboken: Taylor and Francis, 2015: 121; see also H. Johnston (2014) op. cit.: 193.
14 Johnston (2015) op. cit.: 124; see also H. Johnston (2014) op. cit.: 193; Heidensohn (1996) op. cit.
15 H. Johnston (2014) op. cit.: 194; see also J. Sim, *Medical Power in Prisons.* Buckingham: Open University Press, 1990.
16 See Beattie (1986) op. cit.: 113–124; Rabin (2004) op. cit.: 99.
17 M. Jackson (1995) op. cit.: 159.
18 T. Ward (2008) op. cit.: 58.
19 Ibid.: 59.
20 For example, the case of *OBP*, October 28, 1867, Rose Matthews, t18671028-965.

Bibliography

Books

Adam, A., *A History of Forensic Science: British Beginnings in the Twentieth Century*. Abingdon: Routledge, 2016.

—, (ed.), *Crime and the Construction of Forensic Objectivity from 1850*. Basingstoke: Palgrave, Macmillan, 2020.

Allen, C., *The Law of Evidence in Victorian England*. Cambridge: Cambridge University Press, 1997.

Allen, H., *Justice Unbalanced, Gender, Psychiatry and Judicial Decisions*. Milton Keynes: Open University Press, 1987.

Allison, D. and M. Roberts, *Disordered Mother or Disordered Diagnosis? Munchausen by Proxy Syndrome*. Hillsdale, NJ: Analytic Press, 1998.

Anderson, O., *Suicide in Victorian and Edwardian England*. Oxford: Oxford University Press, 1987.

Arnot, M. and C. Usborne, (eds.), *Gender and Crime in Modern Europe*. London: UCL Press, 1999.

Atkinson, S., *Golden Rules of Medical Evidence*. Bristol: John Wright, 1902.

Baker, J., *The Legal Profession and the Common Law: Historical Essays*. London: The Hambeldon Press, 1986.

—, *An Introduction to English Legal History*. Fifth Edition. Oxford: Oxford University Press, 2019.

Ballinger, A., *Dead Woman Walking, Executed Women in England and Wales 1900–1955*. Aldershot: Ashgate/Dartmouth, 2000.

Barron, H. and C. Siebrecht, (eds.), *Parenting and the State in Britain and Europe: Raising the Nation*. Cham, Switzerland: Springer Nature, 2017.

Bartlett, P. and D. Wright, (eds.), *Outside the Walls of the Asylum, the History of Care in the Community 1750–2000*. London: The Athlone Press, 1999.

Battie, W., *The Treatise of Madness*. London: J. Whiston and B. White, 1758.

Beattie, J. M., *Crime and the Courts in England 1660–1800*. Oxford: Clarendon Press, 1986.

—, *Policing and Punishment in London 1660–1750: Urban Crime and the Limits of Terror*. Oxford: Oxford University Press, 2003.

Bechtold, B. H and D. Cooper Graves, (eds.), *Killing Infants: Studies in the Worldwide Practice of Infanticide*. New York: Edwin Mellen Press, 2006: 111.

Berman, H., *Law and Revolution II: The Impact of the Protestant Reformations on the Western Legal Tradition*. Cambridge, MA: Belknap, 2003.

Blackstone, W., *Commentaries on the Laws of England*. Dublin: Printed for John Exshaw [and 3 others], 1771.

Braddick, M. and J. Walter, (eds.), *Negotiating Power in Early Modern Society, Order, Hierarchy and Subordination in Britain and Ireland*. Cambridge: Cambridge University Press, 2001.

Brake, L. and M. Demoor, (eds.), *Dictionary of Nineteenth-Century Journalism in Great Britain and Ireland*. Gent: Academia Press; London: British Library, 2009.

Burch, D., *Digging up the Dead, Uncovering the Life and Times of Astley Cooper, an Extraordinary Surgeon*. London: Vintage Books, 2007.

Burney, I., *Bodies of Evidence, Medicine and the Politics of the English Inquest 1830–1926*. Baltimore: The John Hopkins University Press, 2000.

—–, *Poison, Detection and the Victorian Imagination*. Manchester: Manchester University Press, 2006.

Cairns, D., *Advocacy and the Making of the Adversarial Criminal Trial 1800–1865*. Oxford: Clarendon Press, 1998.

Campbell Hurd-Mead, K., *A History of Women in Medicine, from the Earliest Times to the Beginning of the Nineteenth Century*. Haddam, Conn: The Haddam Press, 1938.

Ceci, S. J. and H. Hembrooke, (eds.), *Expert Witnesses in Child Abuse Cases*. Washington, DC: American Psychological Association, 1998.

Cecil, R., (ed.), *The Anthropology of Pregnancy Loss: Comparative Studies in Miscarriage, Stillbirth and Neonatal Death*. Oxford: Berg, 1996.

Chadwick, E., *Report on the Sanitary Conditions of the Labouring Population of Great Britain*. London: HMSO, 1842.

Chadwick, R., *Bureaucratic Mercy: The Home Office and the Treatment of Capital Cases in Victorian England*. New York and London: Garland, 1992.

Choo, A., *Evidence*. Third Edition. Oxford: Oxford University Press, 2012.

Clark, M. and C. Crawford, (eds.), *Legal Medicine in History*. Cambridge: Cambridge University Press, 1994.

Cockburn, J. S., (ed.), *Crime in England 1550–1800*. London: Methuen, 1977.

—–, *A History of the English Assizes, 1558–1714*. Cambridge: Cambridge University Press, 2011.

Collins, W., *The Moonstone*. London: Oxford University Press, 1928.

Collins, W., *Collins Concise English Dictionary*. Eighth Edition. Glasgow: HarperCollins Publishers, 2012.

Conan Doyle, A., *The Hound of the Baskervilles*. London: Newnes, 1902.

Conway, H., *The Law and the Dead*. Oxford: Routledge, 2016.

Cossins, A., *Female Criminality: Infanticide, Moral Panics and the Female Body*. London: Palgrave Macmillan, 2015.

Cox, D., *Crime in England 1688–1815*. London: Routledge, 2014.

Cunliffe, E., *Murder, Medicine and Motherhood*. Oxford: Hart, 2011.

D'Cruze, S., *Crimes of Outrage: Sex, Violence and Victorian Working Women*. London: UCL Press, 1998.

—–, (ed.), *Everyday Violence in Britain, 1850–1950*. Harlow: Longman, 2000.

D'Cruze, S. and L. Jackson, *Women, Crime and Justice in England since 1660*. Basingstoke: Palgrave Macmillan, 2009.

D'Cruze, S., S. Walklate, and S. Pegg, *Murder: Social and Historical Approaches to Understanding Murder and Murders*. Cullompton: Willan, 2006.

De Groot, J. and S. Morgan, (eds.), *Sex, Gender and the Sacred: Reconfiguring Religion in Gender History*. Chichester: Wiley Blackwell, 2014.

Dickens, C., *Bleak House*. London: Low Chapman and Hall, 1891.
—–, *Oliver Twist*. Second Edition. London: Richard Bentley, New Burlington Street, 1939.
Dixon Mann, J., *Forensic Medicine and Toxicology*. Fourth Edition. London: C. Griffin, 1902.
Dobson, J. and R. M. Walker, *Barbers and Barber Surgeons of London: A History of the Barbers' and Barber Surgeons' Companies*. Oxford: Blackwell, 1979.
Donnison, J., *Midwives and Medical Men: A History of the Struggle for the Control of Childbirth*. New Barnet: Historical Publications, 1988.
Ehrenreich, B. and D. English, *Witches, Midwives and nurses: A History of Women Healers*. London: Writers and Readers Publishing Cooperative, 1976.
Eigen, J. P., *Witnessing Insanity: Madness and Mad-Doctors in the English Court*. New Haven and London: Yale University Press, 1995.
—–, *Unconscious Crime: Mental Absence and Criminal Responsibility in Victorian London*. Baltimore: John Hopkins University Press, 2003.
—–, *Mad-Doctors in the Dock, Defending the Diagnosis, 1760–1913*. Baltimore: John Hopkins University Press, 2016.
Einarsdottir, J., *Tired of Weeping: Mother Love, Child Death and Poverty in Guinea-Bissau*. Wisconsin: University of Wisconsin Press, 2005.
Evenden, D., *The Midwives of Seventeenth-Century London*. Cambridge: Cambridge University Press, 2000.
Finn, M., M. Lobban, and J. Bourne Taylor, (eds.), *Legitimacy and Illegitimacy in Nineteenth-Century Law, Literature and History*. Basingstoke: Palgrave Macmillan, 2010.
Fitzgerald, M., G. McLennan, and J. Pawson, (eds.), *Crime and Society: Readings in History and Theory*. London: Routledge and Kegan Paul, 1981.
Fleischacker, S., *What is Enlightenment?* London: Routledge, 2013.
Ford, B., (ed.), *The New Pelican Guide to English Literature, Volume 6: From Dickens to Hardy*. London: Penguin, 1982.
Forster, C. A., *Court Housing in Kingston upon Hull: An Example of Cyclic Processes in the Morphological Development of Nineteenth-Century Bye-Law Housing*. Hull: University of Hull, 1972.
Foucault, M., *The Birth of the Clinic, An Archaeology of Medical Perspective*. London: Tavistock, 1973.
—–, *Discipline and Punish: The Birth of the Prison*. London: Allen Lane, 1977.
—–, *Madness and Civilization*. London: Routledge, 2001.
—–, *Abnormal*. London: Verso, 2003.
—–, *History of Madness*. London: Routledge, 2006a.
—–, *Psychiatric Power: lectures at the College De France, 1973–1974*. (edited by Jacques Lagrange; translated by Graham Burchell) Basingstoke: Palgrave Macmillan, 2006b.
Freidson, E., *Profession of Medicine: A Study of the Sociology of Applied Knowledge*. New York: Harper and Row Publishers, 1970.
Frith, V., (ed.), *Women and History, Voices of Early Modern England*. Toronto: Coach House Press, 1995.
Frost, G., *Illegitimacy in English Law and Society 1860–1930*. Manchester: Manchester University Press, 2016.
Gaskell, E., *Ruth*. London: Penguin, 1997.
Gaskell, M., *Crime and Mentalities in Early Modern England*. Cambridge; Cambridge University Press, 2002.
Gatrell, V., *'The Hanging Tree': Executions and the English People 1770–1868*. Oxford: Oxford University Press, 1994.

Gatrell, V., B. Lenman, and G. Parker, (eds.), *Crime and the Law: The Social History of Crime in Western Europe since 1500*. London: Europa Publications, 1980.

Gillet, E. and K. MacMahon, *A History of Hull*. Hull: The University of Hull Press, 1989.

Gilman, S., *The Face of Madness: Hugh W. Diamond and the Origin of Psychiatric Photography*, New York: Brunner/Mazel, 1976.

Goc, N., *Women, Infanticide and the Press*. Farnham: Ashgate, 2013.

Godfrey, B. and P. Lawrence, *Crime and Justice* 1750–1950. Second Edition. Oxford: Routledge, 2011.

Golan, T., *Laws of Men and Laws of Nature: The History of Scientific Expert Testimony in England and America,* Cambridge, MA: Harvard University Press, 2004.

Gooch, R., *An Account of Some of the Most Important Diseases Peculiar to Women*. London: John Murray, 1829.

—, *A Practical Compendium of Midwifery; Being a Course on Lectures on Midwifery and on the Diseases of Women and Infants, Delivered at St Bartholomew's Hospital by the Late Robert Gooch, M. D.* London: Longman, Rees, Orme, Brown and Green, 1831.

Goodman, D., *Foul Deeds and Suspicious Deaths in Hull*. Barnsley Wharncliffe Books, 2005.

Gowing, L., *Common Bodies: Women, Touch and Power in Seventeenth-Century England*. London: Yale University Press, 2003.

Gray, D., *Crime, Prosecution and Social Relations: The Summary Courts of the City of London in the Late Eighteenth Century*. London: Palgrave Macmillan, 2009.

—, *London's Shadows: The Dark Side of the Victorian City*. London: Continuum, 2010.

Gregory, J. and J. Stevenson, *The Routledge Companion to Britain in the Eighteenth Century, 1688–1820*. Oxford: Routledge, 2007.

Gutting, G., *Michel Foucault's archaeology of Scientific Reason*. Cambridge: Cambridge University Press, 1989.

—, (ed.), *The Cambridge Companion to Foucault*. Cambridge: Cambridge University Press, 2003.

Hale, M., *History of the Pleas of the Crown ede. Sollom Emlyn*. 2 Vols. London: Printed by E. and R. Nutt, and R. Gosling, (assigns of Edward Sayer, Esq.) for F. Gyles, 1736.

Hardy, T., *Tess of the D'Urbervilles*. London: Penguin, 2011.

Harris, R., *Murders and Madness: Medicine, Law and Society in the Fin de Siècle*. Oxford: Clarendon Press, 1989.

Havard, J., *The Detection of Secret Homicide: A Study of the Medico-Legal System of Investigation of Sudden and Unexplained Death*. London: Macmillan, 1960.

Hawkins, W., *Pleas of the Crown*. London: Professional Books, 1973, [1716].

Hay, D., P. Linebaugh, J. Rule, E. Thompson, and C. Winslow, (eds.), *Albion's Fatal Tree: Crime and Society in Eighteenth-Century England*. London: Verso, 1977.

Heidensohn, F., *Women and Crime*. Second Edition. Basingstoke: Macmillan, 1996.

Helmholz, R. H., *The Oxford History of the Laws of England, Vol. I: The Canon Law and Ecclesiastical Jurisdiction from 597 to the 1640s*. Oxford: Oxford University Press, 2004.

Hillman, R. and P. Ruberry-Blanc, (eds.), *Female Transgressions in Early Modern Britain: Literary and Historical Explorations*. Oxford: Ashgate, 2014.

Hitchcock, T. and R. Shoemaker, *Tales from the Hanging Court*. London: Bloomsbury Academic, 2010.

—, *London Lives: Poverty, Crime and the Making of the Modern City*. 1690–1800. Cambridge: Cambridge University Press, 2015.

Hoffer, P. C. and N. E. H. Hull, *Murdering Mothers: Infanticide in England and New England 1558–1803*. New York: New York University Press, 1981.
Holmes, G., *Augustan England: Professions, State and Society, 1680–1730*. London: Allen & Unwin, 1982.
Hostettler, J., *The Criminal Jury Old and New: Jury Power from Early Times to the Present Day*. Winchester: Waterside Press, 2004.
——, *Champions of the Rule of Law*. Hook, Hampshire: Waterside Press, 2011.
Hougthon, W. E., *Victorian Frame of Mind 1830–1870*. Boston: Yale University Press, 1957.
Hull City Council, *Hull Character Study*. Hull: Hull City Council, 2010.
Hunnisett, R. F., *The Medieval Coroner*. Cambridge: Cambridge University Press, 1961.
Hunt, L., (ed.), *The New Cultural History*. California: University of California Press, 1989.
Hunter, W., *On the Uncertainty on the Signs of Murder: In the Case of Bastard Children*. London: Callow, 1818.
Jackson, G., *Hull in the Eighteenth Century: A Study in Economic and Social History*. London: Oxford University Press, 1972.
Jackson, M., *New-born Child Murder, Women, Legitimacy and the Courts in Eighteenth-Century England*. Manchester: Manchester University Press, 1996.
——, *The Borderland of Imbecility: Medicine, Society and the Fabrication of the Feeble Minded in Late Victorian and Edwardian England*. Manchester: Manchester University Press, 2000.
——, *Infanticide, Historical Perspectives on Child Murder and Concealment, 1550–2000*. Aldershot: Ashgate, 2002.
James, P. D., *Death Comes to Pemberley*. London: Faber, 2012.
James-Fitzpatrick, S., *A History of the Criminal Law in England Volume 3V*. London: Macmillan and Co, 1833.
Jarcho, S., (ed.), *Essays on the History of Medicine*. New York: New York Academy of Medicine, Neale Watson Publications, 1976.
Jasonoff, S., (ed.), *States of Knowledge, the Co-Production of Science and Social Order*. London: Routledge, 2004.
Jenkins, R., *The Law and the Midwife*. Oxford: Blackwell Science, 1995.
Johnson, S., *A Dictionary of Language*. Sixth Edition. London: Consortium, 1786.
Johnston, H., (ed.), *Punishment and Control in Historical Perspective*. Basingstoke: Palgrave Macmillan, 2008.
——, *Crime in England 1815–1880, Experiencing the Criminal Justice System*. Oxford: Routledge, 2015.
Johnstone, G., *Medical Concepts and Penal Policy*. London: Cavendish, 1996.
Johnstone, G. and T. Ward, *Law and Crime*. London: Sage, 2010.
Jones, C., *Expert Witnesses, Science, Medicine and the Practice of Law*. Oxford: Clarendon Press, 1994.
Jones, K., *Lunacy, Law and Conscience, 1744–1845: The Social History of the Care of the Insane*. London: Routledge and Kegan Paul, 1955.
Kahn, V. and L. Hutson, (eds.), *Rhetoric and the Law in Early Modern Europe*. New Haven: Yale University Press, 2001.
Kamm, F., *Creation and Abortion: A Study in Moral and Legal Philosophy*. New York: Oxford University Press, 1992.
Kant, I., *The Metaphysics of Morals*, Immanuel Kant: translated and edited by Mary Gregor; with an introduction by Roger J. Sullivan. Cambridge: Cambridge University Press, 1996.

Kermode, J. and G. Walker, (eds.), *Women, Crime and the Courts in Early Modern England*. London: UCL Press, 1994.

Kilday, A. M., *A History of Infanticide in Britain c.1600 to the Present*. Basingstoke: Palgrave Macmillan, 2013.

Kilday, A. M. and D. Nash, (eds.), *Histories of Crime, Britain, 1600–2000*. Basingstoke: Palgrave Macmillan, 2010.

King, P., *Crime, Justice and Discretion in England, 1740–1820*. Oxford: Oxford University Press, 2000.

Klaver, E., (ed.), *The Body in Medical Culture*. Albany: State University of New York Press, 2009.

Knelman, J., *Twisting in the Wind, the Murderess and the English Press*. Toronto: University of Toronto Press, 1998.

Kramar, K., *Unwilling Mothers, Unwanted Babies: Infanticide in Canada*. Vancouver: UBC Press, 2005.

Lacey, N., *Women, Crime and Character: From Moll Flanders to Tess of the D'Urbervilles*. Oxford: Oxford University Press, 2008.

Landau, N., (ed.), *Law, Crime and English Society, 1660–1830*. Cambridge: Cambridge University Press, 2002.

Langbein, J., *The Origins of the Adversary Criminal Trial*. Oxford: Oxford University Press, 2003.

Lee, A. J., *The Origins of the Popular Press in England, 1855–1914*. London: Croom Helm, 1976.

Leeuwen, G., *The Problem of Certainty in English Thought, 1630–1690*. The Hague: Nijhoff, 1963.

Lemmings, D., (ed.), *Crime, Courtrooms and the Public Sphere in Britain 1700-1850*. Farnham: Ashgate, 2012.

Levene, A., T. Nutt, and S. Williams, (eds.), *Illegitimacy in Britain 1700-1920*. Basingstoke: Palgrave Macmillan, 2005.

Lewis, J., *The Politics of Motherhood: Child and Maternal Welfare in England, 1900–1939*. London: Croom Helm and McGill-Queen's University Press, 1980.

Linebaugh, P., *The London Hanged: Crime and Civil Society in the Eighteenth Century*. London: Verso, 2006.

Lord Cooke, *Turning Points of the Common Law*. London: Sweet and Maxwell, 1997.

Loughnan, A., *Manifest Madness: Mental Incapacity in Criminal Law*. Oxford: Oxford University Press, 2012.

Marland, H., (ed.), *The Art of Midwifery, Early Modern Midwives in Europe*. London: Routledge, 1993.

——, *Dangerous Motherhood: Insanity and Childbirth in Victorian England*. Basingstoke, Hampshire: Palgrave Macmillan, 2004.

McDonagh, J., *Child Murder and British Culture, 1720–1900*. New York: Cambridge University Press, 2003.

McKee, G., *Why Mothers Kill: A Forensic Psychologists Casebook*. New York: Oxford University Press, 2006.

McLynn, F., *Crime and Punishment in Eighteenth-Century England*. Oxford: Oxford University Press, 1991.

McNay, L., *Foucault and Feminism: Power, Gender and Self*. Cambridge: Polity, 1992.

Melling, J. and B. Forsythe, (eds.), *Insanity, Institutions and Society, 1800–1914: A Social History of Madness in Comparative Perspective*. London: Routledge, 1999.

Miller, J., *Cities Divided: Politics and Religion in English Provincial Towns 1660–1722*. Oxford: Oxford University Press, 2010.

Newton, J. L, M. P. Ryan, and J. R. Walkowitz, (eds.), *Sex and Class in Women's History*. London: Routledge, 1983.

Norrie, A., *Crime, Reason and History: A Critical Introduction to Criminal Law*. Cambridge: Cambridge University Press, 2001.

Oakley, A., *The Captured Womb: A History of the Medical Care of Pregnant Women*. Oxford: Blackwell, 1986.

Parry-Jones, W. L., *The Trade in Lunacy: A Study of Private Madhouses in England in the Eighteenth and Nineteenth Centuries*. London: Routledge and Kegan Paul, 1972.

Pelling, M., *The Common Lot: Sickness, Medical Occupations and the Urban Poor in Early Modern England*. London; Longman, 1998.

Porter, R., (ed.), *Patients and Practitioners: Law Perceptions of Medicine in Pre-Industrial Society*. Cambridge: Cambridge University Press, 1988.

—–, (ed.), *Medicine in the Enlightenment*. Amsterdam: Rodopi, 1995.

—–, *A Social History of Madness: Stories of the Insane*. London: Phoenix Giants, 1996.

—–, *London: A Social History*. London: Penguin, 1996.

—–, *Madness: A Brief History*. Oxford: Oxford University Press, 2002.

Porter, R., and D. Wright, (eds.), *In the Confinement of the Insane: International Perspectives 1800–1965*. Cambridge: Cambridge University Press, 2003.

Pritchard, J. C., *A Treatise on Diseases of the Nervous System, part the first*. London: Thomas and George Underwood, 1822.

Pugh, R., *Imprisonment in Medieval England*. Cambridge: Cambridge University Press, 1968.

Rabin, D., *Identity, Crime and Legal Responsibility in Eighteenth-Century England*. Basingstoke: Palgrave Macmillan, 2004.

Rabinow, P., (ed.), *The Foucault Reader*. Harmondsworth: Penguin, 1991.

Radzinowicz, L., *A History of English Criminal Law and its Administration from 1750, Volume 1*. London: Stevens, 1948.

Rattigan, C., *"What Else Could I Do?" Single Mothers and Infanticide, 1900–1950*. Dublin: Irish Academic Press, 2012.

Redmayne, M., *Expert Evidence and Criminal Justice*. Oxford: Oxford University Press, 2001.

Richardson, R., *Death, Dissection and the Destitute*. London: Routledge & Kegan Paul, 1987.

Roberts, H., (ed.), *Women, Health and Reproduction*. London: Routledge & Kegan Paul, 1981.

Rodensky, L., *The Crime in Mind: Criminal Responsibility and the Victorian Novel*. New York: Oxford University Press, 2003.

Rose, L., *The Massacre of the Innocents: Infanticide in Britain 1800-1939*. London: Routledge & Kegan Paul, 1986.

Ross, E., *Love and Toil: Motherhood in Outcast London 1870–1918*. Oxford: Oxford University Press, 1993.

Rowbotham, J. and Stevenson, K., (eds.), *Criminal Conversations: Victorian Crimes, Social Panic, and Moral Outrage*. Columbus: The Ohio State University Press, 2005.

Ryan, W. B., *Infanticide: Its Law, Prevalence, Prevention and History*. London: Churchill, 1862.

Scull, A., *Museums of Madness, The Social Organisation of Insanity in Nineteenth-Century England*. London: Penguin, 1979.

——, *Social Order/Mental Disorder Anglo-American Psychiatry in Historical Perspective*. London: Routledge, 1989.
——, *Madness in Civilization: A Cultural History of Insanity, from the Bible to Freud, from the Madhouse to Modern Medicine*. London: Thames & Hudson, 2015.
Shapiro, B., *Probability and Certainty in Seventeenth-Century England*. Princeton, NJ: Princeton University Press, 1983.
Sharp, J., *The Midwives Book, or The Whole Art of midwifry Discovered*. London: Printed for Simon Miller, at the Star at the West End of St. Pauls, 1671.
Sharpe, J., *Crime in Early Modern England 1550–1750*. Second Edition. Harlow: Addison Wesley Longman, 1999.
Shore, H., *London's Criminal Underworlds, c. 1720-c. 1930*. London: Palgrave MacMillan, 2015.
Shorter, E., *Women's Bodies, A Social History of Women's encounter with Health, Ill Health and Medicine*. New Brunswick; Transaction Publishers, 1991.
Showalter, E., *The Female Malady: Women, Madness and English Culture 1830–1980*. New York: Pantheon Books, 1985.
Sim, J., *Medical Power in Prisons: The Prison Medical Service in England 1774–1989*. Milton Keynes: Open University Press, 1990.
Simpson, K., (ed.), *Modern Trends in Forensic Medicine 2*. London: Butterworths, 1967.
Smart, C., *Women, Crime and Criminology, A Feminist Critique*. London: Routledge & Kegan Paul, 1976.
Smellie, W., *A Treatise on the Theory and Practice of Midwifery*. London: Bailliere Tindall, 1974.
Smith, R., *Trial by Medicine: Insanity and Responsibility in Victorian Trials*. Edinburgh: Edinburgh University Press, 1981.
Smith, R. and B. Wynne, (eds.), *Expert Evidence: Interpreting Science in the Law*. London: Routledge, 1989.
Smith, S., (ed.), *Taylors Principles and Practices of Medical Jurisprudence*. Eighth Edition. London: J. & A. Churchill, 1928.
Smith, S. and J. Glaister, *Recent Advances in Forensic Medicine*. London: J & A Churchill, 1931.
Smith, S. and W. Cook, (eds.), *Taylors Principles and Practices of Medical Jurisprudence*. Vol. II, Eighth Edition. London: J. & A. Churchill, 1928.
Sprigge, S., *The Life and Times of Thomas Wakley*. London: Longmans, Green and Co, 1897.
Spurzheim, J. G., *Observations on the Deranged Manifestations of the Mind, or Insanity*. Boston: Marsh, Capen & Lyon, 1836.
Sweet, M., *Inventing the Victorians* London: Faber, 2001.
Taylor, A. S., *The Principles and Practice of Medical Jurisprudence*. Two Vols, Tenth Edition. London: J. & A Churchill, 1928.
Taylor, A. S., A. Lacassagne, and J. L. Casper, *A Handbook of the Practice of Forensic Medicine*. Vol. 3, Third Edition, trans W. Balfour. London: The New Sydenham Society, 1861.
Teubner, G., *Law as an Autopoietic System* Oxford: Blackwell, 1993.
Thompson, F. M. L., (ed.), *The Cambridge Social History of Britain 1750-1950. Vol. 3: Social Agencies and Institutions*. Cambridge: Cambridge University Press, 2002.
Timmermans, S., *Post-mortem: How Medical Examiners Explain Suspicious Deaths*. Chicago: University of Chicago Press, 2006.
Towler, J., *Midwives in History and Society*. London: Croom Helm, 1986.
Trollope, F., *Jessie Phillips: A Tale of the Present Day*. Stroud: Nonsuch, 2006.

Turner, B., *Medical Power and Social Knowledge*. London: Sage Publications, 1987.
Ussher, J., *Women's Madness: Misogyny or Mental Illness?* Hemel Hempstead: Harvester Wheatsheaf, 1991.
Van Leeuwen, H., *The Problem of Certainty in English Thought 1630–1690*. The Hague: Martinus Nijhoff, 1963.
Vogler, R., *A World View of Criminal Justice*. Aldershot: Ashgate Publishing Limited, 2005.
Waddington, I., *The Medical Profession in the Industrial Revolution*. Dublin: Gill and Macmillan Ltd, 1984.
Waddington, K., *An Introduction to the Social History of Medicine: Europe since 1500*. Basingstoke: Palgrave Macmillan, 2011.
Wade, S., *Yorkshire Murderous Women, Two Centuries of Killings*. Barnsley: Wharncliffe Books, 2007.
Walker, N. and S. McCabe, *Crime and Insanity in England*. Edinburgh: Edinburgh University Press, 1973.
Watson, K., (ed.), *Assaulting the Past, Violence and Civilization in Historical Context*. Newcastle: Cambridge Scholars Publishing, 2007.
—, *Forensic Medicine in Western Society: A History*. Oxford: Routledge, 2011.
—, *Medicine and Justice: Medico-Legal Practice in England and Wales, 1700–1914*. Oxford: Routledge, 2020.
Weisser, M., *Crime and Punishment in Early Modern Europe*. Hassocks: Harvester Press, 1979.
Whitman, J., *The Origins of Reasonable Doubt, Theoretical Roots of the Criminal Trial*. Yale: Yale University Press, 2008.
Wiener, M., *Reconstructing the Criminal: Culture, Law and Policy in England 1830–1914*. Cambridge: Cambridge University Press, 1990.
—, *Men of Blood: Violence, Manliness and Criminal Justice in Victorian England*. Cambridge: Cambridge University Press, 2004.
Wilczynski, A., *Child Homicide*. London: Greenwich Medical Media Limited, 1997.
Williams, R., *Keywords, a Vocabulary of Culture and Society*. London: Fontana Press, 1983.
Wilson, A., (ed.), *Rethinking Social History: English Society, 1570–1920 and Its Interpretation*. Manchester: Manchester University Press, 1993.
—, *The Making of Man-Midwifery: Childbirth in England, 1660–1770*. Cambridge, MA: Harvard University Press, 1995.
Wilson, S. and I. Cumming, (eds.), *Psychiatry in Prisons, A Comprehensive Handbook*. London: Jessica Kingsley Publishers, 2010.
Wohl, A., (ed.), *The Victorian Family: Structure and Stresses*. London: Croom Helm, 1978.
Wolfreys, J., *Dickens to Hardy 1837–1883: The Novel, the Past and Cultural Memory on the Nineteenth Century*. Basingstoke: Palgrave Macmillan, 2007.
Zedner, L., *Women, Crime and Custody in Victorian England*. Oxford: Oxford University Press, 1991.

Chapters in edited collections

Arnot, M., 'Understanding Women Committing New-born Child Murder in Victorian England' in S. D'Cruze, (ed.) *Everyday Violence in Britain, 1850–1950*. Harlow: Pearson Education Limited, 2000.
Bland, L., 'Feminist Vigilantes of Late-Victorian England' in C. Smart, (ed.) *Regulating Womanhood: Historical Essays on Marriage, Motherhood and Sexuality*. London: Routledge, 1992.

Caswell, M., 'Mothers, Wives and Killers: Marital Status and Homicide in London 1674–1790' in R. Hillman and P. Ruberry-Blanc, (eds.) *Female Transgression in Early Modern Britain: Literary and Historical Explorations*. Surrey: Ashgate, 2014.

Cleall, E., '"Deaf to the Word": Gender, Deafness and Protestantism in Nineteenth-Century Britain and Ireland' in J. De Groot and S. Morgan, (eds.) *Sex, Gender and the Sacred: Reconfiguring Religion in Gender History*. Chichester: Wiley Blackwell, 2014.

Cooper Graves, D., '"…In a Frenzy While Raving Mad": Physicians and Parliamentarians Define Infanticide in Victorian England" in B. Bechtold and D. Cooper Graves, (eds.) *Killing Infants: Studies in the Worldwide Practice of Infanticide*. New York: Edwin Mellen Press, 2006.

Cosman, M. P., 'Medieval Medical Malpractice' in S. Jarcho, (ed.) *Essays on the History of Medicine*. New York: New York Academy of Medicine, Neale Watson Publications, 1976.

Davidoff, L., 'Class and Gender in Victorian England' in J. L. Newton, et al. (eds.) *Sex and Class in Women's History*. London: Routledge, 1983.

Dear, P., 'Mysteries of State, Mysteries of Nature: Authority, Knowledge and Expertise in the Seventeenth Century' in S. Jasonoff, (ed.) *States of Knowledge, The Co-Production of Science and Social Order*. London: Routledge, 2004.

Elston, M. A., 'Women Doctors in a Changing Profession: The Case of Britain' in E. Riska and K. Wegar, (eds.) *Gender, Work and Medicine*: Women and the Medical Division of Labour. London: Sage, 1993.

Gowing, L., 'Ordering the Body: Illegitimacy and Female Authority in Seventeenth-Century England' in M. Braddick, and J. Walter, (eds.) *Negotiating Power in Early Modern Society: Order, Hierarchy and Subordination in Britain and Ireland.* Cambridge: Cambridge University Press, 2001.

Grey, D., 'Parenting, Infanticide and the State in England and Wales, 1870–1950' in H. Barron, and C. Siebrecht, (eds.) *Parenting and the State in Britain and Europe, Raising the Nation.* Cham, Switzerland: Springer Nature, 2017.

Harley, D., 'Provincial Midwives in England: Lancashire and Cheshire, 1600–1760,' in H. Marland, (ed.) *The Art of Midwifery, early modern midwives in Europe*. London: Routledge, 1993.

Hay, D., 'Property, Authority and the Criminal Law' in Hay, D et al., (eds.) *Albion's Fatal Tree: Crime and Society in Eighteenth-Century England.* London: Penguin, 1977.

Hobbs, A. and M. Beetham, 'Local Press' in L. Brake and M. Demoor, (eds.) *Dictionary of Nineteenth-Century Journalism in Great Britain and Ireland.* Gent: Academia Press; London: British Library, 2009.

Jackson, M., 'Suspicious Infant Deaths: The Statute of 1624 and Medical Evidence at Coroners' Inquests' in M. Clark and C. Crawford, (eds.) *Legal Medicine in History.* Cambridge: Cambridge University Press, 1994.

——, 'Developing Medical Expertise: Medical Practitioners and the Suspected Murders of New-Born Children,' in R. Porter, (ed.) *Medicine in the Enlightenment.* Amsterdam: Rodopi, 1995.

King, P., 'Gender, Crime and Justice in Late Eighteenth and Early Nineteenth-Century England' in Arnot, M. and Usborne, C. (eds.) *Gender and Crime in Modern Europe.* London: UCL Press, 1999.

Kittredge, K., 'Introduction: Contexts for the Consideration of the Transgressive Antitype' in Kittredge, K. (ed.) *Lewd and Notorious: Female Transgression in the Eighteenth Century.* Michigan: The University of Michigan Press, 2003.

Laqueur, T., 'Bodies, Details and the Human Narrative' in A. Biersack, and L. Hunt, (eds.) *The New Cultural History*. Berkeley: University of California Press, 1989.

Linebaugh, P., 'The Tyburn Riot Against the Surgeon' in D. Hay, P. Linebaugh, J. Rule, E. Thompson, and C. Winslow, (eds.) *Albion's Fatal Tree: Crime and Society in Eighteenth-Century England*. London: Verso, 1977.

Malcolmson, R. W., 'Infanticide in the Eighteenth Century' in J. S. Cockburn, (ed.) Crime *in England 1550–1800*. London: Methuen & Co LTD, 1977.

Marland, H., 'At Home with Puerperal Mania: The Domestic Treatment of the Insanity of Childbirth in the Nineteenth Century' in P. Bartlett and D. Wright, (eds.) *Outside the Walls of the Asylum, the History of Care in the Community 1750–2000*. London: The Athlone Press, 1999.

——, 'Getting Away with Murder' in M. Jackson, (ed.) *Infanticide, Historical Perspectives on Child Murder and Concealment, 1550–2000*. Aldershot: Ashgate, 2002.

Masciola, A. L., 'The Unfortunate Maid Exemplified': Elizabeth Canning and Representations of Infanticide in Eighteenth-Century England' in M. Jackson, (ed.) *Infanticide: Historical Perspectives on Child Murder and Concealment, 1550–2000*. Aldershot: Ashgate, 2002.

May, A., 'Infanticide Trials' in V. Frith, (ed.) *Women and History, Voices of Early Modern England*. Toronto: Coach House Press, 1995.

McGowen, R., 'Cruel Inflictions and the Claims of Humanity in Early Nineteenth-Century England' in K. Watson, (ed.) *Assaulting the Past Violence and Civilization in Historical Context*. Newcastle: Cambridge Scholars Publishing, 2007.

Quinn, C., 'Images and Impulses: Representations of puerperal insanity and infanticide in late Victorian England' in M. Jackson, (ed.) *Infanticide, Historical Perspective on Child Murder and Concealment, 1550–2000*. Aldershot: Ashgate, 2002.

Rabin, D., 'Bodies of Evidence, States of Mind: Infanticide, Emotion and Sensibility in Eighteenth-Century England' in M. Jackson, (ed.) *Infanticide: Historical Perspectives on Child Murder and Concealment 1550–2000*. Aldershot: Ashgate, 2002.

Roberts, H., 'Marriage, Redundancy or Sin' in M. Vicinus, (ed.) *Suffer and be Still, Women in the Victorian Age*. London: Indiana University Press, 1972.

Rubery, M., Siemann, C. and J. Wood, 'Court and Parliamentary Reporting' in L. Brake, and M. Demoor, (eds.) *Dictionary of Nineteenth-Century Journalism in Great Britain and Ireland*. Gent: Academia Press; London: British Library, 2009.

Sharpe, J., 'Enforcing the Law in the Seventeenth-Century English Village' in V. Gatrell, B. Lenman, and G. Parker, (eds.) *Crime and the Law: The Social History of Crime in Western Europe since 1500*. London: Europa Publications, 1980.

——, 'Women, Witchcraft and the Legal Process' in J. Kermode, and G. Walker, (eds.) *Women, Crime and the Courts in Early Modern England*. London: UCL Press, 1994.

Smart, C., 'Disruptive Bodies and Unruly Sex: The Regulation of Reproduction and Sexuality in the Nineteenth Century' in C. Smart, (ed.) *Regulating Womanhood: Historical Essays on Marriage, Motherhood and Sexuality*. London: Routledge, 1992.

Sommers, S., 'Remapping Maternity in the Courtroom, Female Defences and Medical Witnesses in Eighteenth-Century Infanticide Proceedings' in E. Klaver, (ed.) *The Body in Medical Culture*. Albany: State University of New York Press, 2009.

Spencer, J. R., 'The Role of Experts in the Common Law: A Comparison' in S. Ceci, and H. Hembrooke, (eds.) *Expert Witnesses in Child Abuse Cases*. Washington, DC: American Psychological Association, 1998.

Stevenson, K., 'Most Intimate Violations: Contextualising the Crime of Rape' in A. M. Kilday, and D. Nash, (eds.) *Histories of Crime, Britain 1600-2000*. Basingstoke: Palgrave Macmillan, 2010.

Taylor, D., 'Beyond the Bounds of Respectable Society: "The Dangerous Classes" in Victorian and Edwardian England' in J. Rowbotham, and K. Stevenson, (eds.) *Criminal Conversations, Victorian Crimes, Social Panic, and Moral Outrage*. Columbus: The Ohio State University Press, 2005.

Ward, T., 'Legislating for Human Nature: Legal Responses to Infanticide, 1860–1938' in M. Jackson, (ed.) *Infanticide, Historical Perspective on Child Murder and Concealment 1550–2000*. Aldershot: Ashgate, 2002.

—, 'An Honourable Regime of Truth? Foucault, Psychiatry and English Criminal Justice' in H. Johnston, (ed.) *Punishment and Control in Historical Perspective*. Basingstoke: Macmillan, 2008.

Wheelwright, J., '"Nothing in between": Modern Cases of Infanticide' in M. Jackson, (ed.) *Infanticide: Historical Perspectives on Child Murder and Concealment 1550–2000*. Aldershot: Ashgate, 2002.

Articles

Ackerknecht, E., 'Midwives as Expert Witnesses in Court' *Bulletin of the New York Academy of Medicine*, Vol. 52, No. 10, December 1976, pp. 1224–1228.

Allan, K., 'Managing Madness in the Victorian Asylum' *British Journal of Healthcare Management*, Vol. 19, No. 4, 2013, pp.167–169.

Anand, S., 'The Origins, Early History and Evolution of the English Criminal Trial Jury' *Alberta Law Review*, Vol. 43, No. 2, 2005, pp. 407–432.

Atkinson, S., 'Life, Death and Live-Birth' *Law Quarterly Review*, Vol. 20, 1904, pp. 134–159.

Backhouse, C., 'Desperate Women and Compassionate Courts: Infanticide in Nineteenth-Century Canada' *The University of Toronto Law Journal*, Vol. 34, No. 4, 1984, pp. 447–478.

Baines M. A. Mrs., 'A Few Thought's Concerning Infanticide' *Journal of Social Science*, Vol. 10, 1866, pp. 535–540.

Baker, J., 'Female Lunatics: A Sketch' *British Journal of Psychiatry*, Vol. 48, Vol. 200, January 1902, pp. 13–28.

Bartlett, P., 'Legal Madness in the Nineteenth Century' *Social History of Medicine*, Vol. 14, No. 1, 2001, pp. 107–131.

Beattie, J. M., 'The Criminality of Women in Eighteenth-Century England' *Journal of Social History*, Vol. 8, No. 4, 1975, pp. 80–116: 84.

Beattie, J. M., 'Scales of Justice: Defence Counsel and the English Criminal Trial in the Eighteenth and Nineteenth Centuries,' in *Law and History Review* Vol. 9, No. 2, 1991, pp. 221–267.

Bechtold, B. H., 'Infanticide in 19th century France: A Quantitative Interpretation' *Review of Radical Political Economics*, Vol. 33, 2001, pp. 165–187.

Beckett, J., 'The Glorious Revolution, Parliament and the Making of the First Industrial Nation' *Parliamentary History*, Vol. 33, No. 1, 2014, pp. 36–53.

Behlmer, G. K., 'Deadly Motherhood: Infanticide and Medical Opinion in Mid-Victorian England' *Journal of the History of Medicine and Allied Sciences*, Vol. 34, No. 4, 1979, pp. 403–427.

Benedek, T. G., 'The Changing Relationship between Midwives and Physicians during the Renaissance' *Bulletin of the History of Medicine*, Vol. 51, No. 4, 1977, pp. 550–564.

Bosworth, M., 'The Past as a Foreign Country? Some Methodological Implications of Doing Historical Criminology' *British Journal of Criminology*, Vol. 41, 2001, pp. 431–442.

Brown, M. M., 'Puerperal Mania' *Medical and Surgical Reporter*, Vol. 26, 1872, pp. 92–94.

Brown, P., 'Unfitness to Plead in England and Wales: Historical Development and Contemporary Dilemmas,' *Medicine, Science and the Law* Vol. 59, No. 3, 2019, pp.187–196.

Burney, I., 'Viewing Bodies: Medicine, Public Order and English Inquest Practice' *Configurations, Society for Literature and Science*, Vol. 2, No. 1, 1994, pp 33–46.

Burney, I. and N. Pemberton, 'The Rise and Fall of Celebrity Pathology' *British Medical Journal*, Vol. 34, No. 7786, 18–25 December 2010, pp 1319–1321.

Casey, C. A., 'Common Misperceptions: The Press and Victorian Views of Crime' *Journal of Interdisciplinary History*, Vol. 41, No. 3, winter, 2011, pp. 376–391.

Clark, T. T., 'The Law of Infanticide' *The Journal of Jurisprudence*, Vol. 3, No. 25, 1859, pp. 1–9.

Clayton, M., 'Changes in Old Bailey Trials for the Murder of New-born Babies, 1674–1803' *Continuity and Change*, Vol. 24, No. 2, August 2009, pp. 337–359.

Cook, H. J., 'The Rose Case Reconsidered: Physician, Apothecaries and the Law in Augustan England' *Journal of the History of Medicine and Allied Science*, Vol. 45, October 1990, pp. 527–555.

Cornett, J., 'Hoodwink'd by Custom: The Exclusion of Women from Juries in Eighteenth-Century English Law and Literature' *William and Mary Journal of Women and the Law*, Vol. 4, 1997, pp. 17–34.

Cox, G., 'War, Moral Hazard and Ministerial Responsibility: England after the Glorious Revolution' *The Journal of Economic History*, Vol. 71, No. 1, March 2011, pp. 133 –161.

——, 'Was the Glorious Revolution a Constitutional Watershed?' *The Journal of Economic History*, Vol. 72, No. 3, September 2012, pp. 567–600.

Crone, R., 'Crime-and Its Fabrication: A Review of the New Digital Resources in the History of Crime,' *Journal of Victorian Culture*, Vol. 16, No. 1, 2009, pp. 125–134.

Crosby, K., 'Bushell's Case and the Juror's Soul' *The Journal of Legal History*, Vol. 33, No. 3, 2012, pp. 251–290.

Crotty, H., 'The History of Insanity as a Defence to Crime in English Criminal Law' *California Law Review*, Vol. 12, No. 2, January 1924, pp. 105–123.

C.S.A., 'An English County Assizes' *Metropolitan*, Vol. 5, No. 17, 1832, pp.91-98.

Davies, D. S., 'Child-Killing in English Law Part I' *Modern Law Review*, Vol. 1, No. 3, December 1937, pp. 203–223.

——, 'Child-Killing in English Law Part II' *Modern Law Review*, Vol. 1, No. 4, March 1938, pp. 269–287.

Davis, J., 'The Great Fire of London' *History*, Vol. 8, No. 29, April 1923, pp. 40–44.

De Beer, E. S., 'Executions Following the Bloody Assizes' *Historical Research*, Vol. 4, No. 10, 1926, pp. 36–39.

DeLacy, M., 'Puerperal Fever in Eighteenth-Century Britain' *Bulletin of the History of Medicine*, Vol. 63, No. 4, 1989, pp. 521–556.

Dell, S., G. Robertson, K. James, and A Grounds, 'Remands and Psychiatric Assessment in Holloway Prison I: The Psychotic Population' *British Journal of Psychiatry*, Vol. 163, No. 5, 1993, pp. 634–640.

Dentith, S., '"Under the Shadow of the Workhouse:" The Afterlife of a Victorian Institution' *Lit: Literature Interpretation Theory*, Vol. 20, No. 1–2, 2009, pp. 79–91.

Devereaux, S., 'The City and the Sessions Paper: "Public Justice" in London, 1770–1800' *Journal of British Studies*, Vol. 35, No. 4, October 1996, pp. 466–503.

——, 'The Fall of the Sessions Papers: Criminal Trial and Popular Press in late Eighteenth-Century London' *Criminal Justice History*, Vol. 18, 2002, pp. 57–88.

Donovan, J., 'Infanticide and the Juries in France 1825–1913' *Journal of Family History*, Vol. 16, No. 2, 1991, pp. 157–176.

D. R. S. D., 'The Infanticide Act 1938' *The Modern Law Review*, Vol. 2, No. 3, December 1938, p. 229.

Dufraimont, L., 'New Challenges for the Gatekeeper: The Evolving Law on Expert Evidence in Criminal Cases' *Criminal Law Quarterly*, Vol. 58, 2012, pp. 531–558.

Einsiedel, E., K. Salomone, and P. Schneider, 'Crime: Effects of Media Exposure and Personal Experience on Issue Salience' *Journalism Quarterly*, Vol. 61, No. 1, 1984, pp. 131–136.

Evans, T. and P. Thane, 'Lone Mothers' *Women's History Review*, Vol. 20, No. 1, 2011, pp. 3–9.

Faedda, G. L., I. Becker, A. Baroni, L. Tondo, E. Aspland, and A. Koukopoulos, 'The Origins of Electroconvulsive Therapy: Prof. Bini's first Report on ECT' *Journal of Effective Disorders*, Vol. 120, No. 1–3, January 2010, pp. 12–15.

Fife, E., 'Gender and Professionalism in Eighteenth-Century Midwifery' *Women's Writing*, Vol. 11, No. 2, 2004, pp. 185–200.

Foran, D., B. Wills, B. Kiley, C. Jackson, and J. Trestrail, 'The Conviction of Dr Crippen: New Forensic Findings in a Century Old Murder' *Journal of Forensics Sciences*, Vol. 56, No. 1, January 2011, pp. 233–240.

Forbes, T., 'The Regulation of English Midwives in the Sixteenth and Seventeenth Centuries' *Medical History*, Vol. 8, No. 3, July 1964, pp. 235–244.

——, 'Early Forensic Medicine in England: The Angus Murder Trial' *Journal of the History of Medicine*, Vol. 36, No. 3, July 1981, pp. 296–309.

Francus, M., 'Monstrous Mothers, Monstrous Societies: Infanticide and the Rule of Law in Restoration and Eighteenth-Century England' *Eighteenth-Century Life*, Vol. 21, No. 2, 1997, pp. 133–156.

Freemon, F., 'The Origin of the Medical Expert Witness, the Insanity of Edward Oxford' *The Journal of Legal Medicine*, Vol. 22, 2001, pp. 349–373.

Gillon, R., 'Is There a 'New Ethics of Abortion'?' *Journal of Medical Ethics*, Vol. 27, No. supl II, , 2001, ii5–ii9.

Glasgow, G., 'The Campaign for Medical Coroners in Nineteenth-Century England and its Aftermath: A Lancashire Focus on Failure (Part I)' *Mortality*, Vol. 9, No. 2, May 2004a, pp. 150–167.

——, 'The Campaign for Medical Coroners in Nineteenth-Century England and its Aftermath: A Lancashire Focus on Failure (Part II)' *Mortality*, Vol. 9, No. 3, August 2004b, pp. 223–234.

Golan, T., 'The History of Scientific Expert Testimony in the English Courtroom' *Science in Context*, Vol. 12, No. 1, March 1999, pp. 7– 32.

——, 'Revisiting the History of Scientific Expert Testimony' *Brooklyn Law Review*, Vol. 73, No. 3, 2008, pp. 879–942.

Gough, J., 'Fundamental Law in the Seventeenth-Century' *Political Studies*, Vol. 1, No. 2, June 1953, pp. 162–174.

Gowing, L., 'Secret Births and Infanticide in Seventeenth-Century England' *Past and Present*, Vol. 156, August 1997, pp. 87–115: 89.

Green, T. A., 'The Jury and the English Law of Homicide 1200–1600' *Michigan Law Review*, Vol. 74, No. 3, 1976, pp. 413–499.

Grey, D., '"More Ignorant and Stupid than Wilfully Cruel": Homicide Trials and "baby farming" in England and Wales in the Wake of the Children Act 1908' *Crimes and Misdemeanours: Deviance and the Law in Historical Perspective*, Vol. 3, No. 2, 2009, pp. 60–77.

—, 'Women's Policy Networks and the Infanticide Act 1922' *Twentieth Century British History*, Vol. 20, No. 4, 2010, pp. 441–483.

—, 'Gender, Religion and Infanticide in Colonial India, 1870–1906' *Victorian Review*, Vol. 37, No. 2, 2011, pp. 107–120.

—, 'Almost Unknown amongst the Jews': Jewish Women and Infanticide in London, 1890–1918' *The London Journal*, Vol. 37, No. 2, July 2012, 122–35.

—, 'Creating the "Problem Hindu": Sati, Thuggee and Female Infanticide in India 1800–60' *Gender and History*, Vol. 25, No. 3, 2013a, pp. 498–510.

—, '"Liable to Very Gross Abuse": Murder, Moral Panic and Cultural Fears over Infant Life Insurance, 1875-1914' *Journal of Victorian Culture*, Vol. 18, No. 1, 2013b, pp. 54–71.

—, '"What Woman is Safe…?": Coerced Medical Examinations, Suspected Infanticide, and the Response of the Women's Movement in Britain, 1871-1881' *Women's History Review*, Vol. 21, No. 3, 2013c, pp. 403–421.

—, '"Agonised Weeping:" Representing Femininity, Emotion and Infanticide in Edwardian Newspapers' *Media History*, Vol. 21, No. 4, 2015, pp. 468–480.

Hallett, C., 'The Attempts to Understand Puerperal Fever in the Eighteenth and Early Nineteenth Centuries: The Influence of Inflammatory Theory' *Medical History*, Vol. 49, 2005, pp. 1–28.

Halvorsen, V., 'Is It Better that Ten Guilty Persons Go Free than that One Innocent Person Be Convicted?' *Criminal Justice Ethics*, Vol. 23, No. 2, 2004, pp. 3–13.

Hamblin Smith, M., 'Unfitness to Plead in Criminal Trials' *Journal of Mental Sciences*, Vol. 62, No. 259, 1916, pp. 763–774.

Hand, L., 'Historical and Practical Considerations Regarding Expert Testimony' *Harvard Law Review*, Vol. 15, 1901, pp. 40–58.

Hansen, E., 'Overlaying in 19th-Century England: Infant Mortality or Infanticide?' *Human Ecology*, Vol. 7, No. 4, December 1979, pp. 333–352.

Harley, D., 'Historians as Demonologists: The Myth of the Midwife-Witch' *Journal of the Society for the Social History of Medicine*, Vol. 3, 1990, pp. 1–26.

Haskell, T., 'Capitalism and the Origins of the Humanitarian Sensibility, Part 1' *The American Historical Review*, Vol. 90, No. 2, 1985, pp. 339–361.

Hedley-Whyte, T., 'On Being a Pathologist: How Does One Plan a Career, or Does One?' *Human Pathology*, Vol. 39, No. 9, 2008, pp. 1269–1974.

Herrup, C., 'Law and Morality in Seventeenth-Century England' in *Past and Present*, Vol. 106, February 1985, pp.102–123.

Higginbotham, A., 'Sin of Age: Infanticide and Illegitimacy in Victorian London' *Victorian Studies*, Vol. 32, No. 3, 1989, pp. 319–337.

Hopwood, S., 'Child Murder and Insanity' *British Journal of Psychiatry*, Vol. 73, January 1927, pp. 95–108.

Hunt, A., 'Calculations and Concealments: Infanticide in Mid-Nineteenth Century Britain' *Victorian Literature and Culture*, Vol. 34, No. 1, 2006, pp. 71–94.

Hurren, E. T., 'Whose Body is it Anyway?: Trading the Dead Poor, Coroners Disputes, and the Business of Anatomy at Oxford 1885–1929' *Bulletin of the History of Medicine*, Vol. 82, No. 4, 2008, pp. 775–818.

Jackson, J., 'Expert Witnesses. Science, Medicine and the Practice of Law by Carol A. G. Jones' *Journal of Law and Society*, Vol. 22, No. 2, June 1995, pp. 274 –279.

Jansson, M., 'Matthew Hale on Judges and Judging' *The Journal of Legal History*, Vol. 9, 1988, pp. 201–213.

Jefferson, L., K Bloor, and A. Maynard, 'Women in Medicine: Historical Perspectives and Recent Trends' *British Medical Bulletin*, Vol. 115, No. 5, 2015, pp. 5–15.

Johnston, H., 'Gendered Prison Work: Female Prison Officers in the Local Prison System, 1877–1939' *The Howard Journal*, Vol. 53, No. 2, 2014, pp. 193–212.

Jones, K. and C. Chaloner, 'Ethics and Abortion: The Arguments for and Against' *The Nursing Standard*, Vol. 27, No. 47, 2007, pp. 45–48.

Jones, R., 'Puerperal Insanity' *British Medical Journal*, Vol. 1, 1902, pp. 579–586, 646–651.

Kearley, S., 'It's a Hard-Knock Life in Victorian Workhouses' *British Heritage*, Vol. 36, No. 5, 2015, pp. 50–53.

Kellett, R., 'Infanticide and Child Destruction: The Historical, Legal and Pathological Aspects' *Forensic Science International*, Vol. 53, 1992, pp. 1–28.

Kilday, A. M., '"Monsters of the Vilest Kind:" Infanticidal Women and attitudes to their Criminality in Eighteenth-Century Scotland' *Family and Community History*, Vol. 11, No. 2, 2008, pp. 100–115.

Kilday, A. M. and K. Watson, 'Infanticide, Religion and Community in the British Isles 1720–1920: Introduction' *Family and Community History*, Vol. 11, No. 2, 2008, pp. 84–89.

Kord, S., 'Women as Children, Women as Child Killers: Poetic Images of Infanticide in Eighteenth-Century Germany' *Eighteenth-Century Studies*, Vol. 26, No. 3, 1993, pp. 449–466.

Krueger, C., 'Literary Defences and Medical Prosecutions: Representing Infanticide in Nineteenth-Century Britain' *Victorian Studies*, Vol. 40, No. 2, 1997, pp. 271–294.

Landsman, S., 'The Rise of the Contentious Spirit: Adversary Procedure in Eighteenth Century England' *Cornell Law Review*, Vol. 75, 1990, pp. 497–609.

——, 'One Hundred Years of Rectitude: Medical Witnesses at the Old Bailey, 1717–1817' *Law and History Review*, Vol.16, No. 3, 1998, pp. 445–494.

Langbein, J., 'The Criminal Trial before the Lawyers' *University of Chicago Law Review*, Vol. 45, 1978, pp. 263–316.

——,'Shaping the Eighteenth-Century Criminal Trial: A View from the Ryder Sources' *University of Chicago Law Review*, Vol. 50, 1983, pp. 1–136.

——, 'The Historical Foundations of the Law of Evidence: A View from the Ryder Sources' *Columbia Law Review*, Vol. 96, 1996, pp. 1168–1202.

Lemmings, D., 'Criminal Trial Procedure in Eighteenth-Century England: The Impact of Lawyers' *The Journal of Legal History*, Vol. 26, No. 1, 2005, pp. 73–82.

Loar, C., '"Under Felt Hats and Worsted Stockings": The Uses of Conscience in Early Modern English Coroners' Inquests' *Sixteenth Century Journal*, Vol. 41, No. 2, 2010, pp. 393–414.

Loudon, I., 'Puerperal Insanity in the 19th Century' *Journal of Royal Society of Medicine*, Vol. 81, February 1988, pp. 76–79.

Loughnan, A., '"In a Kind of Mad Way": A Historical Perspective on Evidence and Proof of Mental Incapacity' *Melbourne University Law Review*, Vol. 35, Issue 3, 2011, pp. 1049–1070.

——, 'The Strange Case of the Infanticide Doctrine' *Oxford Journal of Legal Studies*, Vol. 32, No. 4, 2012, pp. 685–711.

Loughnan, A. and T. Ward, 'Emergent Authority and Expert Knowledge: Psychiatry and Criminal Responsibility in the UK' *International Journal of Law and Psychiatry*, Vol. 37, 2014, pp. 25–36.

Luddy, M., 'Unmarried Mothers in Ireland, 1880–1973' *Women's History Review*, Vol. 20, No. 1, 2011, pp. 109–126.

Manzo, S., 'Certainty, Laws and Facts in Francis Bacon's Jurisprudence' *Intellectual History Review*, Vol. 24, No. 4, 2014, pp. 457–478.

Marks, L., '"The Luckless Waifs and Strays of Humanity," Irish and Jewish Immigrant Unwed Mothers in London, 1870–1939' *Twentieth Century British History*, Vol. 3, No. 2, 1992, pp. 113–137.

Marks, M. N. and R. Kumar, 'Infanticide in England and Wales' *Medicine, Science and the Law*, Vol. 33, No. 4, 1993, pp. 329–339.

Marland, H., 'Under the Shadow of Maternity: Birth, Death and Puerperal Insanity in Victorian Britain' *History of Psychiatry*, Vol. 23, No. 1, 2012, pp. 78–90.

Marshall Mitnick, J., 'From Neighbor- Witness to Judge of Proofs: The Transformation of the English Civil Juror' *American Journal of Legal History*, Vol. 32, 1988, pp. 201–235.

Martin, P. J., 'Observation on Some of the Accidents of Infanticide' *Edinburgh Medical and Surgical Journal*, Vol. 26, July 1826, pp. 34–37.

Matheson, J. C. M., 'Infanticide' *Medico-Legal and Criminology Review*, Vol. 9, 1941, pp. 135–152.

McIlroy, L., 'The Effects of Parturition upon Insanity and Crime' *The British Medical Journal*, Vol. 1, 1928, pp. 303–304.

McKean, M., 'Re-thinking Late Victorian Fiction: The Crowd and Imperialism at Home' *English Literature in Translation 1880-1920*, Vol. 54, No. 1, 2011, pp. 28.

Miley, F. and A. Read, 'Go Gentle Babe: Accounting and the London Foundling Hospital, 1757–97' *Accounting History*, Vol. 21, No. 2–3, 2016, pp.167–184.

Mooney, G., 'Diagnostic Spaces: Workhouse, Hospital and Home in Mid-Victorian London' *Social Science History*, Vol. 33, No. 3, 2009, pp. 357–390.

Oldham, J., 'On Pleading the Belly: A History of the Jury of Matrons' *Criminal Justice History*, Vol. 6, 1985, pp. 1–64.

Pearson, R., 'Women Defendants in Magistrates' Courts' *British Journal of Law and Society*, Vol. 3, 1976, pp. 265–273.

Pierce, G., 'Homicide by Hyoscine: The Case of Dr Crippen' *Irish Medical Times*, Vol, 44, No. 23, June 4th 2010, pp. 24–25.

Platt, A. and B. Diamond, ''The Origins of the Right and Wrong' Test of Criminal Responsibility and its Subsequent Development in the United States: An Historical Survey' *California Law Review*, Vol. 53, 1966, pp. 1227.

Porter, R., 'Foucault's Great Confinement' *History of Human Sciences*, Vol. 3, No. 1, 1990, pp. 47–54.

Rattigan, C., '"I Thought from Her Appearance that She Was in the Family Way:" Detecting Infanticide Cases in Ireland, 1900–1921' *Family & Community History*, Vol. 11/2, November 2008, pp. 134–151.

Rendel, M., 'Abortion and Human Rights: The European Convention on Human Rights Safeguards the Right to Life' *New Law Journal*, Vol. 141, No. 6520, 1991, pp. 1270.

Resnick, P., 'Murder of the New-born: A Psychiatric Review of Neonaticide' *American Journal of Psychiatry*, Vol. 126, No. 10, 1970, pp. 1414 – 1420.

Richter, J. S., 'Infanticide, Child Abandonment and Abortion in Imperial Germany' *Journal of Interdisciplinary History*, Vol. 28, No. 4, 1998, pp. 511–551.

Rizzo, T., 'Between Dishonor and Death: Infanticides in the *Causes Celebres* of Eighteenth-Century France' *Women's History Review*, Vol. 13, No. 1, 2004, pp. 5–21.

Rosenberg, A., 'The Sarah Stout Murder Case: An Early Example of the Doctor as an Expert Witness' *Journal of the History of Medicine and Allied Sciences*, Vol. 12, No. 1, January 1957, pp. 61–70.

Rustigan, M., 'A Reinterpretation of Criminal Law Reform in Nineteenth Century England' *Journal of Criminal Justice*, Vol. 8, 1980, pp. 205–219.

Sagall, E., 'Forensic Medicine, the Medico-legal History' *Journal of Law, Medicine and Ethics*, Vol. 8, No. 2, 1980, pp. 10–13.

Sauer, R., 'Infanticide and Abortion in Nineteenth-Century Britain' *Population Studies*, Vol. 32, No. 1, March 1978, pp. 81–93.

Scull, A., 'From Madness to Mental Illness: Medical Men as Moral Entrepreneurs' *European Journal of Sociology*, Vol. 16, No. 2, 1975, pp. 218–261.

—, 'Michel Foucault's History of Madness' *History of the Human Sciences*, Vol. 3, No. 1, 1990, pp. 57–67.

Seaborne Davies, D., 'Child Killing in English Law *The Modern Law Review*, Vol. 1, No. 3, December 1937, pp. 203–223.

Shapiro, B., 'Law and Science in Seventeenth-Century England' *The Stanford Law Review*, Vol. 21, April 1969, pp. 726–766.

—, 'Law Reform in Seventeenth-Century England' *The American Journal of Legal History*, Vol. 19, No. 4, October 1975, pp. 280–312.

—, 'To a Moral Certainty: Theories of Knowledge and Anglo-American Juries 1600–1850' *The Hastings Law Journal*, Vol. 38, November 1986, pp. 153–194.

—, 'Testimony in Seventeenth-Century English Natural Philosophy: Legal Origins and Early Development' *Studies in the History and Philosophy of Science*, Vol. 33, no. 2, 2002, pp. 243–263.

—, 'Oaths, Credibility and the Legal Process in Early Modern England: Part One' *Law and Humanities*, Vol. 6, No. 2, 2012, pp. 145–178.

—, 'Oaths, Credibility and the Legal Process in Early Modern England: Part Two' *Law and Humanities*, Vol. 7, No. 1, 2013, pp. 19–54.

Sharpe, J. and J. R. Dickinson, 'Coroners Inquests in an English County, 1600–1800: A Preliminary Survey' *Northern History*, Vol. 47, No. 2, September 2011, pp. 253–269.

Shepherd, J., 'One of the Best Fathers until He Went Out of His Mind': Paternal Child Murder, 1864-1900' *Journal of Victorian Culture*, Vol. 18, No. 1, 2013, pp. 17–35.

—, '"I Am Very Glad and Cheered When I Hear the Flute:" The Treatment of Criminal Lunatics in Late Victorian Broadmoor' *Medical History*, Vol. 60, No. 4, October 2016, pp. 473–491.

Shoemaker, R. B., 'The Old Bailey Proceedings and the Representation of Crime and criminal Justice in Eighteenth-Century London' *The Journal of British Studies*, Vol. 47, No. 3, July 2008, pp. 559–580.

Silies, E. M., 'Taking the Pill after the "Sexual Revolution": Female Contraceptive Decisions in England and West Germany in the 1970s' *European Review of History*, Vol. 22, No. 1, 2015, pp. 41–59.

Smith, S., 'The History and Development of Forensic Medicine' *The British Medical Journal*, Vol 1, no. 4707, 1951, pp. 599–607.

Strachan, B., 'Coroners' Necropsies' *British Medical Journal*, Vol. 2, No. 2168, July 19th 1902, pp. 232.

Teubner, G., 'How the Law Thinks: Towards a Constructivist Epistemology of Law' *Law and Society Review*, Vol. 23, 1989, pp. 727–757.

Thane, P., 'Unmarried Motherhood in Twentieth-Century England' *Women's History Review*, Vol. 21, No. 1, 2011, pp. 11–29.

The British Medical Journal, 'The Abolition of "The View" at Inquests' *The British Medical Journal*, Vol. 2, No. 1970, October 1, 1898, pp. 995–996.

The British Medical Journal, 'Medical Men as Witnesses' *The British Medical Journal,* Vol. 2, No. 2020, September 16, 1899, pp. 741–743.

Ulbricht, O., 'The Debate About Foundling Hospitals in Enlightenment Germany: Infanticide, Illegitimacy, and Infant Mortality Rates' *Central European History*, Vol. 18, No. 3/4, Sept-Dec 1985, pp. 211–256.

Van den Tweel, J. and C. Taylor, 'A Brief History of Pathology' *Virchows Arch*, Vol. 457, 2010, pp. 3–10.

Ward, D., 'The Victorian Slum: An Enduring Myth?' *Annals of the Association of American Geographers*, Vol. 66, No. 2, June 1976, pp. 323–336.

Ward, T., 'Law, Common Sense and the Authority of Science: Expert Witnesses and Criminal Insanity in England, CA, 1840–1940' *Social and Legal Studies*, Vol. 6, No. 3, 1997, pp. 343–362.

——, 'The Sad Subject of Infanticide: Law, Medicine and Child Murder, 1860–1938' *Social and Legal Studies*, Vol. 8, No. 2, 1999, pp. 163–180.

——, 'Standing Mute' *Law and Literature*, Vol. 24, No. 1, 2012, pp. 3–20.

Watson, K. 'Medical and Chemical Expertise in English Trials for Criminal Poisoning, 1750–1914' *Medical History*, Vol. 50, No. 3, 2006, pp. 373–390.

——, 'Religion, Community and the Infanticidal Mother: Evidence From 1840's Rural Wiltshire' *Family and Community History*, Vol. 11, No. 2, 2008, pp. 116–133.

Whittet, T., 'The Apothecary in Provincial Gilds' *Medical History*, Vol. 8, No. 3, July 1964, pp. 245–273.

Wiener, M., 'Judges v Jurors: Courtroom Tensions in Murder Trials and the Law of Criminal Responsibility in Nineteenth-Century Britain' *Law and History Review*, Vol. 17, 1999, pp. 467–506.

Wigmore, J. H., 'The History of the Hearsay Rule' *Harvard Law Review*, Vol. 17, No. 7, May 1904, pp. 437–458.

Williams, S., 'The Experience of Pregnancy and Childbirth for Unmarried Mothers in London, 1760–1866' *Women's History Review*, Vol. 20, No. 1, 2011, pp. 67–86.

Wilson, J., 'History of the Suppression of Infanticide in Western India under the Government of Bombay, including notices of the Provinces and Tribes in which the Practice has prevailed' *The Edinburgh Review*, Vol. 119, No. 244, April 1st 1869, pp. 389–412.

Woodbridge, F., 'Some Unusual Aspects of Mental Irresponsibility in the Criminal Law' *Journal of Criminal Law and Criminology,* Vol. 29, No. 6, March-April 1939 (1931-1951), pp. 822–847.

Zedner, L., 'Women, Crime and Penal Responses: A Historical Account' *Crime and Justice*, Vol. 14, 1991, pp. 307–362.

Unpublished theses and dissertations

Grey, D., "Discourses in Infanticide in England, 1880–1922." PhD Thesis Roehampton University, 2008.

Hatfield, J. A., "An Irresistible Impulse: Puerperal Insanity and Infanticide in Nineteenth-Century England." MA Dissertation, 2014.

Ward, T., "Psychiatry and Criminal Responsibility in England 1843–1939." PhD Thesis De Montfort University, 1996.

Home Office Circulars

Home Office Circulars, *Justice of the Peace*, 53, 1889, pp. 793–794.

Parliamentary papers

Royal Commission, 'Royal commission on the care and control of the feeble-minded vol II minutes of evidence' *Parliamentary Papers*. London: Wyman and Sons, 1908.

Select Committee publications

Select Committee, *The Health of Towns Report Together with the Minutes of Evidence Taken before Them, and an Appendix and Index*. London: HMSO, 1840.

Newspapers

Aberdeen Journal
Bedfordshire Times
Biggleswade Chronicle
Bradford Observer
Cambridge Chronicle and Journal
Chelmsford Chronicle
Driffield Times
Dundee Evening Telegraph
Exeter and *Plymouth Gazette*
Glasgow Herald
Gloucester Citizen
Hull and East Riding Times
Hull Daily Mail
Hull Packet and *East Riding Times*
Illustrated Police News
Lincolnshire Echo
Lloyds Weekly London Newspaper
London Standard
Morning Post
Nottingham Evening Post
Reynolds Newspaper
Sheffield Daily Telegraph
Sheffield Evening Telegraph
South London Chronicle
Sunderland Echo and *Shipping Gazette*
Surrey Mirror
The Derby Daily Telegraph
The Sheffield Independent, Yorkshire, and *Derbyshire Advertiser*

Western Daily Press
York Herald
York Herald and *General Advertiser*
Yorkshire Evening Post
Yorkshire Post and *Leeds Intelligencer*

Websites

https://archive.org/details/medicalsurgicalr26philuoft
http://www.bbc.co.uk/news/uk
http://www.blackkalendar.nl/content.php?key=11109
https://books.google.co.uk/books
http://www.britishnewspaperarchive.co.uk/
http://www.capitalpunishmentuk.org/fem1735.html
http://www.capitalpunishmentuk.org/tyburn1695.html
https://cmis.hullcc.gov.uk/CMIS/Document.
http://www.geocities.ws/lzbthjoachim/Hannah_Samuel.html
http://www.hulldailymail.co.uk/
http://www.hullhistorycentre.org.uk/
http://www.ww1hull.org.uk/index.php/hull-in-ww1/hull-before-1914
http://julieannhatfield.co.uk/ma-in-english-and-american-literature-dissertation-an-irresistible-impulse-puerperal-insanity-and-infanticide-in-nineteenth-century-england/
https://www.justice.gov.uk/courts/procedure-rules/criminal/docs/crim-proc-rules-2014-part-33.pdf.
http://www.legislation.gov.uk/uksi/2005/384/contents/made
http://www.legislation.gov.uk/ukpga/1967/87
https://www.londonlives.org/static/CriminalTrial.jsphttp://medical-dictionary.thefreedictionary.com/neurasthenia http://munksroll.rcplondon.ac.uk/Biography/Details/1385 http://www.mylearning.org/the-hull-blitz/p-1805/
http://www.oed.com
https://www.oldbaileyonline.org/
https://www.oldbaileyonline.org/static/Ordinarys-accounts.jsp
https://www.oldbaileyonline.org/static/Trial-procedures.jsp
http://www.sherlock-holmes.org.uk/conan-doyle/
https://www.theguardian.com/society/2015/nov/28/closure-of-holloway-womens-prison-revolution
https://wonderfulcollection.wordpress.com/tag/penny-hang/

Index

abandonment 33–34, 143
Abortion Act (1967) 2
Ackerknecht, E. 61, 92
adultery 61, 194
Adversarial Revolution 29
Allen, H. 37
anatomical: demonstrations 86; dissection 1–2, 87; examination 189; knowledge 83, 87, 192; post mortem 169; reasoning 191; research 45; studies 60; theatres 86
anatomy 85–86, 88, 101; female 15; human 77; knowledge of 48, 112; pathological 86
Anatomy Act (1832) 88
apothecaries 16, 39, 43, 59–60, 74–75, 84–85, 102, 110, 124, 131; surgeon- 60, 103
Arnot, M. 5, 24
asphyxia 33, 87, 101, 133–134, 151, 179–183
Assizes 6–9, 44, 92, 97, 100, 142, 181; county 27; Hull 7; Leeds 153; Lincolnshire 145, 175, 176–177; Surrey 25; West Riding 146; York 5, 7, 10, 83, 90, 152–154, 183–184; Yorkshire Summer 123
asylum 122, 125, 127, 131–132, 142, 153; county 132; criminal 147; doctors 45–46; female 125; local county 130; lunatic 132, 136, 142, 154; superintendents 127, 131–132
Atkinson, S. 169

baby farming 33, 35
Baker, J. 36–37, 125
Barber-Surgeons Company 84
bastard children 15, 23–24, 28, 58, 109
Battie, W. 122
Beattie, J. M. 25–26, 68
Behlmer, G. K. 94
bestiality 130
The British Medical Journal 35
Brock v Kellock 174
Burney, I. 87, 98
Bushell case 9

cadaver 15–16, 24, 85, 87–88, 95, 121; examination of 192; infant 4–5, 63, 77, 113, 192; new-born 191
Cairns, D. 29
causality 127; pathological 44
Chadwick, R. 143
Children Act (1908) 33
Christian burial 87
Clayton, M. 43, 73
College of Physicians 84
Collins, W. 168
Company of Barbers 84
Company of Surgeons 84
compassion 32, 88; approach 30; defence 89; lack of 26; temper 68; view 30
Conan Doyle, A. 14, 168
concealment of birth 1, 9, 14, 28, 30, 90, 112, 121, 134, 141, 154, 155, 168, 174, 176, 178, 190–193
Concealment of Birth of Bastards Act (1624) 24
Cooper Graves, D. 37
Coroners Act (1887) 100
Coroners (Amendment) Act (1926) 98
Council of Surgeons 84
criminal: asylums 147; charge 128; court 7, 11; deed 128; execution of 30; female 13, 32, 45, 92, 190; homicides 169; insanity trials 132; institutions 132; interference 174; justice process 3, 5, 122, 127–128, 141, 190; justice system

3, 27, 29–30, 48–49, 61; law 11, 45, 108, 146; law reforms 30–31; liability 2, 38; lunatic asylum 132, 154; lunatics 124, 128, 130, 132, 140–141; mentally ill 132; mental state of 16; offences 62; procedure 29; proceedings 24–25, 39; responsibility 128; sanity of 122; state of mind 45; suspected 97; trials 10, 12, 23, 29, 40, 47, 64, 76, 190; wilful negligence 176
Criminal Appeal Act (1907) 11
Criminal Evidence Act (1898) 30
Criminal Lunatics Act (1800) 127–128
Criminal Statute Repeals Act (1827) 31
Crone, R. 11
cruentation test 85
culpability 121, 190; accused's 43; woman's 1, 83, 191
cytology 167

D'Cruze, S. 32
delivery 36, 38, 63, 65, 88–89, 91–92, 107, 124, 145, 174; forthcoming 26; live 175; onset 65; post- 36, 38; precipitous 65, 71; premature 63, 72; rapid 65, 71; recent 5; room 58, 60–61, 74–75, 77, 191; surprise 65, 70; unassisted 88, 92, 172
dementia 45, 127
desperation 4, 35–36
Dickens, C. 4, 95
distressful circumstances 48
distress of reason 48
Driffield Times 143
Dundee Evening Telegraph 180

Eigen, J. P. 44, 122, 128, 132
Enabling Act (1875) 85

fallen woman 30–31
feeblemindedness 150
Fellowship or Guild of Surgeons 84
female impotence 61
Folkes v Chadd 40
Foucault, M. 14, 44–45, 86–87, 122, 131, 192
Freemon, F. 133

Gaols Act (1823) 131
Gaskell, E. 31
Gatrell, V. 92
general practitioner (GP) 85, 137–139, 169–170, 193–194
Glasgow, G. 99
Glorious Revolution 2
Golan, T. 40
Gooch, R. 124, 126
Gowing, L. 63
Green, T. A. 9
Grey, D. 13, 15, 36, 145, 147
guilty but insane 16, 37, 121–122, 128, 130, 132–133, 135, 140–141, 144, 148–149, 151, 154, 156, 166, 181, 193

Hale, M. 25, 43
Hamblin Smith, M. 130
Hanoverian era 31
Hardy, T. 31
Haskell, T. 28–29
Hay, D. 6
The Health of the Prisoners Act (1774) 131
Higginbotham, A. 30, 34, 49
Hoffer, P. C. 24, 27
Holloway Prison 122, 131–132, 134, 139–140, 148, 150
homicide 125, 135, 169
Homicide Act (1957) 38
Hopwood, S. 125
Hull Daily Mail 151, 154
Hull Packet and *East Riding Times* 96
Hull Prison 153
humanitarian 47; approach 28, 49; attitude 36; concerns 41, 109; feeling 109; reform 28–29; sensibilities 38–39; sentiment 26, 29, 145; stance 28; sympathy 69
Hunter, W. 28, 86, 89–90, 94, 175
hydrostatic test (lung test) 16, 43, 76, 83, 92–94, 101, 103–106, 109–110, 112–113, 166, 169, 173–175, 192

Indemnity Act (1827) 31
industrial revolution 4
Infanticide Act (1922) 15, 36–38, 46, 48, 113, 144–148, 155
Infanticide Act (1938) 2, 38–39, 145, 148–149, 151, 154–156
infanticide cases: at the Old Bailey (1763–1813) 102–109; at the Old Bailey (1863–1913) 76–77, 110–112; at the Old Bailey (1914–1955) 149–151; in Hull and the surrounding area (1863–1913); in Hull and the surrounding area (1914–1955) 151–155; in London 6; of the Old Bailey (1688–1738) 63–72; recorded at the Old Bailey (1788–1838) 74–75

insanity 16, 25, 43–44, 46, 49, 64, 69, 121–123, 125–128, 136–137, 139, 141, 148, 155–156; actual 38; concepts of 48; criminal 132; defence 121, 193; depressive 152; developing 132; diagnosis 128; discourse 125; evidence of 68, 131, 134; grounds of 122, 124, 128, 136–137, 139, 142; moral 128; plea of 48, 121, 154, 193; predisposition to 126; of pregnancy 125; sense of 37; symptoms of 64; temporary 47, 122, 125, 134, 143, 155; test of 128; trials 122, 141; verdict of 47; *see also* insanity; puerperal

Jackson, G. 5, 7, 9
Jackson, M. 24, 27–28, 40–41, 49, 93, 95, 101, 109, 192
James, P. D. 95
Johnstone, G. 31
Jones, C. 39, 41–42
Jones, R. 125
Justice Hall 7

Kermode, J. 32
Kilday, A. M. 34–36, 73, 88, 99
King, P. 27
The King v Penn and Mead 9

lactational: disturbances 147; exhaustion 148; insanity 36, 38, 47, 125, 147–148, 156, 193; period 125
Landsman, S. 102
Langbein, J. 29, 71, 189
Law of Property Act (1922) 145
legal abstraction 38–39, 46
Lloyds Weekly London Newspaper 140
Loar, C. 8
London Foundling Hospital 33–34
Lord Ellenborough's Act (1803) 15, 23, 30, 58, 108, 121, 175
Loudon, I. 127
Loughnan, A. 47
lunacy 44, 46, 48, 123

Malcolmson, R. W. 25–26
malnutrition 125, 147
mania 125; homicidal 135, 137; onset of 38; uncontrollable 137; *see also* puerperal
Marks, M. N. 38
Marland, H. 125
Martin, P. J. 190
maternal: instincts 47; mental disorder 38; mental state 36; link 35; qualities 31
Matheson, J. C. M. 132, 150–151, 154
matrons 76, 94; jury of 62
McIlroy, L. 147
McNaughtan: *Rules* 128; sense of insanity 37
medical: discourse 2, 16, 47, 49, 61, 64, 76–77, 83, 88, 112, 127, 131, 144, 169, 192, 194; evidence 2–3, 11, 16, 40–41, 43–44, 48, 74, 77, 83–84, 88, 95–103, 110, 112, 141, 150, 156, 166, 168–169, 174, 177, 181, 184, 189–191, 193–194; testimony 23, 40, 77, 103, 155, 168
Medical Act (1858) 85
medicalisation 47–48, 61, 83, 86, 112
Medical Witnesses Act (1836) 98–99
melancholy 27, 125–126, 136, 137
mental: abnormality 37; attack 126; capacity 128; causes 125; condition 130, 137, 151; confusion 148; defective 150; disease 37, 136; disorder 38, 47; distress 134; disturbance 47; element 43; health 2, 23, 132; illness 122–123, 136, 150–151, 155, 193; imbalance 153, 156; impairment 141; incapacity 45–46, 48, 65, 150; patients 122; shock 133; state 2, 16, 36–38, 42, 44–46, 49, 113, 122–123, 125, 128, 130–135, 140, 144, 151, 153, 155, 166, 170, 193–194; trouble 134; weakness 127; wellbeing 131
Mental Deficiency Act 150
midwife 15, 58–60, 62–77, 83, 93, 103–104, 106, 108–109, 112–113, 138, 191–192; female 39, 58–59, 61, 192; man- 16, 58, 60, 74, 89–90, 103–105, 110, 167, 191; role of 58
Midwifery Charter (rejection of) (1616) 84
Midwives Act (1920) 77
modesty 28, 109
moral 28, 31, 125; being 190; code 31, 191; consideration 33; decisions 9; dilemma 9; duty 33; judgements 150; justice 147; neutrality 12; normative 25; obligation 29; perceptions 189; philosophy 86; problem 184; psychologico- 44; uplifting influence 31; values 31; *see also* insanity
morphology 85
mortality 63, 147, 167
murder: trials 1
Murder Act (1751) 87

Napoleonic Code (*demence*) 45
necropsy 167, 169
Newgate Prison 7, 35, 66, 68, 72, 112, 131, 135, 137
Norrie, A. 38–39, 44, 46

Oakley, A. 61
Offences Against the Person Act (1828) 30–31
Offences Against the Person Act (1861) 34
Oldham, J. 7, 62
overlaying 33, 167, 178, 180

pathologists 16, 166–167, 174, 178, 180, 193
pathology 44, 61, 85, 113, 166–167, 170–172; forensic 88, 99; histo- 167; legal 37
penalty 44, 147, 191; death 6, 37, 129, 155, 189; extreme 108
Pentonville Prison 172
Poor Law Amendment Act (1834) 33
poverty 4, 27, 32, 44, 46, 125, 127, 141, 143, 147, 194
pregnancy 1–2, 26–27, 34–36, 61–63, 65, 91, 98, 125, 127, 145, 155
Prevention of Cruelty to Children Act (1889) 33
prison 6, 34, 44, 95, 97, 130, 132, 146, 149–151, 153, 155, 173, 181, 190–191; commissioners 131; doctor 132, 184; governor 133; inspectorate 131; medical officers 131, 153; psychiatry 131; reform 131; sentence 16, 112, 132, 141, 146, 153, 189–191; surgeons 131, 137; *see also* Holloway Prison; Hull Prison; Newgate Prison; Pentonville Prison
Prisoner's Counsel Act (1836) 29
Prisons Act (1835) 131
Prisons Act (1865) 132
Prisons Act (1877) 131
prostitution 32, 61, 191
Protection of Infant Life Act (1872) 35
psychiatric defence 36
psychosis 125; post-natal 36
puerperal: insanity 38, 47, 122, 124–127, 138, 144, 147–148, 193; mama 139; mania 125, 127, 136–138, 140–141; melancholia 36, 44, 127; period 38, 125
punishment 6, 11, 14, 23–24, 27, 37, 44, 47–48, 65, 74, 101, 121, 141, 146, 155, 184, 189; capital 83, 155, 189; corporal 27; harsh 9, 27; humiliating 23; objects of 30; penal 150

Quinn, C. 123

R v Dyson 128–129
R v Hadfield 128
R v McNaughtan 128
R v Pritchard 130
R v Turner 40
R v Brain 89
Rabin, D. 26, 43, 66
rape 31, 61–62, 102
Resnick, P. 146
respiration 93–94, 111–112, 172–175
Rose Case 84
Royal College of Physicians 60, 84
Royal College of Surgeons 84

scientific experiments 2, 15, 59, 189, 191
Sessions 10; Court 7; House Yard 7; Old Bailey 27; Papers 11; Quarter 7
Sex Disqualification (Removal) Act (1919) 145
sexual: behaviour 24, 27; matters 61; misconduct 31; organs 124; promiscuity 24, 190
Shapiro, B. 68
Sharp, J. 58
Sharpe, J. 4
Shoemaker, R. B. 11
Simpson, K. 178, 180
Smart, C. 32
socio-economic 13, 47
Sommers, S. 92, 112
State Asylum Broadmoor 36–37, 125, 130, 132, 136–137, 139, 151–152, 155
strangulation 63, 104, 107, 151, 171–172, 177, 180, 182–183
suffocation 33, 66, 90, 94, 96–97, 101, 104, 111, 171, 176, 178–179, 183
suicide 33, 38, 125, 127, 136, 142–144, 146, 148, 154

Taylor, A. S. 169, 175
temporary malady 137, 139, 155, 193
Teubner, G. 48
therapeutics 85
therapy 44, 47
Trollope, F. 33
Turner, B. 60

Van den Tweel, J. 170
Victorian era 31–32, 36, 48
violence 67, 94–95, 170, 172, 177; acts of 136–137; evidence of 65, 193; marks of

63, 73, 75, 92, 94–95, 98–99, 104, 106, 172, 176, 179, 182; probability of 172; signs of 28, 63, 72, 90, 94, 183
virginity 61

Walker, N. 130
Ward, T. 29–30, 34, 37–39, 42, 45, 47–48, 121, 125, 130, 145, 147, 155, 192
Watson, K. 121, 156
Wells Harbour 40
West Riding Pauper Asylum 129
Wheelwright, J. 155
Wiener, M. 61
Wilson, A. 60
witchcraft 32, 61
Women's Freedom League 145
Woolmington v DPP 25
workhouse 4–5, 33; infirmaries 131; Islington 111
Worshipful Society of Apothecaries 84–85

York Herald 91, 100, 141

Zedner, L. 45, 127, 190

Milton Keynes UK
Ingram Content Group UK Ltd.
UKHW021133060324
438926UK00006B/41

9 780367 439231